W9-BWN-570

W9-BWN-570

PORTRAIT OF
IRELAND

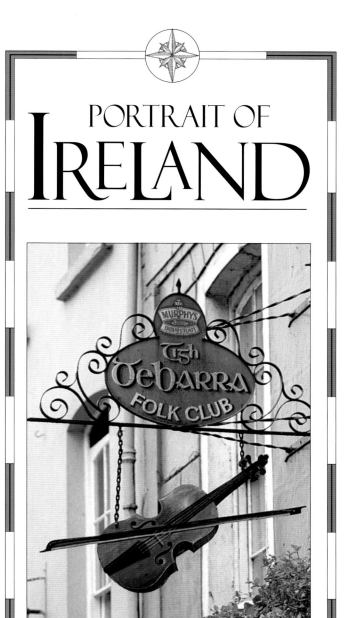

PORTRAIT OF
IRELAND

Main Contributors:
LISA GERARD-SHARP AND TIM PERRY

DORLING KINDERSLEY PUBLISHING, INC.
LONDON • NEW YORK • SYDNEY • DELHI • PARIS
MUNICH • JOHANNESBURG
www.dk.com

DORLING KINDERSLEY PUBLISHING, INC.

www.dk.com

PROJECT EDITORS Claire Folkard, Paul Hines, Ferdie McDonald
ART EDITORS Jo Doran, Elly King, Lisa Kosky, Marisa Renzullo
EDITORS Emily Anderson, Freddy Hamilton
DESIGNERS Joy FitzSimmons, Jaki Grosvenor, Paul Jackson,
Katie Peacock, Jan Richter, Nicola Rodway, Emma Rose

PICTURE RESEARCH Brigitte Arora, Victoria Peel, Ellen Root
DTP DESIGNERS Samantha Borland, Lee Redmond, Rachel Symons,
Ingrid Vienings

CONTRIBUTORS
Gerald Carr, Bonnie Friedman, Rita Goldman,
Clemence McLaren, Melissa Miller, Alex Salkever,
Stephen Self, Greg Ward, Paul Wood

PHOTOGRAPHERS
Joe Cornish, Tim Daly, Rob Reichenfeld, Magnus Rew,
Mike Severns, Antony Souter, Alan Williams

ILLUSTRATORS
Robert Ashby, Richard Bonson, Stephen Conlin, Gary Cross,
Chris Forsey, Stephen Gyapay, Claire Littlejohn, Maltings
Partnership, Chris Orr & Associates, Robbie Polley, Mike Taylor,
John Woodcock

Reproduced by Colourscan, Singapore
Printed and bound by L. Rex Printing Company Limited, China

First American Edition, 2000
2 4 6 8 10 9 7 5 3 1

Published in the United States by
Dorling Kindersley Publishing, Inc.,
95 Madison Avenue, New York, New York 10016

Copyright 2000 © Dorling Kindersley Limited, London

PUBLISHED IN GREAT BRITAIN BY DORLING KINDERSLEY LIMITED.
Library of Congress Cataloging-in-Publication Data
Perry, Tim
Portrait of Ireland / Tim Perry, Lisa Gerard-Sharp – – 1st American ed.
    p.   cm – – (Dorling Kindersley travel guides)
    Includes index
    ISBN 0-7894-6361-X (alk. paper)
    1. Ireland-- Guidebooks. I. Gerard-Sharp, Lisa II
    Title.

DA980.P47 2000
914.1504'824--dc21   99-056184

**The information in every
Dorling Kindersley Travel Guide is checked annually**.
Every effort has been made to ensure that this book is as up-to-
date as possible at the time of going to press. Some details,
however, such as telephone numbers, opening hours, prices,
gallery hanging arrangements and travel information are liable to
change. The publishers cannot accept responsibility for any
consequences arising from the use of this book.
We value the suggestions of our readers very highly. Please write
to: Senior Managing Editor, Dorling Kindersley Travel Guides,
Dorling Kindersley, 9 Henrietta Street, London WC2E 8PS.

CONTENTS

An evangelical symbol from the
Book of Kells (see p62)

INTRODUCING
IRELAND

DUBLIN AREA
BY AREA

Johnson's Court alley behind
Grafton Street in southwest Dublin

Farmer and his sheep in the Caha Mountains *(see p159)*

Façade of a pub in Dingle *(see p217)*

IRELAND REGION BY REGION

Traditional Dublin dish of oysters,
often consumed with Guinness

Castletown House *(see
p159-160)*

HOW TO USE THIS GUIDE

THIS GUIDE helps you to get the most from your visit to Ireland. It provides both expert recommendations and detailed practical information. *Introducing Ireland* maps the country and sets it in its historical and cultural context. The seven regional chapters, plus *Dublin Area by Area*, contain descriptions of all the important sights, with maps, pictures and illustrations. Restaurant and hotel recommendations can be found in *Travellers' Needs*. The *Survival Guide* has tips on everything from the telephone system to transport both in the Republic and in Northern Ireland.

DUBLIN AREA BY AREA

Central Dublin is divided into three sightseeing areas. Each has its own chapter, which opens with a list of the sights described. A fourth chapter, *Further Afield*, covers the suburbs and County Dublin. Sights are numbered and plotted on an *Area Map*. The descriptions of each sight follow the map's numerical order, making sights easy to locate within the chapter.

Sights at a Glance lists the chapter's sights by category: Churches, Museums and Galleries, Historic Buildings, Parks and Gardens.

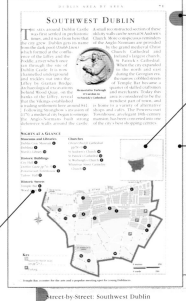

All pages relating to Dublin have red thumb tabs.

A locator map shows where you are in relation to other areas of the city centre.

1 Area Map
For easy reference, the sights are numbered and located on a map. Sights in the city centre are also shown on the Dublin Street Finder *on pages 132–33.*

2 Street-by-Street Map
This gives a bird's-eye view of the key area in each chapter.

A suggested route for a walk is shown in red.

Stars indicate the sights that no visitor should miss.

3 Detailed information
The sights in Dublin are described individually with addresses, telephone numbers and information on opening hours and admission charges.

Story boxes highlight noteworthy features of the sights.

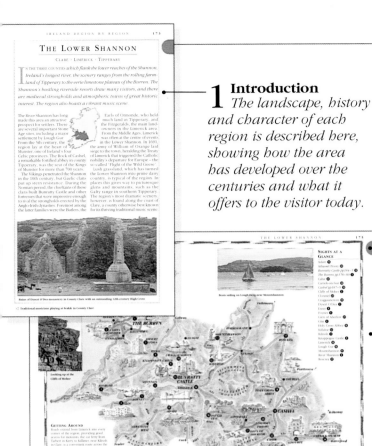

1 Introduction
The landscape, history and character of each region is described here, showing how the area has developed over the centuries and what it offers to the visitor today.

IRELAND REGION BY REGION
Apart from Dublin, Ireland has been divided into seven regions, each of which has a separate chapter. The most interesting towns and places to visit in each area have been numbered on a *Pictorial Map*.

Each region of Ireland can be quickly identified by its colour coding, shown on the inside front cover.

2 Pictorial Map
This shows the road network and gives an illustrated overview of the whole region. All interesting places to visit are numbered and there are also useful tips on getting around the region by car and train.

Getting Around gives tips on travel within the region.

3 Detailed information
All the important towns and other places to visit are described individually. They are listed in order, following the numbering on the Pictorial Map. Within each town or city, there is detailed information on important buildings and other sights.

The Visitors' Checklist provides all the practical information you will need to plan your visit for all the top sights.

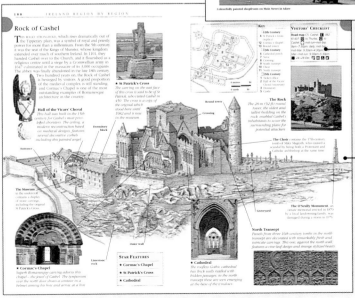

4 Ireland's top sights
These are given two or more full pages. Historic buildings are dissected to reveal their interiors. The most interesting towns or city centres are shown in a bird's-eye view, with sights picked out and described.

Ireland Region by Region

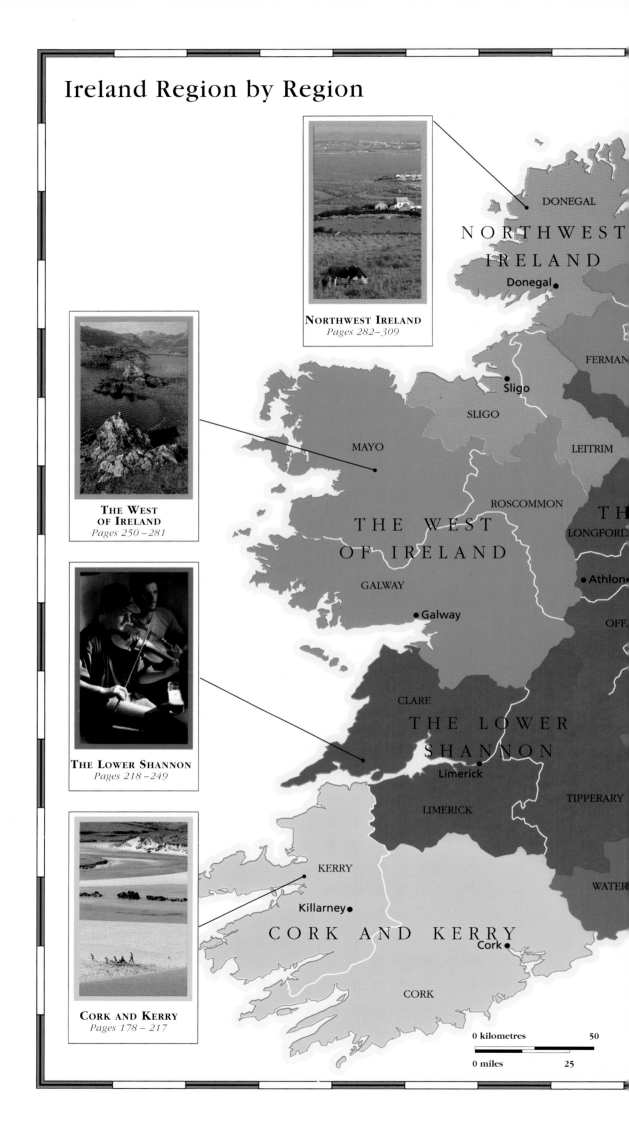

NORTHWEST IRELAND
Pages 282–309

THE WEST OF IRELAND
Pages 250–281

THE LOWER SHANNON
Pages 218–249

CORK AND KERRY
Pages 178–217

DONEGAL

NORTHWEST IRELAND

Donegal

FERMAN

Sligo

SLIGO

LEITRIM

MAYO

ROSCOMMON

TH

LONGFORD

THE WEST OF IRELAND

Athlon

GALWAY

OFF

Galway

CLARE

THE LOWER SHANNON

Limerick

LIMERICK

TIPPERARY

KERRY

WATER

Killarney

CORK AND KERRY

Cork

CORK

0 kilometres   50

0 miles   25

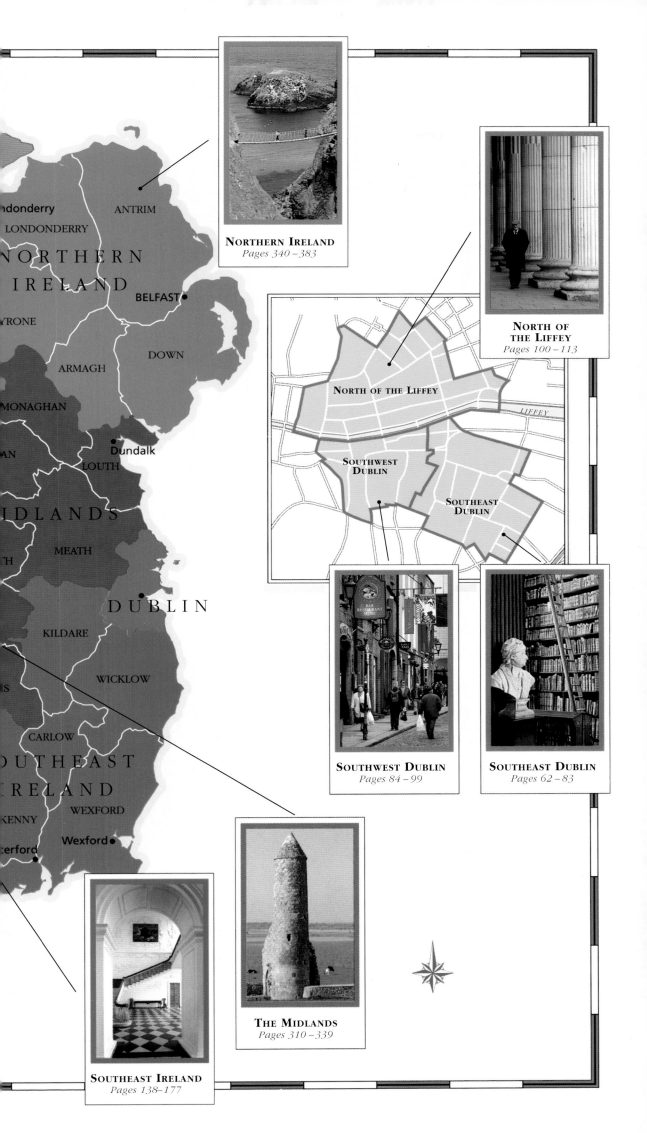

ndonderry
LONDONDERRY
ANTRIM

NORTHERN IRELAND
Pages 340 – 383

NORTHERN
IRELAND

BELFAST

YRONE

DOWN

ARMAGH

MONAGHAN

AN

Dundalk

LOUTH

IDLANDS

MEATH

DUBLIN

KILDARE

WICKLOW

S

CARLOW

OUTHEAST

RELAND

KENNY

WEXFORD

Wexford

terford

NORTH OF THE LIFFEY
Pages 100 – 113

NORTH OF THE LIFFEY

LIFFEY

SOUTHWEST
DUBLIN

SOUTHEAST
DUBLIN

SOUTHWEST DUBLIN
Pages 84 – 99

SOUTHEAST DUBLIN
Pages 62 – 83

THE MIDLANDS
Pages 310 – 339

SOUTHEAST IRELAND
Pages 138–177

INTRODUCING
IRELAND

Putting Ireland on the Map

THE ISLAND OF IRELAND covers an area of 84,430 sq km (32,598 sq miles). Lying in the Atlantic Ocean to the northwest of mainland Europe, it is separated from Great Britain by the Irish Sea. The Republic of Ireland takes up 85 per cent of the island with a population of 3.5 milllion. Northern Ireland, part of the United Kingdom, has 1.5 million people. Dublin is the capital of the Republic and has good international communications.

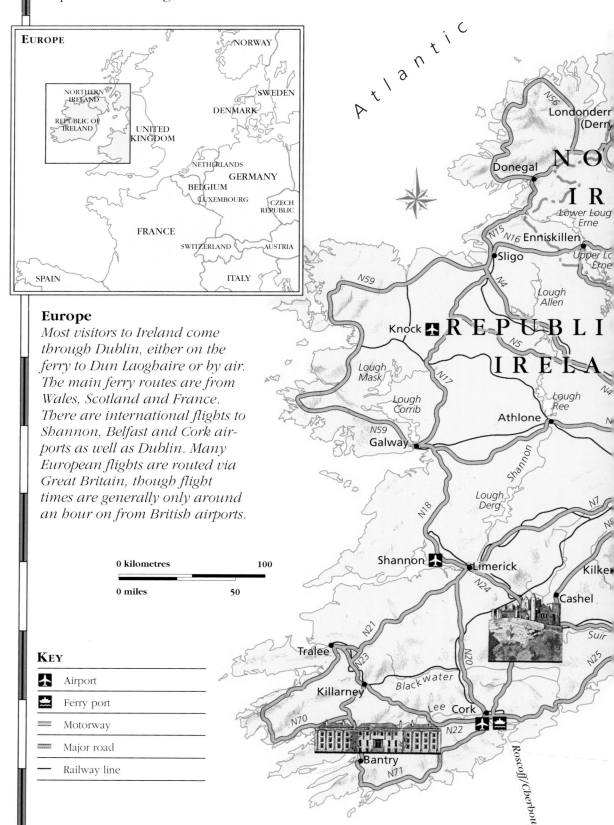

Europe

Most visitors to Ireland come through Dublin, either on the ferry to Dun Laoghaire or by air. The main ferry routes are from Wales, Scotland and France. There are international flights to Shannon, Belfast and Cork airports as well as Dublin. Many European flights are routed via Great Britain, though flight times are generally only around an hour on from British airports.

0 kilometres   100

0 miles   50

KEY

✈ Airport

⛴ Ferry port

═══ Motorway

━━━ Major road

── Railway line

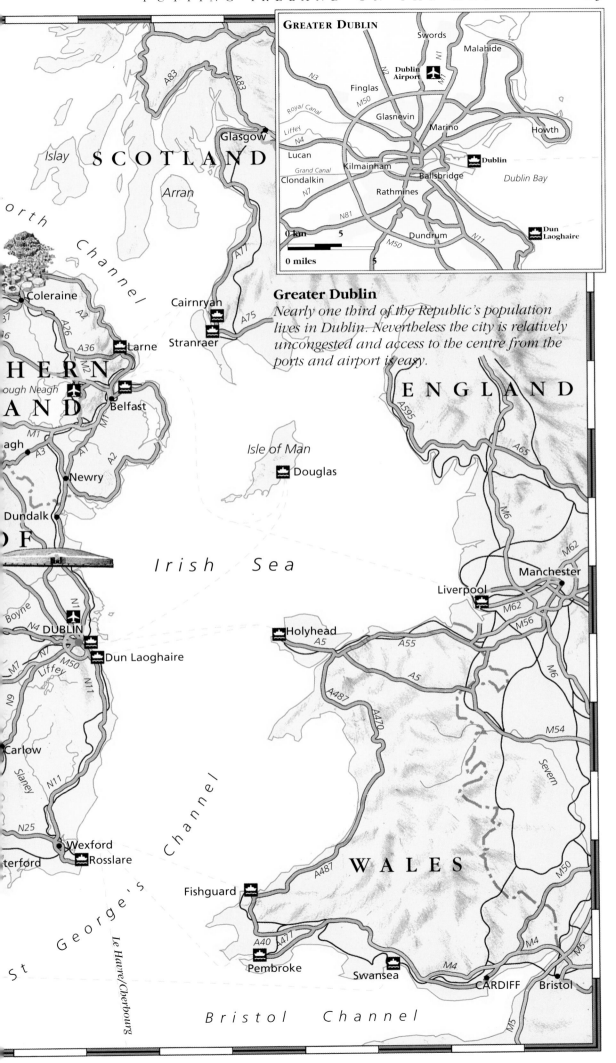

GREATER DUBLIN

Swords
Malahide
Dublin Airport
N1
N2
N3
Finglas
M1
M50
Royal Canal
Liffey
Glasnevin
Marino
Howth
N4
Lucan
Kilmainham
Dublin
Grand Canal
Clondalkin
Ballsbridge
Dublin Bay
N7
Rathmines
N81
Dundrum
N11
M50
Dun Laoghaire
0 km   5
0 miles   5

Islay
S C O T L A N D
Arran
Glasgow
Liffey
North Channel
A83
A83
A77
A77
A75
Cairnryan
Stranraer

Greater Dublin

*Nearly one third of the Republic's population
lives in Dublin. Nevertheless the city is relatively
uncongested and access to the centre from the
ports and airport is easy.*

Coleraine
A2
A26
A36
Larne
M2
HERN
AND
agh
M1
A3
A1
A2
Belfast
ough Neagh
Newry
Dundalk
OF

E N G L A N D
A595
A65
M6
M62

Isle of Man
Douglas

Manchester
Liverpool
M62
M56

I r i s h   S e a

Boyne
N4
N1
DUBLIN
N7
M7
M50
Liffey
N11
N9
Dun Laoghaire
M6
M54
Severn

Holyhead
A5
A55
A5
A487
A470

Carlow
Slaney
N11

St George's Channel

N25

Wexford
Rosslare
terford

W A L E S
A487
M50

Fishguard
A40
A411
A487

Le Havre/Cherbourg

A40
A411
Pembroke
Swansea
M4
M4
CARDIFF
M4
Bristol
M5

B r i s t o l   C h a n n e l
M5

PORTRAIT OF IRELAND

*M*ANY VISITORS *see Ireland as a lush, green island, full of thatched cottages, pubs and poetry. This has some basis in truth, and the tourist industry works to sustain that image. Political challenges and a booming economy add realism to this picture of rural bliss, but the genuine good humour and congeniality of the people always makes Ireland a most welcoming place to visit.*

Cathleen ni Houlihan, personification of Ireland

Ireland is, for the time being at least, a divided island. History and religion have created two communities, with the Protestant majority in the North opposed to the Catholic ideal of a united Ireland. In recent years the Troubles – the politically motivated campaigns of bombings, beatings and shootings in Northern Ireland – have tarnished the world's view of the country, but the Good Friday Agreement of 1998 has brought new hopes for peace, coupled with a fresh determination to take a practical approach to solving some emotive problems.

Ireland has long known its share of tragedy, culminating in the Great Famine of 1845–8, and poverty and emigration have been historical hallmarks of the Irish way of life. Suffering in the name of freedom, as personified by the heroine of WB Yeats's play *Cathleen ni Houlihan* is central to the national consciousness. Yet Irish people retain a relaxed and easy-going attitude that is positive and forward-looking.

Both sections of the island have young, ambitious and educated populations who are working hard to make their country a success, particularly in the context of today's European Union.

Rural areas, especially in the South (which the Industrial Revolution barely touched) are quaint. City life, however, is vibrant, with cultural and leisure scenes rivalling any urban centre in Europe.

Façade of Trinity College, Dublin, the Republic's most prestigious university

◁ **Thatching a traditional cottage in Adare, County Limerick**

Young first communicant in County Kerry

ECONOMIC DEVELOPMENT

Geography was once a barrier to the prosperity of both parts of Ireland. Located on the periphery of Europe, the island was isolated from its main markets and thus suffered high transportation costs. Today, however, Ireland has turned its location to its advantage by positioning itself as a 'hub' between Europe and the global marketplace. Traditionally, Northern Ireland had far more industry than the South, but during the Troubles old heavy industries such as shipbuilding declined and potential investors were scared away.

The Republic of Ireland, formerly among the poorer countries of the EU, has become one of its success stories. In the late 1980s, officials introduced fiscal policies such as tax breaks, wage moderation and low inflation to attract foreign investment to the Republic. The Republic now trades over 153 per cent of its GNP, and generous subsidies from the European Union have improved its transportation infrastructure. Many multinationals, especially computing and chemical companies, have established subsidiaries in

Traditional Irish dancing

Ireland. The advanced telecommunications system has made the country an important centre for teleservices, with more than 30 international companies basing their operations here.

Since 1990, Ireland's economy has been the healthiest in Western Europe. Its annual economic growth has averaged between 7 and 11 per cent, more than three times the EU average. Ireland's labour force grew by 2.5 per cent per annum in the 1990s, and unemployment is falling.

Pundits coined the phrase 'the Celtic Tiger' to describe Ireland's dramatic pounce on the marketplace. The long overdue signs of prosperity can be seen not only in the cities but in bustling provincial shopping streets and the number of large new homes springing up around the country. For many, the happiest legacy of the Celtic Tiger is that it has reversed the tide of emigration, and

Pavement artist on O'Connell Street, Dublin

for the first time in decades young people are not only staying in Ireland but actually returning from abroad.

Despite the growing manufacturing and service industries, agriculture remains vital and now accounts for 10 per cent of exports. Out of the Republic's total land area of around 7 million hectares (17 million acres), 5 million (12.32 million acres) are devoted to forestry and agriculture. Dairying and cattle raising are major agricultural industries, and the main crops are wheat, barley, sugar beet and potatoes. The country's good harbours and long coastline have made fishing significant.

Traditional farming: a field of haystacks overlooking Clew Bay, County Mayo

Another important industry, and one of the fastest growing, is tourism. The Republic receives more than 5.5 million overseas visitors a year, and its strong popularity is reflected not only in the above-average growth in first-time guests from all around the world, but also in the number of people who come back. Among most Europeans, Dublin rates as one of the 'hot' spots for a weekend getaway. Now that the political situation seems to be stabilizing, tourism is renascent in Northern Ireland as well, and the region is ready to welcome tourists. The Irish gift for hospitality is not affected by religious or political divides and makes the people naturals in the tourism industry.

Ireland's challenge today is to determine the best plan for prosperity. While the economy has raced ahead, some housing and infrastructure matters have yet to catch up. But the country will continue to be an important economic partner in the EU. The public backs European Monetary Union as the basis for economic growth. In 1999, Ireland adopted the Euro as its national currency, although the Irish pound is still in use until the new notes and coins come into circulation, which will probably happen in the year 2002.

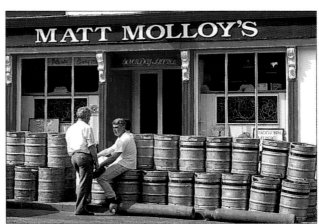

Connemara pony show

RELIGION AND POLITICS

Catholicism remains a strong influence. In the Republic, the Church runs most schools, along with some hospitals and social services. Religion forms a major part of everyday life, and conversations are often peppered with 'God bless you's' or references to the saints. According to some estimates, over 90 per cent of the population attends Mass. Religion also plays an important role in the politics of the Republic and moral

Matt Molloy's pub in Westport, County Mayo

Typically brightly-painted shop selling local wares from Sneem in the Ring of Kerry

Cathedral window

first woman to hold the post, was seen by many people as a sign of more enlightened times. She was succeeded in November 1997 by Mary McAleese. A new political climate has favoured the quiet spread of feminism and challenged the old paternalism of Irish politics, not only in social issues but also in helping break down the exclusivity of the largest of the traditional parties Fianna Fáil and Fine Gael.

Ireland joined the United Nations in 1955 and has served terms on the Security Council. It was elected to membership of the European Economic Community in 1973, and sees the Union as a central to its foreign and economic policies.

Being part of the United Kingdom, Northern Ireland has a separate political system from the South. From partition in 1921 until the escalation of the Troubles in 1972, a virtually autonomous government at Stormont oversaw the affairs of the province. The Unionist Party, whose large majority community supported union with Britain, held power, and the nationalist community, who number around two-fifths of the population and favour a united Ireland, suffered much discrimination. This situation was almost bound to result in violence. In 1972, in response to the threat to civil security posed by the escalating crisis between these

conservatism affects Irish attitudes to issues such as divorce, contraception, abortion and homosexuality. It has also enriched the country's artistic legacy, from the treasures of its early Christian monasteries to the ornate churches that stand today.

The Republic of Ireland is a parliamentary democracy and the president, who is elected for a seven-year term of office by a direct vote of the people, is the head of state. There are two Houses of Parliament, the Dáil Éireann (House of Representatives) and the Seanad (Senate). The head of the government, or prime minister, is called the Taoiseach. The democracy is strong, and five main political parties are currently represented in the Dáil. The election of lawyer Mary Robinson as president in 1990, the

Looking through the trees to Lough Foyle on the Inishowen Peninsula, County Donegal

View of early monastic settlement, County Sligo

between parties and safeguard human rights, and was approved by the people of both North and South. This demand for peace from the people themselves is the single most potent cause for optimism as opposing factions struggle to make the deal workable.

factions, the British government took control of all aspects of government in Northern Ireland.

Since that time, several agreements have been negotiated that attempted to establish the political fate of the province, trying to take into account three sets of relationships: those within Northern Ireland; between North and South; and between Britain and Ireland. In spite of the enormity and complexity of this task, the Good Friday Agreement of 1998 was a genuine leap forward and it set a new political structure for Northern Ireland. Both governments agreed to change their respective constitutions to enable the future status of Northern Ireland to be determined not by the claims of Britain or the Republic to the province, but by the wishes of the people who live there. It was agreed that Northern Ireland will continue to be part of the United Kingdom as long as the majority of people there wish to do so. But if in the future a majority votes to join a united Ireland, both governments must support that course of action. The Good Friday Agreement, also set up commissions in order to promote co-operation

Medieval cross and round tower

LANGUAGE AND CULTURE

Ireland was a Gaelic-speaking nation until the 16th century, when the English ascendancy sent the language into decline. Happily, that decline was not fatal: today the Republic has become officially bilingual and 35 per cent of adults claim to have some knowledge of the Irish language. While many speak it fluently, some figures indicate that only 3 per cent use it with any regularity. That should begin to change as Irish is now a core subject in primary and secondary level schools; some degree of knowledge of Irish is needed for university entrance and for careers in the public sector. There is even a state agency that promotes the language, as well as exclusively Irish broadcast outlets.

Evening descends on the Corkian countryside

Irish culture is as enduring as it is rich. The people love old folk legends, epic poetry and songs; these form the foundation of a world-renowned tradition of literature, which embraces many aspects of Irish history and character and still continues to evolve in fiction and film. Religion had a major influence on art and architecture, from the lavish illustrated medieval manuscripts, best represented by the famous Book of Kells, to the elaborate carved high crosses and unique, slender round towers of the early monasteries.

Bustling Great Victoria Street in Belfast, Northern Ireland

Music is a passion in Ireland, from the rock of U2 to the folk music of Clannad, the Chieftains and Mary Black. The country has a wealth of accomplished local musicians, and traditional music is played in pubs throughout the land. Irish dancing also became one of the great hits of the 1990s when *Riverdance* took to stages all over the world.

Another national passion is horse racing. Ireland's breeders and trainers are masters of their trade and enjoy astonishing international success for such a small country. Other sports are followed with equal intensity, particularly the uniquely Irish sports of hurling and Gaelic football, as well as rugby and football (soccer).

Ireland is great for recreational pursuits, and the country is loaded with golf courses, a great many of them designed by celebrated architects and ranking among the best in the world. With a landscape of green grass, links, rolling hills and other natural features, the country is a highly rated golf destination. Drinking also plays an important part in Irish culture: social life centres on the pub. When the Republic introduced stricter drink driving laws in 1994, rural publicans said traditional Irish society would collapse. Instead, many pubs now serve coffee, tea and more non-alcoholic drinks, as well as food at lunchtime and often in the evenings.

Relaxing in companionable silence

THE LAND

Ireland was once divided into four provinces: Leinster, which included Dublin and the east; Munster in the south; Connaught in the west and Ulster in the north. The island has now been divided into 32 counties – 26 lie in the Republic with 6 located in Northern Ireland.

The Irish have always possessed a sense of belonging to their land, which makes the forced emigrations of the past all the more poignant. Much Irish poetry and literature is a celebration of nature, and inspiration is everywhere. Within this small island lies a kaleidoscope of landscapes: green hills and pasturelands, heather and heath,

Winter scenery in Black Valley, County Kerry

The exquisite furnished dining room of Bantry House, County Cork, once home to the White family, the Earls of Bantry

to strengthen its links with the European Union, more Irish people are also living and working in quite a wide variety of other European countries. Tracing ancestors has become an activity for many visitors from the Irish diaspora worldwide. Most counties have their own heritage centre or genealogical service that can help people locate data from their region. Some 70 million people around the world can claim Irish descent, nowhere more so than in the United States, where 40 million have Irish forebears. People of Irish origin have generally influenced the political and cultural profiles of their new homelands. The Irish-Americans have managed to rise to prominence in American business and politics and often played pivotal roles in US history. The two nations are both politically and culturally compatible, and the Clinton administration has encouraged the Northern Ireland peace process. Anyone who has lived or travelled in the United States before making a visit to Ireland will notice the strong links between the two nations.

dramatic cliffs and rocky coasts, interspersed with numerous lakes, rivers and wetlands. The most unusual geographical feature is the vast expanse of boglands, some of the largest in the world. Ireland has no nuclear power stations, but depends instead on peat harvested from the boglands for the generation of all its electricity. However, the increasing use of this nonrenewable source of energy over the past century has greatly reduced the extent of the boglands.

Modern statuary representing Ireland's timeless love of music

Ireland is a delight for touring by car – indeed this is the only way to see the scenic areas off the beaten track. It is also great walking and hiking country. Touring along the waterways by boat or along the trails on horseback is increasingly popular.

THE IRISH DIASPORA

There may be nearly as many Irish citizens living outside of Ireland as there are dwelling on the emerald isle. Around 2 million live in the United Kingdom, while half a million live in the United States. Up to half a million more are scattered elsewhere, with significant numbers resident in Australia, New Zealand and Canada. As Ireland continues

The rugged coast of the tranquil Fanad peninsula in County Donegal

The Landscape and Wildlife of Ireland

Corncrake

THE LANDSCAPE is one of the Ireland's greatest attractions. It varies from bogs and lakes in the central lowlands to mountains and rocky islands in the west. Between these two extremes, the island has abundant lush, green pastureland, the result of plentiful rainfall, but little natural woodland. Parts of the far west, where the land is farmed by traditional methods, are havens for threatened wildlife, including the corncrake, which needs undisturbed hay fields in which to nest.

THE FAUNA OF IRELAND

Natterjack toad

Many animals (including snakes) did not make it to Ireland before the Irish Sea rose after the Ice Age. Other surprising absentees are the mole, weasel and common toad (the natterjack, however, can be seen). The wood mouse is the only small native rodent, but the once common red squirrel has now been virtually taken over by the grey.

ROCKY COASTS

Chough

The Dingle Peninsula (see pp190–91) is part of a series of rocky promontories and inlets created when sea levels rose at the end of the Ice Age. Cliffs and islands offer many sites for sea birds, with some enormous colonies, such as the gannets of Little Skellig (pp196–97). The chough still breeds on cliffs in the extreme west. Elsewhere in Europe, this rare species of crow is declining in numbers.

Thrift grows in cushion-like clumps, producing its papery pink flowerheads from spring right through to autumn.

Sea campion is a low-growing plant. Its large white flowers brighten up many a cliff top and seaside shingle bank.

LAKES, RIVERS AND WETLANDS

Great crested grebe

This watery landscape around Lough Oughter is typical of the lakelands of the River Erne (pp364–5). Rainfall is high throughout the year, which results in many wetlands, especially along the Shannon (pp228–9) and the Erne. The elegant great crested grebe breeds mainly on the larger lakes in the north.

Water lobelia grows in the shallows of stony lakes. Its leaves remain below the water, while the pale lilac flowers are borne on leafless stems above the surface.

Fleabane, once used to repel fleas, thrives in wet meadows and marshes. It has yellow flowers like dandelions.

Grey seals *are a common sight in the waters off the Atlantic coast, feeding on fish and occasionally on sea birds.*

Red deer *have been introduced into many areas, notably the hills of Connemara.*

Pine martens, *though mainly nocturnal, may be spotted in daytime during the summer.*

Otters *are more likely to be seen in the shallow seas off rocky coasts than in rivers and lakes, though they live in both habitats.*

MOUNTAIN AND BLANKET BOG

As well as the raised bogs of the central lowlands *(p338)*, much of Ireland's mountainous ground, particularly in the west, is covered by blanket bog such as that seen here in Connemara *(pp264–65)*.

Wheatear On drier upland sites this grades into heather moor and poor grassland. The wheatear, which inhabits rocky scree and heathland, is a restless bird with an unmistakeable white rump. It flits about, dipping and bobbing in pursuit of flies.

Bog myrtle *is an aromatic shrub, locally common in Ireland's bogs. Its leaves can be used to flavour drinks.*

Bogbean, *a plant found in fens and wet bogland, has attractive white flowers splashed with pink. Its leaves were once used as a cure for boils.*

PASTURELAND

Rolling pastureland with grazing livestock, as seen here in the foot-hills of the Wicklow Mountains *(pp160–61)*, is a very common sight throughout Ireland. The traditional farming methods employed in many parts of the **Rook** island (particularly in the west) are of great benefit to wildlife. Rooks, for example, which feed on worms and insect larvae found in pasture, are very common.

Meadow vetchling *uses its tendrils to clamber up grasses and other plants. It has clusters of pretty pale yellow flowers.*

Marsh thistle *is a common flower of wet meadows and damp woodland. It is a tall species with small, purple flowerheads.*

Architecture in Ireland

Window of an Irish cottage

IRELAND'S TURBULENT HISTORY has done incalculable damage to its architectural heritage. Cromwell's forces, in particular, destroyed scores of castles, monasteries and towns in their three-year campaign against the Irish in the mid-17th century. However, many fascinating buildings and sites remain, with Iron Age forts being the earliest surviving settlements. Christianity in Ireland gave rise to monasteries, churches and round towers; conflict between Anglo-Norman barons and Irish chieftains created castles and tower houses. The later landlord class built luxurious country mansions, while their labourers had to make do with basic, one-roomed cottages.

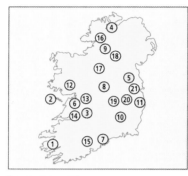

LOCATOR MAP

☐	Iron Age forts
☐	Round towers
☐	Tower houses
☐	Georgian country houses

IRON AGE FORT

Ring forts (raths) were Iron Age farmsteads enclosed by an earth bank, a timber fence and a ditch to protect against cattle-raiders. Inside, people lived in huts with a souterrain (underground passage) for storage and refuge. Some were in use as late as the 17th century, but all you can usually see today are low circular mounds. In the west, stone was used for cahers (stone ring forts) and promontory forts (semi-circular forts built on cliff tops using the sea as a natural defence).

Thatched hut

Entrance　　**Souterrain**

ROUND TOWER

Lookout window　　**Conical roof**

Round towers, often over 30m (100 ft) tall, were built between the 10th and 12th centuries on monastic sites. They were bell towers, used as places of refuge and to store valuable manuscripts. The entrance, which could be as high as 4 m (13 ft) above ground, was reached by a ladder that was hauled up from the inside. Other moveable ladders connected the tower's wooden floors.

Wooden floor

Moveable ladder

TOWER HOUSE

Machicolation

Outer wall around bawn

Spiral staircase

Tower houses were small castles or fortified residences built between the 15th and 17th centuries. The tall square house was often surrounded by a stone wall forming a bawn (enclosure), used for defence and as a cattle pen. Machicolations (projecting parapets from which to drop missiles) were sited at the top of the house.

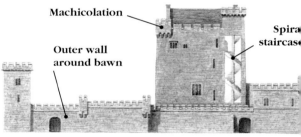

COTTAGE

One-roomed cottages, thatched or slate-roofed, are still a common feature of the Irish landscape. Built of local stone with small windows to retain heat, the cottages were inhabited by farm workers or smallholders.

Bog-oak timbers　　**Thatched, clay-lined chimney**

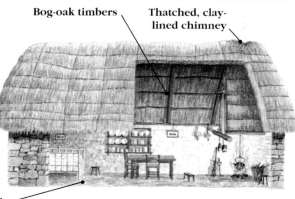

Clay floor

Iron Age Forts

Round Towers

Tower Houses

Georgian Country Houses

The well-preserved round tower at Ardmore

Georgian Country House

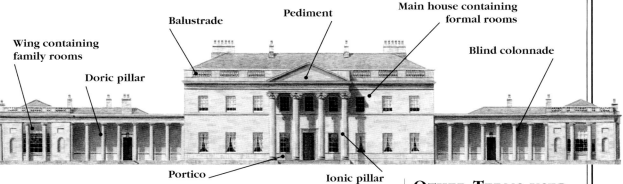

Wing containing family rooms — Doric pillar — Balustrade — Pediment — Main house containing formal rooms — Blind colonnade — Portico — Ionic pillar

Between the 1720s and 1800, prosperous landlords commissioned palatial country mansions in the Palladian and Neo-Classical styles popular in England over that period. Castle Coole (above) has a Palladian layout, with the main house in the centre and a colonnade on either side leading to a small pavilion. The Neo-Classical influence can be seen in the unadorned façade and the Doric columns of the colonnades. Noted architects of Irish country houses include Richard Castle (1690–1751) and James Wyatt (1746–1813).

Stucco

Stucco (decorative relief plasterwork), popular in the 18th century, is found in many Georgian country houses as well as town houses and public buildings. The Italian Francini brothers were particularly sought after for their intricate stuccowork (notably at Castletown and Russborough) as was Irish craftsman Michael Stapleton (Trinity College, Dublin and Dublin Writers Museum).

Trompe l'oeil detail at Emo Court

Ceiling at Dublin Writers Museum

Stucco portrait at Castletown House

Stuccowork at Russborough House

Other Terms Used in this Guide

Beehive hut: Circular stone building with a domed roof created by corbelling (laying a series of stones so that each projects beyond the one below).

Cashel: Stone ring fort.

Crannog: Defensive, partly artificial island on a lake. Huts were often built on crannogs (*see p37*).

Curtain wall: Outer wall of a castle, usually incorporating towers at intervals.

Hiberno-Romanesque: Style of church architecture with rounded arches highly decorated with geometric designs and human and animal forms. Also called Irish-Romanesque.

Motte and bailey: Raised mound (motte) topped with a wooden tower, surrounded by a heavily fenced space (bailey). Built by the Normans in the 12th century, they were quickly erected in time of battle.

Tympanum: Decorated space over a door or window.

Literary Ireland

Fᴏʀ ᴀ ʟᴀɴᴅ the size of Ireland to have produced four Nobel prizewinners in Shaw, Yeats, Beckett and Séamus Heaney is a considerable feat. Yet it is not easy to speak of an "Irish literary tradition" as the concept embraces rural and urban experiences, Protestant and Catholic traditions and the Gaelic and English languages. Irish fiction today, as in the past, is characterized by a sense of community and history, a love of storytelling and a zest for language.

A first edition of *Ulysses*

WB Yeats – Ireland's most famous poet

The Blasket Islands, which provided inspiration for several writers

Gᴀᴇʟɪᴄ Lɪᴛᴇʀᴀᴛᴜʀᴇ

Iʀɪsʜ ʟɪᴛᴇʀᴀᴛᴜʀᴇ proclaims itself the oldest vernacular literature in Western Europe, dating back to early monastic times when Celtic folklore and sagas such as the epics of Cuchulainn *(see p30)* were written down for the first time. The disappearance of Gaelic literature followed the demise, in the 17th century, of the Irish aristocracy for whom it was written. Gaelic literature has had several revivals. Peig Sayers is famous for her accounts of the harsh life on the Blasket Islands *(see p190)* in the early 20th century.

Playwright George Bernard Shaw

Wilde, who entered Oxford University in 1874 and later became the darling of London society with plays such as *The Importance of Being Earnest*. George Bernard Shaw *(see p120)*, writer of *St Joan* and *Pygmalion*, also made London his home. This dramatist, critic, socialist and pacifist continued to write until well into the 20th century.

An early Anglo-Irish writer was satirist Jonathan Swift *(see p95)*, author of *Gulliver's Travels*, who was born in Dublin in 1667 of English parents. Anglo-Irish literature was strong in drama, the entertainment of the cultured classes, and owed little to Irish settings or sensibilities. By the 1700s, Ireland was producing an inordinate number of leading playwrights, many of whom were more at home in London. These included Oliver Goldsmith, remembered for his comedy *She Stoops to Conquer*, and Richard Brinsley Sheridan, whose plays include *The School for Scandal*. Near the end of the century, Maria Edgeworth set a precedent with novels such as *Castle Rackrent*, based on the class divide in Irish society.

Novelist Maria Edgeworth

The 19th century saw an exodus to England of Irish playwrights, including Oscar

Aɴɢʟᴏ-Iʀɪsʜ Lɪᴛᴇʀᴀᴛᴜʀᴇ

Tʜᴇ ᴄᴏʟʟᴀᴘsᴇ of Gaelic culture and the Protestant Ascendancy led to English being the dominant language. Most literature was based around the privileged classes.

20ᴛʜ-Cᴇɴᴛᴜʀʏ Wʀɪᴛᴇʀs

Iɴ 1898, WB Yeats and Lady Gregory founded Dublin's Abbey Theatre *(see p104)*. Its opening, in 1904, heralded the Irish Revival, which focused on national and local themes. Playwright John Millington Synge drew inspiration from a love of the Aran Islands and Irish folklore, but the "immoral language" of his *Playboy of the Western World* caused a riot when first performed at the Abbey Theatre. Along with contemporaries, like Sean O'Casey and WB Yeats, Synge influenced subsequent generations of Irish writers, including novelist Seán O'Faolain, humorous writer and columnist Flann O'Brien, and hard-drinking, quarrelsome playwright Brendan Behan. The literary revival also produced many notable poets in the mid-20th century such as the gifted Patrick Kavanagh and Belfast-born Louis MacNeice, often considered to be one of the finest poets of his generation.

The writer Brendan Behan enjoying the company in a Dublin pub

Caricature of protesters at Dublin's Abbey Theatre in 1907

THREE LITERARY GIANTS

FROM the mass of talent to emerge in Irish literature, three figures stand out as visionaries in their fields. WB Yeats *(see p307)* spent half his life outside Ireland but is forever linked to its rural west. A writer of wistful, melancholic poetry, he was at the forefront of the Irish Revival, helping forge a new national cultural identity. James Joyce *(see p106)* was another trailblazer of Irish literature – his complex narrative and stream of consciousness techniques influenced the development of the modern novel. *Ulysses* describes a day in the life of Joyce's beloved Dublin and shaped the work of generations of writers. Bloomsday, which is named after one of the novel's characters, Leopold Bloom, is still celebrated annually in the city. The last of the three literary giants, novelist and playwright Samuel Beckett *(see p70)*, was another of Dublin's sons, though he later emigrated to France. His themes of alienation, despair, and the futility of human existence pervade his best-known plays, *Waiting for Godot* and *Endgame*.

The poet Patrick Kavanagh celebrating Bloomsday

CONTEMPORARY WRITERS

IRELAND's proud literary tradition is today upheld by a stream of talented writers from both North and South. Among the finest are Cork-born William Trevor, regarded as a master of the short story, and Brian Moore, whose stories of personal and political disillusionment are often based in his native Belfast. Similarly, Dubliner Roddy Doyle mines his working-class origins in novels such as *The Snapper* and *Paddy Clarke Ha Ha Ha*. Other established Irish writers are Brian Friel and Edna O'Brien. Out of Ireland's contemporary poets, the Ulster-born writers Séamus Heaney and Derek Mahon are considered among the most outstanding.

IRELAND IN THE MOVIES

Ireland has long been fertile ground for the world's film makers, and its people have been the subjects of major films, notably *The Crying Game* (1992), *In the Name of the Father* (1994) and *Michael Collins* (1996). Another popular film was *The Commitments* (1991). Filmed on location in and around Dublin with an all-Irish cast, it was based on a novel by Roddy Doyle. More recently, parts of Co Wexford doubled as the beach heads of Normandy in Steven Spielberg's World War II epic *Saving Private Ryan* (1997).

Cast of *The Commitments*, written by Roddy Doyle

The Music of Ireland

IRELAND IS THE ONLY COUNTRY in the world to have a musical instrument – the harp – as its national emblem. In this land, famous for its love of music, modern forms such as country-and-western and rock flourish, but it is traditional music that captures the essence of the country. Whether you are listening to Gaelic love songs that date back to medieval times or 17th- and 18th-century folk songs with their English and Scottish influences, the music is unmistakeably Irish. Dance is an equally important aspect of Irish traditional music, and some of the most popular airs are derived from centuries-old reels, jigs and hornpipes. Nowadays these are mainly performed at *fleadhs* (festivals) and *ceilidhs* (dances).

An Irish jig

Turlough O'Carolan (1670–1738) is the most famous Irish harper. The blind musician travelled the country playing his songs to both the rich and poor. Many of O'Carolan's melodies, such as The Lamentation of Owen O'Neill, *still survive.*

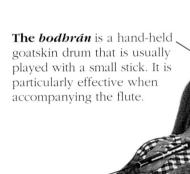

Piano accordion

The *bodhrán* is a hand-held goatskin drum that is usually played with a small stick. It is particularly effective when accompanying the flute.

Flute

John F McCormack (1884–1945) was an Irish tenor who toured America to great acclaim during the early part of this century. His best-loved recordings were arias by Mozart. Another popular tenor was Derry-born Josef Locke. A singer of popular ballads in the 1940s and '50s, he was the subject of the 1992 film, Hear My Song.

Two-row button accordion

THE CURRENT MUSIC SCENE

Mary Black

Ireland today is a melting pot of musical styles. The resurgence of Irish traditional music has produced many highly-respected musicians, such as the pipe-players Liam Ó Floin and Paddy Keenan from Dublin. Groups like the Chieftains and the Fureys have gained worldwide fame by melding old with new. Ireland is also firmly placed on the rock'n'roll map, thanks to bands such as Them in the 1960s and Thin Lizzy a decade later. The most famous rock band to come out of Ireland is Dublin's U2 who, in the 1980s, became one of the world's most popular groups. More recently, the series of albums entitled *A Woman's Heart* has been a showcase for talents such as Mary Black and Sinéad O'Connor, and bands like The Cranberries and Boyzone have conquered the world stage.

Bono of U2

Traditional Irish dancing *is currently enjoying renewed popularity. From the 17th century the social focus in rural areas was the village dance held every Sunday. From these gatherings, Irish dancing became popular.*

LIVE TRADITIONAL MUSIC

Wherever you go in Ireland, you won't be far from a pub with live music. For the Irish traditional musician, there are few set rules – the improvisational nature of the music means that no two performances of any piece are ever likely to be the same.

Violins, or fiddles, can either be tucked under the chin or held against the upper arm, shoulder or chest.

The New National Song—

ERIN REMEMBER 1916

Copyright Jan 3rd 1919

PRICE 2/. NET

Published by
QUINN & COMPANY.
29 UPPER ABBEY ST.,
DUBLIN.

Irish folk songs, *such as this one about the 1916 Easter Rising, tend to have a patriotic theme. But some of the most powerful songs have been written not just about the national struggle, but also on hardship, emigration and the longing for the homeland.*

TRADITIONAL INSTRUMENTS

There is no set line-up in traditional Irish bands. The fiddle is probably the most common instrument used. Like the music, some instruments have Celtic origins – the uillean pipes are related to the bagpipes played in Scotland and Brittany today.

The melodeon *is a basic version of the button accordion. Both these instruments are better suited to Irish music than the piano accordion.*

The uillean pipes *are similar to bagpipes and are generally considered to be one of the main instruments in Irish traditional music.*

The harp *has been played in Ireland since the 10th century. In recent years, there has been a keen revival of harp playing in Irish traditional music.*

The banjo *comes from the Deep South of the US and adds a new dimension to the sound of traditional bands.*

Tin whistle

Flute

The flute and tin whistle *are among the most common instruments used in traditional Irish music. The latter is often called the penny whistle.*

The violin *is called a fiddle by most musicians. The style of playing and sound produced varies from region to region.*

Ireland's Celtic Heritage

Stone carving on Boa Island

IRELAND'S RICH TRADITION of storytelling embraces a folk heritage that abounds with myths and superstitions. Some stories have been in written form since the 8th century, but most originated over 2,000 years ago when druids passed on stories orally from one generation to the next. Like the Gaelic language itself, many of Ireland's legends have links with those of ancient Celtic races throughout Europe. As well as the heroic deeds and fearless warriors of mythology, Irish folklore is also rich in tales of fairies, leprechauns, banshees and other supernatural beings.

The formidable Queen Maeve of Connaught

single-handedly. However, Queen Maeve took revenge on Cuchulainn by using sorcerers to lure him to his death. Today, in Dublin's GPO (see p105), a statue of Cuchulainn commemorates the heroes of the 1916 Easter Rising.

Part of the 2,300-year-old Gundestrup Cauldron unearthed in Denmark, which depicts Cuchulainn's triumph in the Cattle Raid of Cooley

CUCHULAINN

THE MOST FAMOUS warrior in Irish mythology is Cuchulainn. At the age of seven, going by the name of Setanta, he killed the savage hound of Culainn the Smith by slaying it with a hurling stick (one of the first times the sport of hurling is mentioned in folklore). Culainn was upset at the loss so Setanta volunteered to guard the house,

earning himself the new name of Cuchulainn, meaning the hound of Culainn.

Before he went into battle, Cuchulainn swelled to magnificent proportions, turned different colours and one of his eyes grew huge. His greatest victory was in the "Cattle Raid of Cooley" when Queen Maeve of Connaught sent her troops to capture the coveted prize bull of Ulster. Cuchulainn learned of the plot and defeated them

FINN MACCOOL

THE WARRIOR Finn MacCool is the most famous leader of the Fianna, an elite band of troops chosen for their strength and valour and who defended Ireland from foreign forces. Finn was not only strong and bold but also possessed the powers of a seer, and could obtain great wisdom by putting his thumb in his mouth and sucking on it. When they were not at war, the Fianna spent their time hunting. Finn had a hound called Bran which stood almost as high as himself and is said to be the original ancestor of the breed known today as the Irish wolfhound. Many of the

FAIRIES, LEPRECHAUNS AND BANSHEES

The diminutive figure of the leprechaun

The existence of spirits, and in particular the "little people", plays a large part in Irish folklore. Centuries ago, it was believed that fairies lived under mounds of earth, or "fairy raths", and that touching one of these tiny figures brought bad luck. The most famous of the "little people" is the leprechaun. Legend has it that if you caught one of these, he would lead you to a crock of gold, but take your eyes off him and he would vanish into thin air. The banshee was a female spirit whose wailing presence outside a house was said to signal the imminent death of someone within.

A banshee with long flowing hair

Fianna possessed supernatural powers and often ventured into the life beyond, known as the Otherworld. Among these was Finn's son Ossian who was not only a formidable warrior, like his father, but was also renowned as a wise and knowledgeable poet. Through time, Finn has come to be commonly portrayed as a giant. Legend has it that he constructed the Giant's Causeway in County Antrim *(see pp356–7)*.

A 19th-century engraving of Finn MacCool dressed for battle

THE CHILDREN OF LIR

ONE OF the saddest tales in Irish folklore involves King Lir, who so adored his four children that their stepmother was driven wild with jealousy. One day she took the children to a lake and cast a spell on them, turning them into white swans confined to the waters of Ireland for 900 years. However, as soon as she had done the deed, she became racked with guilt and bestowed upon them the gift of exquisite song. The

The children of King Lir being turned into white swans

end of the children's 900-year ordeal coincided with the coming of Christianity. The four children regained human form but were wizened and weak. They died soon afterwards, but not before being baptized. King Lir then decreed that no swan in Ireland should be killed – an act which is still illegal today.

SAINT BRENDAN

BRENDAN THE NAVIGATOR, like many other 6th-century monks, travelled widely. It is known that although he lived in western Ireland he visited Wales, Scotland and France. It is likely, though, that his most famous journey is fictitious. This story tells of a shipload of monks who, after seven years of all kinds of strange encounters designed to test their faith, found the Land of Promise. It is essentially a Christian retelling of the common tales of the Celtic Otherworld. The Feast of St Brendan on 16 May is celebrated in Kerry by the climbing of Mount Brandon.

ORIGINS OF IRISH PLACE NAMES

The names of many of Ireland's cities, towns and villages today are largely based on ancient Gaelic terms for prominent local landmarks, some of which no longer exist. Here are just a few elements of the place names the traveller may come across.

The fort on the Rock of Cashel that gives the town its name

Ar, ard – *high, height*
Ass, ess – *waterfall*
A, ah, ath – *ford*
Bal, bally – *town*
Beg – *small*
Ben – *peak, mountain*
Carrick, carrig – *rock*
Cashel – *stone fort*
Crock, knock – *hill*
Curra, curragh – *marsh*
Darry, derry – *oak tree*
Dun – *castle*
Eden – *hill brow*
Innis, inch – *island*
Inver – *river mouth*
Isk, iska – *water*
Glas, glass – *green*
Glen, glyn – *valley*
Kil, kill – *church*
Lough – *lake, sea inlet*
Mona, mone – *peat bog*
Mor – *great, large*
Mullen, mullin – *mill*
Rath, raha – *ring fort*
Slieve – *mountain*
Toom – *burial ground*
Tul, tulagh – *small hill*

St Canice's Cathedral in Kilkenny (the town's name means "church of Canice")

Engraving showing St Brendan and his monks encountering a siren

The Sporting Year

ALL MAJOR INTERNATIONAL team sports are played in Ireland, but the most popular games are the two uniquely native ones of Gaelic football and hurling. Most of the big games, plus soccer and rugby internationals, are sold out well in advance. However, if you can't get a ticket you'll find plenty of company with whom to watch the event in pubs. Horse racing, with over 240 days of racing a year, attracts fanatical support. For those keen on participatory sports, there are also Ireland's famous fishing waters and golf courses.

The North West 200 *is the fastest motorcycle race in the world over public roads – held near Portstewart* (see p354).

Football Association of Ireland Cup – the Republic's football final

Round-Ireland Yacht Race – held every two years

Four-day national hunt racing festival at Punchestown

The Irish Grand National *is a gruelling steeplechase run at Fairyhouse in County Meath.*

January	February	March	April	May	June

Irish Champion Hurdle, run at Leopardstown, County Dublin

The International Rally of the Lakes is a prestigious car rally around the Lakes of Killarney (see pp194–5).

Start of the salmon fishing season

The Six Nations Rugby Tournament, *between Ireland, Scotland, Wales, England, France and Italy, runs until April. Ireland play their home games at Lansdowne Road, Dublin.*

Irish Football League Cup – Northern Ireland's final

KEY TO SEASONS

	Hurling
	Gaelic football
	Flat racing
	National Hunt racing
	Rugby
	Association football
	Salmon fishing
	Equestrianism

The Irish Derby, *Ireland's premier flat race, attracts many of Europe's best three-year-olds to the Curragh (see p149).*

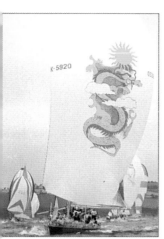

The All-Ireland Football Final *is held at Croke Park in Dublin. The top two counties play for this Gaelic football championship. More people watch the game than any other event in Ireland.*

Cork Week is a biennial regatta, organized by Royal Cork Yacht Club, where crews and boats of all classes meet and compete.

Greyhound Derby, run at Shelbourne Park, Dublin

The Dublin Marathon *is Ireland's foremost marathon event. It attracts a huge field including top-class athletes from around the world.*

Galway Race Week is one of Ireland's premier festival meetings and a popular social event.

Millstreet Indoor International showjumping event

ly	August	September	October	November	December

The Dublin Horse Show *is Ireland's premier horse show and a major event in the social calendar.*

All-Ireland Hurling Final at Croke Park, Dublin

THE GAELIC ATHLETIC ASSOCIATION

The GAA was founded in 1884 to promote indigenous Irish sport and discourage British influences – members were once forbidden from playing foreign games such as cricket. Today, despite heavy competition from soccer, the most popular sport in Ireland remains Gaelic football. However, the more intriguing GAA game is hurling – a fast and physical field sport played with sticks – which is said to have originated in ancient Celtic times. Both Gaelic football and hurling are played at parish and county level on a wholly amateur basis. The season ends with the All-Ireland finals, which draw large and passionate crowds to Dublin.

Camogie, a version of hurling played by women

The Irish Open Golf Champion- ship *is held at a different course each year and attracts a world- class field to courses such as Ballybunion in County Kerry.*

THE HISTORY OF IRELAND

IRELAND'S RELATIVE ISOLATION has cut it off from several of the major events of European history. Roman legions, for example, never invaded and the country's early history is shrouded in myths of warring Gods and heroic High Kings. Nevertheless, the bellicose Celtic tribes were quick to embrace Christianity after the arrival of St Patrick on the island in AD 432.

Until the Viking invasions of the 9th century, Ireland enjoyed an era of relative peace. Huge monasteries like Clonmacnoise and Glendalough were founded, where scholarship and art flourished. The Vikings never succeeded in gaining control of the island but in 1169 the Anglo-Normans arrived with greater ambitions. Many Irish chiefs submitted to Henry II of England, who declared himself Lord of Ireland. He left in 1172, and his knights shared out large baronies between themselves.

Matters changed when Henry VIII broke with the Catholic church in 1532. Ireland became a battleground between native Irish Catholics and the forces of the English Crown. Where the Irish were defeated, their lands were confiscated and granted to Protestants from England and Scotland. England's conquest was completed with the victory of William of Orange over James II at the Battle of the Boyne in 1690. The new order was backed up by repressive Penal Laws, but opposition to English rule was never totally quashed.

South Cross, Clonmacnoise

The Famine of 1845 to 1848 was the bleakest period of Irish history. Over two million either died or were forced to emigrate. Many who stayed were evicted by absentee English landlords. A campaign for Home Rule gathered strength, but it took decades before the Government of Ireland Act of 1920 divided the island. The South became the Irish Free State, gaining full independence in 1937, while the North bacame part of the UK. The IRA waged a bombing campaign for more than 25 years until a ceasefire in 1997, and in 1998 the Good Friday Agreement paved the way for the new Northern Ireland Assembly.

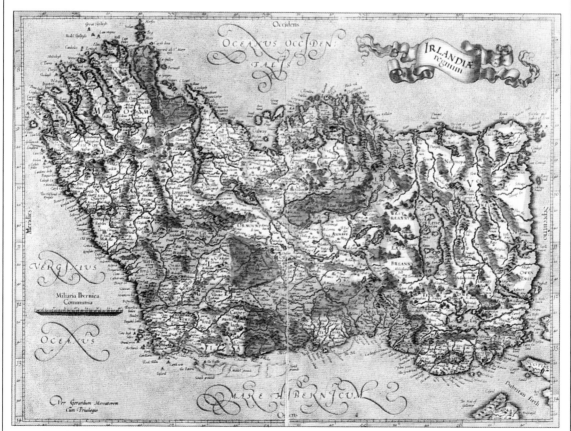

Map of Ireland, printed in 1592, showing the four traditional provinces

◁ *The Feast of St Kevin amid the Ruins of Glendalough* **by Joseph Peacock (1813)**

Prehistoric Ireland

Early Bronze Age stone axe-head

UNTIL ABOUT 9,500 YEARS ago Ireland was uninhabited. The first people, who may have crossed by a land bridge from Scotland, were hunter-gatherers and left few traces of permanent settlement. The 4th millennium BC saw the arrival of Neolithic farmers and herdsmen who built stone field walls and monumental tombs such as Newgrange. Metalworking was brought from Europe around 2000 BC by the Bronze Age Beaker people, who also introduced new pottery skills. The Iron Age reached Ireland in the 3rd century BC along with the Celts, who migrated from Central Europe, via France and Britain, and soon established themselves as the dominant culture.

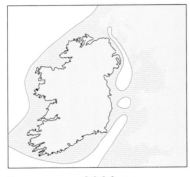

IRELAND C. 8000 BC

☐	*Former coastline*
☐	*Present-day coastline*

The terminal discs were worn on the shoulders.

GLENINSHEEN GORGET

Many remarkable pieces of gold jewellery were created in the late Bronze Age. This gold collar dates from about 700 BC. The Iron Age Celts produced similarly fine metalwork and ornaments.

Three strands of ropework

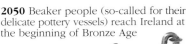

Dolmens or Portal Tombs

These striking megalithic tombs date from around 2000 BC. Legananny Dolmen in the Mountains of Mourne (see p382) is a fine example.

Wooden Idol

This Iron Age fetish would have played a role in pagan fertility rites.

Celtic Stone Idol

This mysterious three-faced head was found in County Cavan. In Celtic religion the number three has always had a special significance.

Bronze Bridle Bit

Celtic chiefs rode into battle on two-horse chariots with beautifully decorated harnesses.

TIMELINE

	8000 BC	6000	4000	2000	1000
	c. 7500 BC First inhabitants of Ireland *Extinct giant deer or "Irish Elk"*	**5000–3000** Ireland covered by dense woodland dominated by oak and elm	**2500** Building of Newgrange passage tomb *(see pp330–1)*	**1500** Major advances in metalworking, especially gold	
	6000 Date of huts excavated at Mount Sandel, Co Londonderry; oldest known dwellings in Europe	**3700** Neolithic farmers reach Ireland; they clear woods to plant cereals	**2050** Beaker people (so-called for their delicate pottery vessels) reach Ireland at the beginning of Bronze Age	

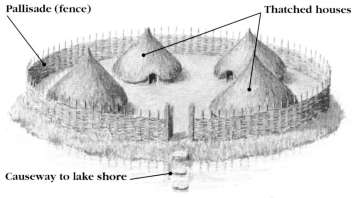

Pallisade (fence)   Thatched houses

Causeway to lake shore

Reconstruction of a Crannog

Originating in the Bronze Age, crannogs were artificial islands built in lakes. At first used for fishing, they soon developed into well-protected homesteads. Some remained in use up to the 17th century.

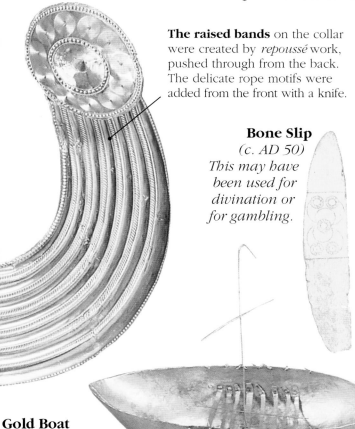

The raised bands on the collar were created by *repoussé* work, pushed through from the back. The delicate rope motifs were added from the front with a knife.

Bone Slip
(c. AD 50)
This may have been used for divination or for gambling.

Gold Boat
Part of a hoard of gold objects found at Broighter, County London-derry, the boat (1st century AD) was made as a votive offering.

WHERE TO SEE PREHISTORIC IRELAND

Prehistoric sites range from individual tombs such as Newgrange, Browne's Hill Dolmen *(see p163)* or Ossian's Grave to whole settlements, as at Céide Fields *(p260)* and Lough Gur *(p244)*. The largest Stone Age cemetery is at Carrowmore *(p308)*. Good reconstructions of prehistoric structures can be seen at Craggaunowen *(p238)* and the Ulster History Park *(p363)*. The National Museum in Dublin *(pp76–7)* houses the finest collection of artifacts, including wonderful gold objects from the Bronze Age.

Newgrange *(pp330–1) is Ireland's finest restored Neolithic tomb. At the entrance lie huge spiral-patterned boulders.*

Ossian's Grave *is a court grave, the earliest kind of Neolithic tomb (p361). An open court stood before the burial mound.*

600 First wave of Celtic invaders	**500** Intertribal warfare; chieftains vie for title of *Ard Rí* (High King)	**AD 80** Roman general Agricola considers invasion of Ireland from Britain		**367** Roman Britain attacked by Irish, Picts and Saxons
750	**500**	**250**	**AD 1**	**AD 250**
Bronze goad decorated with birds	**250** Second wave of Celts, who bring La Tène style of pottery			**c. 150** Greek geographer Ptolemy draws up map and account of Ireland

Bronze sword hilt imported from southern France

Celtic Christianity

Monk illuminating a manuscript

CELTIC IRELAND was divided into as many as 100 chiefdoms, though these often owed allegiance to kings of larger provinces such as Munster or Connaught. At times, there was also a titular High King based at Tara (see p332). Ireland became Christian in the 5th century AD, heralding a golden age of scholarship centred on the new monasteries, while missionaries such as St Columba travelled abroad. At the end of the 8th century, Celtic Ireland was shattered by the arrival of the Vikings.

IRELAND IN 1000

◻ *Viking settlements*

◻ *Traditional Irish provinces*

Ogham Stone
The earliest Irish script, Ogham, dates from about AD 300. The notches correspond to Roman letters, like a form of Morse code.

CELTIC MONASTERY
Monasteries were large centres of population. This reconstruction shows Glendalough (see pp162–3) in about 1100. The tall round tower served as a lookout for Viking raiders.

Craftmen's dwellings

Refectory and kitchen

Round tower

Abbot's house

St Mary's Church

The water-mill is used for grinding wheat and barley.

The Magnus Domus was a large communal building used by the abbot and the monks.

St Kevin's Church

Dry-stone bridge

A High Cross marks the monastery boundary.

Battle of Clontarf
After their defeat by the Irish High King, Brian Boru, in 1014, the Vikings began to integrate more fully with the native population. Brian Boru himself was killed in the battle.

TIMELINE

430 Pope sends first Christian missionary, Palladius

455 St Patrick founds church at Armagh

St Patrick

563 St Columba (Colmcille), the first Irish missionary, founds monastery on Iona in the Hebrides

664 Synod of Whitby decides that Irish Church should conform with Rome over date of Easter

400	500	600	700

432 Start of St Patrick's mission to Ireland

c. 550 Beginning of golden age of Celtic monasticism

615 St Columbanus dies in Italy after founding many new monasteries on the Continent

c. 690 *Book of Durrow* (see p71) completed

Viking Raids and Settlements

The first longships reached Ireland in 795. Though notorious for pillaging monasteries, the Vikings introduced new farming methods and coinage. They also founded walled cities such as Dublin, Waterford and Limerick.

Garryduff Gold Bird

Irish metalwork in the early Christian era was of very high quality. This gold ornament, possibly a wren, dates from around the 7th century AD.

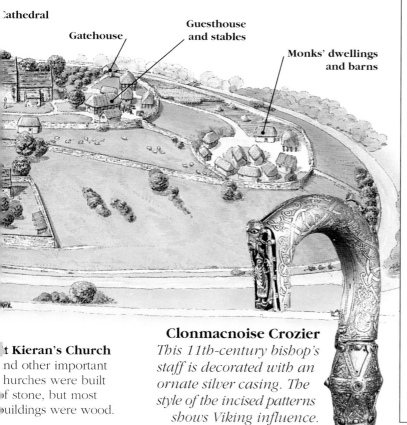

Cathedral

Gatehouse

Guesthouse and stables

Monks' dwellings and barns

t Kieran's Church

nd other important hurches were built f stone, but most uildings were wood.

Clonmacnoise Crozier

This 11th-century bishop's staff is decorated with an ornate silver casing. The style of the incised patterns shows Viking influence.

WHERE TO SEE EARLY CHRISTIAN IRELAND

Important early monastic sites besides Glendalough include Clonmacnoise and Devenish Island. Churches from this period can also be seen at Gallarus *(see p189)*, Clonfert *(p275)* and the Rock of Cashel *(pp246–7)*, while High Crosses *(p325)* and round towers *(p24)* survive all over Ireland. Dublin's National Museum *(pp76–7)* has the best collection of ecclesiastical (and Viking) artifacts and Trinity College *(pp70–1)* houses the finest illuminated manuscripts.

***Devenish Island** has a fine 12th-century round tower and enjoys a peaceful setting on Lower Lough Erne (p365).*

***Clonmacnoise** (pp336–7) lies on the east bank of the Shannon. This Romanesque doorway is part of the ruined Nuns' Church.*

Viking silver brooch

795 First Viking invasion of coastal monasteries

967 Irish warriors sack Limerick and begin military campaign against Viking overlords

999 Sitric Silkenbeard, the Viking king of Dublin, surrenders to Brian Boru

1166 Dermot McMurrough, King of Leinster, flees overseas

1134 Cormac's Chapel is built at Cashel *(see pp246–7)*

800	900	1000	1100

841 A large Viking fleet spends the winter at Dublin

807 Work starts on Kells monastery *(see p321)*

1014 High King Brian Boru of Munster defeats joint army of Vikings and the King of Leinster at Clontarf

Viking coin

1142 Ireland's first Cistercian house founded at Mellifont *(see p327)*

Anglo-Norman Ireland

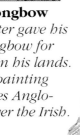

13th-century gold brooch

ANGLO-NORMAN NOBLES, led by Richard de Clare (nicknamed Strongbow), were invited to Ireland by the King of Leinster in 1169. They took control of the major towns and Henry II of England proclaimed himself overlord of Ireland. In succeeding centuries, however, English power declined and the Crown controlled just a small area around Dublin known as the Pale (*see p154*). Many of the Anglo-Norman barons living outside the Pale opposed English rule just as strongly as did the native Irish clans.

IRELAND IN 1488

☐ *Extent of the Pale*

CARRICKFERGUS CASTLE

The first Anglo-Norman forts were wooden structures, but they soon started to build massive stone castles. Carrickfergus (*see p371*) was begun in the 1180s and by 1250 had acquired a keep and a gatehouse.

The keep contained a hall on the first floor and, above that, the lord's private apartments.

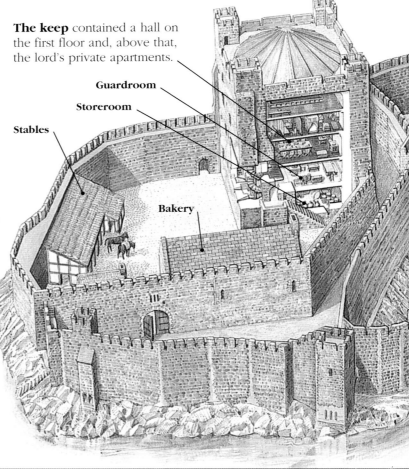

Guardroom
Storeroom
Stables
Bakery

Marriage of Strongbow
The King of Leinster gave his daughter to Strongbow for helping him regain his lands. Daniel Maclise's painting (1854) emphasizes Anglo-Norman power over the Irish.

Norman Weapons
These bows and arrows, unearthed at Waterford, may be relics of Strongbow's assault on the city in 1170.

TIMELINE

Dermot McMurrough, King of Leinster, who invited Strongbow to come to his aid

1172 Pope affirms King Henry II of England's lordship over Ireland

1177 John de Courcy's forces invade Ulster

1169 Strongbow's Anglo-Normans arrive at invitation of exiled King of Leinster, Dermot McMurrough

1224 Dominican order enters Ireland and constructs friaries

1260 Powerful Irish chieftain Brian O'Neill killed at the Battle of Down

1318 Bruce killed in battle

1315 Scots invade Ireland; Edward Bruce crowned king

1297 First Irish Parliament meets in Dublin

| 1200 | 1250 | 1300 |

Richard II's Fleet Returning to England in 1399
Richard made two trips to Ireland – in 1394 and 1399.
On the first he defeated Art McMurrough, King of Leinster,
and other Irish chiefs, but the second was inconclusive.

WHERE TO SEE ANGLO-NORMAN IRELAND

The strength of Norman fortifications is best seen in the castles at Carrickfergus, Limerick *(see p239)* and Trim *(p332)* and in Waterford's city walls. Gothic cathedrals that survive include Dublin's Christ Church *(pp116–17)* and St Patrick's *(pp118–19)* and St Canice's *(p168)* in Kilkenny. There are impressive ruins of medieval Cistercian abbeys at Jerpoint and Boyle *(p281)*.

Kitchen

The gatehouse was the last addition made in the 13th century. The two towers have arrow loops for longbowmen.

Drawbridge

Chapel

The Hall was where the lord of the castle held public court and decided cases brought before him.

Éamonn Burke
The 14th-century Lord of Mayo was a typically independent chieftain of Anglo-Norman descent.

Jerpoint Abbey *(p169) has a well-preserved 15th-century cloister decorated with carvings of curiously elongated figures.*

Waterford's *Anglo-Norman city walls include this sturdy watchtower (pp172–3).*

Great Charter Roll of Waterford (1372) showing portraits of the mayors of four medieval cities

1394 King Richard II lands with army to reassert control; returns five years later but with inconclusive results

1471 8th Earl of Kildare made Lord Deputy of Ireland

1496 Kildare regains Lord Deputy position

1491 Kildare supports Perkin Warbeck, pretender to the English throne

1350

1400

1450

1366 Statutes of Kilkenny forbid marriage between Anglo-Normans and Irish

1348 The Black Death: one third of population killed in three years

English forces (left) confront Irish horsemen on Richard II's return expedition

1487 Kildare crowns Lambert Simnel, Edward VI in Dublin

1494 Lord Deputy Edward Poynings forbids Irish Parliament to meet without royal consent

Protestant Conquest

E NGLAND'S BREAK with the Catholic Church, the dissolution of the monasteries and Henry VIII's assumption of the title King of Ireland incensed both the old Anglo-Norman dynasties and resurgent Irish clans such as the O'Neills. Resistance to foreign rule was fierce and it took over 150 years of war to establish the English Protestant ascendancy. Tudor and Stuart monarchs adopted a policy of military persuasion, then Plantation. Oliver Cromwell was even more forceful. Irish hopes were raised when the Catholic James II ascended to the English throne, but he was deposed and fled to Ireland, where he was defeated by William of Orange (William III) in 1690.

Hugh O'Neill, Earl of Tyrone

IRELAND IN 1625

Main areas of Plantation in the reign of James I

The first relief ship to reach Londonderry was the *Phoenix*. For three months English ships had been prevented from sailing up the Foyle by a wooden barricade across the river.

James II's army on the east bank of the Foyle attack the ship.

Battle of the Boyne
This tapestry, from the Bank of Ireland (see p66), shows William of Orange leading his troops against the army of James II in 1690. His victory is still celebrated by Orangemen in Northern Ireland.

Silken Thomas Fitzgerald
Silken Thomas, head of the powerful Kildares, renounced his allegiance to Henry VIII in 1534. He was hanged along with his five uncles in 1537.

The artist's depiction of 17th-century weapons and uniforms is far from accurate.

TIMELINE

	1541 Henry VIII declared King of Ireland by Irish Parliament	*Sir Thomas Lee, an officer in Elizabeth I's army, dressed in Irish fashion*		**1585** Ireland is mapped and divided into 32 counties	**1592** Trinity College, Dublin founded
Henry VIII					
1500	**1525**	**1550**		**1575**	**16●**
	1534 Silken Thomas rebels against Henry VIII			**1582** Desmond rebellion in Munster	
1504 8th Earl of Kildare becomes master of Ireland after victory at Knocktoe	**1539** Henry VIII dissolves monasteries	**1557** Mary I orders first plantations in Offaly and Laois		**1588** Spanish Armada wrecked off west coast	

The Siege of Drogheda
Between 1649 and 1652 Cromwell's army avenged attacks on Protestant settlers with ruthless efficiency. Here Cromwell himself directs the gunners bombarding Drogheda.

PLANTATION IRELAND
James I realized that force alone could not stabilize Ireland. The Plantation programme uprooted the native Irish and gave their land to Protestant settlers from England and Scotland. London livery companies organized many of the new settlements. The policy created loyal garrisons who supported the Crown.

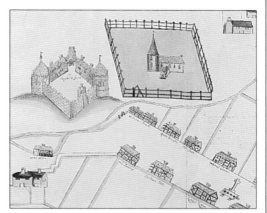

Bellaghy in County Londonderry was settled by the Vintners Company. This map of the neatly planned town dates from 1622.

The Walls of Derry have never been breached by any attacker and many of the original 17th-century gates and bastions that withstood the siege of 1689 are still in place *(see pp350–51).*

St George's flag

Ship Quay

Protestants emerge from the besieged city to greet the English relieving force and to engage the enemy.

Loftus Cup
Adam Loftus, Chancellor of Ireland, used his position to enrich his family. In 1593 he had the Great Seal of Ireland melted down and made into this silver-gilt cup.

THE RELIEF OF DERRY *(1689)*
Some 20,000 Protestants were besieged for 105 days in Londonderry by James II's forces. Thousands died from starvation, until relief finally came from English warships. This 18th-century painting by William Sadler II gives a rather fanciful picture of the ending of the siege.

607 Flight of the Earls: old Irish leaders flee to the Continent; Plantation of Ulster	**1632** Important Irish history, *The Annals of the Four Masters,* written by four Franciscan friars from Donegal	*Protestant apprentice boys closing the gates of Derry before the siege of 1689*	**1690** William of Orange defeats James II at Battle of the Boyne; James's army surrenders the following year in Limerick
1625	**1650**	**1675**	**1700**
03 Earl of Tyrone ends ght years of war by signing e Treaty of Mellifont		**1688** James II, deposed Catholic king of England, flees to Ireland and raises army	**1695** Penal code severely reduces rights of Roman Catholics
1641 Armed rebellion in Ulster opposes Plantation	**1649** Cromwell lands in Dublin; razes Drogheda and Wexford; Catholic landowners transplanted to far west		
			1689 Siege of Derry

Georgian Ireland

Lacquer cabinet in Castletown House

THE PROTESTANT ASCENDANCY was a period of great prosperity for the landed gentry, who built grand country houses and furnished them luxuriously. Catholics, meanwhile, were denied even the right to buy land. Towards the end of the century, radicals, influenced by events in America and France, started to demand independence from the English Crown. Prime Minister Henry Grattan tried a parliamentary route; Wolfe Tone and the United Irishmen opted for armed insurrection. Both approaches ultimately failed.

IRELAND IN 1703

Counties where Protestants owned over 75 per cent of land

The Irish House of Commons
This painting shows Irish leader Henry Grattan addressing the house (see p66). The "Grattan Parliament" lasted from 1782 to 1800, but was then abolished by the Act of Union.

State Bedroom

The saloon, the Casino's main room, was used for formal entertaining. It has a magnificent parquet floor.

Stone lions by Edward Smyth (1749–1812)

The basement contains the servants' hall, the kitchen, pantry and wine cellar.

Surveyors
The 18th century saw work begin on ambitious projects such as the Grand Canal, new roads and Dublin's network of wide streets and squares.

TIMELINE

Jonathan Swift (1667–1745)

1713 Jonathan Swift appointed Dean of St Patrick's Cathedral *(see p95)*

1724 Swift attacks Ireland's penal code in *A Modest Proposal*

1731 First issue of the *Belfast Newsletter,* the world's oldest continually running newspaper

1731 Royal Dublin Society founded to encourage agriculture, art and crafts

1738 Death of Ireland's most famous harper, Turlough O'Carolan *(see p28)*

1742 First performance of Handel's *Messiah* given in Dublin

1751 Dublin's Rotunda Lying-In Hospital is first maternity hospital in the British Isles

1710	1720	1730	1740	1750

Linen Bleaching

Ulster's linen industry flourished thanks to the expertise of Huguenot weavers from France. The woven cloth was spread out in fields or on river banks to bleach it (see p362).

WHERE TO SEE GEORGIAN IRELAND

Dublin preserves many fine Georgian terraces and public buildings such as the Custom House *(see p68)* and the Four Courts *(p112)*. Around Dublin, the grand houses at Castletown *(pp152–3)*, Russ-borough and Powerscourt *(pp156–7)* are fascinating reminders of the lifestyle of the gentry. Other 18th-century country seats open to the public include Emo Court, Westport House *(pp260–1)* and Castle Coole *(p366)*.

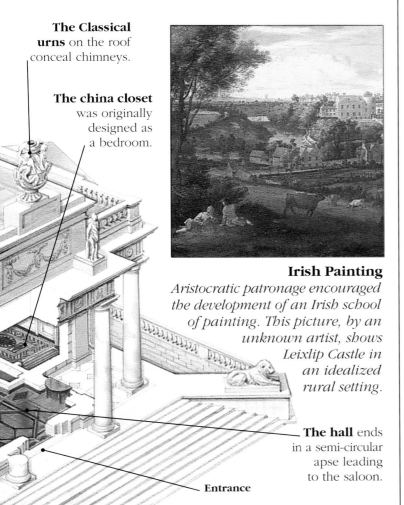

The Classical urns on the roof conceal chimneys.

The china closet was originally designed as a bedroom.

Irish Painting

Aristocratic patronage encouraged the development of an Irish school of painting. This picture, by an unknown artist, shows Leixlip Castle in an idealized rural setting.

The hall ends in a semi-circular apse leading to the saloon.

Entrance

***Emo Court's** façade, with its plain Ionic portico, is by James Gandon, architect of many of Dublin's public buildings (p339).*

***Russborough House** (p154) was built in 1741 by Richard Castle. Elegant niches with Classical busts flank the grand fireplace in the entrance hall.*

MARINO CASINO

This frivolous summer house was built in the 1760s for the first Earl of Charlemont on his estate just north of Dublin *(see p126)*. Palladian architecture of this kind was popular among the Irish aristocracy, who followed 18th-century English fashions.

Guinness Brewery Gate

1782 Parliament gains greater degree of independence from Westminster

The Irish Volunteers, a local militia which pressed Parliament for reform

1798 Rebellion of Wolfe Tone's United Irishmen quashed

1760	1770	1780	1790

Custom House

1791 James Gandon's Custom House built in Dublin

1759 Arthur Guinness buys the St James's Gate Brewery in Dublin

1795 Orange Order formed by Ulster Protestants

1793 Limited emancipation for Irish Catholics

Famine and Emigration

Ration card from Famine period

THE HISTORY of 19th-century Ireland is dominated by the Great Famine of 1845–8, which was caused by the total failure of the potato crop. Although Irish grain was still being exported to England, around one million people died from hunger or disease, with even more fleeing to North America. By 1900, the pre-famine population of eight million had fallen by half. Rural hardship fuelled a campaign for tenants' rights which evolved into demands for independence from Britain. Great strides towards "Home Rule" were made in Parliament by the charismatic politician, Charles Stuart Parnell.

IRELAND IN 1851

Areas where population fell by over 25% during the Famine

The ships that brought the Irish to America were over-crowded and fever-ridden, and known as "coffin ships".

Daniel O'Connell

Known as "The Liberator", O'Connell organized peaceful "monster rallies" of up to a million people in pursuit of Catholic emancipation. He was elected MP for Clare in 1828.

Castle Clinton was used for processing new arrivals to New York prior to the construction of the huge depot on Ellis Island.

The Boycotting of Landlords

In 1880, troops guarded the crops of Captain Boycott, the first notable victim of a campaign to ostracize landlords guilty of evicting tenants. His name later passed into the English language.

TIMELINE

Charles Bianconi's coach service, 1836

1815 First coach service begins in Ireland

1817 Royal Canal is completed

1838 Father Mathew founds temperance crusade – five million Irish take abstinence pledge and whiskey production is reduced by half

1845 Start of Great Famine which lasts for four years

1800	1810	1820	1830	1840

1803 Uprising, led by Robert Emmet, is crushed after feared Napoleonic invasion of England fails to materialize

1800 Act of Union: Ireland legally becomes part of Britain

1828 After a five-year campaign by Daniel O'Connell, Catholic Emancipation Act is passed, giving a limited number of Catholics the right to vote

Father Mathew

Eviction of Irish Farmers
In the late 1870s, agricultural prices plummeted. Starving tenant farmers fell into arrears and were mercilessly evicted. Their plight spawned the Land League, which lobbied successfully for reform.

THE IRISH ABROAD

One result of the Famine was the growth of a strong Irish community in the USA. From the lowest rung of American society, the immigrants rose up the social scale and became rich by Irish Catholic standards. They sent money to causes back home, and as a well-organized lobby group put pressure on the American government to influence British policies in Ireland. A more militant group, Clan na Gael, sent veterans of the American Civil War to fight in the Fenian risings of 1865 and 1867.

New Yorkers *stage a huge St Patrick's Day parade, 17 March 1870.*

The Irish were widely perceived as illiterate peasants in the USA and often met with a hostile reception.

IMMIGRANTS ARRIVE IN NEW YORK

The Irish who survived the journey to America landed at Castle Garden in New York, seen here in a painting by Samuel Waugh (1855). Although mainly country people, most new arrivals settled in Manhattan, often enduring horrific living conditions.

Charles Stuart Parnell
A campaigner for the Land League and Home Rule, Parnell saw his political career ruined in 1890, when he was cited as co-respondent in a divorce case.

1850	1860	1870	1880	1890

53 Dublin Exhibition is opened by Queen Victoria

Dublin Exhibition

1877 Charles Stuart Parnell becomes leader of the new Home Rule Party

1884 Founding of Gaelic Athletic Association, first group to promote Irish traditions

1892 Second Home Rule Bill is defeated

1867 Irish-Americans return home to fight in a rising led by the Irish Republican Brotherhood, also known as the Fenians

848 Failure of the Young Ireland Uprising – a spontaneous response ɔ insurrections elsewhere in Europe

1879–82 Land War, led by Michael Davitt's Land League, campaigns for the reform of tenancy laws

1881 Parnell is jailed in Kilmainham, Dublin

1886 British PM Gladstone sponsors first Home Rule Bill but is defeated by Parliament

War and Independence

Irish Free State stamp of 1922

PLANS FOR IRISH HOME RULE were shelved because of World War I; however, the abortive Easter Rising of 1916 inspired new support for the Republican cause. In 1919 an unofficial Irish Parliament was established and a war began against the "occupying" British forces. The Anglo-Irish Treaty of 1921 divided the island in two, granting independence to the Irish Free State, while Northern Ireland remained in the United Kingdom. There followed a civil war between pro-Treaty and anti-Treaty factions in the South.

IRELAND IN 1922

▨	*Northern Ireland*
☐	*Irish Free State*

The Unionist Party
Leader of the campaign against Home Rule was Dublin barrister Edward Carson. In 1913 the Ulster Volunteer Force was formed to demand that six counties in Ulster remain part of the UK.

The 1916 Service Medal,
issued to all who fought in the Easter Rising, depicts, on one side, the mythical Irish warrior Cuchulainn.

Sean J Heuston

Thomas McDonough

Major John McBride

William Pearse

Patrick Pearse, a poet, read the Proclamation of the Republic from the steps of the GPO on Easter Monday.

The Black and Tans
Named for their makeshift uniforms, these British troops – mostly demobbed World War I soldiers – carried out savage reprisals against the Irish in 1920–21.

TIMELINE

The Titanic

1913 General strike in Dublin

1912 Belfast-built *Titanic* sinks on her maiden voyage

1918 Sinn Féin wins 73 seats at Westminster; Constance Markievicz elected first woman MP

1916 Easter Rising quashed

1919 Fir meeting indepen parliame (*Dáil Éir*

1905	1910	1915	19

1905 Sinn Féin (We Ourselves) party founded

1904 Dublin's Abbey Theatre opens

1912 Edward Carson rallies Ulster Protestants; solemn covenant to defeat Home Rule signed by 471,414 people

Despatch bag carried by Constance Markievicz during Easter Rising

1920 Government of Ireland Act proposes partition of the island

1921 Anglo-Irish Treaty sign de Valera resigns; southe Ireland plunged into civil v

The General Post Office, Easter 1916
What was supposed to be a national uprising was confined to 2,500 armed insurgents in Dublin. They managed to hold the GPO and other public buildings for five days.

This Mauser rifle, smuggled in from Germany in 1914, was used by rebels in the Rising.

Tom Clarke

James Connolly

Joseph Plunkett

EAMON DE VALERA (1882–1975)

After escaping execution for his part in the Easter Rising, American-born de Valera went on to dominate Irish politics for almost 60 years. The opposition of his party, Sinn Fein, to the Anglo-Irish Treaty of 1921 plunged the new Irish Free State into civil war. After forming a new party, Fianna Fáil, he became Prime Minister (*Taioseach*) in 1932. De Valera remained in office until 1948, with further terms in the 1950s. Between 1959 and 1973 he was President of Ireland.

Mementoes of the Rising at Dublin's Kilmainham Gaol *(see p117)* include this crucifix made by a British soldier from rifle bullets.

Election Poster
Cumann na nGaedheal, the pro-Treaty party in the Civil War, won the Free State's first general election in 1923. It merged with other parties in 1933 to form Fine Gael.

LEADERS OF THE 1916 RISING

This collage portrait shows 14 leaders of the Easter Rising, who were all court-martialled and shot at Kilmainham Gaol. The brutality of their executions (the badly injured James Connolly was tied to a chair before being shot) changed public opinion of the Rising and guaranteed their status as martyrs.

22 Irish Free State inaugurated; Michael Collins shot dead in ambush in Co Cork

Michael Collins (1890–1922), hero of the War of Independence, became chairman of the Irish Free State and Commander-in-Chief of the Army

1932 Fianna Fáil sweep to victory in general election, and de Valera begins 16-year term as *Taioseach* (Prime Minister)

1936 IRA proscribed by Free State Government

1939 Éire declares neutrality during World War II

1925	1930	1935

1923 WB Yeats wins Nobel prize for Literature

1925 GB Shaw also receives Nobel prize

1926 De Valera quits Sinn Féin; sets up Fianna Fáil (Soldiers of Destiny) party

1929 Work started on River Shannon hydro-electric power scheme

1933 Fine Gael (United Ireland) party formed to oppose Fianna Fáil

1937 New constitution declares complete independence from Britain; country's name changes to Éire

Modern Ireland

Mary Robinson, Ireland's first woman President

Since joining the European Economic Community (now called the European Union) in 1973, the Irish Republic has done much to modernize its traditional rural-based economy. There have been social changes too, and laws prohibiting abortion and divorce have slowly been relaxed. Meanwhile, Northern Ireland has lived through more than 25 years of bombings and shootings. But recent peace agreements have brought new hope to the province, especially since the inauguration in 1998 of the new Northern Ireland Assembly.

1972 Bloody Sunday – British soldiers shoot dead 13 demonstrators in Derry. Northern Ireland Parliament is suspended and direct rule from Westminster imposed

1970 Reverend Ian Paisley, a radical Protestant Unionist, wins the Bannside by-election

1969 Violent clashes between the police and demonstrators in Belfast and Derry. British troops sent to restore order

1956 IRA launches a terrorism campaign along the border with Northern Ireland which lasts until 1962

1967 Northern Ireland Civil Rights Association is set up to fight discrimination against Catholics

NORTHERN IRELAND		
1945	1955	1965
REPUBLIC OF IRELAND		

1959 Eamon de Valera resigns as *Taoiseach* (Prime Minister) and is later elected President

1949 New government under John A Costello. Country changes name from Éire to Republic of Ireland and leaves British Commonwealth

1955 Republic of Ireland joins United Nations. Irish troops have played an important role in UN peace-keeping missions around the world ever since

1969 Samuel Beckett, seen here rehearsing one of his own plays, is awarded the Nobel prize for literature, but does not go to Stockholm to receive it

1947 Statue of Queen Victoria is removed from the courtyard in front of the Irish Parliament in Dublin

1963 John F Kennedy, the first American President of Irish Catholic descent, visits Ireland. He is pictured here with President Eamon de Valera

1973 Republic of Ireland joins the European Economic Community at same time as the UK. Membership has given the country access to much-needed development grants

74 Power-sharing experiment is ught down by a devastating ke, organized by Protestant rkers. Direct rule is reimposed

1976 Organizers of the Ulster Peace Movement, Mairead Corrigan and Betty Williams, are awarded the Nobel Peace Prize in Oslo

1982 De Lorean car factory in Belfast closes just four years after £17 million investment by British government

1981 Hunger-striker Bobbie Sands dies in Maze Prison

1985 Barry McGuigan beats the Panamanian, Eusebio Pedroza, for world featherweight boxing title

1986 Bitter Loyalist opposition follows the previous year's signing by the British and Irish governments of the Anglo-Irish Agreement

1987 IRA bomb explodes during Enniskillen's Remembrance Day parade, killing 11 people

1991 Peace talks instituted by Westminster between the main political parties of Northern Ireland (except Sinn Féin) and the British and Irish governments

1994 IRA and Protestant cease-fires. Gerry Adams, Sinn Féin leader, allowed to speak on British radio and television

1995 For the first time in 25 years, there are no troops on daylight patrols in Northern Ireland

1998 The Good Friday agreement sets out proposed framework for self-government in Northern Ireland

NORTHERN IRELAND

| 1975 | 1985 | 1995 |

REPUBLIC OF IRELAND

1979 Pope John Paul II visits Ireland and celebrates Mass in Dublin's Phoenix Park, in front of more than a million people

1988 Dublin's millennium is celebrated, boosting the city's image

1991 Mary Robinson becomes first female President of the Republic, succeeded by Mary McAleese in 1998

1992 In a referendum, 62 per cent of the Irish vote in favour of allowing pregnant women to seek an abortion abroad. A vote in favour of divorce follows in 1997

1994 Republic of Ireland football team reaches quarterfinals of World Cup in the USA. Here, Ray Houghton is congratulated on scoring the winning goal against Italy

1999 Ireland joins the single European currency on 1 January

1985 Irish pop singer Bob Geldof organizes Live Aid concerts in London and Philadelphia; £40 million is raised for African famine relief

1987 Dubliner Steven Roche wins the Tour de France, Giro d'Italia and World Championship in one incredible season

IRELAND THROUGH THE YEAR

POPULAR MONTHS for visiting Ireland are July and August, though whatever the season it's rarely crowded. June and September can be pleasant but never count on the weather, for Ireland's lush beauty is the product of a wet climate. Be aware that most tourist sights are open from Easter to September but have restricted opening hours or close in the low season. During spring and summer, festivals are held in

honour of everything from food to religion. A common thread is music, and few festivities are complete without musical accompaniment. Ireland is at its best when it has something to celebrate, so is an inspired choice for Christmas or New Year. Look out for the word *fleàdh* (festival) on your travels but remember, too, that the Irish are a spontaneous people: festivities can spring from the air, or from a tune on a fiddle.

Ladies' Day at Dublin Horse Show

Dublin's annual parade to celebrate St Patrick's Day (17 March)

SPRING

ST PATRICK'S DAY is often said to mark the beginning of the tourist season. Later, the spring bank holiday weekend in May, when accommodation is in short supply, is celebrated with music in most places. After the quiet winter months, festivals and events start to become more common.

MARCH

Adare Jazz Festival (*mid-Mar, see p244*). Staged in pubs and hotels throughout the town over five days.
St Patrick's Day (*17 Mar*). Parades and pilgrimages held at Downpatrick, Armagh, Dublin, Cork, Limerick and many other places.
Horse Ploughing Match and Heavy Horse Show, Bally-castle (*17 Mar, see p360*). The annual competition is more than 100 years old.

A St Patrick's Day float advertising Guinness

APRIL

Feis Ceoil, Dublin (*early Apr*). A classical music festival held at many different venues throughout the city.
Pan Celtic Festival, Tralee (*mid-Apr, see p188*). A lively celebration of Celtic culture, with music, dance and song.
Cork Choral Festival (*late Apr–May, see pp212–13*).

MAY

Belfast Civic Festival and Lord Mayor's Show (*mid-May, see pp372–3*). Street parade with bands and floats.
Royal Ulster Agriculture Society Show, Belfast (*mid-May*). A three-day show with diverse events ranging from sheep-shearing competitions to fashion shows.
"A Taste of Baltimore" Shellfish Festival (*end May, see p206*).
Fleadh Nua, Ennis, *end May, see p235*). Four days of traditional Irish music, songs and dance.

SUMMER

FOR THE VISITOR, summer represents the height of the festive calendar. This is the busiest time of year for organized events, from music and arts festivals to lively local race meetings, summer schools and matchmaking festivals. Book accommodation if your plans include a popular festival.

Beach races at Laytown (June)

JUNE

Laytown Beach Races, Co Meath (*late May or early June*). Horse races on the sand.
County Wicklow Garden Festival (*all month*). Held at private and public gardens around the county, including Powerscourt (*see pp156–7*).
An Tostal, Drumshanbo, Co Leitrim (*mid-Jun*). A pageant of Irish music and dance.
Maracycle, Belfast and Dublin (*mid-Jun*). Many thousands of people cycle each way between the two cities.
Bloomsday, Dublin (*16 Jun*). Lectures, pub talks, readings, dramatizations and walks to celebrate James Joyce's greatest novel, *Ulysses*.

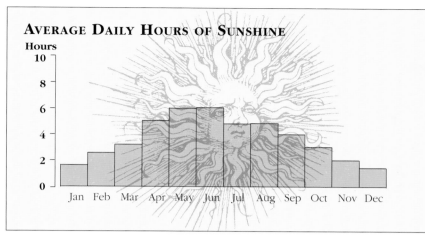

AVERAGE DAILY HOURS OF SUNSHINE

Hours

Jan Feb Mar Apr May Jun Jul Aug Sep Oct Nov Dec

Sunshine Chart
The chart gives figures for Dublin, though conditions are similar around the country. The Southeast enjoys more sunshine hours than any other part of Ireland, while Northern Ireland receives marginally fewer hours of sun than the Republic.

Scurlogstown Olympiad Celtic Festival, Trim *(mid-Jun, see p332)*. Traditional Irish music, dance, fair and selection of a festival queen.
Music in Great Irish Houses *(second and third weeks)*. Classical music recitals in grand settings at various venues.
Castle Ward Opera, Strangford *(end Jun, see p382)*. Opera festival in the grounds of 18th-century stately home.
County Wexford Strawberry Fair, Enniscorthy *(end Jun–early Jul, see p175)*. Includes a craft fair, music, street theatre and, of course, strawberries.

JULY

Battle of the Boyne Day *(12 Jul, see p326)*. Members of the Orange Order march in towns across Northern Ireland to celebrate the Protestants' landmark victory over King James II's Catholic army in 1690.
Cork Regatta Week, Crosshaven, Co Cork *(mid-Jul)*.
Galway Arts Festival *(third & fourth weeks, see pp270–1)*. Processions, concerts, street theatre, children's shows and

Traditional sailing craft in the Cruinniú na mBad at Kinvarra (August)

many other events in the medieval city centre. Followed immediately by Galway's popular five-day race meeting.
Mary from Dungloe International Festival, Dungloe *(last week, see p300)*. Dancing, music and selection of "Mary", the beauty queen.
Lughnasa Fair, Carrickfergus Castle *(end Jul, see p371)*. A popular medieval-style fair.
Ballyshannon International Folk Festival *(end Jul, see p303)*. Three days of traditional Irish music.
O'Carolan Harp and Traditional Music Festival, Keadue, Co Roscommon *(end Jul–early Aug)*. Music and traditional dance.

AUGUST

Stradbally Steam-engine Rally, Co Laois *(early Aug)*. Many types of steam-engine join this rally.

Orangemen parading on Battle of the Boyne Day

Letterkenny Folk Festival, Co Donegal *(early Aug, see p297)*. A week of celebration.
Dublin Horse Show *(first or second week)*. A premier showjumping competition and social event.
Puck Fair, Killorglin, Co Kerry *(mid-Aug, see p197)*. A wild goat is crowned "king" at this two-day-long traditional festival.
Blessing of the Sea *(second or third Sunday)*. Held in seaside towns all over Ireland.
Oul' Lammas Fair, Ballycastle *(mid-Aug, see p360)*. A popular fair that is particularly famous for its edible seaweed.
Kilkenny Arts Week *(third or fourth week, see pp166–8)*. A major arts festival including poetry, film and crafts.
Rose of Tralee Festival, *(end Aug, see p188)*. Bands, processions, dancing and selection of the "Rose".
Cruinniú na mBad, Kinvarra *(end Aug, see pp271–4)*. Various types of traditional sailing craft take part in this "gathering of the boats".

Steam-engine at Stradbally Rally (August)

AVERAGE MONTHLY RAINFALL

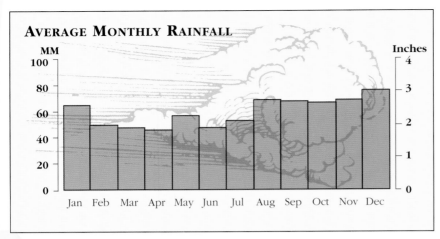

MM
100
80
60
40
20
0

Inches
4
3
2
1
0

Jan Feb Mar Apr May Jun Jul Aug Sep Oct Nov Dec

Rainfall Chart
Ireland is one of the wettest countries in Europe, with rainfall distributed evenly through the year – the figures displayed here are for Dublin. The West has the heaviest annual rainfall, while the Southeast receives marginally less rain than other regions.

Galway Oyster Festival (September)

AUTUMN

O YSTERS AND OPERA are the two big events in autumn. There are also festivals devoted to jazz, film and music. The October bank holiday week-end is celebrated with music in many towns; though it is low season, it can be difficult to find accommodation.

SEPTEMBER

All-Ireland Hurling Final, Croke Park, Dublin *(first or second Sunday, see p33).*
Lisdoonvarna Matchmaking Festival *(all month and first*

week of Oct, see p234). Single people gather together for traditional music and dance.
Waterford International Festival of Light Opera *(mid-Sep – early Oct).* Musicals and operettas at the Theatre Royal.
All-Ireland Football Final, Croke Park, Dublin *(3rd Sunday, see p33).* Gaelic football final.
Sligo Arts Festival *(last week, see p308).* Street entertainment, jazz, Irish music and dance.
Galway Oyster Festival *(end Sep, see pp270–1).* Oyster tastings at different venues.

All-Ireland Hurling at Croke Park, Dublin

OCTOBER

Octoberfest, London-derry *(all month, see pp350–51).* Dance, poetry, film, comedy, theatre and music.
Cork Film Festival *(early Oct, see pp212–13).* Irish and international films.
Kinsale Gourmet Festival *(early Oct, see pp208–9).* Superb food is served in the

Horse and trap at Lisdoonvarna fair

hotels, restaurants and pubs of Ireland's "Gourmet Capital".
Ballinasloe Fair, Co Galway *(first week).* One of Europe's oldest horse fairs, staged amid lively street entertainment.
Dublin Theatre Festival *(first and second week).* Features works by both Irish and foreign playwrights.
Wexford Opera Festival *(last two weeks in Oct).* A festival of lesser known operas.
Hallowe'en (Sham-hana) *(31 Oct).* An occasion celebrated all over the country.
Cork Jazz Festival *(end Oct, see pp212–13).* An extremely popular festival, with music all over the city.

NOVEMBER

Sligo International Choral Festival *(early Nov, see p308).* Choirs from around the world in concert and competition.
Carrick Theatre Festival, Carrick-on-Shannon, Co Leitrim *(mid-Nov, see p309).* One-act plays in qualifying festival for the All-Ireland Drama Festival.
Belfast Festival at Queen's, Queen's University *(last three weeks, see pp372–75).* Arts festival featuring drama, ballet, cinema and all types of music from classical to jazz.

Traditional horse fair at Ballinasloe in County Galway (October)

AVERAGE MONTHLY TEMPERATURE

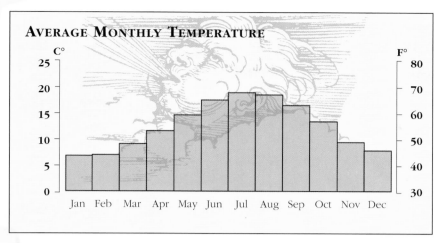

Temperature Chart
This chart gives the average minimum and maximum temperatures for the city of Dublin. Winter is mild throughout Ireland, except in the high mountain ranges, while the warmest summer temperatures are in the Southeast.

WINTER

ALTHOUGH a quiet time for festivals, there's a range of entertainment including musical and theatrical events. Christmas is the busiest social period and there are plenty of informal celebrations. There is also a wide choice of National Hunt race meetings *(see p32)*.

DECEMBER

Pantomime Season *(Dec–Jan)*. Traditional pantomime performed at many theatres throughout Ireland.
Leopardstown Races *(26 Dec, see p149)*. The biggest meeting held on this traditional day for racing. There are other fixtures at Limerick and Down Royal.
St Stephen's Day *(26 Dec)*. Catholic boys traditionally dress up as Wren boys (chimney sweeps with blackened faces) and sing hymns to raise money for charitable causes.

Young boys dressed up as Wren boys on St Stephen's Day

JANUARY

Salmon and Sea Trout Season *(1 Jan–end Sep)*. Start of the season for one of the most popular pastimes in Ireland.

FEBRUARY

Dublin Film Festival *(end Feb–early Mar)*. International films at various venues.
Belfast Music Festival *(end Feb–mid-Mar)*. Young people take part in music (and speech and drama) competitions.
Six Nations Rugby Tournament, Lansdowne Road, Dublin *(varying Saturdays Feb–Apr, see p32)*.

PUBLIC HOLIDAYS

New Year's Day (1 Jan)
St Patrick's Day (17 Mar)
Good Friday
Easter Monday
May Day (first Mon in May)
Spring Bank Holiday (Northern Ireland: last Mon in May)
June Bank Holiday (Republic: first Mon in Jun)
Battle of the Boyne Day (Northern Ireland: 12 Jul)
August Bank Holiday (first Mon in Aug)
Summer Bank Holiday (Northern Ireland: last Mon in Aug)
October Bank Holiday (last Mon in Oct)
Christmas Day (25 Dec)
St Stephen's Day (Republic: 26 Dec)
Boxing Day (Northern Ireland: 26 Dec)

Glendalough *(see pp162–3)* in the snow

DUBLIN AREA
BY AREA

Dublin at a Glance

IRELAND'S CAPITAL has a wealth of attractions, most within walking distance of each other. For the purpose of this guide, central Dublin has been divided into three sections: *Southeast Dublin*, heart of the modern city and home to the prestigious Trinity College; *Southwest Dublin*, site of the old city around Dublin Castle; and *North of the Liffey*, the area around the imposing O'Connell Street. The map references given for sights in the city refer to the *Dublin Street Finder* on pages 132–133.

DUBLIN

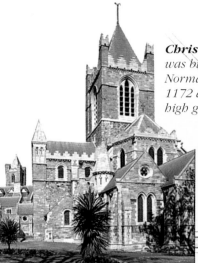

Christ Church Cathedral
was built by Dublin's Anglo-Norman conquerors between 1172 and 1220. It stands on high ground above the River Liffey. Much of the cathedral's present appearance is due to restoration carried out in the 1870s. (See pp98–9.)

NORTH OF THE LIFFEY
Pages 100–113

L I F F E

SOUTHWEST DUBLIN
Pages 84–99

Dublin Castle *stands in the heart of old Dublin. St Patrick's Hall is part of the suite of luxury State Apartments housed on the upper floors on the south side of the castle. Today, these rooms are used for functions of national importance such as presidential inaugurations.* (See pp88–9.)

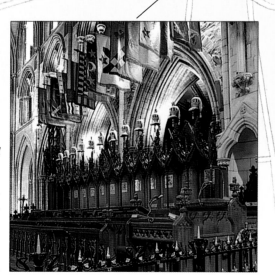

St Patrick's Cathedral
has a spectacular choir featuring banners and stalls decorated with the insignia of the Knights of St Patrick. The cathedral also holds Ireland's largest and most powerful organ, as well as memorials to Dean Jonathan Swift and prominent Anglo-Irish families. (See p95.)

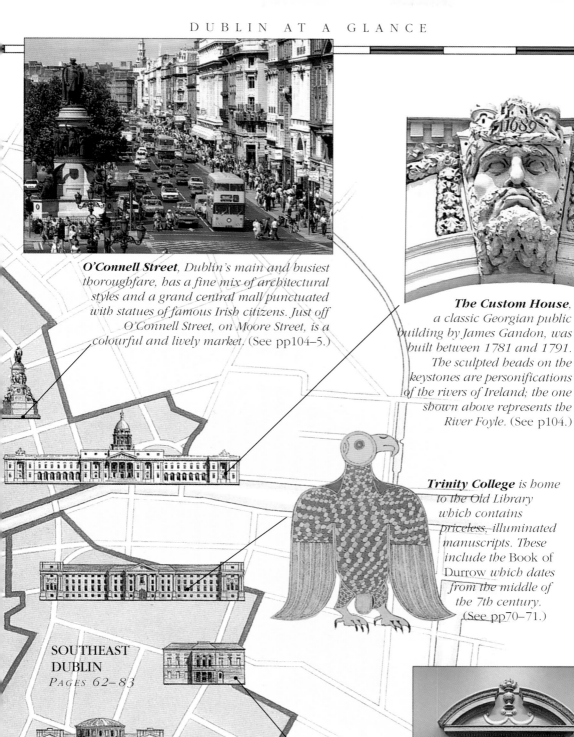

O'Connell Street, Dublin's main and busiest thoroughfare, has a fine mix of architectural styles and a grand central mall punctuated with statues of famous Irish citizens. Just off O'Connell Street, on Moore Street, is a colourful and lively market. (See pp104–5.)

The Custom House, a classic Georgian public building by James Gandon, was built between 1781 and 1791. The sculpted heads on the keystones are personifications of the rivers of Ireland; the one shown above represents the River Foyle. (See p104.)

Trinity College is home to the Old Library which contains priceless, illuminated manuscripts. These include the Book of Durrow which dates from the middle of the 7th century. (See pp70–71.)

SOUTHEAST DUBLIN
Pages 62–83

0 metres 400
0 yards 400

The National Gallery was opened in 1864. Housed on two floors, the well-organized gallery holds an eclectic collection, particularly strong on Irish and Italian paintings. The gallery's most prized painting is its recent acquisition The Taking of Christ by Caravaggio. (See pp80–1.)

The National Museum has an impressive collection of artifacts dating from the Stone Age to the 20th century. The Ardagh Chalice (c. AD 800) is one of the many Celtic Christian treasures on display. (See pp76–7.)

Dublin's Best: Pubs

EVERYONE KNOWS that Dublin is famous for its vast number of drinking establishments but, on arrival in the city, the choice can seem overwhelming. All the pubs are different – they range from vibrant, trendy bars to smoky traditional pubs. Whatever your choice of environment and beverage, you can be guaranteed to find it in Dublin. These pages offer no more than a taster of the most popular pubs in the city and what they are famous for, but there are many more to choose from.

Slattery's
A very traditional Dublin pub. North of the Liffey, Slattery's attracts fewer tourists than the Temple Bar and Grafton Street pubs. It is considered to be the best pub in the city for live music.

NORTH OF THE LIFFEY

SOUTHWEST DUBLIN

The Stag's Head

This gorgeous Victorian pub has a long mahogany bar and has retained its original mirrors and stained glass. Located down an alley off Dame Street, this atmospheric pub is well worth seeking out.

The Brazen Head

Reputedly the oldest pub in Dublin. The present building, still with its courtyard for coach and horses, dates back to 1750. The interior is full of dark wood panelling and old photographs of Dublin.

Hogan's

A café bar rather than a pub, Hogan's is a stylish establishment serving excellent drinks, and is popular with a young, trendy crowd. It is centrally situated on George's Street.

Oliver St John Gogarty

This famous old pub in the heart of Temple Bar is renowned for its live music throughout the day, and good food. It is named after the poet and friend of James Joyce. The atmosphere is relaxed and it is popular with visitors keen to sample a part of traditional Dublin.

O'Neill's

Just round the corner from Grafton Street, O'Neill's is one of the best places in the city for pub food. Its cosy atmosphere and location close to Trinity College make it a favourite with Dublin's student population.

LIFFEY

SOUTHEAST DUBLIN

0 metres 200

0 yards 200

McDaid's

Playwright Brendan Behan downed many a pint in this pub, which dates from 1779. Though on the tourist trail, McDaid's retains a bohemian charm, and bars upstairs and downstairs provide space for a leisurely drink.

O'Donoghue's

A good mix of locals and tourists, young and old, frequent this pub in the heart of Georgian Dublin which has been a city favourite for years. Famous as the pub where the Dubliners folk group began in the 1960s, it is known today for its live traditional music.

SOUTHEAST DUBLIN

DESPITE ITS location close to the old walled city, this part of Dublin remained virtually undeveloped until the founding of Trinity College in 1592. Even then, it was almost a hundred years before the ancient common land further south was enclosed to create St Stephen's Green, a spacious city park.

The mid-18th century saw the beginning of a construction boom in the area. During this time, magnificent public buildings such as the Old Library at Trinity College, Leinster House and the Bank of Ireland were built. However, the most conspicuous reminders of Georgian Dublin are the beautiful squares and terraces around

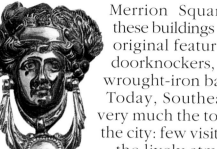

Georgian doorknocker in Merrion Square

Merrion Square. Many of these buildings still have their original features, including doorknockers, fanlights and wrought-iron balconies.

Today, Southeast Dublin is very much the tourist heart of the city: few visitors can resist the lively atmosphere and attractive shops of Grafton Street. The area is also home to much of Ireland's cultural heritage. The National Gallery has a good collection of Irish and European paintings while the National Museum has superb displays of Irish Bronze Age gold and early Christian treasures. Nearby, the fascinating Natural History Museum has preserved its wonderful Victorian interior.

SIGHTS AT A GLANCE

Museums, Libraries and Galleries
National Gallery pp80–1 ⓫
National Library ❽
National Museum pp76–7 ❼
Natural History Museum ❿
Royal Hibernian Academy ⓭

Historic Buildings
Bank of Ireland ❶
Leinster House ❾
Mansion House ❺
Trinity College pp70–1 ❷

Historic Streets
Fitzwilliam Square ⓮
Grafton Street ❸
Merrion Square ⓬

Churches
St Ann's Church ❻

Parks and Gardens
St Stephen's Green ❹

KEY

▨	Street-by-Street map *See pp64–5*
🚉	Railway station
🚈	DART station
🅿	Parking
ℹ	Tourist information

0 metres 250
0 yards 250

◁ **Marble bust of Jonathan Swift in the Old Library, Trinity College**

Street-by-Street: Southeast Dublin

THE AREA AROUND COLLEGE GREEN, dominated by the façades of the Bank of Ireland and Trinity College, is very much the heart of Dublin. The alleys and malls cutting across busy pedestrianized Grafton Street boast many of Dublin's better shops, hotels and restaurants. Just off Kildare Street are the Irish Parliament, the National Library and the National Museum. To escape the city bustle many head for sanctuary in St Stephen's Green, which is overlooked by fine Georgian buildings.

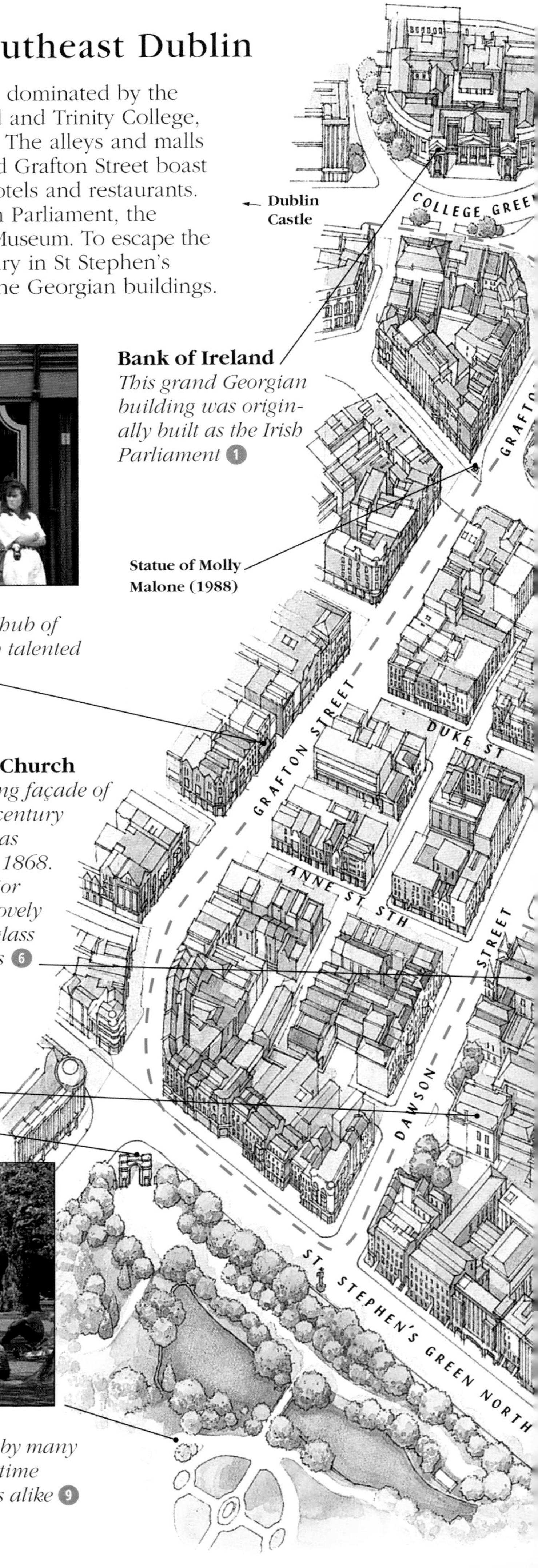

← **Dublin Castle**

Bank of Ireland
This grand Georgian building was origin-ally built as the Irish Parliament ❶

Statue of Molly Malone (1988)

Grafton Street
Bewley's Oriental Café is the social hub of this pedestrianized street, alive with talented buskers and pavement artists ❹

St Ann's Church
The striking façade of the 18th-century church was added in 1868. The interior features lovely stained-glass windows ❻

Mansion House
This has been the official residence of Dublin's Lord Mayor since 1715 ❼

Fusiliers' Arch (1907)

★ **St Stephen's Green**
The relaxing city park is surrounded by many grand buildings. In summer, lunchtime concerts attract tourists and workers alike ❾

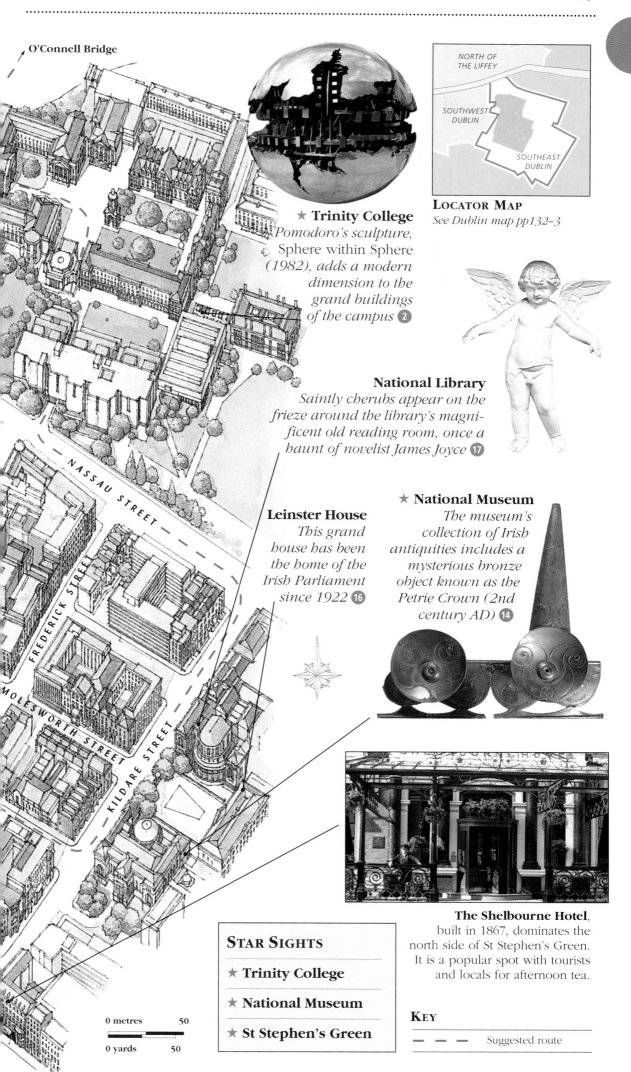

← O'Connell Bridge

LOCATOR MAP
See Dublin map pp132–3

★ **Trinity College**
Pomodoro's sculpture,
Sphere within Sphere
(1982), adds a modern
dimension to the
grand buildings
of the campus ②

National Library
Saintly cherubs appear on the
frieze around the library's magni-
ficent old reading room, once a
haunt of novelist James Joyce ⑰

Leinster House
This grand
house has been
the home of the
Irish Parliament
since 1922 ⑯

★ **National Museum**
The museum's
collection of Irish
antiquities includes a
mysterious bronze
object known as the
Petrie Crown (2nd
century AD) ⑭

The Shelbourne Hotel,
built in 1867, dominates the
north side of St Stephen's Green.
It is a popular spot with tourists
and locals for afternoon tea.

STAR SIGHTS

★ **Trinity College**

★ **National Museum**

★ **St Stephen's Green**

0 metres   50

0 yards   50

KEY

– – – – – – Suggested route

Original Chamber of the Irish House of Lords at the Bank of Ireland

Bank of Ireland ❶

2 College Green. 📞 *661 5933 ext 2265.* ⭕ *10am–4pm Mon– Wed & Fri, 10am–5pm. Thu.* ⚫ *public hols.* **House of Lords** 📷 *10:30am, 11:30am & 1:45pm Tue or by appt.*

THE PRESTIGIOUS offices of Ireland's national bank began life as the first purpose-built parliament house in Europe. The original central section was started by Irish architect Edward Lovett Pearce and completed in 1739 after his death. Sadly, Pearce's masterpiece, the great octag-onal chamber of the House of Commons, was destroyed by fire in 1792. The House of Lords, however, remains intact. Attendants lead tours that point out the coffered ceiling and oak panelling. There are also huge tapestries of the *Battle of the Boyne* and the *Siege of Londonderry*, and a splendid 1,233-piece crystal chan-delier that dates from 1788.

James Gandon added the east portico in 1785. Further additions were made around 1797. After the dissolu-tion of the Irish Parliament in 1800, the Bank of Ireland bought the building. The present structure was completed in 1808 with the transformation

of the former lobby of the House of Commons into a cash office and the addition of a curving screen wall and the Foster Place annexe.

At the front of the bank on College Green is a statue by John Foley of Henry Grattan *(see p44)*, the most formidable leader of the old parliament.

Trinity College ❷

See pp70–1.

St Teresa's Church ❸

Clarendon St or Johnson Court. 📞 *671 8466.* ⭕ *6:45am–6:30pm Mon–Fri, 6:45am–7:30pm Sat, 8:15am–7pm Sun.*

THE FOUNDATION stone of St Teresa's was laid in 1793, making it the first post-Penal Law church to be legally planned and built in the city after the passing of the Catholic Relief Act the same year. The land was bought by a brewer named John Sweetman and was given to the Discalced Carmelite Fathers. The church did not in fact open until several years later, in 1810. The eastern transept was

Statue of the Virgin and child in St Teresa's Church

added in 1863 and the western transept in 1876, at which stage it reached the form it remains in today.

Located in the middle of Dublin, St Teresa's is a relatively busy place of worship. Its T-shaped interior means that, if you enter through the main door on Claren-don Street and walk through the church, you will arrive in the tight alleyway of Johnson Court, a few yards from the heart of bustling Grafton Street. There are seven stained-glass windows in the church by Phyllis Burke, which were made in the 1990s, and a fine sculpture of Christ by John Hogan beneath the altar.

Street musicians outside Brown Thomas on Grafton Street

Grafton Street ❹

THE SPINE OF DUBLIN'S most popular and stylish shop-ping district runs south from Trinity College to the glass-covered St Stephen's Green Shopping Centre. At the north end, at the junction with Nassau Street, is a bronze statue by Jean Rynhart of *Molly Malone* (1988), the celebrated "cockles and mussels" street trader from the traditional Irish folk song.

This busy pedestrianized strip, characterized by numerous energetic buskers and talented street theatre artists, boasts many shops, including many British chain stores. Its most exclusive, however, is Brown Thomas, which is one of Dublin's most elegant department stores, selling designer clothes and exclusive perfumery. Grafton Street's most famous

Monkeys playing billiards outside the Heraldic Museum

landmark is Bewley's Oriental Café at No. 78. Although not the oldest branch of this 150-year-old Dublin institution, this is Bewley's most popular location and a favourite meeting spot for Dubliners and visitors alike throughout the day. It stands on the site of Samuel Whyte's school, whose illustrious roll included Robert Emmet *(see p89)*, leader of the 1803 Rebellion, and the Duke of Wellington.

Despite the removal of the old wooden pews, this large café retains its pleasant Victorian ambience, especially in the James Joyce Room upstairs. The balcony on the first floor, which looks down on the shop area at the entrance to the café, is a good spot for people-watching.

On many of the sidestreets off Grafton Street there are numerous pubs which provide an alternative to Bewley's for the exhausted shopper, among them is the famous Davy Byrne's, which for years has been frequented by Dublin's literati.

Heraldic Museum and Genealogical Office ⑤

2 Kildare St. 📞 *603 0200.* ⏰ *10am–12:20pm, 2–4pm Mon–Fri.*

THE GENEALOGICAL OFFICE helps anyone with an Irish background assemble facts about their ancestors, responding to great interest from North America. Inexpensive consultations are available but they recommend that the more you have found out about your ancestry beforehand (they offer a handy questionnaire) the better.

The Heraldic Museum offers a small but interesting collection of seals, stamps, regimental colours, coins, porcelain, paintings, family crests and county shields.

The building that houses the museum is a red-brick structure in the Venetian style, which is unusual for Dublin. On the exterior, it features some fanciful decorative aspects such as three monkeys playing billiards and bears playing violins just to the right of the entrance.

Window depicting Faith, Hope and Charity in St Ann's Church

St Ann's Church ⑥

Dawson St. 📞 *676 7727.* ⏰ *10am–4pm Mon–Fri (also for Sun service, phone to check).*

FOUNDED IN 1707, St Ann's striking Romanesque façade was added by the architects Deane and Woodward in 1868. The best view of the façade is from Grafton Street, looking down Anne Street South. Inside the church are many colourful stained-glass windows that date back to the mid-19th century. St Ann's has a long tradition of charity work: in 1723 Lord Newton left a bequest specifically to buy bread for the poor. The original shelf used for the bread still stands adjacent to the altar.

There are numerous famous past parishioners of St Ann's including the Irish patriot Wolfe Tone *(see p45)*, who was married here in 1785, Douglas Hyde, the first president of Ireland, and Bram Stoker (1847–1912), the author of *Dracula*.

The milling crowds filling the pedestrianized Grafton Street

Trinity College ❷

Trinity College coat of arms

T RINITY COLLEGE was founded in 1592 by Queen Elizabeth I on the site of an Augustinian monastery. Originally a Protestant college, it was not until the 1970s that Catholics started entering the university. Among the many famous students to attend the college were playwrights Oliver Goldsmith and Samuel Beckett, and political writer Edmund Burke. Trinity's lawns and cobbled quads provide a pleasant haven in the heart of the city. The major attractions are the Old Library and the *Book of Kells*, housed in the Treasury.

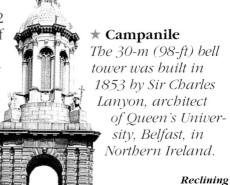

★ **Campanile**
The 30-m (98-ft) bell tower was built in 1853 by Sir Charles Lanyon, architect of Queen's University, Belfast, in Northern Ireland.

Reclining Connected Forms (1969) by Henry Moore

Dining Hall (1761)

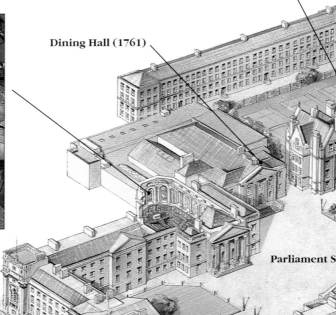

Parliament Square

Provost's House (c. 1760)

Chapel *(1798)*
This is the only chapel in the Republic to be shared by all denominations. The painted window above the altar dates from 1867.

Statue of Edmund Burke (1868) by John Foley

Main entrance

Statue of Oliver Goldsmith (1864) by John Foley

SAMUEL BECKETT (1906–89)

Nobel prizewinner Samuel Beckett was born at Foxrock, south of Dublin. In 1923 he entered Trinity, where he was placed first in his modern literature class. He was also a keen member of the college cricket team. Forsaking Ireland, Beckett moved to France in the early 1930s. Many of his works such as *Waiting for Godot* (1951) were written first in French, and then later translated, by Beckett, into English.

Examination Hall
Completed in 1791 to a design by Sir William Chambers, the hall features a gilded oak chandelier and ornate ceilings by Michael Stapleton.

◁ **Relaxing in the park, St Stephen's Green**

Library Square
The red-brick building (known as the Rubrics) on the east side of Library Square was built around 1700 and is the oldest surviving part of the college.

VISITORS' CHECKLIST

College Green. 📞 677 2941. 🚉 DART to Tara Street. 🚌 14, 15, 46 & many other routes. **Old Library and Treasury** ◯ 9:30am– 5:30pm Mon–Sat (last adm: 5pm), noon–5pm Sun & some public hols (last adm: 4:30pm). ● 10 days at Christmas. 🏷 📷 ♿ 📖 by arrangement. **Chapel** ◯ by appt. **Douglas Hyde Gallery** ◯ for exhibitions only.

Shop and entrance to Old Library

The Museum Building, completed in 1857, is noted for its Venetian exterior, and its magnificent multicoloured hall and double-domed roof.

New Square

Sphere within Sphere
(1982) was given to the college by its sculptor Arnaldo Pomodoro.

Berkeley Library Building by Paul Koralek (1967)

Fellows' Square

Entrance from Nassau Street

The Douglas Hyde Gallery was built in the 1970s to house temporary art exhibitions.

★ **Treasury**
This detail is from the Book of Durrow, *one of the other magnificent illuminated manuscripts housed in the Treasury along with the celebrated* Book of Kells *(see p72).*

★ **Old Library** *(1732)*
The spectacular Long Room measures 64 m (210 ft) from end to end. It houses 200,000 antiquarian texts, marble busts of scholars and the oldest surviving harp in Ireland.

STAR FEATURES

★ **Old Library**

★ **Treasury**

★ **Campanile**

The Book of Kells

THE MOST RICHLY decorated of Ireland's illuminated manuscripts, the *Book of Kells*, may have been the work of monks from Iona, who fled to Kells, near Newgrange *(see pp330–1)*, in AD 806 after a Viking raid. The book, which was moved to Trinity College *(see pp70–1)* in the 17th century, contains the four gospels in Latin. The scribes who copied the texts embellished their calligraphy with intricate spirals as well as human figures and animals. Some of the dyes used were imported from as far as the Middle East.

Pair of moths

Stylized angel

The Greek letter "X"

The symbols *of the four evangelists are used as decoration throughout the book. The figure of the man symbolizes St Matthew.*

The letter that looks like a "P" is a Greek "R".

The letter "I"

Interlacing motifs

Cat watching rats

Rats eating bread could be a reference to sinners taking Holy Communion. The symbolism of the animals and people decorating the manuscript is often hard to interpret.

MONOGRAM PAGE
This, the most elaborate page of the book, contains the first three words of St Matthew's account of the birth of Christ. The first word "XRI" is an abbreviation of "Christi".

A full-page portrait *of St Matthew, shown standing barefoot in front of a throne, precedes the opening words of his gospel.*

The text *is in a beautifully rounded Celtic script with brightly ornamented initial letters. Animal and human forms are often used to decorate the end of a line.*

Mansion House ⑦

Dawson St. ◉ *to the public.*

Sᴇᴛ ʙᴀᴄᴋ from Dawson Street
with a neat cobbled fore-
court, the Mansion House is
an attractive Queen Anne-
style building. It was built in
1710 for the aristocrat Joshua
Dawson, after whom the street
is named. The Dublin Corporation bought it from him five
years later as the official
residence of the city's Lord
Mayor. A grey stucco façade
was added in Victorian times.

The Dáil Éireann *(see p78)*,
which adopted the Declaration
of Independence, first met here
on 21 January 1919. The building is now used mostly for
civic functions and receptions.

Royal College of Surgeons ⑧

Dawson St. ◉ *to the public.*
🖾 *2pm Sun (Oct–May: groups only).*

Aʟᴛʜᴏᴜɢʜ ᴛʜᴇ ᴡᴇsᴛ side of
St Stephen's Green is its
scruffiest, it is home to the
most striking building of the
square, namely the squat
granite-faced Royal College of
Surgeons. The college opened
in 1810 and 15 years later its
façade was extended from
three to seven bays when a
central pediment was added.
On top of this are three
statues which from left to
right are Hygieia, goddess
of health, Asclepius, god of

Royal College of Surgeons, which overlooks St Stephen's Green

medicine and son of Apollo,
and Athena, the goddess of
wisdom and patron of the
arts. Today, the main entrance
is through the modern exten-
sion on York Street. The academy has almost 1,000 students
from all over the world.

The building itself played
an important part in Irish history. During the 1916 Easter
Rising *(see p48)*, a section of
the Irish Citizen Army under
Michael Mallin and Countess
Constance Markievicz were in
control of the college. They
were the last detachment of
rebels to surrender and,
although Mallin was executed, Markievicz escaped sen-
tence because of her gender
and public status. She was
later to become the first
woman to be elected as an
MP at Westminster in London.
The front columns of the
building still feature the old
bullet holes, an ever-present
reminder of its colourful past.

St Stephen's Green ⑨

◻ *daylight hours.*

Oʀɪɢɪɴᴀʟʟʏ ᴏɴᴇ of three
ancient commons in the
old city, St Stephen's Green
was enclosed in 1664. The
9-ha (22-acre) green was laid
out in its present form in 1880,
using a grant given by Lord
Ardilaun, a member of the
Guinness family. Landscaped
with flowerbeds, trees, a
fountain and a lake, the green
is dotted with memorials to
eminent Dubliners, including
Ardilaun himself. There is a
bust of James Joyce *(see p106)*,
and a memorial by Henry
Moore (1967) dedicated to
WB Yeats *(see p26)*. At the
Merrion Row corner stands a
massive monument (1967) by
Edward Delaney to 18th-
century nationalist leader
Wolfe Tone – it is known
locally as "Tonehenge". The
1887 bandstand still has free
daytime concerts in summer.

The busiest side of the
Green is the north, known
during the 19th century as the
Beaux' Walk and still home to
several gentlemen's clubs.
The most prominent building
is the venerable Shelbourne
Hotel. Dating back to 1867, its
entrance is adorned by
statues of Nubian princesses
and attendant slaves. It is well
worth popping in for a look
at the chandeliered foyer and
for afternoon tea in the Lord
Mayor's Lounge.

Dubliners relaxing by the lake in St Stephen's Green

Stucco work in the Apollo room of No. 85 in Newman House

Newman House 🔟

85 & 86 St Stephen's Green.
📞 706 7422. ⏰ Jun–Aug: Tue–Fri
12–5pm, Sat 2–5pm, Sun 11am–
2pm. 📷

NUMBERS 85 AND 86 on the south side of St Stephen's Green are collectively known as Newman House, named for John Henry Newman, later Cardinal Newman and the first rector of the Catholic University of Ireland.

Founded as an alternative to the Protestant Trinity College, it became part of University College Dublin in the 1920s and is still owned by that institution.

During the 1990s it has seen one of the most painstaking and diligent restorations ever undertaken in the city. It is the much smaller No. 85, designed by Richard Castle in 1738, that contains the most beautiful rooms with plaster-work by the Franchini brothers. Of particular interest are the Apollo Room, with a figure of the god above the mantle, and the upstairs Saloon. In the late 1800s the Jesuits covered the naked plaster bodies on the ceiling of the Saloon with rudimentary plaster casts to conceal what they thought to be shameful nudity. One of the figures is still covered today. A class-room, decorated as it would have been in the days when James Joyce was a student

here, is open to the public, as is the study used by the poet Gerard Manley Hopkins, who was a professor here in the late 19th century. Other famous past pupils include the writer Flann O'Brien and former president Eamon de Valera.

Iveagh House and Iveagh Gardens ⑪

80 & 81 St Stephen's Green. 🌑 to
the public. **Gardens** ⬜ daily.

IVEAGH HOUSE, on the south of St Stephen's Green, was originally two free-standing town houses. No. 80 was designed in 1730s by Richard Castle – his first commission in the city. The houses were combined in the 1860s when Sir Benjamin Guinness bought the properties. None of the original façade remains as Guinness linked the proper-ties under a Portland stone façade and had the family arms engraved on the pedi-ment. The Guinness family also carried out much interior reconstruction, including a large new ball-room, with a domed ceiling and liberal amounts of marble and onyx, added to the rear of the house. Iveagh House was given to the state by Rupert Guinness, the second Earl of Iveagh, in 1939. It is now used by the Department of Foreign Affairs, both as the office of the minister and as a venue for state receptions.

Enjoying the secluded peace of Iveagh Gardens

The rear of Iveagh House faces out onto the peaceful Iveagh Gardens, an almost secret Dublin park, which offers a quiet alternative to the busy St Stephen's Green. It owes its tranquility partly to the fact that its two en-trances are discreet: one is behind the National Concert Hall on Earlsfort Terrace, the other is off Clonmel Street.

Ely Place ⑫

A CUL-DE-SAC with several well-preserved Georgian houses, Ely Place is at the end of Merrion Street Upper. Most of the houses along the street were built in the 1770s and Ely Place soon became one of the most desirable addresses in the city at this time. Behind its red brick façade, 8 Ely Place, known as Ely House, has elegant plasterwork by the stucco-dore Michael Stapleton and an ornate staircase covered with engravings of characters taken from the tales of the Labours of Hercules below the banister rail.

Modern buildings seal the end of the street. The Royal Hibernian Academy Gallagher Gallery (see p 79) was built in 1973 and may look somewhat out of place on this otherwise rather grand stretch, but it offers one of the best gallery spaces in the city, exhibiting mostly 20th-century Irish art.

Detail of stucco from Ely House, featuring the mythical dog Cerberus

The elegant, Neo-Classical façade of the Government Buildings

Government Buildings ⑬

Upper Merrion Street.
📞 662 4888. 🕐 Sat 10:30am–
12:30pm and 1:30–4:30pm. (Tickets
available from the National Gallery.)
🎟 obligatory.

IN BETWEEN the Natural History Museum and the National Gallery on Upper Merrion Street, facing the Georgian town houses, stand the imposing Government Buildings, built in a Neo-Georgian style.

The complex was opened in 1911 as the Royal College of Science (RCS) and it has the distinction of being the last major project planned by the British in Dublin. In 1922 the Irish government took over the north wing as offices and the RCS became part of University College Dublin. Academic pursuits continued here until 1989, when the government moved into the rest of the buildings and ordered a massive restoration of the façade. The city grime on the Portland stone was blasted away to restore it to its original near-white appearance.

The elegant domed buildings are set apart from the street by a cobbled courtyard and a large colonnade with columns that are strongly reminiscent of Gandon's Custom House (see p104). The tour takes in the office of the Taoiseach (pronounced Tee-Shuck) and the cabinet office. The interior is decorated with examples of works by contemporary Irish artists, most notably a huge stained-glass window, situated above the grand staircase, called My Four Green Fields by Dublin artist Evie Hone, which depicts the island's four provinces. This was designed for the 1939 World's Fair in New York. It was displayed in the Irish Pavilion there and afterwards returned to Dublin. For a number of years it lay packed away. In the 1960s, it was displayed for a while in the Dublin Bus offices in O'Connell Street. It was eventually moved to its present home in the Government Buildings in 1991.

National Museum ⑭

See pp76–7.

Natural History Museum ⑮

Merrion St. 📞 677 7444.
🕐 10am–5pm Tue–Sat, 2–5pm Sun.
⬤ public hols. ♿ ground floor only.
🎫 May–Sep.

KNOWN AFFECTIONATELY as the "Dead Zoo" by Dublin residents, this museum is crammed with antique glass cabinets containing stuffed animals from around the world. The museum was opened to the public in 1857 with an inaugural lecture by Dr David Livingstone on African fauna. It remains virtually unchanged from Victorian times.

On the ground floor, the Irish room holds exhibits on local wildlife. Inside the front door are three skeletons of the extinct giant deer known as the "Irish elk". Also on this floor are shelves with jars of octopuses, leeches and worms, preserved in embalming fluid.

The upper gallery is home to the Blaschka Collection of interesting glass models of marine life, and a display of buffalo and deer trophies. Hanging from the ceiling are the skeletons of a fin whale and a humpback whale.

The advances made in taxidermy over the years are emphasized by a stuffed rhinoceros and an Indian elephant, both so heavily lacquered that they seem to be covered in tar.

Lawn and front entrance of the Natural History Museum on Merrion Street Upper

National Museum ⑭

T HE NATIONAL MUSEUM OF IRELAND was built in the 1880s to the design of Sir Thomas Deane. Its splendid domed rotunda features marble pillars and a zodiac mosaic floor. The Treasury houses priceless items such as the Broighter gold boat, while an exhibition on Ireland's Bronze Age gold contains some beautiful jewellery. Many collections have now moved to the recently opened annexe of the museum at the impressive Collins Barracks *(see pp124–5).*

Egyptian Mummy
This mummy of the lady Tentdinebu is thought to date back to c.945–716 BC. Covered in brilliant colours, it is part of the stunning Egyptian collection.

★ Ór – Ireland's Gold
This is one of the most extensive collections of Bronze Age gold in Western Europe. This gold lunula (c.1800 BC), found in Athlone, is one of many pieces of ancient jewellery in this exhibition.

KEY TO FLOORPLAN

☐	The Road to Independence
☐	Ór – Ireland's Gold
☐	The Treasury
☐	Prehistoric Ireland
☐	Viking Exhibition
☐	Ancient Egypt
☐	Temporary exhibition space
☐	Non-exhibition space

Flag from 1916 Rising
The Road to Independence *exhibition covers historical events between 1900 and 1921. This flag flew over Dublin's GPO during the Easter Rising* (see p48).

Main entrance

GALLERY GUIDE
The ground floor holds The Treasury, Ór – Ireland's Gold exhibition, The Road to Independence and the Prehistoric Ireland display. The first floor houses Viking artifacts and displays of silver, glass and ceramics. There may be other new displays, while some rooms may be closed to the public – this is due to the continuing reorganization of the museum.

The domed rotunda, based on the design of the Altes Museum in Berlin, makes an impressive entrance hall.

The Treasury houses masterpieces of Irish crafts including the Ardagh Chalice.

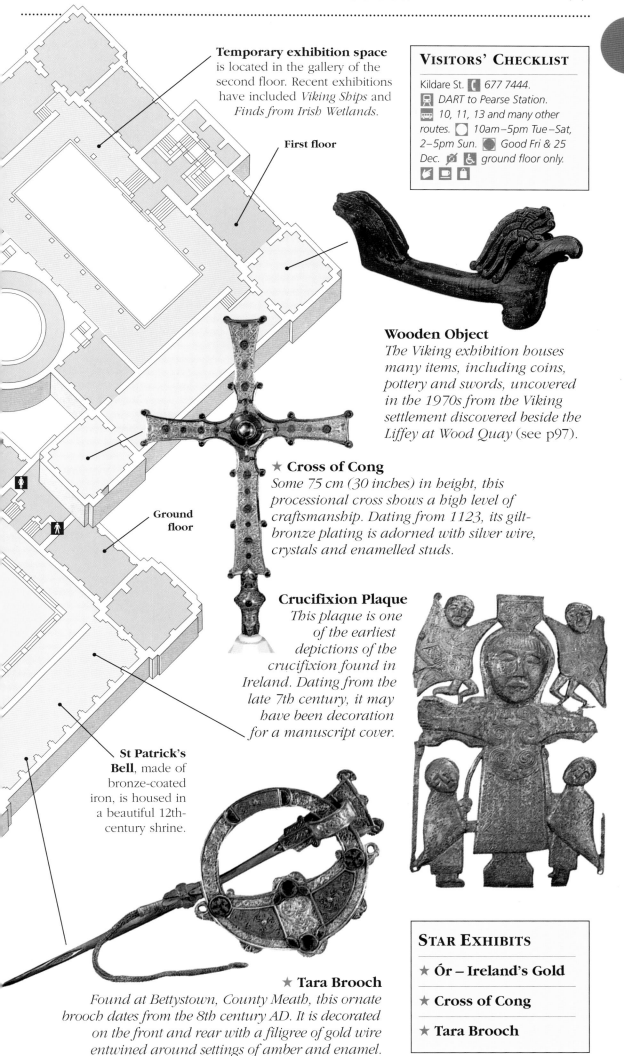

Temporary exhibition space is located in the gallery of the second floor. Recent exhibitions have included *Viking Ships* and *Finds from Irish Wetlands*.

First floor

VISITORS' CHECKLIST

Kildare St. 677 7444. DART to Pearse Station. 10, 11, 13 and many other routes. 10am–5pm Tue–Sat, 2–5pm Sun. Good Fri & 25 Dec. ground floor only.

Wooden Object
The Viking exhibition houses many items, including coins, pottery and swords, uncovered in the 1970s from the Viking settlement discovered beside the Liffey at Wood Quay (see p97).

★ **Cross of Cong**
Some 75 cm (30 inches) in height, this processional cross shows a high level of craftsmanship. Dating from 1123, its gilt-bronze plating is adorned with silver wire, crystals and enamelled studs.

Ground floor

Crucifixion Plaque
This plaque is one of the earliest depictions of the crucifixion found in Ireland. Dating from the late 7th century, it may have been decoration for a manuscript cover.

St Patrick's Bell, made of bronze-coated iron, is housed in a beautiful 12th-century shrine.

★ **Tara Brooch**
Found at Bettystown, County Meath, this ornate brooch dates from the 8th century AD. It is decorated on the front and rear with a filigree of gold wire entwined around settings of amber and enamel.

STAR EXHIBITS

★ **Ór – Ireland's Gold**

★ **Cross of Cong**

★ **Tara Brooch**

Domed reading room on the first floor of the National Library

Leinster House 16

Kildare St. (681 3000.) to the public. by arrangement, phone for details.

THIS STATELY MANSION houses the *Dáil* and the *Seanad* – the two chambers of the Irish Parliament. It was originally built for the Duke of Leinster in 1745. Designed by Richard Castle, the Kildare Street façade resembles that of a large town house. The rear, which looks out on to the attractive Merrion Square, has the air of a country estate. The Royal Dublin Society bought the building in 1815. The government obtained a part of it in 1922 and bought the entire building two years later.

Visitors can arrange to tour the main rooms, including the *Seanad* chamber.

National Library 17

Kildare St. (661 8811.) 10am–9pm Mon–Wed, 10am–5pm Thu & Fri, 10am–1pm Sat. public hols.

DESIGNED BY Sir Thomas Deane, the National Library was opened in 1890. It was built to house the collection of the Royal Dublin Society *(see p121)*. In the entrance hall are exhibitions from the library's archive, including manuscripts by George Bernard Shaw, and politician Daniel O'Connell

(see p46). Prized exhibits include photographs of Victorian Ireland and the 13th-century manuscript of Giraldus Cambrensis's *Topographia Hiberniae*.

The first-floor Reading Room has green-shaded lamps and well-worn desks. To go in, ask an attendant for a visitor's pass.

National Gallery 18

See pp80–1.

Merrion Square 19

MERRION SQUARE is one of Dublin's largest and grandest Georgian squares. Covering about 5 ha (12 acres), the square was laid out by John Ensor around 1762.

On the west of the square are the impressive façades of

Statue of Oscar Wilde by Danny Osbourne in Merrion Square

THE IRISH PARLIAMENT

The Irish Free State, the forerunner of the Republic of Ireland, was inaugurated in 1922 *(see p16)*, although an unofficial Irish parliament, the *Dáil*, had already been in existence since 1919. Today, parliament is made up of two houses: the *Dáil* (House of Representatives) and the *Seanad Eireann* (Senate). The Prime Minister is the *Taoiseach* and the deputy, the *Tánaiste*. The *Dáil's* 166 representatives – *Teachta Dala*, commonly known as TDs – are elected by proportional representation every five years. The 60-strong *Seanad* is appointed by various individuals and authorities, including the *Taoiseach* and the University of Dublin.

The first parliament of the Irish Free State in 1922

the Natural History Museum, the National Gallery and the front garden of Leinster House. However, this august triumvirate does not compare with the attractive Georgian town houses on the other three sides of the square. Many have brightly painted doors with original features such as wrought-iron balconies, ornate doorknockers and fanlights. The oldest and finest houses are on the north side.

Many of the houses – now predominantly used as office space – have plaques detailing the rich and famous who once lived in them. These include Catholic emancipation leader Daniel O'Connell *(see p46)*, who lived at No. 58 and poet WB Yeats *(see p27)*, who lived at No. 82. Oscar Wilde *(see p27)* spent his childhood at No. 1.

The attractive central park features colourful flower and shrub beds. In the 1840s it served a grim function as an emergency soup kitchen, feeding the hungry during the Great Famine *(see p46)*. On the northwest side of the park stands the restored Rutland Fountain. It was originally erected in 1791 for the sole use of Dublin's poor.

Just off the square, at No. 24 Merrion Street Upper, is the birthplace of the Duke of Wellington, who, when he was teased about his Irish background, famously said, "Being-born in a stable does not make one a horse."

Royal Hibernian Academy 20

15 Ely Place. 661 2558. 11am–5pm Tue–Sat, 11am–9pm Thu, 2–5pm Sun. public hols.

THE ACADEMY is one of the largest exhibition spaces in the city. It puts on touring exhibitions and mounts shows of painting, sculpture and other work by Ireland's best young art and design students. This modern brick-and-plate-glass building does,

The recreated Georgian kitchen of Number 29, Fitzwilliam Street Lower

however, look out of place at the end of Ely Place, which is an attractive Georgian cul-de-sac.

Number 29 21

29 Fitzwilliam Street Lower. 702 6165. 10am–5pm Tue–Sat, 2–5pm Sun. Two weeks prior to Christmas.

NUMBER 29 IS A corner townhouse, built in 1794 for a Mrs Elizabeth Beattie whose late husband was a wine and paper merchant. While the period furniture comes from the collection of the National Museum, the main purpose of this exhibit is to give visitors a behind-the-scenes look at how middle-class Georgians went

about their daily business. Tours start with a short slide show and then work their way through the building from the cellar upwards. Along the way are mahogany tables, chandeliers, Turkish carpets and landscape paintings (by Thomas Roberts amongst others) but of most interest are some of the quirkier items. Guides point out rudimentary hostess trolleys, water filters and even a Georgian pushchair, as well as an early exercise machine, used to tone up the muscles for horse riding. A tea caddy takes pride of place in one of the reception rooms: at today's prices a kilo of tea would have cost IR£1,000 and hence the lady of the house kept the key to the caddy on her person at all times.

The elegant gardens in Merrion Square, a quiet backwater in the centre of Dublin

National Gallery ⑱

THIS PURPOSE-BUILT gallery was opened to the public in 1864. It houses many excellent exhibits, largely due to generous bequests, such as the Milltown collection of works of art from Russborough House (*see p154*). Playwright George Bernard Shaw was also a benefactor, leaving a third of his estate to the gallery. More than 500 works are on display in the gallery and, although there is much emphasis on Irish art, every major school of European painting is well represented.

The Houseless Wanderer by John Foley

★ **For the Road**
A whole room is dedicated to the works of Jack Yeats (1871–1957). This mysterious late painting reflects the artist's obsession with the Sligo countryside.

GALLERY GUIDE
The collection is housed on two floors. On the ground floor are the Irish and British rooms: Room 32 has portraits of Irish sitters by artists from all schools. The first floor features works hung in broadly chronological order according to nation. The Italian, French, Dutch and Flemish collections account for most of the space.

STAR PAINTINGS

★ **The Taking of Christ by Caravaggio**

★ **Castle of Bentheim by Ruisdael**

★ **For the Road by Jack Yeats**

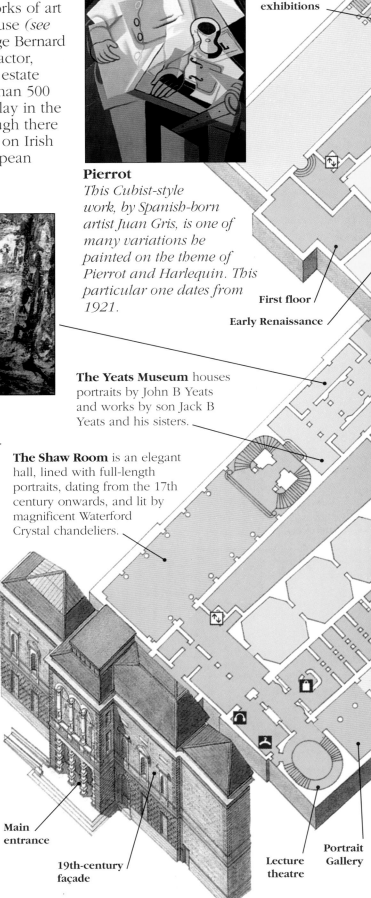

Pierrot
This Cubist-style work, by Spanish-born artist Juan Gris, is one of many variations he painted on the theme of Pierrot and Harlequin. This particular one dates from 1921.

Stairs to temporary exhibitions

First floor

Early Renaissance

The Yeats Museum houses portraits by John B Yeats and works by son Jack B Yeats and his sisters.

The Shaw Room is an elegant hall, lined with full-length portraits, dating from the 17th century onwards, and lit by magnificent Waterford Crystal chandeliers.

Main entrance

19th-century façade

Lecture theatre

Portrait Gallery

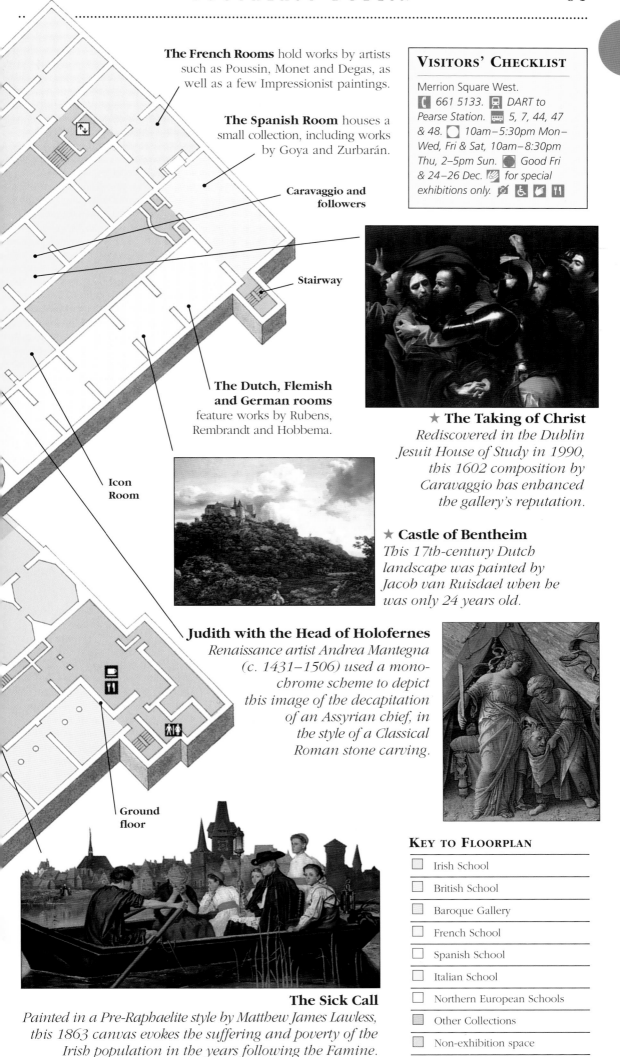

The French Rooms hold works by artists such as Poussin, Monet and Degas, as well as a few Impressionist paintings.

The Spanish Room houses a small collection, including works by Goya and Zurbarán.

Caravaggio and followers

VISITORS' CHECKLIST

Merrion Square West.
(661 5133. **🚋** DART to Pearse Station. **🚌** 5, 7, 44, 47 & 48. **◯** 10am–5:30pm Mon–Wed, Fri & Sat, 10am–8:30pm Thu, 2–5pm Sun. **●** Good Fri & 24–26 Dec. **🖋** for special exhibitions only. 🚫 ♿ 🖊 🍴

Stairway

The Dutch, Flemish and German rooms feature works by Rubens, Rembrandt and Hobbema.

Icon Room

Ground floor

★ **The Taking of Christ**
Rediscovered in the Dublin Jesuit House of Study in 1990, this 1602 composition by Caravaggio has enhanced the gallery's reputation.

★ **Castle of Bentheim**
This 17th-century Dutch landscape was painted by Jacob van Ruisdael when he was only 24 years old.

Judith with the Head of Holofernes
Renaissance artist Andrea Mantegna (c. 1431–1506) used a monochrome scheme to depict this image of the decapitation of an Assyrian chief, in the style of a Classical Roman stone carving.

KEY TO FLOORPLAN

☐	Irish School
☐	British School
☐	Baroque Gallery
☐	French School
☐	Spanish School
☐	Italian School
☐	Northern European Schools
☐	Other Collections
☐	Non-exhibition space

The Sick Call
Painted in a Pre-Raphaelite style by Matthew James Lawless, this 1863 canvas evokes the suffering and poverty of the Irish population in the years following the Famine.

Exploring the National Gallery

The EXHIBITIONS IN the gallery are laid out in a clear, easy-to-follow way and there are some excellent pieces of art on display. Modern Irish art, including the *Four Seasons* installation by Felim Egan, occupies the airy Atrium, a recent addition to the gallery's space. In addition to the major schools, there are rooms devoted to religious icons, and a modern print gallery which houses temporary exhibitions.

IRISH SCHOOL

This IS THE largest collection on display and the richest part of the gallery. Stretching back to the late 17th century, works range from landscapes such as *A View of Powerscourt Waterfall* by George Barret to paintings by Nathaniel Hone the Elder, including *The Conjuror*. Portraiture includes work by James Barry and Hugh Douglas Hamilton.

The Romantic movement made a strong impression on artists in the early 19th century; Francis Danby's *The Opening of the Sixth Seal*, an apocalyptic interpretation from the Book of Revelations, is the best example of this genre. Other examples are the Irish landscapes of James Arthur O'Connor.

In the late 19th century many Irish artists lived in Breton colonies, absorbing Impressionist influences. Roderic O'Conor's *Farm at Lezaven, Finistère* and William Leech's *Convent Garden, Brittany*, with its refreshing tones of green and white, are

Convent Garden, Brittany, **by William Leech (1881–1968)**

two of the best examples from this period.

The foundation in 1920 of the Society of Dublin Painters promoted work by the likes of Paul Henry and Jack B Yeats, also on display in the gallery. Other exponents of modern Irish works of art can be found on display at The Hugh Lane Gallery in Parnell Square *(see p107)*.

In 1999 a new Yeats gallery opened, displaying not just the work of Jack B Yeats but also other members of this talented Irish family.

A View of Powerscourt Waterfall **by George Barret the Elder (c.1728–84)**

BRITISH SCHOOL

Works DATING from the 18th century dominate in those rooms that are devoted to British artists. In particular William Hogarth, Thomas Gainsborough and Joshua Reynolds are well represented, accounting for over 15 items on display. Reynolds was one of the great portrait painters of his time and other portraits, by artists including Philip Reinagle, Francis Wheatley and Henry Raeburn, perfectly capture the family, military and aristocratic life of that period.

BAROQUE GALLERY

This LARGE ROOM accommodates 17th-century paintings, many by lesser-known artists. It also holds enormous canvases by more famous names such as Lanfranco, Jordaens and Castiglione, which are too big to fit into the spaces occupied by their respective schools. *The Annunciation* and *Peter Finding the Tribute Money* by Rubens are among the gallery's most eye-catching paintings.

FRENCH SCHOOL

The PAINTINGS IN the rooms devoted to the French school are separated into the 17th and 18th centuries (in the Milltown Rooms) and the Barbizon, Impressionist, post-Impressionist and Cubist collections (in the Dargan Wing).

Among the earlier works is *The Annunciation*, a fine 15th-century panel by Jacques Yverni and the *Lamentation over the Dead Christ* by the 17th-century Nicolas Poussin.

The early 19th century saw the French colonization of North Africa. Many works were inspired by it, including *Guards at the Door of a Tomb* by Jean-Léon Gérôme. Another fine 19th-century work is *A Group of Cavalry in the Snow* by Jan Chelminski.

The Impressionist paintings are always amongst the most popular in the gallery. These

A Group of Cavalry in the Snow by Jan Chelminski (1851–1925)

include Monet's *A River Scene, Autumn* from 1874. Works by Degas, Pissarro and Sisley are also displayed in this set of rooms. Jacques Emile Blanche's famous 1934 portrait of James Joyce is in Room 10.

Guards at the Door of a Tomb by Jean-Léon Gérôme (1824–1904)

SPANISH SCHOOL

WORKS FROM the Spanish school occupy comparatively little space, but they are rich and varied. One of the early pieces of note is El Greco's *St Francis Receiving the Stigmata*, a particularly dramatic work, dating from around 1595. Other notable acquisitions from this period are by Zurbarán, Velázquez and Murillo. There are four works by Francisco de Goya (1746–1828) on display including a portrait of the actress Doña Antonia Zárata. Pablo Picasso's *Still Life With A Mandolin* and *Pierrot* by Juan Gris represent 20th-century Spanish art.

ITALIAN SCHOOL

AS A RESULT of a successful purchasing strategy at the time of the gallery's inauguration, and various bequeathments, there is a strong collection of Italian art in the gallery.

Works of the Italian School spread over six rooms. Andrea Mantegna's *Judith with the Head of Holofernes* is done in *grisaille*, a technique that creates a stone-like effect. Famous pieces by Uccello, Titian, Moroni and Fontana hang in this section, but it is Caravaggio's *The Taking of Christ* (1602) which is the most important item. It was discovered by chance in a Dublin Jesuit house where it had hung in obscurity for many years. It was first hung in the National Gallery in 1993.

Constantinople School icon

NORTHERN EUROPEAN SCHOOLS

THE EARLY Netherlandish School is comprised largely of paintings with a religious theme. One exception is Brueghel the Younger's lively *Peasant Wedding* (1620). In the Dutch collection there are many 17th-century works, including some by Rembrandt. Other highlights include *A Wooded Landscape* by Hobbema and *Lady Writing a Letter With Her Maid* by Vermeer. Rubens and van Dyck are two more famous names here, but there are also fine works by lesser known artists, such as van Uden's *Peasants Merrymaking*. Portraits by such names as Faber and Pencz from the 15th and 16th centuries dominate the German collection, though Emil Nolde's colourful *Two Women in the Garden* dates from 1915.

OTHER COLLECTIONS

THE IMPRESSIVE Shaw Room is home to some exceptionally fine historical portraits. One of the most interesting pieces is Reynolds' portrait of Charles Coote, the first Earl of Bellamont, dressed up in flamboyant pink ceremonial robes. Another famous picture here is *The Marriage of Strongbow and Aoife*, by Maclise.

Peasant Wedding by Pieter Brueghel the Younger (1564–1637)

SOUTHWEST DUBLIN

THE AREA around Dublin Castle was first settled in prehistoric times, and it was from here that the city grew. Dublin gets its name from the dark pool (*Dubh Linn*) which formed at the confluence of the Liffey and the Poddle, a river which originally ran through the site of Dublin Castle. It is now channelled underground. Archaeological excavations behind Wood Quay, on the banks of the river Liffey, reveal that the Vikings had a settlement here as early as AD 841.

Following Strongbow's invasion of 1170, a medieval city began to emerge; the Anglo-Normans built strong defensive walls around the castle.

Logo of the children's centre, The Ark, in Temple Bar

A small reconstructed section of these old city walls can be seen at St Audoen's Church. More conspicuous reminders of the Anglo-Normans appear in the medieval Christ Church Cathedral and St Patrick's Cathedral. When the city expanded during the Georgian era, the narrow cobbled streets of Temple Bar became a quarter inhabited by skilled craftsmen and merchants. Today this area is considered to be the trendiest part of town, and is home to a variety of alternative shops and cafés. The Powerscourt Townhouse is an elegant 18th-century mansion that has been converted into one of the city's best shopping centres.

SIGHTS AT A GLANCE

Museums and Libraries
Chester Beatty Library ❷
Dublin Civic Museum ❻
Dublinia ⓭
Marsh's Library ❽

Historic Buildings
City Hall ❸
Dublin Castle pp88–9 ❶
Powerscourt Townhouse ❺
Tailors' Hall ⓫

Historic Areas
Temple Bar pp90–1 ❹

Churches
Christ Church Cathedral pp98–9 ⓮
St Audoen's Church ⓬
St Patrick's Cathedral ❾
St Werburgh's Church ❿
Whitefriar Street Carmelite Church ❼

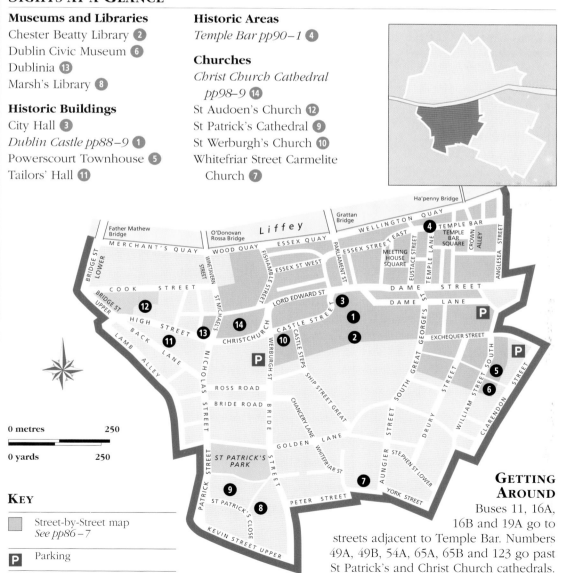

KEY

▨	Street-by-Street map *See pp86–7*
🅿	Parking

0 metres   250
0 yards   250

GETTING AROUND
Buses 11, 16A, 16B and 19A go to streets adjacent to Temple Bar. Numbers 49A, 49B, 54A, 65A, 65B and 123 go past St Patrick's and Christ Church cathedrals.

◁ **Colourful street in bustling Temple Bar**

Street-by-Street: Southwest Dublin

ESPITE ITS WEALTH of ancient buildings, such as Dublin Castle and Christ Church Cathedral, this part of Dublin lacks the sleek appeal of the neighbouring streets around Grafton Street. In recent years, however, redevelopment has rejuvenated the area, especially around Temple Bar, where the attractive cobbled streets are lined with shops, futuristic arts centres, galleries, bars and cafés.

Sunlight Chambers were built in 1900 for the Lever Brothers company. The delightful terracotta decoration on the façade advertises their main business of soap manufacturing.

Wood Quay is where the Vikings established their first permanent settlement in Ireland around 841.

Dublin Viking Adventure

★ **Christ Church Cathedral**
Huge family monuments, including that of the 19th Earl of Kildare, can be found in Ireland's oldest cathedral, which also has a fascinating crypt ⑭

St Werburgh's Church
An ornate interior hides behind the somewhat drab exterior of this 18th-century church ⑩

Dublinia
Medieval Dublin is the subject of this interactive museum, located in the former Synod Hall of the Church of Ireland. It is linked to Christ Church by a bridge ⑬

City Hall
Originally built as the Royal Exchange in 1779, the city's municipal headquarters is fronted by a huge Corinthian portico ❸

★ **Dublin Castle**
The Drawing Room, with its Waterford crystal chandelier, is part of a suite of luxurious rooms built in the 18th century for the Viceroys of Ireland ❶

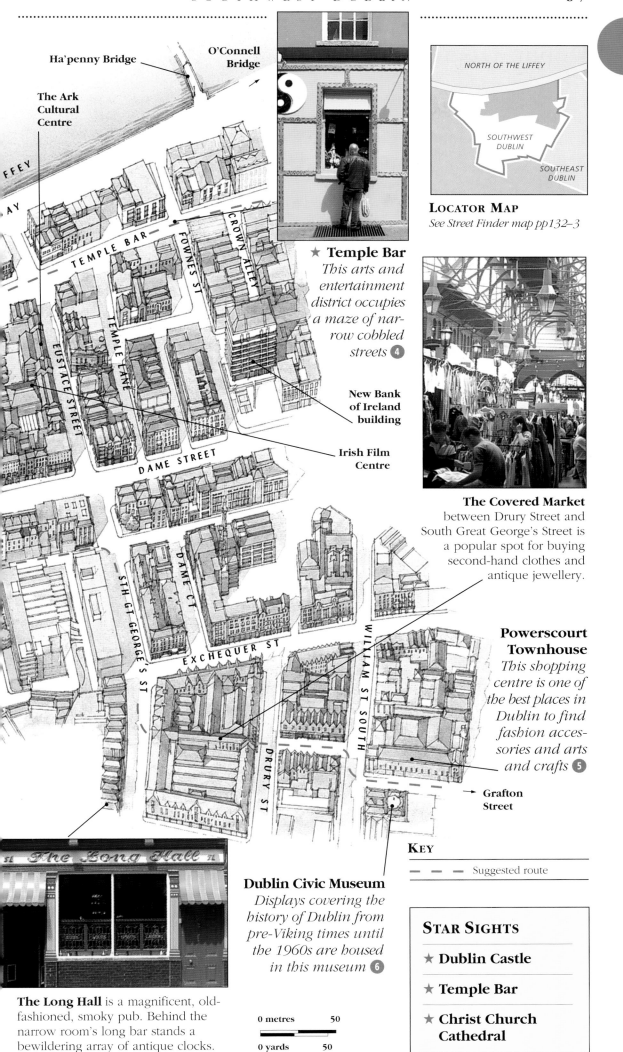

Ha'penny Bridge

O'Connell Bridge

The Ark Cultural Centre

LOCATOR MAP
See Street Finder map pp132–3

★ **Temple Bar**
This arts and entertainment district occupies a maze of narrow cobbled streets ❹

New Bank of Ireland building

Irish Film Centre

The Covered Market
between Drury Street and South Great George's Street is a popular spot for buying second-hand clothes and antique jewellery.

Powerscourt Townhouse
This shopping centre is one of the best places in Dublin to find fashion accessories and arts and crafts ❺

→ Grafton Street

Dublin Civic Museum
Displays covering the history of Dublin from pre-Viking times until the 1960s are housed in this museum ❻

The Long Hall is a magnificent, old-fashioned, smoky pub. Behind the narrow room's long bar stands a bewildering array of antique clocks.

KEY

— — — Suggested route

STAR SIGHTS

★ **Dublin Castle**

★ **Temple Bar**

★ **Christ Church Cathedral**

0 metres 50

0 yards 50

Dublin Castle ❶

FOR SEVEN CENTURIES Dublin Castle was a symbol of English rule, ever since the Anglo-Normans built a fortress here in the 13th century. Nothing remains of the original structure except the much-modified Record Tower. Following a fire in 1684, the Surveyor-General, Sir William Robinson, laid down the plans for the Upper and Lower Castle Yards in their present form. On the first floor of the south side of the Upper Yard are the luxury State Apartments, including St Patrick's Hall. These rooms, with Killybegs carpets and chandeliers of Waterford glass, served as home to the British-appointed Viceroys of Ireland.

St Patrick by Edward Smyth

Figure of Justice
Facing the Upper Yard above the main entrance from Cork Hill, this statue aroused much cynicism among Dubliners, who felt she was turning her back on the city.

★ **Throne Room**
Built in 1740, this room contains a throne said to have been presented by William of Orange after his victory at the Battle of the Boyne (see p13).

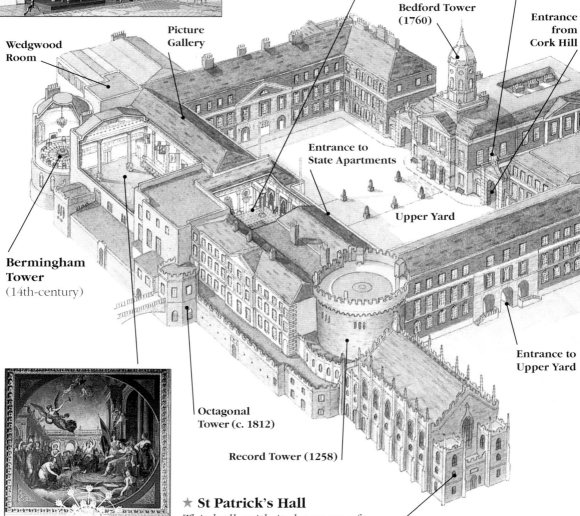

Wedgwood Room

Picture Gallery

Bedford Tower (1760)

Entrance from Cork Hill

Entrance to State Apartments

Upper Yard

Bermingham Tower (14th-century)

Entrance to Upper Yard

Octagonal Tower (c. 1812)

Record Tower (1258)

★ **St Patrick's Hall**
This hall, with its banners of the now defunct Knights of St Patrick, has ceiling paintings by Vincenzo Valdré (1778), symbolizing the relationship between Britain and Ireland.

The Church of the Most Holy Trinity was completed in 1814 by Francis Johnston. The 100 heads on the exterior of this Neo-Gothic church were carved by Edward Smyth.

ROBERT EMMET

Robert Emmet (1778–1803),
leader of the abortive 1803
rebellion, is remembered
as a heroic champion of
Irish liberty. His plan was
to capture Dublin Castle
as a signal for the country
to rise up against the Act
of Union (see p44). Emmet
was caught and publicly
hanged, but the defiant,
patriotic speech he made
from the dock helped to
inspire future generations
of Irish freedom fighters.

Government
offices

wer Yard

Dame Street

STAR FEATURES

★ **St Patrick's Hall**

★ **Throne Room**

Manuscript (1874) from the Holy Koran written by calligrapher Ahmad Shaikh in Kashmir, Chester Beatty Library

Chester Beatty Library ②

Clock Tower Building, Dublin Castle.
📞 677 7129. ○ ring for details.

THIS COLLECTION of Oriental
manuscripts and art was
bequeathed to Ireland by the
American mining magnate and
art collector Sir Alfred Chester
Beatty, who died in 1968.
This generous act no doubt
led to his selection as Ireland's
first honorary citizen in 1957.
  During his lifetime Beatty
accumulated almost 300 copies
of the Koran, representing the
works of master calligraphers
from Iran, Turkey and the
Arab world. Other exhibits
include some 6,000-year-old
Babylonian stone tablets,
Greek papyri dating from the
2nd century AD and biblical
material written in Coptic, the
original language of Egypt.
  In the Far Eastern collection
is a display of Chinese jade
books – each leaf is made from
thinly cut jade. Other displays
include Chinese snuff bottles
and imperial robes. Burmese
and Siamese art is represented
in the fine collection of 18th-
and 19th-century Parabaiks,
books of folk tales illustrated
with colourful paintings. The
Japanese collection also
includes many books as well
as paintings from the 16th to
the 18th centuries.
  Not to be overlooked is the
collection of western European
manuscripts. One of the most
beautiful of which is the

Coëtivy Book of Hours, an
illuminated French prayer
book, dating from the 15th
century. There is also a
collection of printed books,
many with fine engravings.

City Hall ③

Lord Edward St. ● to the public.

DESIGNED BY Thomas Cooley,
this imposing building
was built between 1769 and
1779 as the Royal Exchange.
It was taken over by Dublin
Corporation in 1852 as a meeting place for the city council,
a role it keeps to this day.
  Beyond the façade is the
entrance rotunda with its
attractive illuminated dome.
The city's coat-of-arms and
motto Obedientia Civium
Urbis Felicitas (Happy the
city where citizens obey) is
depicted in mosaic form on
the floor of the rotunda. A
pair of magnificent oval
staircases leads up to the
Council Chamber.

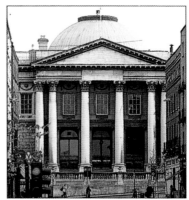

Façade of City Hall

Temple Bar ④

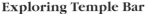

Palm tree seat

THE COBBLED streets between Dame Street and the Liffey are named after Sir William Temple who acquired the land in the early 1600s. The term "bar" meant a river-side path. In the 1800s it was home to small businesses but over the years went into decline. In the early 1960s the land was bought up with plans to build a new bus station. Artists and retailers took short term leases but stayed on when the redevelopment plans were scrapped. Temple Bar prospered and Dublin's selection as the 1991 European City of Culture has added impetus to its transformation. Today it is an exciting place, with bars, restaurants, shops and galleries.

Modern, floor-lit entrance hall of the Irish Film Centre

Exploring Temple Bar

For a first-time visitor, the most dramatic way to enter Temple Bar is through the **Merchants' Arch** opposite Ha'penny Bridge *(see p113)*. Underneath the arch is a short, dark alley lined with bazaar-like retail outlets. The alley then opens out into the modern airy space of **Temple Bar Square**, a popular lunch-time hangout. In the south-west corner is the **Temple Bar Gallery and Studios**, a renovated factory that combines exhibition and studio spaces. Along the east side of the square is the colourful **Crown Alley** with its brightly-painted stores and cafés.

Curved Street is the heart of Temple Bar with its modern cultural institutions. The **Temple Bar Music Centre**, a resource centre and music venue, is here. The **DESIGNyard** has exhibitions of, and sells, modern Irish jewellery and furniture from Ireland's top designers. A good source of information about the area is the **Temple Bar Information Centre** where you can pick up maps and leafets about galleries and restaurants.

In the evening, there is a huge choice of restaurants, bars and pubs to choose from and entertainment ranges from avant-garde performance art at the **Project Arts Centre**, to musicals, plays and rock concerts at the **Olympia Theatre**. The Kitchen, a club owned by Bono, and the Edge of U2, situated under the band's Clarence Hotel offer the latest dance sounds.

Bird from DESIGNyard

Temple Bar Information Centre

18 Eustace Street. **[** 671 5717.
○ *daily.* www.temple-bar.ie

Irish Film Centre

6 Eustace Street. **[** 679 5744.
○ *daily.*
Opened in November 1992, this was the first major cultural project completed in Temple Bar. A neon art sign indicates the main entrance which runs through a floor-lit corridor before opening into an airy atrium where visitors can browse in the bookstore or have a snack. Irish film-making has come to the fore in recent years with such international hits as *The Commitments* (1991). The centre's two screens focus on cult, arthouse and independent films as well as showing archive screenings and documentaries. The IFC's programme also includes seminars and workshops, seasons on various themes, nations or directors, and it hosts the Junior Dublin Film Festival each year.

Arthouse Multimedia Centre for the Arts

Curved Street. **[** 605 6800.
Exhibition areas ○ *daily.*
Standing on Curved Street opposite the Temple Bar Music Centre, Arthouse is a centre for the arts, bringing art and technology together through multimedia. On the ground floor and in the basement, exhibition space is host to touring displays. Arthouse also offers training courses, workshops and seminars in multimedia. There is an Internet café, Cyberia, on the top floor of the building.

Shoppers in the streets of Temple Bar

Meeting House Square

Named after a Quaker place of worship which once stood here, this outdoor performance space is a wonderful asset to the city. In the summer there are lunchtime and evening classical concerts, with the orchestra playing on a stage which folds away into a wall when it is not being used. There are also outdoor screenings of films (these are free, but it is necessary to get a ticket from the Temple Bar Information Centre in advance), family events, and an organic food market is held every Saturday.

Gallery of Photography

Meeting House Square.
671 4654. ◯ *Mon–Sat.*
The only gallery in the country devoted solely to photography, this bright, contemporary space runs exhibitions, workshops and special events. Its bookshop stocks a good array of photos and postcards from the exhibitions.

National Photographic Archive

Meeting House Square. **603 0200.** ◯ *Mon–Fri.*
Housed in the Photography Centre which opened in 1998, the NPA spreads over three floors of exhibition space.

Cheese stall at the weekly organic market in Meeting House Square

The exhibitions, covering a vast range of subjects, change four times a year. The photographs come from the National Library's archives of around a quarter of a million pictures.

Dublin's Viking Adventure

Essex Street West. **679 6040.** ◯ *Mar–Oct: Tue–Sat.*
This multimedia reconstruction of life in Dublin during the 9th century is, appropriately, adjacent to Wood Quay, where the Vikings first settled. The entertaining tours start off with visitors boarding a boat which runs on rollers through a "storm" before docking at a Viking village complete with re-created houses and actors dressed in period costume. The special effects are authentic right down to the smells. Guides then lead visitors through corridors explaining the Wood Quay dig and into a room of Viking artifacts. There is also a film show for visitors to watch, projected onto the side of a replica longship. In the evenings, a feast of Irish food and entertainment is laid on around the longship – tickets must be purchased in advance.

Situated directly opposite the Viking Adventure are excavation sites of Viking dwellings. It is hoped that part of this area will be open to public view in the future.

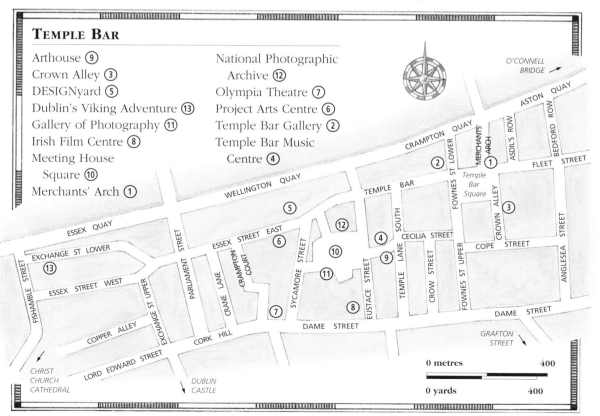

TEMPLE BAR

Arthouse ⑨
Crown Alley ③
DESIGNyard ⑤
Dublin's Viking Adventure ⑬
Gallery of Photography ⑪
Irish Film Centre ⑧
Meeting House Square ⑩
Merchants' Arch ①
National Photographic Archive ⑫
Olympia Theatre ⑦
Project Arts Centre ⑥
Temple Bar Gallery ②
Temple Bar Music Centre ④

The light and airy interior of Powerscourt Townhouse shopping centre

Powerscourt Townhouse 5

South William St. 679 4144.
9am–6pm Mon–Sat
(9am–7pm Thu).

COMPLETED IN 1774 by Robert Mack, this grand mansion was originally built as the city home of Viscount Powerscourt, who also had a country estate at Enniskerry just south of Dublin. Granite from the Powerscourt estate was used in its construction. Today the building houses one of Dublin's most interesting shopping centres. The interior still features the original grand staircase, which is made of mahogany, and finely detailed plasterwork by stuccodore Michael Stapleton.

The building became a drapery warehouse in the 1830s, and major restoration in the 1960s turned it into a centre for specialist galleries, antique shops, jewellery stalls, cafés and other shop units. The central courtyard, topped by a glass dome, is popular with many Dubliners as a place to have a snack and a coffee.

The Townhouse can also be reached by an entrance on the narrow Johnson Court alley, just off bustling Grafton Street.

Dublin Civic Museum 6

58 South William St. 679 4260.
10am–6pm Tue– Sat, 11am–2pm Sun. 10 days at Christmas & public hols.

THIS SMALL MUSEUM, housed in the former Georgian City Assembly House, depicts Dublin's history from Viking times through to the 20th century by means of photographs, paintings, old newspaper cuttings and an

Shoes of an Irish Giant in Dublin Civic Museum

assortment of very unusual objects, including the old shoes of an Irish giant. One of the star exhibits is the head from the 40-m (134-ft) high Nelson Pillar. This massive monument was erected in 1808, and predated Nelson's Column in London's Trafalgar Square by several decades. It loomed high over O'Connell Street until it was destroyed in an explosion by anti-British protestors on 8 March 1966.

Whitefriar Street Carmelite Church 7

56 Aungier St. 475 8821.
8am– 6:30pm Mon & Wed–Fri,
8am–9pm Tue, 8am–7pm Sat,
8am–7:30pm Sun.

DESIGNED BY George Papworth, this Catholic church was built in 1827. It stands on the site of a 16th-century Carmelite priory of which nothing remains.

In contrast to the two Church of Ireland cathedrals, St Patrick's and Christ Church, which are usually full of tourists, this church is frequented by local worshippers. Every day they come to light candles to various saints, including St Valentine – the patron saint of lovers. His remains, previously buried in the cemetery of St Hippolytus in Rome, were offered to the church as a gift from Pope Gregory XVI in 1836. Today they rest beneath the commemorative statue to the saint, which stands in the northeast corner of the church beside the high altar.

Nearby is a Flemish oak statue of the Virgin and Child, dating from the late 15th or early 16th century. It may have belonged to St Mary's Abbey *(see p112)* and is believed to be the only wooden statue of its kind to escape destruction when Ireland's monasteries were sacked during the time of the Reformation *(see p70)*.

Statue of Virgin and child in Whitefriar Street Carmelite Church

◁ **The atmospheric Temple Bar district**

The entrance to Marsh's Library, adjacent to St Patrick's Cathedral

Marsh's Library ⑧

St Patrick's Close. ☏ 454 3511.
🕐 10am–12:45pm & 2–5pm Mon &
Wed–Fri, 10:30am– 12:45pm Sat. ●
Christmas Eve– 2 Jan & public hols. ⌨

BUILT IN 1701 for Archbishop Narcissus Marsh, this is the oldest public library in Ireland. It was designed by Sir William Robinson, architect of the Royal Hospital Kilmainham (see p120).

To the rear of the library are wired alcoves where readers who wanted to read any of the rare books were locked in. The collection of books from the 16th–18th centuries includes a volume of Clarendon's *History of the Rebellion*, with margin notes by Jonathan Swift.

St Patrick's Cathedral ⑨

St Patrick's Close. ☏ 475 4817.
🕐 Apr–Oct: 9am– 6pm Mon–Fri,
9am–5pm Sat, 10–11am
& 12:45–3pm Sun; Nov–Mar: 9am–
6pm Mon–Fri, 9am–4pm Sat, 10am–
11am & 12:45–3pm Sun. ⌨

IRELAND'S LARGEST CHURCH was founded beside a sacred well where St Patrick is said to have baptized converts around AD 450. The original building was just a wooden chapel and remained so until 1192 when Archbishop John Comyn rebuilt it in stone.

In the mid-17th century, Huguenot refugees from France arrived in Dublin, and were given the Lady Chapel by the Dean and Chapter as

JONATHAN SWIFT (1667–1745)

Jonathan Swift was born in Dublin and educated at Trinity College (see pp70–71). He left for England in 1689, but returned in 1694 when his political career failed. He began a life in the church, becoming Dean of St Patrick's in 1713. In addition, he was a prolific political commentator – his best-known work, *Gulliver's Travels*, contains a bitter satire on Anglo-Irish relations. Swift's personal life, particularly his friendship with two younger women, Ester Johnson, better known as Stella, and Hester Vanhomrigh, attracted criticism. In later life, he suffered from Menière's disease – an illness of the ear which led many to believe he was insane.

their place of worship. The chapel was separated from the rest of the cathedral and used by the Huguenots until the late 18th century. Today St Patrick's is the Protestant Church of Ireland's national cathedral.

Much of the present building dates back to work completed between 1254 and 1270. The cathedral suffered over the centuries from desecration, fire and neglect but, thanks to Sir Benjamin Guinness, it underwent extensive restoration during the 1860s. The building is 91 m (300 ft) long; at the western end is a 43-m (141-ft) tower, restored by Archbishop Minot in 1370 and now known as Minot's Tower. The spire was added in the 18th century.

The interior is dotted with memorial busts, brasses and monuments. A leaflet available at the front desk helps identify and locate them. Famous citizens remembered in the church include the harpist Turlough O'Carolan (1670–1738), Douglas Hyde (1860–1949), the first President of Ireland and of course Jonathan Swift and his beloved Stella.

At the west end of the nave is an old door with a hole in it – a relic from a feud between the Lords Kildare and Ormonde in 1492. The latter took refuge in the Chapter House, but a truce was soon made and a hole was cut in the door by Lord Kildare so that the two could shake hands in friendship.

St Patrick's Cathedral with Minot's Tower and spire

Nave of St Werburgh's Church, showing gallery and organ case

St Werburgh's Church ⑩

Entrance through 7–8 Castle St.
℘ *478 3710.* ○ *10am– 4pm Mon–Fri, ring bell if doors locked.*

BUILT ON LATE 12th-century foundations, St Werburgh's was designed by Thomas Burgh in 1715, after an act of parliament which appointed commissioners to build a new church. Around eighty-five people made donations. By 1719 the church was complete but had an unfinished tower. Then in 1728 James Southwell bequeathed money for a clock and bells for the church on condition that the tower was completed within three years of his death. It was finally finished in 1732. After a fire in 1754 it was rebuilt with the financial help of George II. It served as the parish church of Dublin Castle, hosting many state ceremonies, including the swearing-in of viceroys. However, this role was later taken over by the Church of the Most Holy Trinity within the castle walls.

Beyond the shabby pallor of its exterior walls lies some fine decorative work. There are massive memorials to members of the Guinness family, and a finely carved Gothic pulpit by Richard Stewart. Also worth seeing are the 1767 organ case and the beautiful stuccowork in the chancel.

Beneath the church lie 27 vaults including that of Lord Edward Fitzgerald, who died during the 1798 Rebellion *(see p45)*, and also Sir James Ware. The body of Fitzgerald's captor, Major Henry Sirr, is in the graveyard. John Field, the creator of the nocturne, was baptized here in 1782.

Tailors' Hall ⑪

Back Lane. ◉ *to the public.*

DUBLIN'S ONLY surviving guildhall preserves a delightful corner of old Dublin in an otherwise busy redevelopment zone. Built in 1706, it stands behind a limestone arch in a quiet cobbled yard. The building is the oldest guildhall in Ireland and was used by various trade groups including hosiers, saddlers and barber-surgeons as well as tailors. It was regarded as the most fashionable venue in Dublin for social occasions such as balls and concerts for many years until the New Music Hall in Fishamble Street opened and the social scene transferred to there. It also hosted many political meetings – the Protestant leader of the United Irishmen, Wolfe Tone, famously made a speech at the convention of the Catholic Committee on 2nd December 1792 before the 1798 rebellion *(see p45)*.

The building closed in the early 1960s as a result of neglect, but a successful appeal by Desmond Guinness saw the hall completely refurbished. Since 1985 is has been the home of *An Taisce* (the Irish National Trust).

Façade of Tailors' Hall, today the home of the Irish National Trust

St Audoen's Church ⑫

High St. ◉ *for restoration.*

DESIGNATED A national monument and currently under restoration, St Audoen's is Dublin's earliest surviving medieval church. The 12th-century tower is believed to be the oldest in Ireland, and its three bells date from 1423. The 15th-century nave also remains intact.

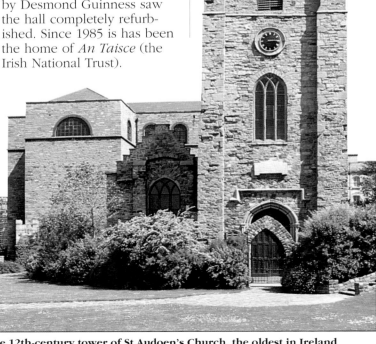

The 12th-century tower of St Audoen's Church, the oldest in Ireland

The church stands in an attractive churchyard with well-maintained lawns and shrubs. To the rear, steps lead down to St Audoen's Arch, the last remaining gateway of the old city. Flanking the gate are restored sections of the 13th-century city walls.

Next door stands St Audoen's Roman Catholic Church, which was begun in 1841 and completed in 1847. It was built by Patrick Byrne, of Talbot Street, who studied at the Dublin Society School. The parish priest, Patrick Mooney, completed the plasterwork and also installed the organ. In 1884 the dome of the church collapsed and was replaced with a plaster circle. The portico was added to the building in 1899. The Great Bell, dedicated on All Saints Day in 1848 and known as The Liberator after Daniel O'Connell, rang to announce his release from prison and also tolled on the day of his funeral. The two large Pacific clam shells situated next to the front door of the church hold holy water. In the basement there is an audio-visual presentation on pre-Viking Ireland.

Dublinia ⑬

St Michael's Hill. 📞 679 4611.
◯ Apr–Sep: 10am–5pm daily; Oct–Mar: 11am–4pm Mon–Sat, 10am–4:30pm Sun. ◐ 24–26 Dec. 🖼 includes entry to Christ Church Cathedral via bridge. ♿

MANAGED BY the non-profit-making Medieval Trust, the Dublinia exhibition covers the formative period of Dublin's history from the arrival of the Anglo-Normans in 1170 to the closure of the monasteries in the 1540s. The exhibition is housed in the Neo-Gothic Synod Hall, which, up until 1983, was home to the ruling body of the Church of Ireland. The building and the bridge linking it to Christ Church Cathedral date from the 1870s. Before Dublinia was

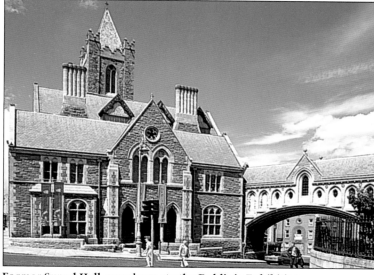
Former Synod Hall, now home to the Dublinia Exhibition

established in 1993, the Synod Hall was briefly converted into a nightclub.

The exhibition is entered via the basement where an audiotape-guided tour takes visitors through exhibits of life-size reconstructions, complete with realistic sounds and smells.

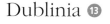
Medieval key in the Dublinia exhibition

These depict major events in Dublin's history, such as the Black Death and the rebellion of Silken Thomas (see p40). The ground floor houses a large scale model of Dublin as it was around 1500, and recon-structions including the inside of a late medieval merchant's kitchen. There is also a display of artifacts from the Wood Quay excavation. This was the site of the first Viking settlement in Ireland. Excavations in the 1970s revealed remains of Norse and Norman villages, and artifacts includ-ing pottery, swords, coins and leatherwork. Many of these finds are on display at the National Museum (see pp 76–7) as well as here in Dublinia. However, the city chose not to develop the Wood Quay site, but instead built two large civic offices there. If you go to Wood Quay today all you will find is a plaque and an unusual picnic site by the Liffey in the shape of a Viking longboat.

Also in the exhibition are in-formation panels on the themes of trade, merchants and religion. On the first floor is the wood-panelled Great Hall, where there is a multi-screen presentation, set up to illus-trate Dublin's medieval history.

Mid 13th-century jug in Dublinia

The Malton Room contains a set of prints by James Malton, the Eng-lish artist who spent ten years in Dublin and did work for James Gandon in the 18th century. The 60-m (200-ft) high St Michael's Tower above Dublinia offers one of the best vantage points across the city.

Reconstruction of a Viking street in Dublinia

Christ Church Cathedral ⑭

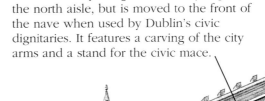

Arms on Lord Mayor's pew

Cʜʀɪsᴛ ᴄʜᴜʀᴄʜ ᴄᴀᴛʜᴇᴅʀᴀʟ was commissioned in 1172 by Strongbow, Anglo-Norman conqueror of Dublin (*see p40*), and Archbishop Laurence O'Toole. It replaced an earlier wooden church built by the Vikings in 1038. At the time of the Reformation (*see p42*), the cathedral passed to the Protestant Church of Ireland. By the 19th century it was in a bad state of repair, but was completely remodelled by architect George Street in the 1870s. In the crypt are monuments removed from the cathedral during its restoration.

★ Medieval Lectern
This beautiful brass lectern was hand-wrought during the Middle Ages. It stands on the left-hand side of the nave, in front of the pulpit. The matching lectern on the right-hand side is a copy, dating from the 19th century.

Great Nave
The 25-m (68-ft) high nave has some fine early Gothic arches. On the north side, the original 13th-century wall leans out by as much as 50 cm (18 in) due to subsidence.

The Lord Mayor's pew is usually kept in the north aisle, but is moved to the front of the nave when used by Dublin's civic dignitaries. It features a carving of the city arms and a stand for the civic mace.

Entrance

★ Strongbow Monument
The large effigy in chain armour is probably not Strongbow. However, his remains are buried in the cathedral and the curious half-figure may be part of his original tomb.

The bridge to the Synod Hall was added when the cathedral was being rebuilt in the 1870s.

Sᴛᴀʀ Fᴇᴀᴛᴜʀᴇs

★ **Strongbow Monument**

★ **Crypt**

★ **Medieval Lectern**

Chapel of St Laud
The casket on the wall contains the heart of St Laurence O'Toole. The chapel features original medieval floor tiles.

The Lady Chapel is used for Eucharist celebrations and is the chapel of the St John Ambulance Brigade.

★ **Crypt**
The cavernous crypt contains several oddities, including this mummified cat and rat, found in an organ pipe in the 1860s.

Stairs to crypt

Crypt

The foundations of the original Chapter House date back to the early 13th century.

Romanesque Doorway
Leading to the south transept, this ornately carved doorway is one of the finest examples of 12th-century Irish stonework.

TIMELINE

1038 Construction of original wooden Viking cathedral

1240 Completion of stone cathedral

1600 Shopkeepers rent crypt space

1541 King Henry VIII alters constitution of cathedral

1689 King James II of England worships in cathedral

1983 Cathedral ceases using Synod Hall

1000	1200	1400	1600	1800

1172 St Laurence O'Toole and Strongbow commission the new stone cathedral

Meeting takes place between Lambert Simnel and the Earl of Kildare

1742 Choir participates in first performance of Handel's *Messiah*

1487 Coronation of 10-year-old Lambert Simnel as "King of England"

1871 Major rebuilding of the cathedral begins, including Synod Hall and bridge

NORTH OF THE LIFFEY

DUBLIN'S NORTHSIDE was the last part of the city to be developed during the 18th century. The city authorities envisioned an area of leafy avenues, but the reality of today's traffic has rather spoiled their original plans. Nonetheless, O'Connell Street is an impressive thoroughfare, lined with department stores, monuments and historic public buildings.

Some of these buildings, such as James Gandon's glorious Custom House and majestic Four Courts, together with the famous General Post Office *(see p105)*, add grace to the area.

The Rotunda Hospital, Europe's first purpose-built maternity hospital, is another fine building. Dublin's two most celebrated theatres, the Abbey and the Gate, act as cultural magnets, as does the Dublin Writers' Museum and also the James Joyce Cultural Centre, two museums that are dedicated to writers who spent most of their lives in the city.

**Bookshop sign on
Ormond Quay Lower**

SIGHTS AT A GLANCE

Historic Buildings
Custom House ①
Four Courts ⑫
King's Inns ⑨
Tyrone House ④

Historic Streets and Bridges
Ha'penny Bridge ⑯
O'Connell Street ③
Parnell Square ⑦
Smithfield ⑩

Theatres
Abbey Theatre ②

Churches
St Mary's Church ⑮
St Mary's Pro-Cathedral ⑤
St Michan's Church ⑬

Museums and Galleries
Old Jameson Distillery ⑪
James Joyce Cultural Centre ⑥
World of Wax ⑧
St Mary's Abbey Exhibition ⑭

GETTING AROUND
Buses 3, 10, 11A, 13, 16A, 16B, 19A, 22A, 22B and 123 go along O'Connell Street and round Parnell Square. To get to St Michan's Church, Smithfield and Old Jameson Distillery, take a number 67A, 68, 69, 79 or 90.

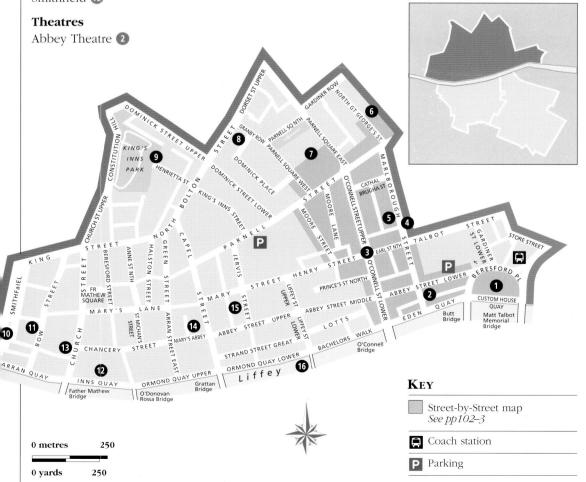

KEY

Street-by-Street map
See pp102–3

🚌 Coach station

🅿 Parking

0 metres   250

0 yards   250

◁ **The impressive columns of the General Post Office on O'Connell Street**

Street-by-Street: Around O'Connell Street

THROUGHOUT THE Georgian era, O'Connell Street was very much the fashionable part of Dublin in which to live. However, the 1916 Easter Rising destroyed many of the fine buildings along the street, includ-

Pavement mosaic, Moore Street

ing much of the General Post Office – only its original façade remains. Today, this main thoroughfare is lined with shops and businesses. Other attractions nearby include St Mary's Pro-Cathedral and James Gandon's Custom House, overlooking the Liffey.

James Joyce Cultural Centre
This well-restored Georgian town house contains a small Joyce museum **6**

Parnell Monument (1911)

The Gate Theatre was founded in 1928 and is renowned for its productions of contemporary drama.

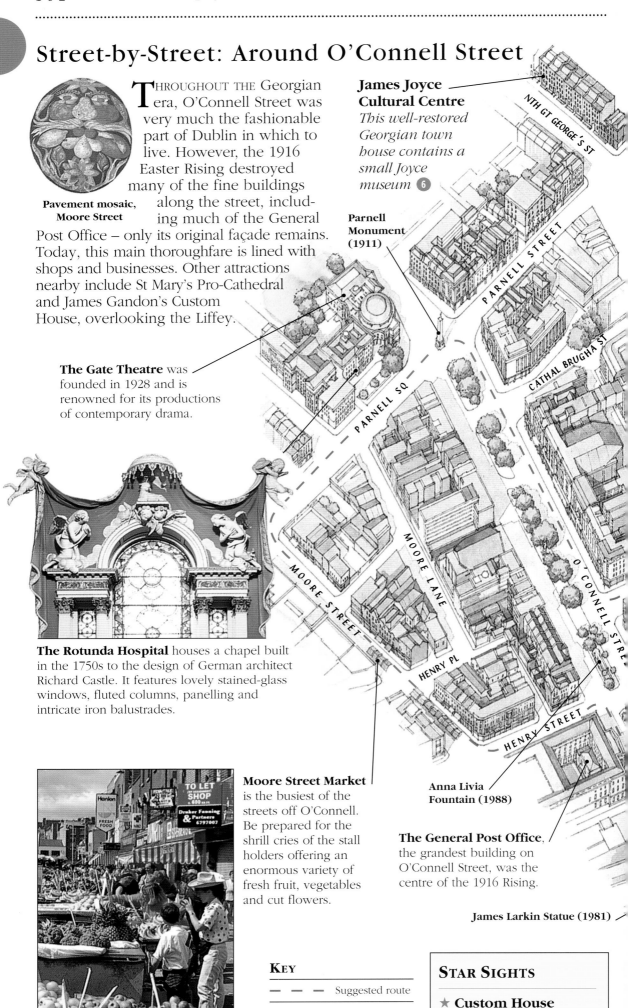

The Rotunda Hospital houses a chapel built in the 1750s to the design of German architect Richard Castle. It features lovely stained-glass windows, fluted columns, panelling and intricate iron balustrades.

Moore Street Market is the busiest of the streets off O'Connell. Be prepared for the shrill cries of the stall holders offering an enormous variety of fresh fruit, vegetables and cut flowers.

Anna Livia Fountain (1988)

The General Post Office, the grandest building on O'Connell Street, was the centre of the 1916 Rising.

James Larkin Statue (1981)

KEY

‒ ‒ ‒ Suggested route

0 metres   50

0 yards   50

STAR SIGHTS

★ **Custom House**

★ **O'Connell Street**

St Mary's Pro-Cathedral
Built around 1825, this is Dublin's main place of worship for Catholics. The plaster relief above the altar in the sanctuary depicts The Ascension **5**

The statue of James Joyce (1990), by Marjorie Fitzgibbon, commemorates one of Ireland's most famous novelists. Born in Dublin in 1882, he catalogued the people and streets of Dublin in *Dubliners* and in his most celebrated work, *Ulysses*.

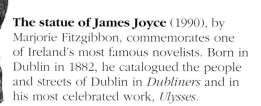

Abbey Theatre
Ireland's national theatre is known throughout the world for its productions by Irish playwrights, such as Sean O'Casey and JM Synge **2**

★ **O'Connell Street**
This monument to Daniel O'Connell by John Foley took 19 years to complete from the laying of its foundation stone in 1864 **3**

Butt Bridge

O'Connell Bridge

Trinity College

★ **Custom House**
This striking head, by Edward Smyth, symbolizes the River Liffey. It is one of 14 carved keystones that adorn the building **1**

Illuminated façade of the Custom House reflected in the Liffey

Custom House ❶

Custom House Quay. ◐ *to the public.*

THIS MAJESTIC BUILDING was designed as the Custom House by the English architect James Gandon. However, just nine years after its completion, the 1800 Act of Union *(see p44)* transferred the custom and excise business to London, rendering the building practically obsolete. In 1921, supporters of Sinn Fein celebrated their election victory by setting light to what they saw as a symbol of British imperialism. The fire blazed for five days causing extensive damage. Reconstruction took place in 1926, although further deterioration meant that the building was not completely restored until 1991, when it reopened as government offices.

The main façade is made up of pavilions at each end with a Doric portico in its centre. The arms of Ireland crown the two pavilions, and a series of 14 allegorical heads by Dublin sculptor Edward Smyth form the keystones of arches and entrances. These heads depict Ireland's main rivers

and the Atlantic Ocean. A statue of Commerce tops the central copper dome.

The best view of the building is from the south of the Liffey beyond Matt Talbot Bridge, especially at night.

Logo of the Abbey Theatre

Abbey Theatre ❷

Lower Abbey St. ☎ *878 7222.*
◐ *for performances only.* **Box office**
◐ *10:30am–7pm Mon–Sat.*
See also **Entertainment** *pp140–5.*

FOUNDED in 1898 with WB Yeats and Lady Gregory as co-directors, the Abbey staged its first play in 1904. The early years of this much lauded national theatre witnessed works by WB Yeats, JM Synge and Sean O'Casey. Many were controversial: nationalist sensitivities were severely tested in 1926 in the premiere of O'Casey's *The Plough and the Stars*, when the flag of the Irish Free State appeared on stage in a scene which featured a pub frequented by prostitutes.

The Abbey Theatre remains best known for its excellent productions of early 20th-century Irish work, though in recent years it has done much to encourage new writing talent, particularly in the small Peacock Theatre downstairs. One of the most acclaimed performances in the main theatre was Brian Friel's *Dancing At Lughnasa* (1990). The walls in the theatre bar are lined with portraits of famous names that were once connected with the theatre.

O'Connell Street ❸

O'CONNELL STREET is very different from the original plans of Irish aristocrat Luke Gardiner. When he bought the land in the 18th century, Gardiner envisioned a grand residential parade with an elegant mall running along its centre. Such plans were short-lived. The construction of Carlisle (now

O'Connell Bridge spanning the Liffey, viewed from the Butt Bridge

O'Connell) Bridge in 1790 transformed the street into the city's main north-south route. Also, several buildings were destroyed during the 1916 Easter Rising and the Irish Civil War. Since the 1960s many of the old buildings have been replaced by the plate glass and neon of fast food joints and amusement arcades.

A few venerable old buildings remain, including the General Post Office (1818), Gresham Hotel (1817), Clery's department store (1822) and the Royal Dublin Hotel, part of which occupies the street's only original town house.

A walk down the central mall is the most enjoyable way to see the street's mix of architectural styles. At the south end stands a huge monument to Daniel O'Connell *(see p46)*, unveiled in 1882. The street, which throughout the 19th century had been called Sackville Street, was renamed for O'Connell in 1922. Higher up, almost facing the General Post Office, is an expressive statue of James Larkin (1867–1943), leader of the

Clock outside Clery's department store

Dublin general strike in 1913. The next statue is of Father Theobald Mathew (1790–1856), founder of the Pioneer Total Abstinence Movement. At the north end of the street is the obelisk-shaped monument to Charles Stewart Parnell (1846–91), who was leader of the Home Rule Party and known as the "uncrowned King of Ireland" *(see p46)*. Also on O'Connell Street, at the junction of Cathedral Street, is the Anna Livia Millennium Fountain, which was unveiled during the city's millennium celebrations in 1988. It is supposed to represent the River Liffey, however, most Dubliners dismiss it simply as the "Floozie in the Jacuzzi".

Tyrone House ④

Marlborough Street. 🚫 *to the public.*

CONSIDERED TO BE the most important Dublin building by German-born Richard Castle (also known as Cassels) after Leinster House, this

Palladian-style structure was completed around 1740 as a town house for Sir Marcus Beresford, later Earl of Tyrone. Its interior features elaborate plasterwork by the Swiss Francini brothers, as well as a grand mahogany staircase. The premises were bought by the government in the 1830s and today house a section of the Department of Education; the minister has one of the most ornate state offices in what used to be a reception room.

Austere Neo-Classical interior of St Mary's Pro-Cathedral

St Mary's Pro-Cathedral ⑤

Marlborough St. 📞 *874 5441.* ⏰ *9:30am–5pm daily.*

DEDICATED in 1825 before Catholic emancipation was fully effected *(see p45)*, St Mary's is Dublin's Catholic cathedral. Its backstreet site was the best the city's Anglo-Irish leaders would allow.

The façade is based on the Temple of Theseus in Athens. Its six Doric columns support a pediment with statues of St Laurence O'Toole, 12th-century Archbishop of Dublin and patron saint of the city, St Mary and St Patrick. The most striking feature of the interior is the intricately carved high altar.

St Mary's is home to the famous Palestrina Choir, started in 1902. In 1904 the great Irish tenor, John McCormack, began his career with the choir, which can be heard every Sunday at 11am.

THE GENERAL POST OFFICE (GPO)

Built in 1818 halfway along O'Connell Street, the GPO became a symbol of the 1916 Irish Rising. Members of the Irish Volunteers and Irish Citizen Army seized the building on Easter Monday, and Patrick Pearse *(see p15)* read out the Proclamation of the Irish Republic from its steps. Shelling from the British finally forced the rebels out after a week. At first, many Irish people viewed the Rising unfavourably. However, as WB Yeats wrote, matters "changed utterly" and a "terrible beauty was born" when, during the

Irish Life magazine cover showing the 1916 Easter Rising

following weeks, 14 of the leaders were shot at Kilmainham Gaol *(see p79)*. Inside the GPO is a sculpture of the Irish mythical warrior Cuchulainn, dedicated to those who died.

James Joyce Cultural Centre ⑥

35 North Great George's St.
☎ 878 8547. ◯ 9:30am–5pm Mon–Sat, 12:30–5pm Sun. ● Good Fri & 23–27 Dec. ▨ ☐

Although born in Dublin, Joyce spent most of his adult life in Europe. He used Dublin as the setting for his major works, including *Ulysses*, *A Portrait of the Artist as a Young Man* and *Dubliners*.

This centre is located in a 1784 town house which was built for the Earl of Kenmare. Michael Stapleton, one of the greatest stuccodores of his time, contributed to the plaster-work, of which the friezes are particularly noteworthy.

The main literary display is an absorbing set of biographies of around 50 characters from *Ulysses*, who were based on real Dublin people. Professor Dennis J Maginni, a peripheral character in *Ulysses*, ran a dancing school from this town house. Leopold and Molly Bloom, the central characters of *Ulysses*, lived a short walk away at No. 7 Eccles Street. The centre also organizes walking tours of Joyce's Dublin, so a visit is a must for all Joycean zealots.

At the top of the road, on Great Denmark Street, is the Jesuit-run Belvedere College attended by Joyce between 1893 and 1898. He recalls his unhappy schooldays there in *A Portrait of the Artist as a Young Man*. The college's interior contains some of Stapleton's best and most colourful plasterwork (1785).

Portrait of James Joyce (1882–1941) by Jacques Emile Blanche

Parnell Square ⑦

Once as affluent as the now-restored squares to the south of the Liffey, Parnell Square is today sadly neglected. However, it still holds many points of interest, including the historic Gate Theatre and the peaceful Garden of Remembrance. There are hopes that this once-elegant part of the city will one day be renovated and restored to its original splendour.

Stained-glass window (c. 1863) in the Rotunda Hospital's chapel

Gate Theatre

1 Cavendish Row. ◯ for performances only. **Box office** ☎ 874 4045. ◯ 10am–7pm Mon–Sat. Originally, this was the grand supper room in the Rotunda, but today the Gate Theatre is renowned for its staging of contemporary international drama in Dublin. It was founded in 1928 by Hilton Edwards and Mícheál Mac Liammóir. The latter is now best remembered for *The Importance of Being Oscar*, his long-running one-man show about the writer Oscar Wilde *(see p26)*. An early success was Denis Johnston's *The Old Lady Says No*, so-called because of the margin notes made on one of his scripts by Lady Gregory, founding director of the Abbey Theatre *(see p104)*. Although still noted for staging productions of new plays, the Gate's current output often includes classic Irish plays including Sean O'Casey's *Juno and the Paycock*. Many famous names in the acting world were given their first real break at the Gate Theatre, including James Mason and a teenage Orson Welles.

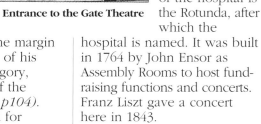

Entrance to the Gate Theatre

Rotunda Hospital

Parnell Square West. ☎ 873 0700. Standing in the middle of Parnell Square is Europe's first purpose-built maternity hospital. Founded in 1745 by Dr Bartholomew Mosse, the design of the hospital is similar to that of Leinster House *(see p78)*. The German-born architect Richard Castle designed both buildings. At the east end of the hospital is the Rotunda, after which the hospital is named. It was built in 1764 by John Ensor as Assembly Rooms to host fund-raising functions and concerts. Franz Liszt gave a concert here in 1843.

On the first floor is a chapel which features striking stained-glass windows and Rococo plasterwork and ceiling (1755) by the stucco-dore Bartholomew Cramillion.

On the other side of the road from the hospital is Conway's Pub. Opened in 1745, it has been popular with expectant fathers for years.

Garden of Remembrance

Parnell Square. ◯ *dawn–dusk daily.*
At the northern end of Parnell Square is a small, peaceful park, dedicated to the men and women who have died in the pursuit of Irish freedom. The Garden of Remembrance marks the spot where several leaders of the Easter Rising were held overnight before being taken to Kilmainham Gaol *(see p117)*, and is also where the Irish Volunteers movement was formed in 1913.

Designed by Daithí Hanly, the garden was opened by President Eamon de Valera *(see p49)* in 1966, to mark the 50th anniversary of the Easter Rising. In the centre is a cruciform pool with a mosaic depicting broken swords, shields and spears, symbolizing peace. At one end of the garden is a large bronze sculpture by Oisín Kelly (1971) of the legendary *Children of Lir*, the daughters of King Lir who were changed into swans by their jealous stepmother.

Gallery of Writers at Dublin Writers' Museum

Dublin Writers' Museum

18 Parnell Square North. ◖ *872 2077.* ◯ *10am–5pm (Jun–Aug: 10am–6pm, except Sat 10am–5pm) Mon–Sat, 11am–5pm Sun & public hols.* ◉ *25 & 26 Dec.* 🔖
Opened in 1991, the museum occupies an 18th-century town house. There are displays relating to Irish literature over the last thousand years, although there is little about writers in the latter part of the 20th century. The exhibits include paintings, manuscripts, letters, rare editions and mementoes of Ireland's finest authors.

Children of Lir in the Garden of Remembrance

There are many temporary exhibits and a lavishly decorated Gallery of Writers upstairs. The museum also hosts frequent poetry readings and lectures.

The pleasant café and a specialist bookstore, which provides a useful out-of-print book search service, both help to enhance the relaxed and friendly ambience of this interesting museum.

Hugh Lane Municipal Gallery of Modern Art

Charlemont House, Parnell Square North. ◖ *874 1903.* ◯ *9:30am–6pm Tue–Thu, 9:30am–5pm Fri & Sat, 11am–5pm Sun.* ◉ *23–25 Dec & public hols.*
Noted art collector Sir Hugh Lane donated his valuable collection of Impressionist paintings, including *Le Concert aux Tuileries* by Manet and *Sur La Plage* by Degas, to Dublin Corporation in 1905. However, the failure to find a suitable location for them prompted Lane to consider transferring his gift to the National Gallery in London. The Corporation then proposed Charlemont House, the town house of Lord Charlemont, who built Marino Casino *(see p126)* and Lane relented. However, in 1915, before Lane's revised will could be witnessed, he died on board the torpedoed liner *Lusitania*. This led to a 50-year dispute which has been resolved by Dublin Corporation and the National Gallery swapping the collection every five years.

As well as the Lane bequest the gallery also has a sculpture hall with work by Rodin and others. There is also an extensive collection of modern Irish canvases including Michael Farrell's *Madonna Irlanda* (1977) and Patrick Graham's *Ire/land III* (1982).

Sur la Plage **(c. 1876) by Edgar Degas, Hugh Lane Municipal Gallery**

The impressive façade of the King's Inns, on Constitution Hill

National Wax Museum ⑧

Granby Row, Parnell Square. ⬛ 872 6340. ⬤ Mon–Sat 10am-5:30pm, Sun noon–5:30pm. 🗓

JUST OFF THE northwest edge of Parnell Square, this museum firmly sets its sights on attracting children. Significant space is given over to fairytale and cartoon characters such as the Flintstones, Ninja Turtles and the Simpsons. Further amusement comes in the form of a hall of mirrors while the dimly-lit Chamber of Horrors is good fun. The largest area traces Ireland's history and culture with characters from the past almost to the present day. The wax dummies of all the figures, from Wolfe Tone to recent President Mary Robinson, make the subjects look incredibly young – including the Reverend Ian Paisley and Pope John Paul II (who appears complete with replica Popemobile). Irish cycling legend Sean Kelly is set racing up a steep climb.

Many of the displays, encased behind glass screens, offer an audio definition of their cultural or historical importance; a useful feature as some of the subjects are not particularly well known outside Ireland. The final section groups together several leading lights in the entertainment world including U2, Garth Brooks and Madonna.

King's Inns ⑨

Henrietta St/Constitution Hill. ⬤ to the public.

THIS CLASSICALLY proportioned public building was founded in 1795 as a place of both residence and study for barristers in Dublin. The King's Inns was the name taken by the Irish lawyers' society upon Henry VIII declaring himself King of Ireland. To build it, James Gandon, famous as the architect of the Custom House *(see p104)*, chose to seal off the end of Henrietta Street, which was Dublin's first Georgian street and, at the time, one of the city's most fashionable addresses. Francis Johnston added the graceful cupola in 1816, and the building was finally completed in 1817. Inside there is a fine Dining Hall, and the Registry of Deeds (formerly the Prerogative Court). The

Statue at the entrance to King's Inns

west façade has two doorways flanked by elegant Classical caryatids (statues used in place of pillars) carved by sculptor Edward Smyth. The male figure, holding book and quill, is representative of the law.

Sadly, much of the area around Constitution Hill today is less attractive than it was in Georgian times. However, the King's Inns' gardens, which are open to the public, are still pleasant to stroll around.

Smithfield ⑩

LAID OUT in the mid-17th century as a marketplace, this vast, cobbled expanse is a welcome respite from central Dublin's traffic-laden streets. Most of the time Smithfield is relatively tranquil, though on the first Sunday of each month it springs to life when it hosts the long-established horse and pony sale. This is an exciting, vibrant place to visit.

Children riding saddle-free through the cobbled streets of Smithfield market

Horses tethered for sale at Smithfield's exuberant market

Old Jameson Distillery ⑪

Bow St. ☎ 807 2355. ○ daily 9.30am–6pm (last tour at 5pm). ● 25 Dec and Good Fri. 🎫 📷

Proof of significant investment in the emerging Smithfield area of Dublin's northside (and, indeed, of the renascent whiskey industry) is evident in this large exhibition, arranged in a restored building that formed part of John Jameson's distillery. Whiskey was produced here from 1780 until 1971.

Although the establishment is owned and run by Irish Distillers Limited, who are obviously keen to talk up their company's products (the four main brand names are Jameson, Paddy, Bushmills and John Power), the sell is distinctly on the soft side and visitors are treated to an impressive, entertaining and educational experience. People are free to investigate the Distillery on their own or take advantage of the guided tour. The latter starts with an eight-minute audiovisual tape, *Uisce Beatha* (the Water of Life; *uisce* meaning "water" and the origin of the word "whiskey"), which provides much factual and anecdotal background information on the great tradition of distilling in Ireland, which stretches back 1,500 years. Further whiskey-related facts are then explained during the 20-minute tour. This moves around displays set out as a working distillery, with different rooms devoted to the various stages of whiskey production, from grain storage right through to bottling (there is even a display item on the poteen manufacturing process). This is very much an interactive tour, with opportunities to view, smell and, ultimately, taste the

Sampling different whiskeys at the Old Jameson Distillery

products of a working mash tun, a huge, ancient wooden fermentation vessel, original copper pot stills, a re-created maturing warehouse and a working bottling line. The tour culminates in the Tasting Room, where there is a welcome opportunity for the newly-created expert to enjoy a sip of the finished product. The tour guides are particularly keen to point out to visitors how the barley drying process differs from that used in the production of Scotch whisky: in Ireland the grain is dried through clean dry air, while in Scotland it is smoked over peat. The Irish claim that their method results in a tipple that is very much smoother than its rather more smoky Scottish counterpart.

Label for John Jameson & Son Irish Whiskey

COOPERAGE

Although much of the demand for coopers has dwindled since Ireland's whiskey manufacturing industry fell into decline, their craft is still vital to distilleries. The type of wood used – and even the shape of the barrel itself – gives the product all of its colour and much of its flavour. The curved shape of the barrels is achieved by fashioning split oak over a wood-burning brazier, and then metal bands are added to hold the barrel in shape and keep it water-tight.

Coopers making barrels at the Bow Street Jameson Distillery, c. 1920

James Gandon's Four Courts overlooking the River Liffey

Four Courts ⑫

Inns Quay. 872 5555.
10am–1pm, 2–4:30pm Mon–Fri
(when courts in session).

COMPLETED IN 1802 by James Gandon, this majestic building was virtually gutted 120 years later during the Irish Civil War *(see p48)* when government forces bombarded anti-Treaty rebels into submission. The adjacent Public Records Office, with documents dating back to the 12th century, was destroyed by fire. In 1932, the main buildings were restored using Gandon's original design. A copper-covered lantern dome rises above the six-columned Corinthian portico, which is crowned with the figures of Moses, Justice and Mercy. This central section is flanked by two wings containing the four original courts: Common Pleas, Chancery, Exchequer and King's Bench. It is possible to walk in to the central waiting hall under the grand dome. An information panel to the right of the entrance gives details of the building's history and functions.

St Michan's Church ⑬

Church St. 872 4154. mid-Mar–Oct: 10am–12:45pm & 2–4:45pm Mon–Fri, 10am–12:45pm Sat; Nov–mid-Mar: 12:30–3:30pm Mon–Fri, 10am–12:45pm Sat.

LARGELY REBUILT in 1686 on the site of an 11th-century Hiberno-Viking church, the dull façade of St Michan's hides a more exciting interior. Deep in its vaults lie a number of bodies that have barely decomposed because of the dry atmosphere created by the church's magnesian limestone walls. Their wooden caskets, however, have cracked open, revealing the preserved bodies, complete with skin and hair. Among those thought to have been mummified in this way are the brothers Henry and John Sheares, leaders of the 1798 rebellion *(see p45)*, who were executed that year.

Other, less gory, attractions include the magnificent wood carving of fruits and violins and other instruments above the choir. There is also an organ (1724) on which Handel is said to have played.

St Mary's Abbey Exhibition ⑭

Meetinghouse Lane. 872 1490.
mid-Jun–mid-Sep: 10am–5pm Wed.

FOUNDED BY Benedictine monks in 1139, but then transferred to the Cistercian order just eight years later, this was one of the largest and most important monasteries in medieval Ireland. When it was built, the surrounding land was peaceful countryside; today, what is left of this historically important abbey is hidden away in

Detail of wood carving (c. 1724) at St Michan's Church

◁ **Ha'penny Bridge on the Liffey**

the sprawling backstreets that are found on the north side of the river Liffey.

As well as having control over extensive estates, including whole villages, mills and fisheries, the abbey acted as state treasury and meeting place for the Council of Ireland. It was during a council meeting in St Mary's that "Silken Thomas" Fitzgerald *(see p40)* renounced his allegiance to Henry VIII and marched out to raise the short-lived rebellion of 1534. The monastery was dissolved a few years later in 1539 and, during the 17th century, the site served as a quarry. Stone from St Mary's was pillaged and used in the construction of Essex Bridge (which was later replaced by Grattan Bridge in 1874), just to the south of the abbey.

Sadly, all that remains of the abbey today is the vaulted chamber of the old Chapter House. This houses a display on the history of the abbey and a model of how it would have looked 800 years ago.

The old vaulted Chapter house in St Mary's Abbey

St Mary's Church ⑮

Mary Street (at Wolfe Tone Street).
☏ *872 4088.*

Ⅰ N AMONGST THE produce stalls and family-run stores in the warren of streets to the west of O'Connell Street stands what was once one of the most important society churches in 18th and 19th century Dublin. Dating back to 1697, its design is usually credited to Sir William Robinson, the Surveyor General who also built the beautiful Royal Hospital Kilmainham *(see p120)*, and it is reckoned to be the first church in the city with a gallery. Famous

Impressive organ in St Mary's Church

past parishioners here include Arthur Guinness, who got married here in 1793, and Wolfe Tone, the leader of the United Irishmen, who was born within a stone's throw of the church and baptised here in the 1760s. The cross street and the small park to the rear of the church are named in his honour today. The playwright Sean O'Casey was also baptized at St Mary's in 1880. Church services finally ceased in the mid-1980s and, in recent years, St Mary's has gone through many incarnations, including a bookshop, with cheap shelves standing where the pews once were. The church has recently been renovated and turned into a pub. However, the impressive stained-glass windows and the organ remain intact.

Detail of carving in St Mary's Church

Ha'penny Bridge ⑯

Ⅼ INKING Temple Bar and Liffey Street on the north bank of the river, this very attractive high-arched foot bridge is made of cast-iron and is used by thousands of people every day to cross Dublin's river. It was built by John Windsor, who was an ironworker from Shropshire, England. One of Dublin's most popular and most photographed sights, it was originally named the Wellington Bridge, after the Duke of Wellington. Its official name today is in fact the Liffey Bridge, but it is also known simply as the Metal Bridge. Originally opened in 1816, the bridge got its better-known nickname from the halfpenny toll that was first levied on it. The toll was scrapped in 1919 but the nickname stuck and is still used with some fondness by Dubliners and visitors alike.

A recent restoration project on the bridge, which included the installation of original period lanterns, has made it even more attractive. This is particularly true at night when it is lit up as people cross over it to go through Merchant's Arch and into the bustling nightlife of the Temple Bar area *(see pp90–1)* with all its pubs, clubs and restaurants.

The Ha'penny Bridge looking from Temple Bar to Liffey Street

FURTHER AFIELD

THERE ARE many interesting sights just outside Dublin. In the western suburbs is the Museum of Modern Art, housed in the splendid setting of the Royal Hospital Kilmainham. Phoenix Park, Europe's largest city park, offers the opportunity for a stroll in a leafy setting. Further north are the National Botanic Gardens, home to over 20,000 plant species from around the world. Nearby, Marino Casino is a fine example of Palladian architecture. The magnificent coastline is easily admired by taking the DART railway. The highlight of the riviera-like southern stretch is around Dalkey village, especially lovely Killiney Bay. One of the many Martello towers built as defences now houses a museum to James Joyce. To the northeast, slightly further from the centre, is Malahide Castle, once home of the Talbot family.

Michael Collins' gravestone

SIGHTS AT A GLANCE

Museums and Galleries
Collins Barracks ⑤
Fry Model Railway Museum ⑭
Guinness Hop Store ④
James Joyce Tower ⑰
Kilmainham Gaol ③
Royal Hospital Kilmainham ⑥
Shaw's Birthplace ⑦
Waterways Visitors' Centre ⑨

Parks and Gardens
Dublin Zoo ②
Glasnevin Cemetery ⑫
National Botanic Gardens ⑪
Phoenix Park ①

Historic Buildings
Malahide Castle ⑬
Marino Casino ⑩

Towns and Villages
Ballsbridge ⑧
Dalkey ⑱
Dun Laoghaire ⑯
Howth ⑮
Killiney ⑲

CENTRAL DUBLIN

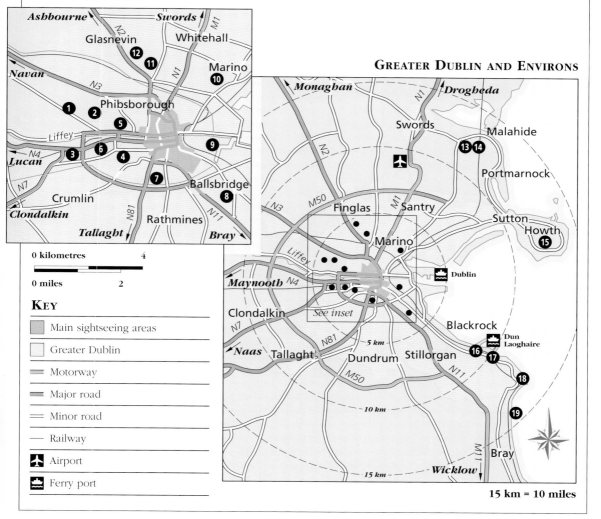

0 kilometres 4
0 miles 2

KEY

	Main sightseeing areas
	Greater Dublin
	Motorway
	Major road
	Minor road
	Railway
✈	Airport
⛴	Ferry port

GREATER DUBLIN AND ENVIRONS

15 km = 10 miles

◁ **Boat moored in Dun Laoghaire harbour at dusk**

Phoenix Park 1

Park Gate, Conyngham Rd, Dublin 8.
10, 25, 26, 37, 38, 39. ○ *6:30am–11pm daily.* **Phoenix Park Visitor Centre** *677 0095.* ○ *mid-Mar–May: 9:30am–5:30pm daily; Jun–Sep: 10am–6pm daily; Oct: 9:30am–5pm daily; Nov to mid-Mar: 9:30am–4:30pm Sat & Sun (last adm 45 mins before closing).*

A LITTLE to the west of the city centre, ringed by a wall 11 km (7 miles) long, is Europe's largest enclosed city park. Phoenix Park is over 700 ha (1700 acres) in size. The name "Phoenix" is said to be a corruption of the Gaelic *Fionn Uisce*, meaning "clear water". This refers to a spring that rises near the **Phoenix Column** which, to add confusion, is crowned by a statue of the mythical bird.

Jogging in Phoenix Park

The Phoenix Column marking the site of the *Fionn Uisce* spring

Phoenix Park originated in 1662, when the Duke of Ormonde turned the land into a deer park. Deer still roam in the park today. In 1745 it was landscaped and opened to the public by Lord Chesterfield.

Near Park Gate is the lakeside **People's Garden** – the only part of the park which has been cultivated. A little further on is the famous **Dublin Zoo**.

In addition to the Phoenix Column, the park has two other striking monuments. The **Wellington Testimonial**, a 63-m (204-ft) obelisk, was begun in 1817 and completed in 1861. It allegedly took so long to be built because of the Duke of Wellington's fall from public favour. Its bronze bas-reliefs were made from captured French cannons. The 27-m (90-ft) steel **Papal Cross** marks the spot where the Pope celebrated Mass in front of one million people in 1979. Buildings within the park include two 18th-century houses. **Áras an Uachtaráin**, the Irish President's official residence, was built in 1751 and was home to various British viceroys until it became the residence of the president in 1937. The other is **Deerfield**, the residence of the US Ambassador and once the home of Lord Cavendish, the British Chief Secretary for Ireland who was murdered in 1882 by an Irish nationalist. The only building open to the public is **Ashtown Castle**, a restored 17th-century tower house which contains the Phoenix Park Visitor Centre.

PHOENIX PARK

Áras An Uachtaráin ⑤
Ashtown Castle ①
Deerfield ②
Dublin Zoo ⑥
Papal Cross ③
People's Garden ⑧
Phoenix Column ④
Wellington Testimonial ⑦

KEY

🚌	Bus stop
🅿	Parking
ℹ	Tourist information
⠿	Park wall

0 metres   500

0 yards   500

Orang-utang mother and baby at Dublin Zoo

Five times the size of Hyde Park in London and over double the size of New York's Central Park, Phoenix Park is large enough to accommodate playing fields for Gaelic football, hurling and polo, and running and cycling trails. It also has a motor racing track and facilities for horse riding.

Visitors at the giraffe compound in Dublin Zoo

Dublin Zoo ❷

Phoenix Park, Dublin 8. 🕿 677 1425.
🚌 10 from O'Connell St or 25 & 26 from Middle Abbey Street. ◯ Apr–Oct: Mon–Sat 9.30am–6pm, Sun 10.30am–6pm; Nov–Mar: Mon–Fri 9.30am–4pm, Sat 9.30am–5pm, Sun 10.30am–5pm. ♿

O PENED IN 1830 with one wild boar and an admission price of 6d (2.5 pence), Dublin Zoo was one of the world's first zoos and was the birthplace of the lion that roars at the beginning of MGM movies. The big cat compound in the southeast sector of Phoenix Park, set around two lakes, has been recently renovated. The lion breeding programme began here in 1857.

Nowhere is the zoo's venerable status better seen than in the old, ornate South America House, home to such enchanting creatures as golden lion tamarins, squirrel monkeys and two-toed sloths. Dublin Zoo has always prided itself on its breeding programme and today it concentrates on several endangered species including the snow leopard. Education is another important aspect of the zoo's work: a Discovery Centre where exhibits include the world's biggest egg, and a Meet The Keeper programme where you can see the animals being fed and chat to the keepers. Another attraction for children is the Zoo Train that runs all day in summer and at weekends in winter. Several hairy two-humped Bactrian camels, a pair of polar bears and a pool of hippos are among the most popular sights.

Kilmainham Gaol ❸

Inchicore Rd, Kilmainham, Dublin 8.
🕿 453 5984. 🚌 23, 51, 51A, 78, 79. ◯ May–Sep: 9:30am–6pm daily; Oct–Apr: 9:30am–5pm Mon–Fri, 10am–4:30pm Sun (last adm 1hr 15mins before closing). ◯ 25 & 26 Dec. ♿ 🎫

A LONG TREE-LINED avenue runs from the Royal Hospital Kilmainham to the grim, grey bulk of Kilmainham Gaol. The building dates from 1789, but was restored in the 1960s.

During its 130 years as a prison, it housed many of those involved in the fight for Irish independence, including Robert Emmet (see p89) and Charles Stewart Parnell (p47). The last prisoner held during the Civil War was Eamon de Valera (p49), the future President of Ireland, who was released on 16 July 1924, just prior to the Gaol's closure.

The tour of the Gaol starts in the chapel, where Joseph Plunkett married Grace Gifford just a few hours before he faced the firing squad for his part in the 1916 Rising (see p48). The tour ends in the prison yard where Plunkett's badly wounded colleague James Connolly, unable to stand up, was strapped into a chair before being shot. It also passes the dank cells of those involved in the 1798, 1803, 1848 and 1867 uprisings, as well as the punishment cells and hanging room. Fourteen of the 16 executions that took place in the few days after the Easter Rising were carried out here. There is a video presentation, and in the central hall are exhibits depicting various events which took place in the Gaol until it finally closed in 1924. There are also personal mementoes of some of the former inmates.

Standing in the courtyard is the ship *Asgard* which carried arms from Germany to the Nationalists in 1914. It famously broke through the British blockade in order to do so.

Doorway and gates of the historic Kilmainham Gaol

Sampling Guinness at the Hop Store

Guinness Hop Store 4

Crane St, Dublin 8. 453 6700 ext 5155. 78A, 68A, 123. Apr–Oct: 9:30am–5pm Mon–Sat, 10:30am–4:30pm Sun; Nov–Mar: 9:30am–4pm Mon–Sat, 12–4pm Sun. Good Fri, 25 & 26 Dec.

THE "WORLD OF GUINNESS" exhibition is housed in a 19th-century warehouse, which was used for storing bales of hops until the 1950s.

A self-guided tour takes the visitor through displays which chronicle 200 years of brewing at St James's Gate. The tour starts in a Victorian kieve (or mash tun), and goes on to examine all other stages of the brewing process. Displays show how production has changed over the years from when Arthur Guinness took over the backstreet brewery in 1759, to today's state-of-the-art techniques. There is also a cooperage display with life-size models showing the skills involved in making the wooden barrels used for storage. Since the 1950s metal containers have been used.

On the ground floor, in the Transport Gallery, is a narrow-gauge steam locomotive which once ferried materials around the factory site. Other displays include models of the company's fleet of barges that plied the Grand Canal, ocean tankers, and the once-familiar dray horses which transported the stout to the ports.

The tour ends with an audio-visual show on the company's development, followed by a visit to the sampling bar where you can enjoy a couple of glasses of draught Guinness.

The Brewing of Guinness

Label from a Guinness bottle

GUINNESS IS A BLACK BEER, known as "stout", renowned for its distinctive malty flavour and smooth, creamy head. From its humble beginnings over 200 years ago, the Guinness brewery site at St James's Gate now covers 26 ha (65 acres) and has its own water and electricity supply. It is the largest brewery in Europe and exports beers to more than 120 countries. Other brands owned by Guinness include Harp Lager and Smithwick's Ale.

HOW GUINNESS IS MADE

The four main ingredients used to brew Guinness are barley, hops, yeast and water which, contrary to popular belief, comes from the Wicklow Mountains rather than the River Liffey.

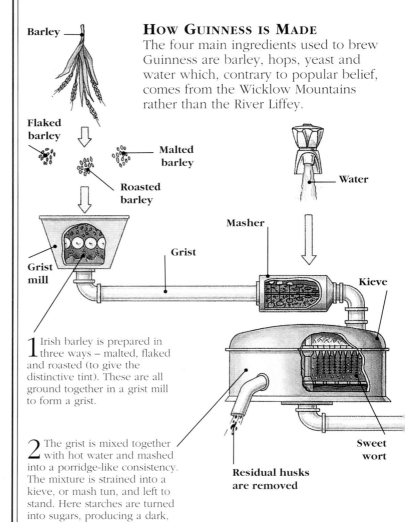

Barley

Flaked barley

Malted barley

Roasted barley

Water

Masher

Grist

Grist mill

Kieve

Sweet wort

Residual husks are removed

1 Irish barley is prepared in three ways – malted, flaked and roasted (to give the distinctive tint). These are all ground together in a grist mill to form a grist.

2 The grist is mixed together with hot water and mashed into a porridge-like consistency. The mixture is strained into a kieve, or mash tun, and left to stand. Here starches are turned into sugars, producing a dark, sweet wort, or an infusion of malt.

GUINNESS FOR STRENGTH

Guinness advertising has become almost as famous as the product itself. Since 1929, when the first advertisement announced that "Guinness is Good for You", poster and television advertising campaigns have employed many amusing images of both animals and people.

ARTHUR GUINNESS

Arthur Guinness

In December 1759, 34-year-old Arthur Guinness signed a 9,000-year lease at an annual rent of £45 to take over St James's Gate Brewery, which had lain vacant for almost ten years. At the time the brewing industry in Dublin was at a low ebb – the standard of ale was much criticized and in rural Ireland beer was virtually unknown, as whiskey, gin and poteen were the more favoured drinks. Furthermore, Irish beer was under threat from imports. Guinness started brewing ale, but was also aware of a black ale called porter, produced in London. This new beer was so called because of its popularity with porters at Billingsgate and Covent Garden markets. Guinness decided to stop making ales and develop his own recipe for porter (the word "stout" was not used until the 1920s). So successful was the switch that he made his first export shipment in 1769.

Engraving (c. 1794) of a satisfied customer

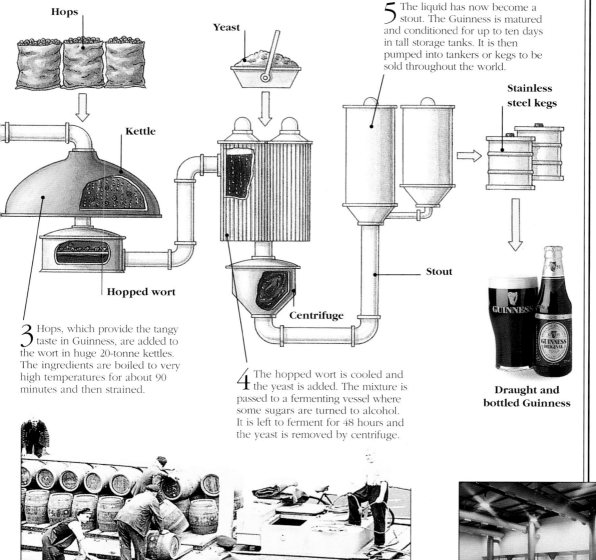

Hops

Yeast

Kettle

Hopped wort

Centrifuge

Stainless steel kegs

Stout

5 The liquid has now become a stout. The Guinness is matured and conditioned for up to ten days in tall storage tanks. It is then pumped into tankers or kegs to be sold throughout the world.

3 Hops, which provide the tangy taste in Guinness, are added to the wort in huge 20-tonne kettles. The ingredients are boiled to very high temperatures for about 90 minutes and then strained.

4 The hopped wort is cooled and the yeast is added. The mixture is passed to a fermenting vessel where some sugars are turned to alcohol. It is left to ferment for 48 hours and the yeast is removed by centrifuge.

Draught and bottled Guinness

***The Guinness brewery** has relied heavily on water transport since its first export was shipped to England in 1769. The barges which, up until 1961, made the short trip with their cargo down the Liffey to Dublin Port, were a familiar sight on the river. Once at port, the stout would be loaded onto huge tanker ships for worldwide distribution.*

Steel kettles used in modern-day brewing

The elegant façade of the Royal Hospital Kilmainham

National Museum at Collins Barracks ⑤

See pp124–5.

The Royal Hospital Kilmainham ⑥

Kilmainham, Dublin 8. 📞 *671 8666.*
🚌 *24, 78, 90.* **Irish Museum of
Modern Art** 🕐 *10am–5:30pm
Tue–Sat, noon–5:30pm Sun & public
hols.* ⚫ *Good Fri & 24–26 Dec.* 📷

I RELAND'S FINEST SURVIVING
17th-century building was
laid out in 1680, and styled
on Les Invalides in Paris.
It was built by Sir William
Robinson, who also built
Marsh's Library *(see p95)*, as
a home for 300 wounded
soldiers, rather than as a
hospital as its name suggests.
It retained this role until 1927
and was the first such institution in the British Isles, erected even before the famous
Chelsea Hospital in London.
When it was completed,
people were so impressed by
its elegant Classical symmetry
that it was suggested it would
be better used as the main
campus of Trinity College.
In contrast to the functional
design of the building, the
Baroque chapel has fine wood
carvings and intricate heraldic
stained glass. The plaster ceiling is a replica of the original,
which fell down in 1902.
    In 1991, the hospital's
former residential quarters
were converted to house the

**Irish Museum of Modern
Art**. Corridors were painted
white and floors were uni-
formly covered in grey to
create a stunning home for
the museum. Since its opening the museum has established a collection through pur-
chases, donations and long-
term loans. The exhibits,
which include a cross section
of Irish and international art,
are shown on a rotating
basis and there are regular
temporary exhibitions.

Shaw's Birthplace ⑦

33 Synge St, Dublin 8. 📞 *475 0854.*
🚌 *16, 19, 22.* 🕐 *May–Oct: 10am–
1pm, 2–5pm Mon–Sat, 11:30am–
1pm, 2–6pm Sun & public hols.* 📷

P LAYWRIGHT and Nobel prizewinner George Bernard
Shaw was born in this Victorian house on 26 July 1856.
In 1876 he followed his
mother to London. She had
left four years earlier with her
daughters, fed up with her

**The re-created Victorian kitchen
in Shaw's Birthplace**

husband's drinking habits.
It was in London that Shaw
met his wife-to-be Charlotte
Payne-Townsend. He remained
in England until his death.
    Inside the house, visitors
can see the young Shaw's
bedroom and the kitchen
where the author remembered he drank "much tea out
of brown delft left to 'draw'
on the hob until it was pure
tannin". Also on view are the
nursery, the maid's room and
the drawing room, all furnished in period style.
    Although there is little in the
museum on Shaw's productive
years, the house does give
an interesting insight into the
lives of a typical middle-class
Victorian family.

GEORGE BERNARD SHAW

Born in Dublin in 1856,
Shaw moved to England
at the age of 20 where he
began his literary career
somewhat unsuccessfully
as a critic and novelist. It
was not until his first play
was produced in 1892
that his career finally took
off. One of the most pro-
lific writers of his time,
Shaw's many works in-
clude *Heartbreak House*,
Man and Superman, and,
perhaps most famously,
Pygmalion, which was
later adapted into the successful musical *My Fair
Lady*. He often attacked
conventional thinking
and was a supporter of
many causes, including
vegetarianism and fem-
inism. He lived an ab-
stemious life and died
in 1950 at the age of 94.

Ballsbridge ⑧

Co Dublin. 🚌 *5,7, 7A, 8, 18, 45.*

LAID OUT mostly between 1830 and 1860, the suburb of Ballsbridge is a very exclusive part of Dublin, attracting many wealthy residents. Many of the streets are named after military heroes. Running off Pembroke Road the elegant tree-lined streets such as Raglan Road and Wellington Road are lined with prestigious red-brick houses. The area is also home to several foreign embassies – look for the striking cylindrical US Embassy building at the junction of Northumberland and Eglin roads – as well as a number of upmarket hotels and guesthouses.

Close to Baggot Street Bridge is a statue of the poet Patrick Kavanagh, depicted reclining on a bench. This attractive stretch of the Grand Canal at Lower Baggot Street was one of the poet's favourite parts of Dublin.

The southeast sector of Ballsbridge, just across the River Dodder, is dominated by the Royal Dublin Society Showgrounds (often simply abbreviated to RDS). Founded in 1731 to promote science, the arts and agriculture, the Royal Dublin Society was an instrumental mover behind the creation of most of Ireland's national museums

Late 18th-century engraving of a passenger ferry passing Harcourt Lock on the Grand Canal, taken from a painting by James Barralet

DUBLIN'S CANALS

The affluent Georgian era witnessed the building of the Grand and Royal canals linking Dublin with the River Shannon and the west coast. These two canals became the main arteries of trade and public transport in Ireland from the 1760s until the coming of the railways, which took much of the passenger business, almost a century later. However, the canals continued to carry freight until after World War II, finally closing to commercial traffic in 1960. Today the canals are well maintained and used mainly for pleasure-boating, cruising and fishing.

and galleries. The two major events at the sprawling yet graceful showgrounds are the Spring Show in May and the Horse Show in August *(see p33)*. Throughout the rest of the year the showground plays host to various conventions, exhibitions and concerts.

The Lansdowne Road stadium, the home of the Irish national rugby team, is another Ballsbridge landmark. Rugby supporters in the team's orange, green and white colours can often be seen in the area.

Stretch of the Grand Canal near the Waterways Visitors' Centre

Waterways Visitors' Centre ⑨

Grand Canal Quay, Dublin 2.
📞 *677 7510.* 🚌 *3.* ⭕ *Jun–Sep: 9:30am–6:30pm daily; Oct–May: 12:30–5pm Wed–Sun.* ⬤ *25 Dec.*
♿ 🏷 *on request.*

FIFTEEN MINUTES' walk from Trinity College along Pearse Street, the Waterways Visitors' Centre overlooks the Grand Canal Basin. Audio-visual displays and models illustrate the history of Ireland's inland waterways. One of the most interesting focuses on their construction: in the 18th century, canals were often called "navigations" and the men who built them were "navigators", a term shortened to "navvies". There are also exhibits on the wildlife found in the canals and surrounding marshlands.

The Royal Dublin Showground at Ballsbridge

The judging process at a horse show in Dublin ▷

The National Museum at Collins Barracks ⑤

Silver coffee pot

COMMISSIONED BY William III in 1700, this was the largest barracks in his domain, with living accommodation for over 5,000 soldiers. Originally known as Dublin Barracks it was renamed Collins Barracks after Michael Collins *(see p49)* following Irish independence. This refurbished annexe of the National Museum *(see pp76–7)* displays the fine exhibits, from furniture to silver, by making full use of up-to-date technology including a multimedia catalogue and clever lighting. Currently occupying only two blocks, the museum is planned to extend eventually to fill all four wings.

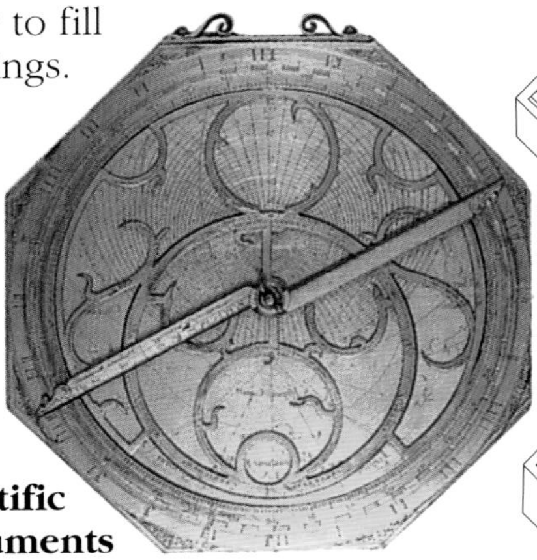

Scientific Instruments
The fascinating display of surveying and navigation instruments includes this astrolabe (c.1580–90), which was made in Prague by Erasmus Habermel.

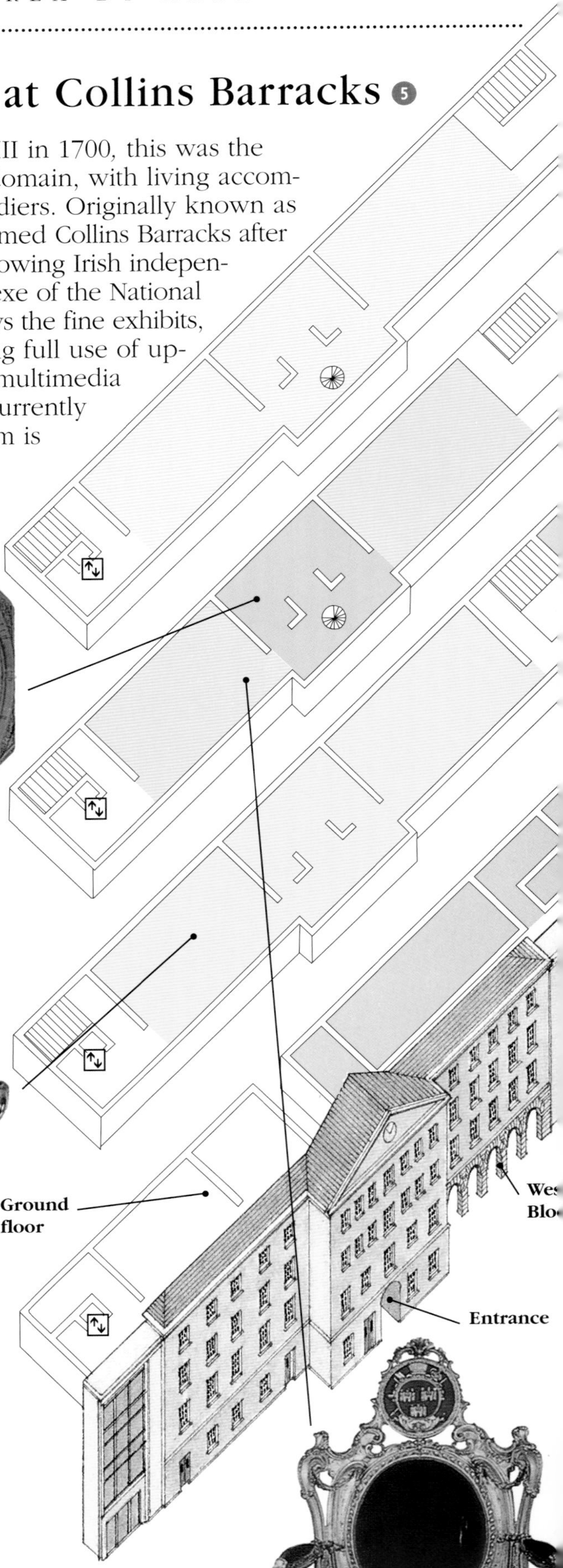

Ground floor

Wes Blo

Entrance

★ Irish Silver
This silver-gilt bowl by Thomas Bolton dates from 1703. Also known as a monteith, it was used for cooling wine glasses.

STAR EXHIBITS

★ **William Smith O'Brien Gold Cup**

★ **Irish Silver**

★ **The Fonthill Vase**

Skinners Alley Chair
Dating back to c.1730, this gilt chair is part of the furniture collection and was made for the Protestant aldermen of Skinners Alley who were removed from the Dublin Assembly by James II.

Third floor

Second floor

★ **The Fonthill Vase**
This beautiful 14th-century Chinese vase takes its name from Fonthill Abbey, near Salisbury in England, one of its many homes before it came to this museum.

★ **William Smith O'Brien Gold Cup**
After an uprising in 1848, O'Brien was sent to Australia and imprisoned. On his release he was presented with this 22-carat gold cup by his supporters in Australia.

GALLERY GUIDE
Furniture, silver and scientific instrument collections are in the South Block. In the West Block the Out of Storage exhibits include musical instruments and glass. The Curators' Choice section displays 25 unusual objects, individually chosen by the curators of the museum for their cultural significance.

First floor

South Block

Main entrance

KEY TO FLOORPLAN

☐ Irish Silver

☐ Period Furniture

☐ Scientific Instruments

☐ Fonthill Vase

☐ Irish Country Furniture

☐ Out of Storage

☐ The Museum at Work

☐ Exhibition Development

☐ Origin of National Collections

☐ Curators' Choice

☐ Temporary exhibition space

☐ Non-exhibition space

Crucifixion Stone
Part of the Curators' Choice, this was found in County Meath. It dates from the time of Catholic persecution, c.1740.

Giant water lilies in the Lily House, National Botanic Gardens

gardens still exude something of an old-world feel, thanks in part to the beautiful cast-iron Palm House and other curvilinear glasshouses. These were built between 1843 and 1869 by Richard Turner, who was also responsible for the Palm House at Kew Gardens, London, and the glasshouses in Belfast's Botanic Gardens. The atmosphere of serenity is, of course, also partly attributable to the beautiful flora on show.

The 20-ha (49-acre) park contains over 20,000 different plant species. A particularly stunning feature is the quite gloriously colourful display of Victorian carpet bedding plants. Other highlights include a renowned rose garden and rich collections of cacti and orchids. The gardens have a significant reputation for horticultural development. The Pampas grass and the giant lily were first grown in Europe here.

One path, known as Yew Walk, has trees that date back to the early 18th century and there is also a giant redwood that towers to 30 m (100 ft).

Marino Casino ⑩

Fairview Park, off Malahide Rd, Dublin 3. ☎ *833 1618.* ▭ *20A, 20B, 27, 42, 42B, 43.* ◯ *May–Oct: 10am– 6:30pm daily; Nov, Feb–Apr: noon– 4pm Wed & Sun.* ▨ ▮ *obligatory.*

THIS DELIGHTFUL little villa, built by Sir William Chambers in the 1760s for Lord Charlemont, now sits next to a busy road. Originally built as a summer house for the Marino Estate, the villa survives today although the main house was pulled down in 1921. The Casino is acknowledged to be one of the finest examples of Palladian architecture in Ireland. Some fascinating innovative features were used in its construction, including chimneys disguised

Carved stone lion at Marino Casino

as urns and hollow columns that accommodate drains. Outside, four fine carved stone lions, thought to be by English sculptor Joseph Wilton, stand guard at each of the corners. The building's squat, compact exterior conceals eight rooms built on three floors around a central staircase. The ground floor comprises a spacious hall and a saloon, with beautiful silk hangings, parquet flooring and a coffered ceiling. On the first floor is the State Room, decorated in green and white.

National Botanic Gardens ⑪

Botanic Ave, Glasnevin, Dublin 9. ☎ *837 4388.* ▭ *13, 19, 19A, 134.* ◯ *Mar–Oct: 9am–6pm Mon–Sat, 11am–6pm Sun; Nov–Feb: 10am– 4:30pm Mon–Sat, 11am–4:30pm Sun.* ● *25 Dec.*

OPENED IN 1795, these gardens are home to Ireland's foremost centre of botany and horticulture.
Of interest to sightseers and botanists alike, the

Glasnevin Cemetery ⑫

Finglas Rd, Glasnevin. ☎ *830 1133.* ◯ *daily.* ▭ *40 from Parnell St.*

ORIGINALLY KNOWN as Prospect Cemetery, this is Ireland's largest graveyard, with approximately 1.2

Impressive gravestones in Glasnevin Cemetery

million people buried here. It was established by Daniel O'Connell in 1832 and was viewed as a great achievement on his part, since Catholics were previously unable to conduct graveside ceremonies because of the Penal Laws.

O'Connell's endeavours have been rewarded with the most conspicuous monument – a 51 m (167 ft) tall round-tower in the early Irish Christian style stands over his crypt.

While the maze of head-stones exhibits a tremendous variety of designs, none, apart from O'Connell's, has been allowed by the cemetery's committee to be too resplendent. However the graves conjure up a very Irish feel with high crosses and insignia such as shamrocks, harps and Irish wolfhounds.

The most interesting sector is the oldest part by Prospect Square, on the far right-hand side. Look for the two watch-towers built into the medieval-looking walls. These were erected as lookouts for the bodysnatchers hired by 19th century surgeons. Before the Anatomy Act permitted corpses to be donated to science, this was the only way medical students could learn. Staff at the cemetery office will gladly give directions to graves of famous people such as Charles Stewart Parnell, Eamon De Valera, Michael Collins and Brendan Behan. A small Republican plot holds the remains of Countess Constance Markievicz and Maud Gonne MacBride, while the grave of poet Gerard Manley Hopkins is situated in the Jesuit Plot.

Glasnevin also reveals some interesting landscaping; the paths that run between the plots follow the same routes as the original woodland trails. Copses of mature syca-more and oak have been maintained while some of the more interesting imports among the thousand trees to be found here include a Californian Giant Sequoia and a Cedar of Lebanon.

The oak-beamed Great Hall at Malahide Castle

Malahide Castle ⑬

Malahide, Co Dublin. 🚉 🚌 42.
📞 846 2184. ◯ Apr–Oct: 10am–5pm Mon–Sat, 11am–6pm Sun & public hols; Nov–Mar: 10am–5pm Mon–Fri, 2–5pm Sat, Sun & public hols. 🎫

N**EAR THE SEASIDE** dormitory town of Malahide stands a huge castle set in 100 ha (250 acres) of grounds. The castle's core dates from the 14th century but later additions, such as its rounded towers, have given it a classic fairy-tale appearance. Originally a fortress, the building served as a stately home for the Talbot family until 1973. They were staunch supporters of James II: the story goes that, on the day of the Battle of the Boyne in 1690 (see p53), 14 members of the family breakfasted here; none came back for supper. Guided tours take in the impressive oak-beamed Great Hall and the Oak Room with its carved panelling as well as the castle's collection of 18th-century Irish furniture. Part of the Portrait Collection, on loan from the National Gallery (see pp80–3), can be seen at the castle. It includes portraits of the Talbot family, as well as other figures such as Wolfe Tone (see p72).

Candelabra at Malahide Castle

Fry Model Railway ⑭

Malahide Castle grounds, Malahide, Co Dublin. 🚌 42 from Beresford Place, near Busaras. 🚉 from Connolly Station. 📞 846 3779. ◯ Apr–Sep: 10am–6pm Mon–Thu, 10am–5pm Sat, 2–6pm Sun & public hols (Jun–Jul: also 10am–6pm Fri); Oct–Mar: 2–5pm Sat, Sun & public hols. 🅿 12:45–2pm daily. 🎫 combined ticket with Malahide Castle available.

S**ET IN THE** grounds of Mala-hide Castle, this collection of handmade models of Irish trains and trams was started by Cyril Fry, a railway engin-eer and draughtsman, in the 1920s. It is one of the largest such displays in the world. Running on a 32 mm-wide (0-gauge) track, each detailed piece is made to scale and journeys through a landscape featuring the major Dublin landmarks, including the River Liffey with model barges. As well as historic trains, there are also models of the DART line, buses and ferries. A smaller room exhibits static displays of memorabilia and larger scale models.

Howth ⓯

Co Dublin. 🚊 *DART.* **Howth Castle grounds** ◯ *8am–sunset daily.*

T HE COMMERCIAL fishing town of Howth marks the northern limit of Dublin Bay. Before Dun Laoghaire, or Kingstown as it was known then, took over, Howth was the main harbour for Dublin. Howth Head, a huge rocky mass, has lovely views of the bay. A footpath runs around the tip of Howth Head, which is known locally as the "Nose". Nearby is Baily Lighthouse (1814). Sadly, much of this area – some of Ireland's prime real estate – has suffered from building development.

To the west of the town is Howth Castle, which dates back to Norman times. Its grounds are particularly beautiful in May and June when the rhododendrons and azaleas are in full bloom.

A short boat ride out from the harbour is the rocky islet, Ireland's Eye, which is a bird sanctuary where puffins nest. Boat trips from Howth run there throughout the summer.

Yachts anchored in Dun Laoghaire harbour

Dun Laoghaire ⓰

Co Dublin. 🚊 *DART.* **National Maritime Museum of Ireland**
📞 *280 0969.* ◯ *May–Sep: 1–5pm Tue–Sun (Oct: 1–5pm Sun).* ♿

I RELAND'S MAJOR passenger ferry port and yachting centre, with its brightly painted villas, parks and palm trees, makes a surprising introduction to Ireland, usually known for its grey dampness. On a warm, sunny day it exudes a decidedly continental feel.

It was once known as Kingstown, after a visit from King George IV of England in 1821. The name lasted for around 100 years, up until the Free State was established in 1921. The harbour at Dun Laoghaire was designed by John Rennie and built between 1817 and 1859. A rail connection with the centre of Dublin was established in 1834. As a result of the railway being built, however, the original *dún* or fort after which Dun Laoghaire is named, was destroyed.

Many visitors to Ireland head straight out of Dun Laoghaire (pronounced Dunleary) upon alighting from the ferry and head for Dublin or the countryside. However, the town offers some magnificent walks around the harbour and to the lighthouse along the east pier. The outlying villages of Sandycove and Dalkey can be reached via "The Metals"; a footpath that runs along the disused railway.

Located in the Mariners' Church, built in 1837, is the **National Maritime Museum**. Exhibits tell the story of Robert Halpin, who captained the *Great Eastern*, the steam vessel built in 1858 by the English engineer Brunel, that successfully laid the first transatlantic telegraph cable in 1866. Also on show in the museum are an enormous clockwork-driven lighthouse lens formerly used at Howth, and a longboat used by French officers during Wolfe Tone's unsuccessful invasion at Bantry in 1796.

Martello Tower at Howth Head just north of Dublin

James Joyce Tower 17

Sandycove, Co Dublin. 280 9265. DART to Sandycove. Apr–Oct: 10am–1pm & 2–5pm Mon–Sat, 2–6pm Sun & public hols.

STANDING ON A rocky promontory above the village of Sandycove is this Martello tower. It is one of 15 defensive towers which were erected between Dublin and Bray in 1804 to withstand a threatened invasion by Napoleon. They were named after a tower on Cape Mortella in Corsica. One hundred years later James Joyce *(see p27)* stayed in this tower for a week as the guest of Oliver St John Gogarty, poet and model for the *Ulysses* character Buck Mulligan. Gogarty rented the tower for a mere £8 per year. Today, inside the squat 12-m (40-ft) tower's granite walls is a small museum with some of Joyce's correspondence, personal belongings, such as his guitar, cigar case and walking stick, and his death mask. There are also photographs and several first editions of his works, including a deluxe edition (1935) of *Ulysses* illustrated by Henri Matisse. The roof, originally a gun platform but later used as a sunbathing deck by Gogarty, affords mar-

Guitar on show at James Joyce Tower

vellous views across Dublin Bay. Directly below the tower is the Forty Foot Pool, which was traditionally an all-male nude bathing spot, but is now open to both sexes.

Dalkey 18

Co Dublin. DART.

DALKEY WAS ONCE known as the "Town of Seven Castles", but only two of these fortified mansions, dating from the 15th and 16th centuries, now remain. They are both on the main street of this attractive village whose tight, winding roads and charming villas give it a Mediterranean feel. A little way offshore is tiny Dalkey Island, a rocky bird sanctuary with a Martello tower and a medieval Benedictine church, both now in a poor state of repair. In summer the island can be reached by a boat ride from the town's Coliemore Harbour. The island was, at one time, held by Danish pirates. In the 18th century, a Dublin club used to gather on the island to crown a mock "King of Dalkey" and his officers of state. Originally done simply for fun, the ceremony was stopped in 1797 by Lord Clare when it became a political issue. It began again in the late 1970s.

Shopfronts lining the main street of Dalkey village

Killiney 19

Co Dublin. DART to Dalkey or Killiney.

SOUTH OF DALKEY, the coastal road climbs uphill before tumbling down into the winding leafy lanes around Killiney village. The route offers one of the most scenic vistas on this stretch of the east coast, with views that are often compared to those across the Bay of Naples in Italy. Howth Head is clearly visible to the north, with Bray Head *(see p155)* and the foothills of the Wicklow Mountains *(see p161)* to the south. There is another exhilarating view from the top of windswept Killiney Hill Park, off Victoria Road. It is well worth tackling the steep trail up from the village to see it. Down below is the popular pebbly beach, Killiney Strand.

View southwards from Killiney Hill over Killiney Bay towards the Wicklow Mountains

Street Finder Index

KEY TO THE STREET FINDER

☐ Major sight		🚕 Taxi rank		⊠ Post office	
☐ Place of interest		🅿 Main car park		═ Railway line	
☐ Railway station		ℹ Tourist information office		One-way street	
Ⓡ DART station		✚ Hospital with casualty unit		Pedestrian street	
🚌 Main bus stop		👮 Police station			
🚌 Coach station		✝ Church			

0 metres   200
0 yards   200
1:11,500

KEY TO ABBREVIATIONS USED IN THE STREET FINDER

Ave	Avenue	**E**	East	**Pde**	Parade	**Sth**	South
Br	Bridge	**La**	Lane	**Pl**	Place	**Tce**	Terrace
Cl	Close	**Lr**	Lower	**Rd**	Road	**Up**	Upper
Ct	Court	**Nth**	North	**St**	Street/Saint	**W**	West

A

Abbey Street Lower	D2
Abbey Street Middle	D2
Abbey Street Old	E2
Abbey Street Upper	C2
Abbey Theatre	D2
Adair Lane	D3
Adelaide Hospital	C4
Amiens Street	F1
Anglesea Row	C2
Anglesea Street	D3
Anne Street South	D4
Anne Street North	B2
Anne's Lane	D4
Ardee Row	A5
Ardee Street	A4
Arran Quay	A3
Arran Street East	B2
Asdill's Row	D3
Ash Street	A4
Aston Place	D3
Aston Quay	D3
Aungier Place	C5
Aungier Street	C5

B

Bachelors Walk	D3
Back Lane	B3
Baggot Court	F5
Baggot Street Lower	F5
Baggot Rath Place	E5
Ball's Lane	B2
Bank of Ireland	D3
Bass Place	F4
Beaver Street	F1
Bedford Row	D3
Bella Place	E1
Bella Street	E1
Bell's Lane	E5
Benburb Street	A2
Beresford Lane	E2
Beresford Place	E2
Beresford Street	B2
Bewley's Oriental Café	D4
Bishop Street	C5
Blackhall Parade	A2
Blackhall Place	A2
Blackhall Street	A2
Blackpitts	B5
Bolton Street	B1
Bonham Street	A3
Borris Court	B3
Bow Lane East	C4
Bow Street	A2
Boyne Street	F4
Brabazon Row	A5
Brabazon Street	A4
Bracken's Lane	E3
Braithwaite Street	A4
Bride Road	B4

Bride Street	C4
Bride Street New	C5
Bridge Street Lower	A3
Bridge Street Upper	A3
Bridgefoot Street	A3
Britain Place	D1
Brown Street North	A2
Brown Street South	A5
Brunswick Street North	A2
Buckingham Street Lower	F1
Bull Alley Street	B4
Burgh Quay	D3
Busáras	E2
Butt Bridge	E2
Byrne's Lane	C2

C

Camden Place	C5
Camden Row	C5
Camden Street Lower	C5
Capel Street	C2
Carman's Hall	A4
Carmelite Church	C4
Castle Market	D4
Castle Steps	C3
Castle Street	C3
Cathal Brugha Street	D1
Cathedral Lane	B5
Cathedral Street	D2
Cathedral View Court	B5
Chamber Street	A5
Chancery Lane	C4
Chancery Place	B3
Chancery Street	B3
Chapel Lane	C2
Charles Street West	B3
Chatham Row	D4
Chatham Street	D4
Christ Church Cathedral	B3
Christchurch Place	B4
Church Avenue West	B2
Church Lane South	C5
Church Street	B3
Church Street New	A2
Church Street Upper	B2
Church Terrace	B2
City Hall	C3
City Quay	F2
Clanbrassil Street Lower	B5
Clarence Mangan Road	A5
Clare Lane	E4
Clare Street	E4
Clarendon Row	D4
Clarendon Street	D4
Clonmel Street	D5
Coke Lane	A3
Coleraine Street	B1
College Green	D3
College Lane	E3
College Street	D3
Commons Street	F2

Constitution Hill	B1
Convent Close	F5
Connolly	F1
Cook Street	B3
Coombe Court	A4
Cope Steet	D3
Copper Alley	C3
Cork Hill	C3
Cork Street	A5
Corporation Street	E1
Crane Lane	C3
Creighton Street	F3
Crown Alley	D3
Cuckoo Lane	B2
Cuffe Street	C5
Cumberland Street North	D1
Cumberland Street South	F4
Curved Street	C3
Custom House	E2
Custom House Quay	E2

D

D'Olier Street	D3
Dame Lane	C3
Dame Street	C3
Dawson Lane	D4
Dawson Street	D4
Dean Street	B4
Dean Swift Square	B4
Denzille Lane	F4
Diamond Park	E1
Digges Lane	C4
Digges Street Upper	C5
Dominick Lane	C1
Dominick Place	C1
Dominick Street Lower	C1
Dominick Street Upper	B1
Donore Road	A5
Dorset Street Upper	C1
Dowlings Court	F3
Drury Street	D4
Dublinia	B4
Dublin Castle	C3
Dublin Civic Museum	D4
Dublin Writers' Museum	C1
Duke Lane	D4
Duke Lane Upper	C1
Duke Street	D4

E

Earl Place	D2
Earl Street North	D2
Earl Street South	A4
Earlsfort Terrace	D5
Ebenezer Terrace	A5
Eden Quay	D2
Ellis Quay	A3
Ely Place	E5
Erne Place Lower	F3
Erne Street Upper	F4

Erne Terrace Front	F3
Essex Quay	C3
Essex Street East	C3
Essex Street West	C3
Eustace Street	C3
Exchange Street Lower	C3
Exchange Street Upper	C3
Exchequer Street	D4

F

Fade Street	C4
Father Matthew Bridge	A3
Father Matthew Square	B2
Fenian Street	F4
Fishamble Street	B3
Fitzwilliam Lane	E4
Fitzwilliam Square	E5
Fitzwilliam Square North	E5
Fitzwilliam Square West	E5
Fitzwilliam Street Lower	F5
Fitzwilliam Street Upper	F5
Fleet Street	D3
Foley Street	E1
Foster Place	D3
Fountain Place	A2
Four Courts	B3
Fownes Street	D3
Francis Street	B4
Frederick Street South	E4
Frenchman's Lane	E2
Friary Avenue	A2
Fumbally Lane	B5

G

Garden Lane	A4
Garden of Remembrance	C1
Gardiner Street Lower	E1
Gardiner Street Middle	D1
Gate Theatre	D1
General Post Office	D2
Geoffrey Keating Road	A5
George's Dock	F2
George's Hill	B2
George's Lane	A2
George's Quay	E2
Gloucester Diamond	E1
Gloucester Place	E1
Gloucester Street South	E3
Glovers Alley	D4
Golden Lane	C4
Grafton Street	D4
Granby Lane	C1
Granby Place	C1
Granby Row	C1
Grangegorman Upper	A1
Grant's Row	F4
Grattan Bridge	C3
Gray Street	A4
Greek Street	B2
Green Street	B2

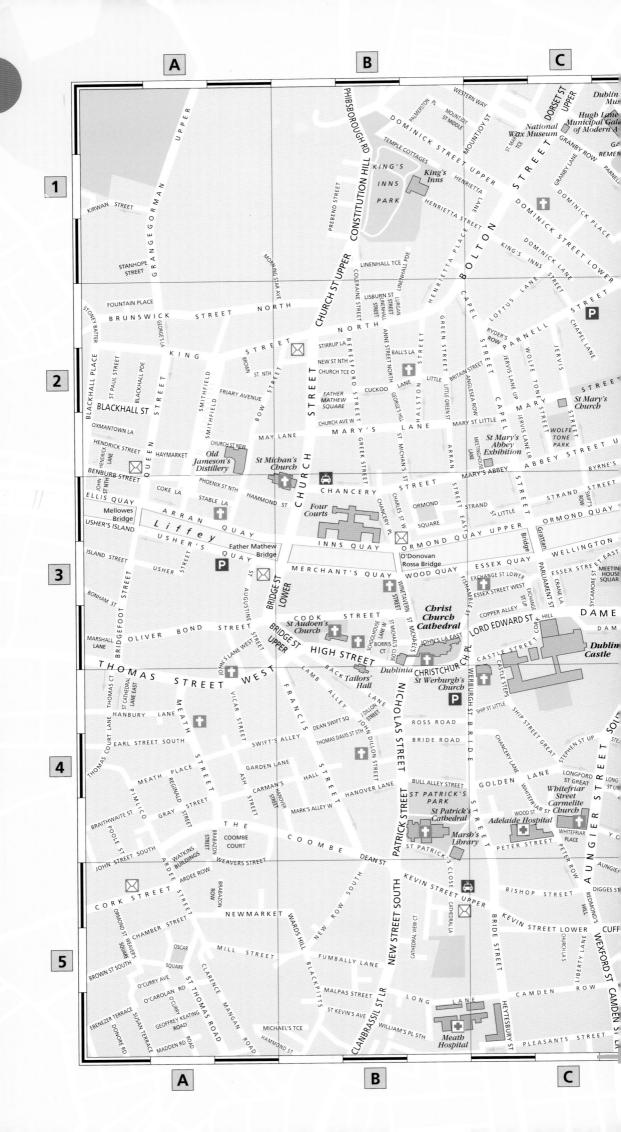

IRELAND REGION BY REGION

Ireland at a Glance

T HE LURE of Ireland's much-vaunted Atlantic
shores, from the wild coastline of Cork and
Kerry to the remote peninsulas of the Northwest,
is strong. However, to neglect the interior would
be to miss out on Ireland's equally characteristic
landscapes of lush valleys, dark peatlands and
unruffled loughs. Most regions are rich in historic
sights: from world-famous Neolithic sites in the
Midlands to imposing Norman castles in the
North and Palladian mansions in the Southeast.

*Yeats Country is a
charming part of County
Sligo closely associated
with WB Yeats. The
poet was born here
and is buried within
sight of Ben Bulben's
ridge. (See pp306–7.)*

NORTHW
IRELAN
(See pp282–

Connemara National Park *in County
Galway boasts stunning landscapes in which
mountains and lakes are combined with a
dramatic Atlantic coastline. The extensive
blanket bogs and moorland are rich in
wildlife and unusual plants. (See p268.)*

**THE WEST
OF IRELAND**
(See pp250–281)

Bunratty Castle
(See pp240–1)

The Rock of Cashel, *a
fortified medieval abbey,
perches on a limestone
outcrop in the heart of
County Tipperary. It boasts
some of Ireland's finest
Romanesque sculpture.
(See pp246–7.)*

**THE LOWER
SHANNON**
(See pp218–49)

CORK AND KERRY
(See pp178–217)

Bantry House
(See pp202–3)

The Lakes of Killarney, *flanked by
the lush, wooded slopes of some of the
country's highest mountains, are the
principal attraction in the southwest
of Ireland. (See pp194–5.)*

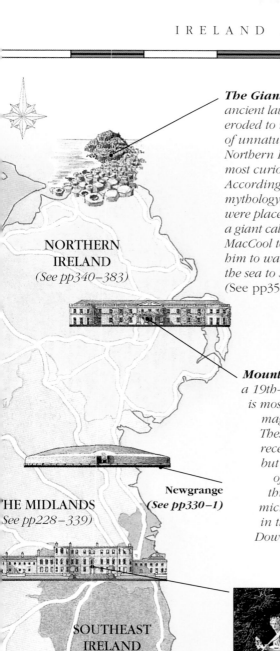

The Giant's Causeway, *where ancient lava flows have been eroded to reveal columns of unnatural regularity, is Northern Ireland's most curious sight. According to local mythology, the rocks were placed here by a giant called Finn MacCool to enable him to walk across the sea to Scotland.* (See pp356–7.)

NORTHERN IRELAND
(See pp340–383)

Mount Stewart House, *a 19th-century mansion, is most renowned for its magnificent gardens. These were created as recently as the 1920s, but a colourful array of exotic plants has thrived in the warm microclimate enjoyed in this part of County Down.* (See pp378–9.)

Newgrange
(See pp330–1)

THE MIDLANDS
See pp228–339)

SOUTHEAST IRELAND
(See pp138–77)

Powerscourt *is a large estate in superb countryside on the edge of the Wicklow Mountains. Its grounds rank among the last great formal gardens of Europe. Originally planted in the 1730s, they were restored and embellished in the 19th century.* (See pp156–7.)

0 kilometres   50

0 miles   25

Kilkenny Castle *was for centuries the stronghold of the Butler dynasty, which controlled much of southeast Ireland in the Middle Ages. The vast Norman fortress was remodelled during the Victorian period and still dominates Kilkenny – one of the country's most historic and pleasant towns.* (See pp166–7.)

The Wicklow Way, County Wicklow ▷

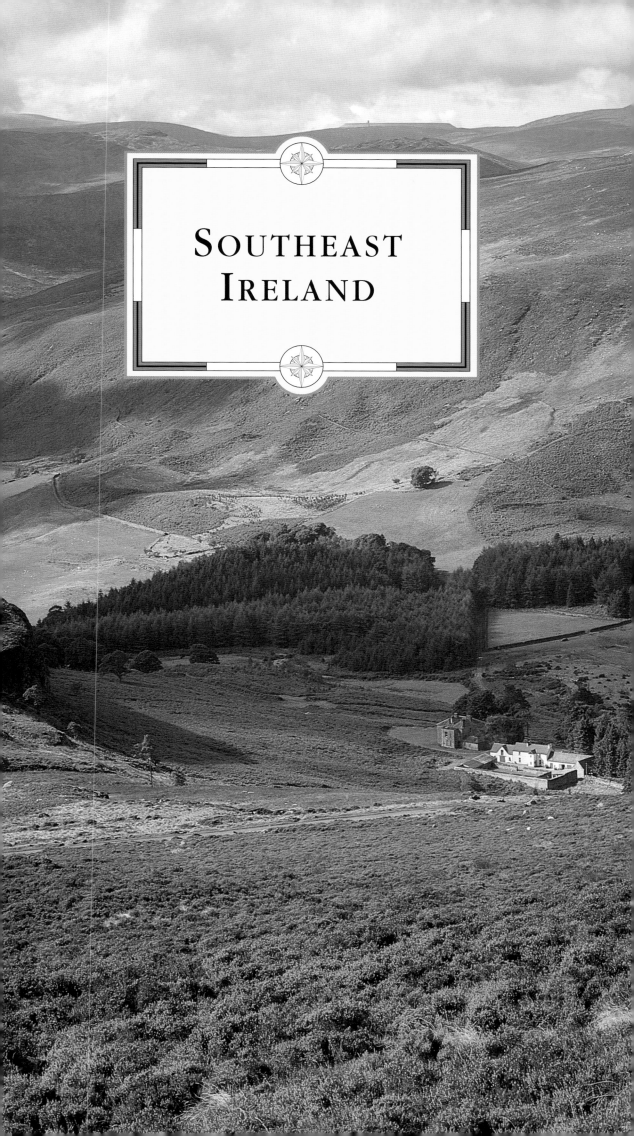

SOUTHEAST
IRELAND

SOUTHEAST IRELAND

KILDARE · WICKLOW · CARLOW · KILKENNY
WATERFORD · WEXFORD

BLESSED WITH *the warmest climate in Ireland, the Southeast has always presented an attractive prospect for settlers. Landscapes of gently rolling hills have been tamed by centuries of cultivation, with lush farmland, imposing medieval castles and great houses enhancing the region's atmosphere of prosperity.*

The Southeast's proximity to Britain often made it invaders' first port of call. Vikings arrived in the 9th century, founding some of Ireland's earliest towns, including Waterford and Wexford. In 1169 came the Anglo-Normans whose cultural influence is still felt; around Wexford, one may hear traces of the authentic old Norman dialect, Yola. The Hook Peninsula, site of the first Norman landing, is dotted with ruined abbeys and a Norman lighthouse.

The busy port of Waterford, only 39 miles (63 km) to the west of Wexford, is also steeped in history. It played a pivotal role in the ascendency of the English overlords when the warrior Strongbow married the King of Leinster's daughter here in 1170 and then succeeded to the throne.

The strategically important Southeast was heavily protected by Anglo-Norman lords loyal to England. Castle remains show the power of the Fitzgeralds of Kildare and the Butlers of Kilkenny, who between them virtually controlled the region in the Middle Ages. In the 18th century, wealthy Anglo-Irish families were attracted by the stability of the area, and built the fine Palladian mansions of Russborough and Castletown.

The English were not universally welcomed by the Irish, and the Wicklow Mountains became a refuge for rebels, including those who fled Enniscorthy during the uprising against the English in 1798. The Wexford peasants, armed only with pikes, held off the English forces for six weeks, an event which

Traditional thatched cottages in Dunmore East, County Waterford

◁ **Staircase hall with ornate 18th-century stuccowork in Castletown House, County Kildare**

The prosperous town of Waterford, reflected in the stillness of the River Suir

very much lives on in the local consciousness, and has inspired memorials in towns and the countryside. Many of the towns in this region have maintained their heritage. Kilkenny has a fine castle, which was once the stronghold of the Butler family, and radiating from it are shopping streets with narrow passageways, historic buildings, a brewery and an old coaching inn. Located just at the foot of the Knockmealdown Mountains is another town with historical remains, Lismore, with its castle and Cathedral of St Carthage.

A traditional Irish pub in peaceful County Wicklow

Though archaeological sights are comparatively rare in this region, Browne's Hill Dolmen near Carlow town is topped with the biggest capstone in Ireland, and prehistoric life has been re-created at the Irish National Heritage Park, just outside Wexford.

There are several religious sites in the Southeast, such as the cathedral at Kildare in honour of St Brigid, one of the country's three patron saints, who founded a religious community here in the late 5th century. The settlement established by St Kevin at Glendalough in the 6th century spread along the valley and was a place of pilgrimage until Victorian times. On the south coast, Ardmore had a fine towered monastery which was founded by St Declan. The remains of Jerpoint Abbey have sculpted cloisters, and St Canice's Cathedral at Kilkenny, one of Ireland's largest, has impressive tombs and many medieval treasures.

The Southeast is the first destination for many of today's visitors to Ireland, via the ferry terminal in Rosslare Harbour, which provides access to the town of Wexford, a former port with medieval alleys and historic buildings.

The Wicklow Way walking route, starting in south Dublin and running to County Carlow, is one of Ireland's most popular treks. South of this route, the rugged interior gives way to the lush wooded glens that follow the rivers of Avonmore and Avonbeg through the vales of Clara

Glendalough in the fertile and tranquil landscape of County Wicklow, the "Garden of Ireland"

and Avoca. Nestling quietly amid this altogether gentler landscape is the beautiful County Wicklow, justifiably labelled as the "Garden of Ireland".

The Southeast has outstanding gardens, from the wonderful, sweeping vistas of Powerscourt below the Great Sugar Loaf Mountain to the romantic Mount Usher Gardens, with its bridges over the River Vartry. The 17th-century Classical French gardens at Kilruddery are among the finest in Ireland,

The charming vista of the Italianate Powerscourt house and gardens

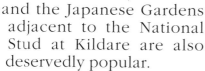

Waterford Crystal

and the Japanese Gardens adjacent to the National Stud at Kildare are also deservedly popular.

An air of prosperity pervades the bustling towns and fertile countryside of the Southeast. This region enjoys more days of sunshine than anywhere else on the island, and its resorts are frequented as much by Irish holidaymakers as by foreigners. Beaches stretch along the eastern shore between Dublin and Rosslare, where the 6-mile stretch of dune-backed sand is augmented by a championship golf course. The Victorian resort of Bray is an escape for Dubliners, and its cliffs offer fine coastal walks. The south coast has sandy stretches, most notably at the resorts of Ardmore and Tramore, but

here the shore is broken by rocky cliffs and small peninsulas. Minor roads meander through the countryside and lead to attractive coastal villages such as Kilmore Quay and Dunmore East.

The coast and inland waterways of the Southeast are a haven for wildlife, and the Saltee Islands, off Wexford's south coast, and the Wexford Wildfowl Reserve (which is particularly noted for its geese) are among the country's major bird sanctuaries. Anglers find a relaxing, rewarding retreat at rivers such as the Slaney, Barrow and Blackwater, and deep-sea fishing excursions sail from many villages and resorts in the region. The historic inland port town of New Ross has now become the centre for river cruising trips along the Barrow and the Nore.

Crafts at Kilkenny Design Centre

The Southeast is the home of some of Ireland's finest crafts. Waterford Crystal is famous worldwide, and its production has played a vital role in the region's growing economical prosperity. The Kilkenny Design Centre and Avoca Handweavers are known for quality goods and have outlets in Ireland and abroad. Kilkenny is a centre for crafts and design in a variety of media, and Enniscorthy has a pottery tradition, particularly for terracotta, which has lasted for more than 300 years.

The Classical French gardens of Kilkenny Castle, stronghold of the Butler family

Horses and Racing in Ireland

ORSES ARE SAID TO BE the second citizens of Ireland, and following racing is almost an alternative national religion. The equine obsession has inspired devotees for thousands of years: the pre-Christian Celts were fanatics, and in medieval times, long before permanent courses were created, the "hobby" (a pony-like horse) competed at fairs and on beaches. Today, the lush pasture and rolling, open countryside of Ireland is considered to be among the finest in the world for every variety of horse, from children's ponies to show-jumpers and classic racehorses worth many millions of pounds.

Young people developing their equestrian skills at a pony club

Ballsbridge Horse Fair, with its colourful salestalk and energetic bargaining, is an example of the type of gathering that used to be such a vital feature of Irish life.

THE CURRAGH AND THE TURF CLUB

The epicentre of Ireland's flat racing culture is at the Curragh in County Kildare, headquarters of the sport's governing body, the Turf Club, which was founded in the 1760s. The Club provides course stewards and takes responsibility for ensuring fair play at a total of 26 flat and jump racecourses, where 4,500 horses take more than a million racegoers each year through the gamut of the gambler's emotions.

Ballymoss, one of Vincent O'Brien's many champions

Two racing legends, Nijinsky and jockey Lester Piggott

CHAMPIONS ON THE FLAT

There are few training establishments more impressive than Ballydoyle, where the trainer Vincent O'Brien reared some of the finest classic horses of the post-war era, among them Sir Ivor, Nijinsky and Alleged. Another Irish champion was Shergar, bred at the Aga Khan's Irish stud but trained in England. Shergar was kidnapped by terrorists in Ireland in 1983 and was never seen again.

BETTING AT THE RACES

Racing without bookmakers (quite often abbreviated to "bookies" but occasionally grandiloquently referred to as "turf accountants") is unimaginable. The betting ring, with its milling crowds, where bookies call the odds, gesticulate wildly, chalk their boards and enter bets in ledgers, is an essential feature of every race meeting. Betting is not just a way of making rich men paupers and injecting additional excitement into the sport: in various ways, the Irish betting industry contributes significantly to racing's annual pot of £16 million prize money.

Bookies orchestrating the betting at Galway races

Thoroughbred sale rings are part of the way of life at fairs and livestock auctions across the country. Ireland's studs – many little more than family farms – produce almost 8,000 thoroughbred foals in a year and have nurtured generations of champions to contest the world's great races.

Jockey dynasties are not a rare phenomenon in professional racing. The Beasley dynasty, riding both flat and jump racers in Ireland and abroad, has been outstanding for more than a century now, especially in such major jump races as the Irish and Aintree Grand Nationals. Such dynasties are a breed apart; the venerable Harry Beasley rode his final race, a "bumper", (National Hunt flat race) at the Curragh, in 1939, at the age of 83.

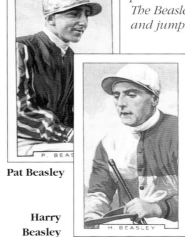

Pat Beasley

Harry Beasley

CHAMPIONS OVER THE JUMPS

Reckless, hell-for-leather cross-country "pounding matches" were organized centuries before the world's first steeple chase was run in Cork in 1752. The popularity of jump-racing today is much in evidence at Irish courses such as Fairyhouse and Punchestown, and every year there is a migration of tens of thousands of Irish people to cheer home Irish-trained runners at England's Cheltenham National Hunt Racing Festival.

Arkle, the supreme steeplchaser, ridden by Pat Taafe

Dawn Run, winner of the Gold Cup at Cheltenham

Exploring Southeast Ireland

THE SOUTHEAST has something for everyone, from busy seaside resorts to quaint canalside villages, Norman abbeys and bird sanctuaries. The Wicklow Mountains, the location of several major sights such as the monastic complex of Glendalough and the magnificent gardens of Powerscourt, provide perfect touring and walking territory. Further south, the most scenic routes cut through the valleys of the Slaney, Barrow and Nore rivers, flanked by historic ports such as New Ross, from where you can explore local waterways by boat. Along the south coast, which is more varied than the region's eastern shore, beaches are interspersed with rocky headlands, and quiet coastal villages provide good alternative bases to the busy towns of Waterford and Wexford. Further inland, the best places to stay include Lismore and Kilkenny, which is one of the finest historic towns in Ireland.

Graiguenamanagh, on the Barrow north of New Ross

SIGHTS AT A GLANCE

Ardmore ⑲
Avondale House ⑭
Bray ⑧
Browne's Hill Dolmen ⑮
Castletown House pp152–3 ❶
Dunmore East ㉑
Enniscorthy ㉔
Glendalough ⑬
Hook Peninsula ㉒
Irish National Heritage Park ㉕
Jerpoint Abbey ⑰
Johnstown Castle ㉗
Kildare ❺
Kilkenny pp166–8 ⑯
Killruddery House ⑨
Lismore ⑱
Monasterevin ❹
Mount Usher Gardens ⑫
New Ross ㉓
Peatland World ❸
Powerscourt pp156–7 ❼
Robertstown ❷
Rosslare ㉙

Russborough House ❻
Saltee Islands ㉘
Waterford pp172–3 ⑳
Wexford ㉖
Wicklow Mountains ⑪

Tours
Military Road ⑩

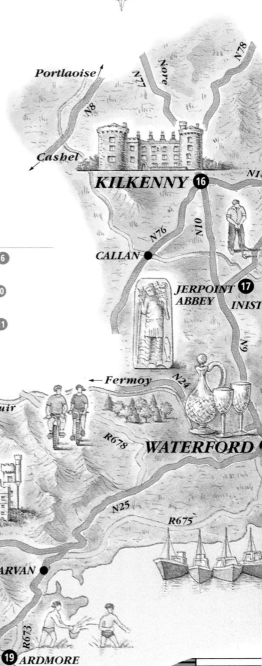

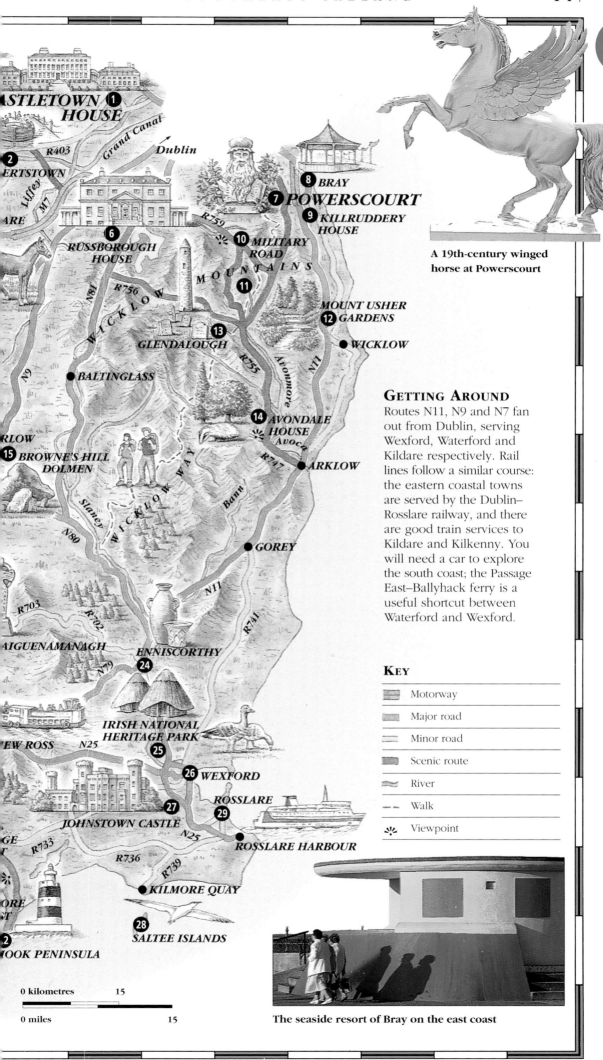

A 19th-century winged horse at Powerscourt

GETTING AROUND

Routes N11, N9 and N7 fan out from Dublin, serving Wexford, Waterford and Kildare respectively. Rail lines follow a similar course: the eastern coastal towns are served by the Dublin–Rosslare railway, and there are good train services to Kildare and Kilkenny. You will need a car to explore the south coast; the Passage East–Ballyhack ferry is a useful shortcut between Waterford and Wexford.

KEY

▨	Motorway
▨	Major road
═	Minor road
▨	Scenic route
∿	River
– –	Walk
☀	Viewpoint

The seaside resort of Bray on the east coast

Castletown House ❶

See pp152–3.

Robertstown ❷

Co Kildare. 👥 240. 🚌

TEN LOCKS WEST along the Grand Canal from Dublin, Robertstown is a characteristic 19th-century canalside village, with warehouses and cottages flanking the waterfront. Freight barges plied the route until about 1960, but pleasure boats have since replaced them. Visitors can take barge cruises from the quay and the Grand Canal Company's Hotel, built in 1801 for canal passengers, is now used for banquets.

Near Sallins, about 8 km (5 miles) east of Robertstown, the canal is carried over the River Liffey along the **Leinster Aqueduct**, an impressive structure built in 1783.

The Grand Canal Company's Hotel in Robertstown

Peatland World ❸

Lullymore, Co Kildare. 📞 045 860133. 🚌 🚌 to Newbridge. 🕐 9am–4:30pm Mon–Fri (Apr–Oct: 2–6pm Sat, Sun also). 🌑 10 days at Christmas. 📷 ♿ limited.

ANYONE INTERESTED in the natural history of Irish bogs should visit Peatland World, an exhibition in an old farm at Lullymore, 9 km (6 miles) northeast of Rathangan. It lies at the heart of the Bog of Allen, a expanse of raised bog *(see p338)* that extends across the counties of Offaly, Laois and Kildare.

There is an exhibition of the history and ecology of the bog, with displays of flora and fauna and archaeological finds from the surrounding area. Guided walks across the peatlands are also organized to introduce visitors to the bog's delicate ecosystem.

Stacking peat for use as fuel

Monasterevin ❹

Co Kildare. 👥 2,200. 🚌

THIS GEORGIAN market town lies west of Kildare, where the Grand Canal crosses the River Barrow. Waterborne trade brought prosperity to Monasterevin in the 18th century, but the locks now see little traffic. However, you can still admire the aqueduct, which is a superb example of canal engineering. **Moore Abbey**, next to

the church, was built in the 18th century on the site of a monastic establishment, however, the grand Gothic mansion owes much to Victorian remodelling. Once the ancestral seat of the Earls of Drogheda, in the 1920s Moore Abbey became the home of the celebrated tenor, John McCormack *(see p30)*. It is now a hospital.

Kildare ❺

Co Kildare. 👥 4,200. 🚌 🚌 ℹ️ Market House (Jun–Sep: 045 522696). 🛍️ Thu.

THE CHARMING and tidy town of Kildare (the 'Church of the Oakwood') is dominated by **St Brigid's Cathedral**, which commemorates the saint who founded a religious community on this site in 490. Unusually, monks and nuns lived there under the same roof, but this was not the only unorthodox practice associated with the community. Curious pagan rituals, including the burning of a perpetual fire, continued until the 16th century. The fire pit is visible in the grounds today. So too is a round tower,

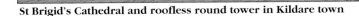
St Brigid's Cathedral and roofless round tower in Kildare town

Japanese Gardens at Tully near Kildare

which was probably built in the 12th century and has a Romanesque doorway, 4 m (13 ft) from the ground. The cathedral was rebuilt in the Victorian era by George Street, the renowned architect responsible for the restoration of Christ Church Cathedral in Dublin, but he largely adhered to the original 13th-century design.

🔼 St Brigid's Cathedral
Market Square. 📞 045 521229.
⭕ May–Oct: daily. **Donation**. ♿

ENVIRONS: Kildare lies at the heart of racing country: the Curragh racecourse, venue for all the Irish flat-racing classics, is nearby; leading stables are scattered all around; and bloodstock sales take place at Kill, northeast of town.

The **National Stud** is a state-run bloodstock farm at Tully, just south of Kildare. It was founded in 1900 by an eccentric Anglo-Irish colonel called William Walker. He sold his foals on the basis of their astrological charts, and put skylights in the stables to allow the horses to be "touched" by sunlight or moonbeams. Walker's views on breeding are variously regarded as being preposterous, eccentric and inspired. Walker received

the title Lord Wavertree in reward for bequeathing the farm to the British in 1915.

Visitors can explore the 400-ha (1,000-acre) grounds and watch the horses being exercised. The whole breeding process is scientifically organized: mares are normally kept in a separate paddock from the stallions, though a "teaser" stallion is cunningly introduced to discover when the mares come into season, and to give some indication of his suspicions. Breeding stallions wait patiently in the covering shed: each one is expected to cover 50 mares per season. There is a special foaling unit where the mare and foal can remain undisturbed for a few days after the birth.

The farm has its own forge and saddlery, and also a most fascinating Horse Museum. Housed in an old stable block, this illustrates the importance of horses in Irish life. Exhibits include the frail skeleton of Arkle, the champion steeplechaser who shot to fame in the 1960s.

Sharing the same estate as the National Stud are the **Japanese Gardens** (also known as the Gardens of Tully). They were originally commissioned by Lord Wavertree at the height of the Edwardian penchant for Orientalism. The gardens were devised by Colonel William Hallwalker, a wealthy Scot, and were laid out in 1906–10 by a Japanese landscape gardener called Tassa Eida, with the help of his son Minoru and 40 assistants. The Gardens have impressive array of trees and shrubs includes maples, mulberries, bonsai, magnolias, sacred bamboos and cherry trees.

The gardens take the form of an allegorical journey symbolizing the experiences of the human soul as it journeys through the path of life, with such areas as The Hill of Learning, The Parting of the Ways, The Hill of Ambition, the Well of Wisdom and the Garden of Peace and Contentment. The route incorporates a variety of elaborate rockeries, symbolic stone lanterns and wonderful miniature bridges.

🍁 National Stud and Japanese Gardens
Tully. 📞 045 521617.
⭕ mid-Feb–mid-Nov: 9:30am–6pm daily. 🖊 ♿ 📷 National Stud only.
💻 📷

Horses hurtling towards the finishing line at the Curragh racecourse, where the big races attract many of Europe's finest thoroughbreds

Killiney Bay, County Wicklow ▷

Castletown House ❶

★ **Long Gallery**
Pompeiian-style friezes adorn the cobalt-blue walls of this magnificent room. The niches frame statues of figures from Classical mythology.

BUILT IN 1722–32 for William Conolly, Speaker of the Irish Parliament, Castletown was the grandest house in the country at the time. The work of Florentine architect, Alessandro Galilei, the building gave Ireland its first taste of Palladianism. The magnificent interiors date from the second half of the 18th century. They were commissioned by Lady Louisa Lennox, wife of William Conolly's great-nephew, Tom, who took up residence here in 1758. Castletown remained in the family until 1965, when it was taken over by the Irish Georgian Society. The house now belongs to the state and is open to the public.

Conolly crest on an armchair

Red Drawing Room
The room takes its name from the red damask on the walls, which is probably French and dates from the 1820s. This exquisite mahogany bureau was made for Lady Louisa in the 1760s.

Green Drawing Room

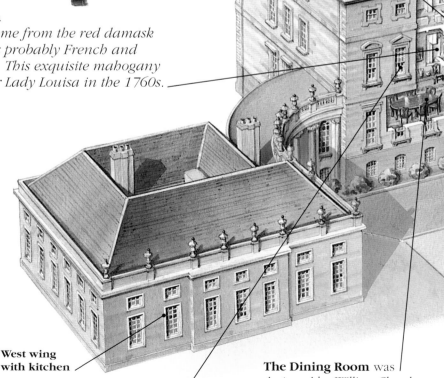

West wing with kitchen

Boudoir Wall Paintings
The boudoir's decorative panels, moved here from the Long Gallery, were inspired by the Raphael Loggia in the Vatican.

The Dining Room was designed by William Chambers, architect of the Marino Casino (*see pp44–5*). The mantelpiece and door cases show his strong Neo-Classical inspiration.

★ Print Room
In this, the last surviving print room in Ireland, Lady Louisa indulged her taste for Italian engravings. In the 18th century, it was fashionable for ladies to paste prints directly on to the wall and frame them with elaborate festoons.

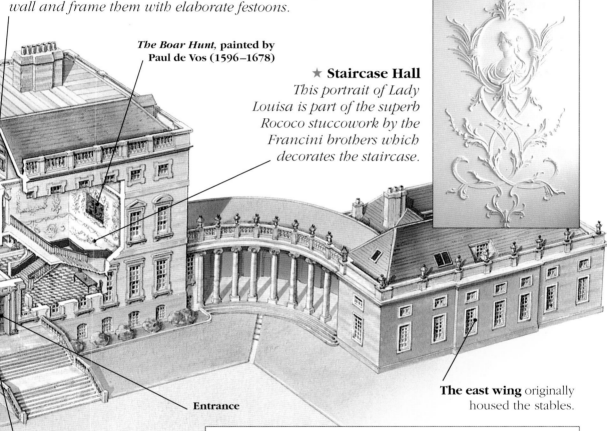

*The Boar Hunt, painted by
Paul de Vos (1596–1678)*

★ Staircase Hall
*This portrait of Lady
Louisa is part of the superb
Rococo stuccowork by the
Francini brothers which
decorates the staircase.*

The east wing originally
housed the stables.

Entrance

The Entrance Hall is an
austere Neo-Classical room.
Its most decorative feature is
the delicate carving on the
pilasters of the upper gallery.

STAR FEATURES

★ **Long Gallery**

★ **Print Room**

★ **Staircase Hall**

CONOLLY'S FOLLY

This folly, which lies just
beyond the grounds of
Castletown House, provides
the focus of the view from
the Long Gallery. Speaker
Conolly's widow, Katherine,
commissioned it in 1740
as a memorial to her late
husband, and to provide
employment after a harsh
winter. The unusual structure of superimposed arches
crowned by an obelisk was
designed by Richard Castle,
architect of Russborough
House (*see p154*).

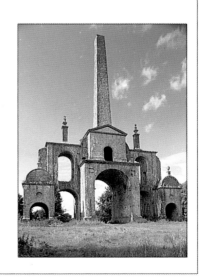

Saloon in Russborough House with original fireplace and stuccowork

Russborough House 6

Blessington, Co Wicklow. 045
865239. 65 from Dublin.
May–Sep: daily; Easter–Apr & Oct:
Sun & public hols.

THIS PALLADIAN MANSION, built
in the 1740s for Joseph
Leeson, Earl of Milltown, is
one of Ireland's finest houses.
Its architect, an anglicized
German called Richard Castle,
also designed Powerscourt
House (see pp156–7) and is
credited with introducing the
Palladian style to Ireland.

Unlike many grand estates
in the Pale, Russborough has
survived magnificently, both
inside and out. The house
claims the longest frontage in
Ireland, with a façade adorned
by heraldic lions and curved
colonnades. The interior is
even more impressive.
Many rooms feature
superb stucco dec-
oration, which was
done largely by
the Italian Francini
brothers, who also
worked on Castle-
town House (see
pp152–3). The best
examples are found
in the music room,
saloon and library,
which are embellished with
exuberant foliage and cherubs.
Around the main staircase, a
riot of Rococo plasterwork

depicts a hunt, with hounds
clasping garlands of flowers.
The stucco mouldings in the
drawing room were designed
especially to enclose marine
scenes by the French artist,
Joseph Vernet (1714–89). The
paintings were sold in 1926,
but were tracked down more
than 40 years afterwards and
returned to the house.

Russborough has many other
treasures, including finely
worked fireplaces of Italian
marble, imposing mahogany
doorways and priceless
collections of silver, porcelain
and Gobelins tapestries.

Such riches aside, one of the
principal reasons to visit Russborough is to see the **Beit Art
Collection**, famous for its
Flemish, Dutch and Spanish
Old Master paintings. These
include fine works by Goya,
Velázquez, Hals, Rubens and
Vermeer. Sir Alfred Beit, who
bought the house in 1952,
inherited the pictures from his
uncle – also named
Alfred Beit and co-
founder of the de
Beer diamond
mining empire
in South Africa.
In 1974, several
masterpieces
were taken by the
IRA, but they were
later retrieved.
Several pictures
are still missing,
following a second robbery in
1986. Only a selection of
paintings is on view in the
house at any one time, while

**Vernet seascape in
the drawing room**

THE HISTORY OF THE PALE

The term "Pale" refers to an area around
Dublin which marked the limits of English
influence from Norman to Tudor times. The
frontier fluctuated, but at its largest the Pale
stretched from Dundalk in County Louth to
Waterford town. Gaelic chieftains outside the
area could keep their lands provided they
agreed to bring up their heirs within the Pale.

The Palesmen supported their rulers' interests
and considered themselves the upholders of
English values. This widened the gap between
the Gaelic majority and the Anglo-Irish, a fore-
taste of England's doomed involvement in the
country. Long after its fortifications were
dismantled, the idea of the Pale lived on as a
state of mind. The expression "beyond the
pale" survives as a definition of those outside
the bounds of civilized society.

**An 18th-century family enjoying the privileged
lifestyle typical within the Pale**

Tourist road train on the beachfront esplanade at Bray

others are on permanent loan to the National Gallery in Dublin *(see pp80–1)*.

Russborough enjoys a fine position near the village of **Blessington**, with a good view across to the Wicklow Mountains. The house lies amid wooded parkland rather than elaborate flower gardens. As Alfred Beit said of Irish Palladianism, "Fine architecture standing in a green sward was considered enough."

ENVIRONS: The **Poulaphouca Reservoir**, which was formed by the damming of the River Liffey, extends south from Blessington. The placid lake is popular with watersports enthusiasts, while other visitors come simply to enjoy the lovely mountain views.

Powerscourt ❼

See pp156–7.

Bray ❽

Co Wicklow. 🏛 *33,000.* 🚆 *DART.* 🚌 🛈 *Old Court House, Main St (01 2867128).*

ONCE A REFINED Victorian resort, Bray is nowadays a brash holiday town, with amusement arcades and fish and chip shops lining the seafront. Its beach attracts large crowds in summer, including many young families. Anyone in search of peace and quiet can escape to nearby Bray Head, where there is scope for bracing cliffside walks. Bray also makes a good base from which to explore Powerscourt Gardens, the Wicklow Mountains and the delightful coastal villages of Killiney and Dalkey *(see p129)*.

Killruddery House ❾

Bray, Co Wicklow. 🕿 *01 2867128.* **House** ⬜ *May–Jun & Sep: daily (pm only).* **Gardens** ⬜ *Apr–Sep: daily (pm only).* 🎫 ♿ *limited.*

KILLRUDDERY HOUSE lies just to the south of Bray, in the shadow of Little Sugar Loaf Mountain. Built in 1651, it has been the family seat of the Earls of Meath ever since, although the original mansion was remodelled in an Elizabethan Revival style in the early 19th century. The house contains some good carving and stuccowork, but it is a rather faded stately home. The real charm of Killruddery lies in the 17th-century formal gardens, regarded as the finest French Classical gardens in the country. They were laid out in the 1680s by a French gardener named Bonet, who also worked at Versailles.

The gardens, planted with great precision, feature romantic parterres, a whole array of different hedges and many fine trees and shrubs, both native and foreign. The sylvan theatre, a small enclosure surrounded by a bay hedge, is the only known example of its kind in Ireland.

The Long Ponds, a pair of canals which extend 165 m (550 ft), were once used to stock fish. Beyond, a pool enclosed by two circular hedges leads to an arrangement of paths flanked by statues and hedges of yew, beech, lime and hornbeam created in the Victorian period.

View across the Long Ponds to Killruddery House

Powerscourt ⑦

THE GARDENS AT POWERSCOURT are probably the finest in Ireland, both for their design and their dramatic setting at the foot of Great Sugar Loaf Mountain. The house and grounds were commissioned in the 1730s by Richard Wingfield, the 1st Viscount Powerscourt. New ornamental gardens were completed in 1858–75 by the 7th Viscount, who added gates, urns and statues collected during his travels in Europe. The house was gutted by an accidental fire in 1974, but the ground floor has been beautifully renovated and now accommodates an upmarket shopping centre with an excellent restaurant and café.

Laocoon statue on upper terrace

Bamberg Gate
Made in Vienna in the 1770s, this gilded wrought-iron gate was brought to Powerscourt by the 7th Viscount from Bamberg Church in Bavaria.

The Walled Gardens include a formal arrangement of clipped laurel trees but are also used for growing plants for Powerscourt's nursery.

The Pets' Cemetery contains the graves of Wingfield family dogs, cats and even horses and cattle.

Statue of Laocoon

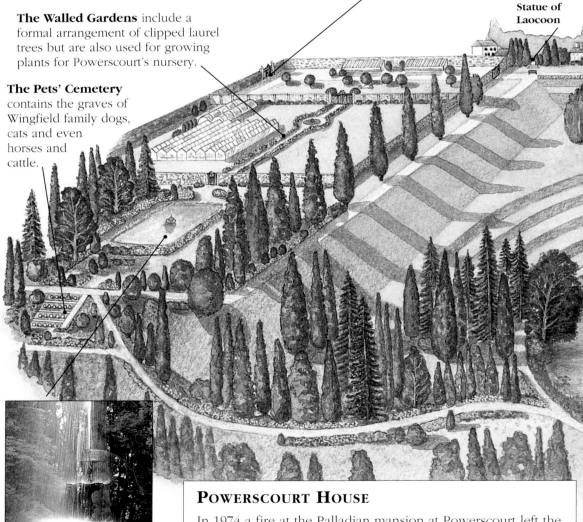

Dolphin Pond
This pool, designed as a fish pond in the 18th century, is enclosed by exotic conifers in a lovely secluded garden.

POWERSCOURT HOUSE

In 1974 a fire at the Palladian mansion at Powerscourt left the fine building a burnt-out shell. In recent years the Slazenger family, who now own the estate, have restored the ground floor and the ballroom up-stairs, although much work remains to be done to the rest of the house. Originally built in 1731 on the site of a Norman castle, the house was designed by Richard Castle, who was also the architect of Russborough House (*see p154*).

Powerscourt ablaze in 1974

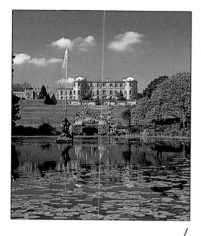

★ The Perron
Leading down to Triton Lake is the Perron, a beautiful Italianate stairway added in 1874. Beside the lake, it is guarded by two statues of Pegasus – the mythical winged horse and emblem of the Wingfield family.

The Italian Garden
is laid out on terraces which were first cut into the steep hillside in the 1730s.

Pebble Mosaic
Many tonnes of pebbles were gathered from nearby Bray beach to build the Perron and to make this mosaic on the terrace.

VISITORS' CHECKLIST

Enniskerry, Co Wicklow.
☎ 01 2046000. 🚌 85 from Bray, 44 from Dublin to Enniskerry. ⊙ 9:30am–5:30pm (dusk Oct–Mar) daily. ● 25 & 26 Dec. 🚫 📷 ♿ 🍴 🎁

The Pepper Pot Tower was built in 1911.

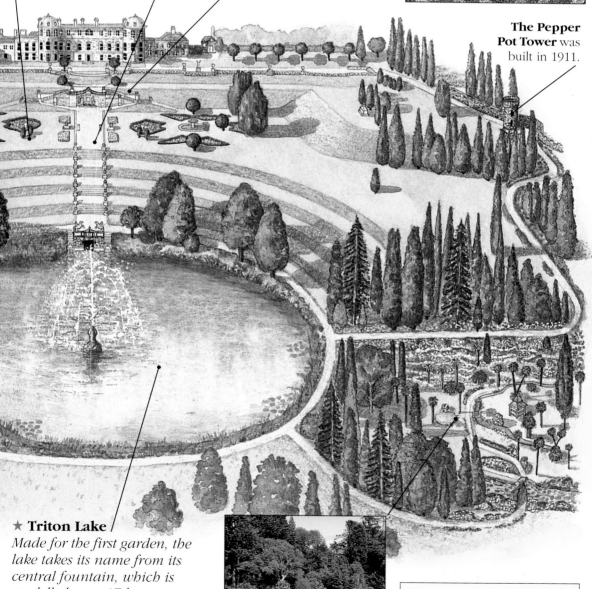

★ Triton Lake
Made for the first garden, the lake takes its name from its central fountain, which is modelled on a 17th-century work by Bernini in Rome.

★ Japanese Gardens
These enchanting Edwardian gardens, created out of bogland, contain Chinese conifers and bamboo trees.

STAR FEATURES

★ **The Perron**

★ **Japanese Gardens**

★ **Triton Lake**

Powerscourt Gardens with Great Sugar Loaf Mountain beyond ▷

A Tour of the Military Road ❿

Rare red squirrel

THE BRITISH BUILT the Military Road through the heart of the Wicklow Mountains during a campaign to flush out Irish rebels after an uprising in 1798 *(see p175)*. Now known as the R115, this road takes you through the emptiest and most rugged landscapes of County Wicklow. Fine countryside, in which deer and other wildlife flourish, is characteristic of the whole of this tour.

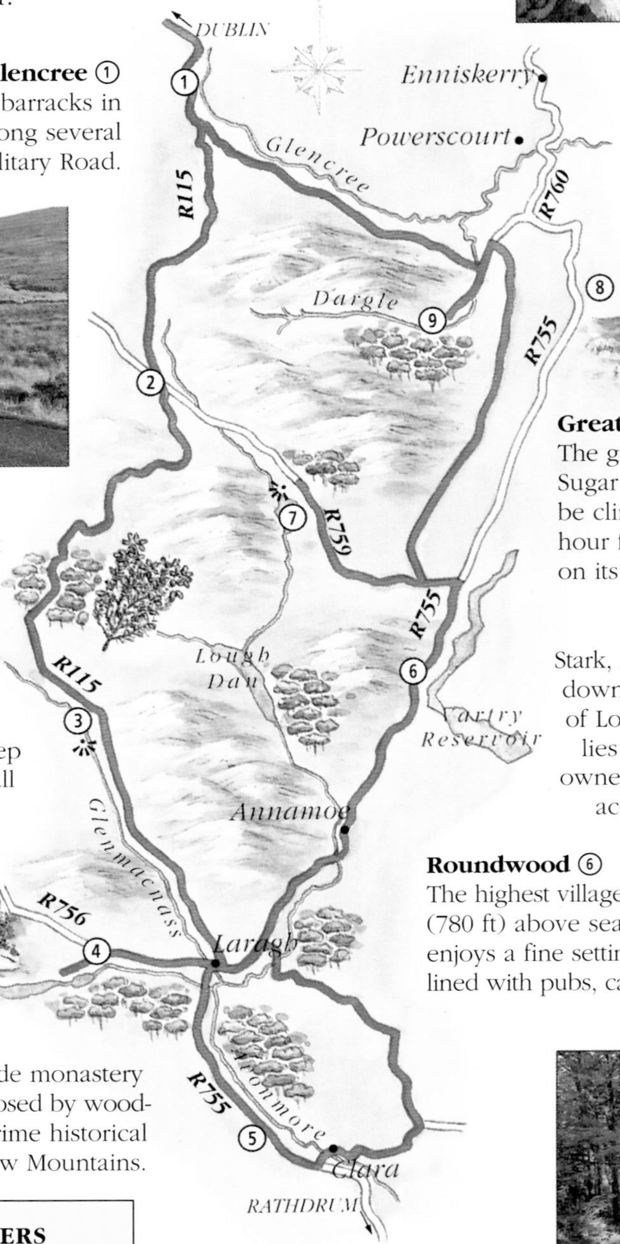

Glencree ①
The former British barracks in Glencree are among several found along the Military Road.

Sally Gap ②
This remote pass is surrounded by a vast expanse of blanket bog dotted with pools and streams.

Glenmacnass ③
After Sally Gap, the road drops into a deep glen where a waterfall spills dramatically over rocks.

Glendalough ④
This ancient lakeside monastery *(see pp162–3)*, enclosed by wooded slopes, is the prime historical sight in the Wicklow Mountains.

Powerscourt Waterfall ⑨
The River Dargle cascades 130 m (425 ft) over a granite escarpment to form Ireland's highest waterfall.

Great Sugar Loaf ⑧
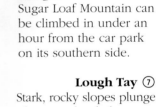
The granite cone of Great Sugar Loaf Mountain can be climbed in under an hour from the car park on its southern side.

Lough Tay ⑦
Stark, rocky slopes plunge down to the dark waters of Lough Tay. Though it lies within a Guinness-owned estate, the lake is accessible to walkers.

Roundwood ⑥
The highest village in Ireland at 238 m (780 ft) above sea level, Roundwood enjoys a fine setting. Its main street is lined with pubs, cafés and craft shops.

Map labels: DUBLIN · Enniskerry · Powerscourt · Glencree · R115 · Dargle · R760 · R755 · Lough Dan · R759 · Annamoe · Vartry Reservoir · Glenmacnass · R756 · Laragh · Avonmore · R755 · Clara · RATHDRUM

TIPS FOR DRIVERS

Length: 96 km (60 miles).
Stopping-off points: There are several pubs and cafés in Enniskerry (including Poppies, an old-fashioned tearoom), and also in Roundwood, but this area is better for picnics. There are several marked picnic spots south of Enniskerry.

```
0 kilometres        5
0 miles          3
```

KEY

⬛ Tour route

═══ Other roads

✳ Viewpoint

Vale of Clara ⑤
This picturesque wooded valley follows the River Avonmore. It contains the tiny village of Clara, which consists of two houses, a church and a school.

Wicklow Mountains ⑪

🚉 to Rathdrum & Wicklow.
🚌 to Enniskerry, Wicklow, Glendalough, Rathdrum & Avoca.
ℹ️ Rialto House, Fitzwilliam Square, Wicklow (0404 69117).

STANDING AMID the rugged wilderness of the Wicklow Mountains, it can be hard to believe that Dublin is under an hour's drive away. The inaccessibility of the mountains meant that they once provided a safe hideout for opponents of English rule. When much of the Southeast was obedient to the English Crown, within an area known as the Pale *(see p154)*, warlords such as the O'Tooles held sway in the Wicklow Mountains. Rebels who took part in the 1798 uprising *(see p45)* sought refuge here too. One of their leaders, Michael Dwyer, remained at liberty in the hills around Sally Gap until 1803.

The building of the **Military Road**, started in 1800, made the area more accessible, but the mountains are still thinly populated. There is little traffic to disturb enjoyment of the exhilarating scenery of rock-strewn glens, lush forest and bogland where heather gives a purple sheen to the land. Turf-cutting is still a thriving cottage industry, and you often see peat stacked up by the road. Numerous walking trails weave through these landscapes. Among them is the **Wicklow Way**, which extends 132 km (82 miles) from Marlay Park in Dublin to Clonegal in County Carlow. It is marked but not always easy to follow, so do not set out without a decent map. Although no peak exceeds 915 m (3,000 ft), the Wicklow Mountains can be dangerous in bad weather.

Hiking apart, there is plenty to see and do in this region. A good starting point for exploring the northern area is the picture-postcard estate village of **Enniskerry**. In summer, it is busy with tourists who come to visit the gardens at Powerscourt *(see pp156–7)*. From Laragh, to the south, you can reach Glendalough *(see pp162–3)* and the **Vale of Avoca**, where cherry trees are laden with blossom in the spring. The beauty of this gentle valley was captured in the poetry of Thomas Moore (1779–1852):

Road sign in the Wicklow Mountains

"There is not in the wide world a valley so sweet as that vale in whose bosom the bright waters meet" – a reference to the confluence of the Avonbeg and Avonmore rivers, the so-called **Meeting of the Waters** beyond Avondale House *(see p162)*. Nestled among wooded

Mount Usher Gardens, on the banks of the River Vartry

hills at the heart of the valley is the hamlet of Avoca, where the **Avoca Handweavers** produce colourful tweeds in the oldest hand-weaving mill in Ireland, in operation since 1723.

Further north, towards the coast near Ashford, the River Vartry rushes through the deep chasm of the **Devil's Glen**. On entering the valley, the river falls 30 m (100 ft) into a pool known as the Devil's Punchbowl. There are good walks around here, with fine views of the coast.

🏠 **Avoca Handweavers**
Avoca. 📞 0402 35105. ⏰ daily.
🔴 25 & 26 Dec. 🍴 🏠

Mount Usher Gardens ⑫

Ashford, Co Wicklow. 📞 0404 40205. 🚌 to Ashford. ⏰ Mar–Nov: daily. 📷 ♿ limited.

SET BESIDE the River Vartry just east of Ashford are the Mount Usher Gardens. They were designed in 1868 by a Dubliner, Edward Walpole, who imbued them with his strong sense of romanticism.

The gardens contain many rare shrubs and trees, from Chinese conifers and bamboos to Mexican pines and pampas grass. There is also a Maple Walk, which is glorious in autumn. The river provides the main focus of the Mount Usher Gardens, and amid the exotic vegetation you can glimpse herons on the weirs.

Colourful moorland around Sally Gap in the Wicklow Mountains

Glendalough ⓭

Co Wicklow. 🚌 *St Kevin's Bus from Dublin.* **Ruins** ◯ *daily.* 🎫 *in summer.* **Visitors' Centre** ☎ *0404 45325.* ◯ *daily.* ● *10 days at Christmas.* 🎫 ♿

Tʜᴇ sᴛᴇᴇᴘ, ᴡᴏᴏᴅᴇᴅ slopes of Glendalough, the "valley of the two lakes", harbour one of Ireland's most atmospheric monastic sites. Established by St Kevin in the 6th century, the settlement was sacked time and again by the Vikings but nevertheless flourished for over 600 years. Decline set in only after English forces partially razed the site in 1398, though it functioned as a monastic centre until the Dissolution of the Monasteries in 1539 *(see p42).* Pilgrims kept on coming to Glendalough even after that, particularly on St Kevin's feast day, 3 June, which was often a riotous event *(see p34).*

The age of the buildings is uncertain, but most date from the 8th to 12th centuries. Many were restored during the 1870s.

View along the Upper Lake at Glendalough

Remains of the Gatehouse, the original entrance to Glendalough

The main group of ruins lies east of the Lower Lake, but the earliest buildings associated with St Kevin are by the Upper Lake. Here, where the scenery is much wilder, you are better able to enjoy the tranquillity of Glendalough and to escape the crowds which inevitably descend on the site. Try to arrive as early as possible in the day, particularly during the peak tourist season. You enter the monastery through the double stone arch of the **Gatehouse**, the only surviving example in Ireland of a gateway into a monastic enclosure.

A short walk leads to a graveyard with a **Round tower** in one corner. Reaching 33 m (110 ft) in height, this is one of the finest of its kind in the country. Its cap was rebuilt in the 1870s using stones found inside the tower. The roofless **Cathedral** nearby dates mainly from the 12th century and is

St Kevin's Kitchen

the valley's largest ruin. At the centre of the churchyard stands the tiny **Priest's House**, whose name derives from the fact that it was a burial place for local clergy. The worn carving of a robed figure above the door is possibly of St Kevin, flanked by two disciples. East of here, **St Kevin's Cross** dates from the 12th century and is one of the best preserved of Glendalough's various High Crosses. Made of granite, the cross may once have marked the boundary of the monastic cemetery. Below, nestled in the lush valley, a minuscule oratory with a steeply pitched stone roof is a charming sight. Erected in the 11th century or even earlier, it is popularly known as **St Kevin's Kitchen**; this is perhaps because its belfry, thought to be a later addition, resembles a chimney. One of the earliest churches at Glendalough, **St Mary's**, lies across a field to the west.

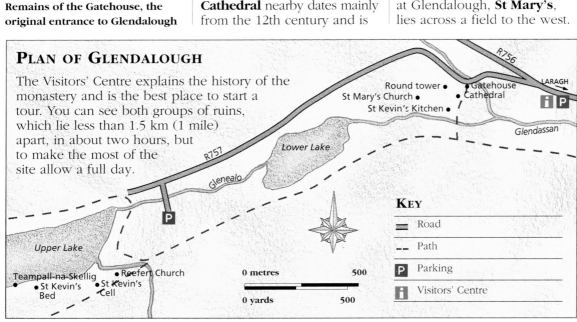

Pʟᴀɴ ᴏғ Gʟᴇɴᴅᴀʟᴏᴜɢʜ

The Visitors' Centre explains the history of the monastery and is the best place to start a tour. You can see both groups of ruins, which lie less than 1.5 km (1 mile) apart, in about two hours, but to make the most of the site allow a full day.

R756

LARAGH

Round tower ●
St Mary's Church ●
St Kevin's Kitchen ●

● Gatehouse
● Cathedral

ℹ 🅿

Glendassan

Lower Lake

R757

Glenealo

🅿

Upper Lake

Teampall-na-Skellig
● St Kevin's Bed

● Reefert Church
● St Kevin's Cell

Kᴇʏ

═══	Road
---	Path
🅿	Parking
ℹ	Visitors' Centre

0 metres   500

0 yards   500

Round tower at Glendalough

Some traces of Romanesque moulding are visible outside the east window. Following the path along the south bank of the river, you reach the Upper Lake. This is the site of more monastic ruins and is also the chief starting point for walks through the valley and to a number of abandoned lead and zinc mines.

Situated in a grove not far from the Poulanass waterfall are the ruins of the **Reefert Church**, a simple Romanesque building. Its unusual name is a corruption of *Righ Fearta*, meaning "burial place of the kings"; the church may mark the site of an ancient cemetery. Near here, on a rocky spur overlooking the Upper Lake, stands **St Kevin's Cell**, the ruins of a beehive-shaped structure which is thought to have been the hermit's home.

There are two sites on the south side of the lake which cannot be reached on foot but are visible from the opposite shore. **Teampall-na-Skellig**, or the "church on the rock", was supposedly built on the site of the first church that St Kevin founded at Glendalough. To the east of it, carved into the cliff, is **St Kevin's Bed**. This small cave, in reality little more than a rocky ledge, may have been used as a tomb in the Bronze Age, but it is more famous as St Kevin's favourite retreat. It was from here that the saint allegedly rejected the advances of a naked woman by tossing her into the lake.

St Kevin at Glendalough

St Kevin was born in 498, a descendant of the royal house of Leinster. He rejected his life of privilege, however, choosing to live instead as a hermit in a cave at Glendalough. He later founded a monastery here, and went on to create a notable centre of learning devoted to the care of the sick and the copying and illumination of manuscripts. St Kevin attracted many disciples to Glendalough during his lifetime, but the monastery became more celebrated as a place of pilgrimage after his death in around 618.

Colourful legends about the saint make up for the dearth of facts about him. That he lived to the age of 120 is just one of the stories told about him. Another tale claims that one day, when St Kevin was at prayer, a blackbird laid an egg in one of his outstretched hands. The saint remained in the same position until it was hatched.

Avondale House 14

Co Wicklow. **0404 46111.** 🚆 🚌 *to Rathdrum.* **House** ◯ *daily.* Good Fri & 23–28 Dec. 🎟 **Grounds** ◯ *daily.*

LYING JUST south of Rathdrum, Avondale House was the birthplace of the 19th-century politician and patriot, Charles Stewart Parnell *(see p47)*. The Georgian mansion is now a museum dedicated to Parnell and the fight for Home Rule.

The state owns Avondale and runs a forestry school here, but the public is free to explore the grounds. Known as **Avondale Forest Park**, the former estate includes an impressive arboretum first planted in the 18th century and much added to since 1900. There are some lovely walks through the woods, with pleasant views along the River Avonmore.

Browne's Hill Dolmen 15

Co Carlow. 🚆 🚌 *to Carlow.* ◯ *daily.*

IN A FIELD 3 km (2 miles) east of Carlow, along the R726, stands a dolmen boasting the biggest capstone in Ireland. Weighing a reputed 100 tonnes, this massive stone is embedded in the earth at one end and supported at the other by three much smaller stones. Dating back to 2000 BC, Browne's Hill Dolmen is thought to mark the tomb of a local chieftain. A path leads to it from the road.

Browne's Hill Dolmen, famous for its enormous capstone

Street-by-Street: Kilkenny ⑯

Kilkenny coat of arms

KILKENNY is undoubtedly Ireland's loveliest inland city. It rose to prominence in the 13th century, when the Irish Parliament often met at Kilkenny Castle. The Anglo-Norman Butler family came to power in the 1390s and held sway over the city for 500 years. Their power has gone but their legacy is visible in the city's historic buildings, many of which have been restored. Kilkenny is proud of its heritage and every August hosts the Republic's top arts festival.

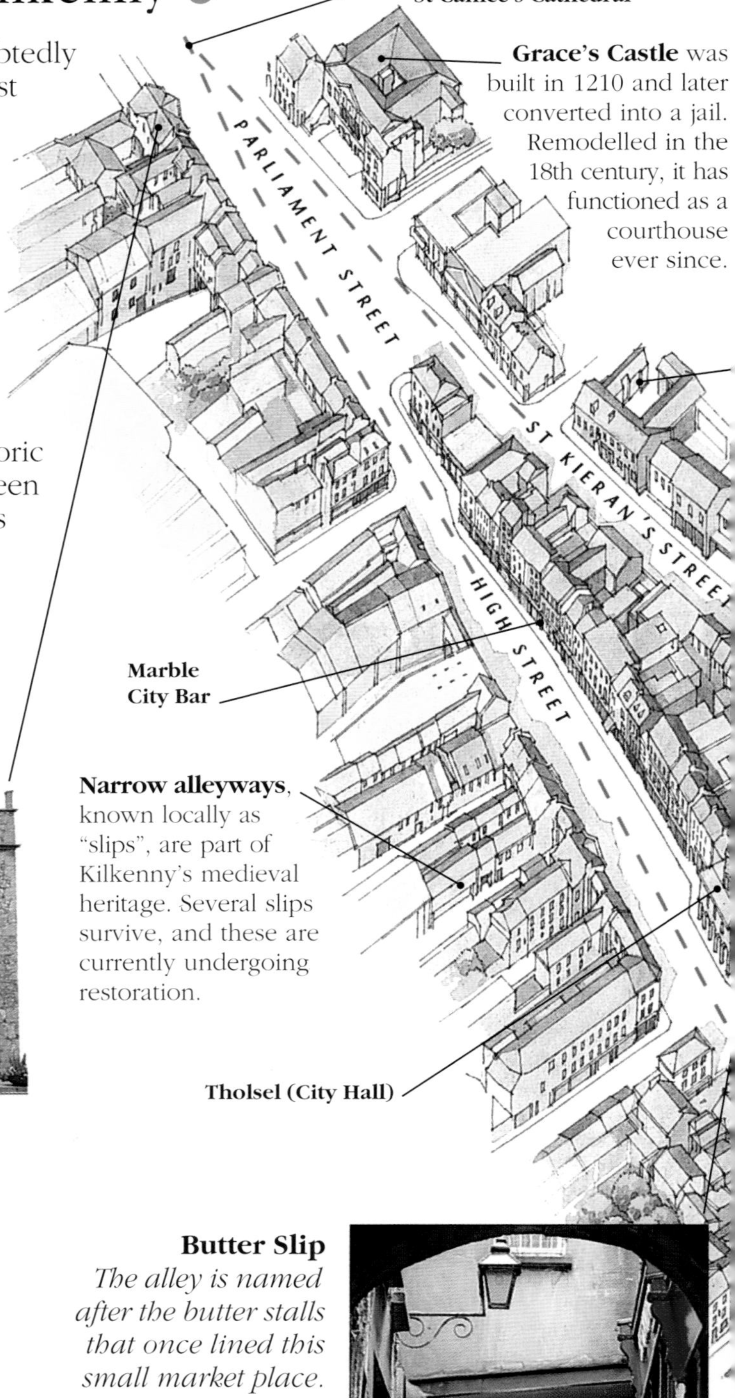

To Irishtown, St Canice's Cathedral

Grace's Castle was built in 1210 and later converted into a jail. Remodelled in the 18th century, it has functioned as a courthouse ever since.

PARLIAMENT STREET

ST KIERAN'S STREET

HIGH STREET

Marble City Bar

Narrow alleyways, known locally as "slips", are part of Kilkenny's medieval heritage. Several slips survive, and these are currently undergoing restoration.

Tholsel (City Hall)

★ Rothe House
This fine Tudor merchant's house, built around two court-yards, is fronted by arcades once typical of Kilkenny's main streets. A small museum inside the house contains a display of local archaeological artifacts and a costume collection.

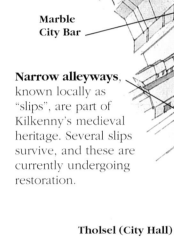

Butter Slip
The alley is named after the butter stalls that once lined this small market place.

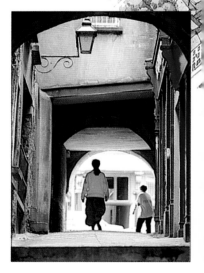

View of the High Street
The 18th-century Tholsel, with its distinctive clock tower and arcade, is the main landmark on the High Street. Its elegant Georgian chamber is used by city councillors to this day.

STAR SIGHTS

★ **Kilkenny Castle**

★ **Rothe House**

Kyteler's Inn

This medieval coaching inn is named after Dame Alice Kyteler, a 14th-century witch who once lived in the building. Like most of the pubs in the city, Kyteler's Inn sells Smithwick's beer, which has been brewed in Kilkenny since 1710.

The Shee Almshouse is one of Ireland's few surviving Tudor alms-houses. Inside, the Cityscope Exhibition illustrates life in 17th-century Kilkenny using a model of the city.

St Mary's Hall

St John's Bridge

To train and bus stations, Dublin

★ **Kilkenny Castle**
Set in a commanding position overlooking the River Nore, this Norman fortress is one of Ireland's most famous castles. The Long Gallery, the finest room in the house, has a striking 19th-century hammer beam and glass roof.

CANAL SQ

NORE

ROSE INN STREET

THE PARADE

PATRICK STREET

To Cork, Waterford

0 metres 50
0 yards 50

KEY

P	Parking
i	Tourist information
– – –	Suggested route

Kilkenny Design Centre
Housed in Kilkenny Castle's stable block, the centre has a nationwide reputation. You can see craftspeople in action and also buy their work.

Exploring Kilkenny

In a lovely spot beside a kink in the River Nore, Kilkenny is of great architectural interest, with much use made of the distinctive local black lime-stone, known as Kilkenny marble. A tour of the town also reveals many unexpected treasures: a Georgian façade often seems to conceal a Tudor chimney, a Classical interior or some other surprise.

The survival of the Irishtown district, now dominated by St Canice's Cathedral, recalls past segregation in Kilkenny. The area once known as English-town still boasts the city's grandest public buildings.

As a brewery city, Kilkenny is a paradise for keen drinkers. Not counting the popular private drinking clubs, there are about 80 official pubs.

North side of Kilkenny Castle showing Victorian crenellations

Sign of the Marble City Bar on Kilkenny's High Street

♠ Kilkenny Castle

The Parade. 📞 *056 21450.*
◯ *Apr–Sep: daily; Oct–Mar: Tue–Sun.* ● *10 days at Christmas.* 🎫
🎫 *obligatory.* ♿ *limited.*
Built in the 1190s, Kilkenny Castle was occupied right up until 1935. The powerful Butler family *(see p166)* lived in it from the late 14th century, but because of the exorbitant run-ning costs, their descendants eventually donated Kilkenny Castle to the nation in 1967. With its drum towers and solid walls, the castle retains its

medieval form, but has under-gone many alterations. The Victorian changes made in Gothic Revival style have had the most enduring impact, and are even more impressive since recent restoration work. The castle is a tremendously popular sight, so be prepared to queue during the summer.

High spots of a tour include the library, the wood-panelled dining room and the Chinese bedroom. Best of all, however, is the Long Gallery, rebuilt in the 1820s to house the Butler art collection. Its elaborate painted ceiling has a strong Pre-Raphaelite feel, with many of the motifs inspired by the *Book of Kells (see p72).*

The castle grounds have shrunk over the centuries, but the French Classical gardens remain, with terraces opening onto a woodland walk and pleasant rolling parkland.

♦ St Canice's Cathedral

Irishtown. ◯ *daily.* **Donation.** ♿
The hilltop cathedral, flanked by a round tower that you can climb for a good view over Kilkenny, was built in the 13th century in an Early English

Gothic style. It was sacked by Cromwell's forces in 1650, but has survived as one of Ireland's medieval treasures. Walls of the local Kilkenny marble and pil-lars of pale sandstone combine to create an interior of simple grandeur. There is a finely sculpted west door, but the cream of the carving lies inside. An array of splendid 16th-century tombs includes the beautiful effigies of the Butler family in the south transept.

♦ Black Abbey

Abbey St. 📞 *056 21279.* ◯ *daily.* ♿
Lying just west of Parliament Street, this Dominican abbey was founded in 1225. It was turned into a courthouse in the 16th century, but is once again a working monastery. The church boasts a fine vaulted undercroft and distinctive, though perhaps over-restored, stonework. There are also some beautiful stained-glass windows, several of which date back to the 14th century.

ENVIRONS: Just north of the town lies **Dunmore Cave**, a limestone cavern with an impressive series of chambers, noted for its steep descent and curious rock formations.

Bennettsbridge, on the Nore 8 km (5 miles) south of Kilkenny, is famous for its ceramics. The Nicholas Mosse Pottery specializes in colourful earthenware made from the local clay.

⚒ Dunmore Cave

Ballyfoyle. 📞 *056 67726.*
◯ *Mar–Oct: daily; Nov–Feb: Sat, Sun & public hols.* 🎫

Tomb of 2nd Marquess of Ormonde in St Canice's Cathedral

Jerpoint Abbey 🄗

Thomastown, Co Kilkenny. ☎ 056 24623. 🚃 🚌 to Thomastown. ○ Mar–Nov: daily. 🖼 🎫 ♿

LYING ON THE BANKS of the Little Arrigle just south of Thomastown, Jerpoint Abbey ranks among the finest Cistercian ruins in Ireland, despite the loss of many of its domestic buildings. Founded in about 1160, the fortified medieval complex rivalled nearby Duiske Abbey (see p175) in prestige. Jerpoint flourished until the Dissolution of the Monasteries (see pp40–1), when it passed to the Earl of Ormonde.

The 15th-century cloisters have not survived as well as some earlier parts of the abbey. Even so, they are the highlight of Jerpoint, with their amusing sculptures of knights, courtly ladies, bishops and dragons. The church itself is well preserved. The Irish-Romanesque transepts date back to the earliest period and contain several 16th-century tombs with exquisite stylized carvings. The north side of the nave is also intact, with a rich array of decorated Romanesque capitals. There are tombs and effigies of early bishops and patrons throughout the abbey. The battlemented crossing tower was added during the 1400s.

Stylized carving of saints on 16th-century tomb in Jerpoint Abbey

Lismore 🄘

Co Waterford. 🚹 1,100. 🚌 🛈 Apr–Oct: Lismore Heritage Centre (058 54975).

THIS GENTEEL riverside town is dwarfed by **Lismore Castle**, perched romantically above the River Blackwater. Built in 1185 but re-modelled in the 19th century, the castle is the Irish seat of the Duke of Devonshire and is closed to the public. However, you can visit the sumptuous gardens, which include a lovely riverside walk. **Lismore Heritage Centre** tells the story of St Carthage, who founded a monastic centre here in the 7th century. The town has two cathedrals dedicated to him. The Protestant **Cathedral of St Carthage** is the more interesting. It dates from 1633 but incorporates older elements and was later altered to suit the Neo-Gothic tastes of the Victorians. There is some fine

Burne-Jones window in St Carthage's Cathedral, Lismore

Gothic vaulting, and two stained-glass windows in the south transept are by the Pre-Raphaelite artist, Sir Edward Burne-Jones.

⛲ **Lismore Castle Gardens** ☎ 058 54424. ○ Easter–Sep: daily (pm only). 🖼

ENVIRONS: From Lismore you can follow a picturesque route through the **Blackwater Valley** (see p215). This runs from Cappoquin, in an idyllic woodland setting just east of Lismore, down to the estuary at Youghal (see p217).

Ardmore 🄙

Co Waterford. 🚹 450. 🚌 🛈 May–Sep: Main St (024 94444).

ARDMORE is a popular seaside resort with a splendid beach, lively pubs, good cliff walks and some interesting architecture. The hill beside the village, which provides fine views of the beach, is the site of a monastery established in the 5th century by St Declan, the first missionary to bring Christianity to this area.

Most of the buildings, including the ruined **St Declan's Cathedral**, date from the 12th century. The cathedral's west wall has fine Romanesque sculptures, arranged in a series of arcades. The scenes include The *Archangel Michael Weighing Souls* in the upper row, and below this *The Adoration of the Magi* and *The Judgment of Solomon*.

The adjacent round tower is one of the best preserved examples in Ireland, and rises to a height of 30 m (95 ft). An oratory nearby is said to mark the site of St Declan's grave.

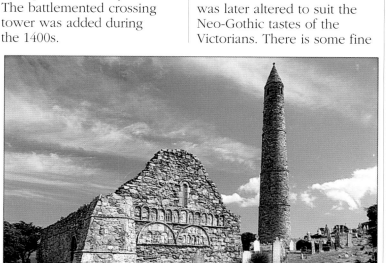
St Declan's Cathedral at Ardmore, with its near-perfect round tower

Johnston Castle, County Wexford ▷

Waterford ⑳

Waterford city coat of arms

WATERFORD WAS FOUNDED in 853 by the Vikings and later extended by the Anglo-Normans. Set in a commanding position by the estuary of the River Suir, it became southeast Ireland's main seaport. From the 18th century, the city's prosperity was consolidated by local industries, including the glassworks for which Waterford is famous. The strong commercial tradition persists today and Waterford's port is still one of Ireland's busiest. While the city has been somewhat tarnished by industrialization, great efforts are now being made to salvage what remains of its heritage, with further excavations of the old Viking city and the creation of pedestrian precincts in the historic quarter.

Reginald's Tower on the quayside

Jenkin's Lane, a quiet corner of Waterford off George's Street

Exploring Waterford

The extensive remains of the city walls clearly define the area originally fortified by the Vikings. The best-preserved section runs northwest from the **Watch Tower** on Castle Street, although Reginald's Tower, overlooking the river, is the largest structure in the old defences. In the Reginald Bar you can see the arches through which boats sallied forth down the river; these sallyports are one of several Viking sections of the largely Norman fortifications.

Although Waterford retains its medieval layout, most of the city's finest buildings are Georgian. Some of the best examples can be seen on the Mall, which runs southwest from Reginald's Tower, and in the lovely Cathedral Square. The latter takes its name from **Christchurch Cathedral**,

which was built in the 1770s to a design by John Roberts, a local architect who contributed much to the city's Georgian heritage. It is fronted by a fine Corinthian colonnade. A grim 15th-century effigy of a rotting corpse is an unexpected sight inside. Heading down towards the river, you pass the 13th-century ruins of **Grey Friars**, often known as the French Church after it became a Huguenot chapel in 1693.

West along the waterfront, a Victorian clock tower stands at the top of Barronstrand Street. Rising above the busy shops is the **Holy Trinity Cathedral**, which has a rich Neo-Classical interior. George's Street, which runs west from here, is dotted with period houses and cosy pubs. It leads to O'Connell Street, whose partially restored warehouses contrast with the shabbier buildings on the quay. In the summer, you can enjoy another view of the waterfront by taking a cruise on the river.

⚓ **Reginald's Tower**
The Quay. 〔 *051 304220.*
◯ *Apr–Oct: daily.*
The Vikings erected a tower on this spot in 1003, but it was the Normans who built the solid structure you see now. With impregnable walls 3 m (10 ft) thick, it is said to be the first Irish building to use mortar, a primitive concoction of blood, lime, fur and mud. The tower has in its time been a fortress, a mint, an arsenal and a prison. It also contains Waterford's civic museum.

🏛 **Waterford Heritage Museum**
Grey Friars St. 〔 *051 871227.*
◯ *Apr–Oct: daily; Nov–Mar: Mon–Fri.*
This excellent museum tells the story of Waterford using models and a reconstruction of the early city. It has a fine display of Viking and medieval artifacts which were discovered during recent excavations.

View of the city of Waterford across the River Suir

⛰ Waterford Crystal Factory

Kilbarry. ☎ *051 373311.* ◐ *Apr–Oct: daily; Nov–Mar: Mon–Fri.* 📷 ♿ ✓

A visit to the Waterford Crystal Factory, just 2.5 km (1.5 miles) south of the centre, is strongly recommended for the insight it gives into the city's special process of crystal-making.

The original glass factory was founded in 1783 by two brothers, George and William Penrose, who chose Waterford because of its port. For many decades their crystal enjoyed an unrivalled reputation, but draconian taxes caused the firm to close in 1851. A new factory was opened in 1947, however, and master blowers and engravers were brought from the Continent to train local apprentices. Competition from Tipperary and Galway Crystal hit sales in the early 1990s, but these have revived recently, largely due to an upturn in the North American market.

Visitors can follow all stages of production, observing the process by which sand, lead and potash are transformed by fire into sparkling crystal. The main difference between ordinary glass and crystal is the latter's high lead content, 30 per cent in Waterford's case. The glass-blowers require great skill to create walls of the right thickness to take the heavy incisions typical of Waterford Crystal. The factory's other main hallmark is the Waterford signature, which is engraved on the base of each piece.

In the gallery showroom, a crystal chandelier lights up a dining table laden with Wedgwood pottery and Waterford glass, tempting visitors to buy.

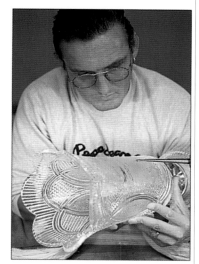

Craftsman engraving a vase at the Waterford Crystal Factory

VISITORS' CHECKLIST

Co Waterford. 👥 *44,000.*
✈ *10 km (6 miles) S.* 🚉 *Plunkett Station, The Bridge (051 873401).* 🚌 *Plunkett Station (051 879000).* ℹ️ *41 The Quay (051 875788).* 🖂 *(051 21723): Jun–Aug.* 🏛 *Fri.* 🎭 *International Festival of Light Opera (Sep).*

Ballyhack port, across Waterford Harbour from Passage East

ENVIRONS: The small port of **Passage East**, 12 km (7 miles) east of Waterford, witnessed the landing of the Normans in 1170 *(see p40)*, but little has happened since. A car ferry links the village to Ballyhack in County Wexford, providing a scenic shortcut across Waterford Harbour as well as an excellent entry point to the Hook Peninsula *(see p174).*

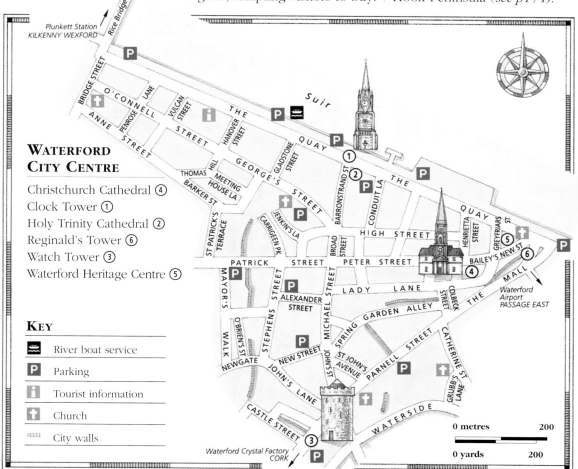

WATERFORD CITY CENTRE

Christchurch Cathedral ④
Clock Tower ①
Holy Trinity Cathedral ②
Reginald's Tower ⑥
Watch Tower ③
Waterford Heritage Centre ⑤

KEY

🚤	River boat service
🅿	Parking
ℹ️	Tourist information
✝	Church
⫞⫞⫞	City walls

0 metres 200
0 yards 200

Dunmore East ㉑

Co Waterford. 🚶 *1,500.* ▣

THE APPEAL of Dunmore East, Waterford's most charming fishing village, lies chiefly in its red sandstone cliffs and bustling harbour. Paths run along the foot of the cliffs, but for the best views take the road that winds uphill from the beach, past tidy cottages and the ivy-clad Ship Inn to the Haven Hotel. A gate nearby leads to delightful gardens overlooking the fishing boats below. If you climb further, up steps cut into the rock, then you will be rewarded by views of the cliffs and noisy kittiwake colonies.

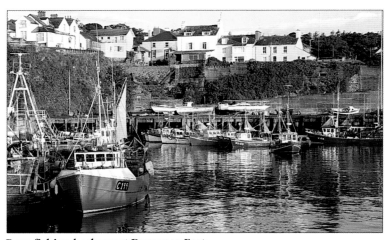
Busy fishing harbour at Dunmore East

Hook Peninsula ㉒

Co. Wexford. ▣ *to Duncannon.* ⛴ *from Passage East to Ballyhack (051 382480).* ⓘ *Fethard-on-Sea (051 397502).*

THIS TAPERING HEADLAND of gentle landscapes scattered with ancient ruins and quiet villages is perfect for a circular tour. The "Ring of Hook" route begins south of New Ross at **Dunbrody Abbey**, the ruins of a 12th-century Cistercian church, but **Ballyhack** is another good place to start. Once a fortified crossing point into County Waterford, the town still has a ferry service to neighbouring Passage East *(see p173)*. **Ballyhack Castle**, built by the Knights Templar in about 1450, contains a small museum. About 4 km (2.5 miles) beyond is the small

resort of **Duncannon**, with a broad sandy beach and a star-shaped fort, which was built in 1588 in expectation of an attack by the Spanish Armada.

The coast road continues south to **Hook Head**. Here, perched on red sandstone, sits what is almost certainly the oldest lighthouse in Europe, dating from 1172. Paths skirt the coast, which attracts many seabirds and seals and is also famous for its fossils.

Just 2 km (1.5 miles) east is the picturesque village of **Slade**. A ruined 15th-century tower house, **Slade Castle**, presides over the tiny harbour where fishing boats cluster around the slipways. The road proceeds along the rugged coastline, past the resort of Fethard-on-Sea and Saltmills to the dramatic ruin of **Tintern Abbey**. This 13th-century Cistercian foundation was built by William Marshall, Earl of Pembroke, in fulfilment of a vow made when his boat was caught in a storm off the coast nearby. The west end has been restored, but excavation work

continues. Fields lead to an old stone bridge and views over **Bannow Bay**, where it is thought the Normans made their first landing in 1169.

🏚 **Dunbrody Abbey**
Campile. 📞 *051 388603.* ○ *Apr–Sep: daily.* 📷
⚓ **Ballyhack Castle**
Ballyhack. 📞 *051 389468.* ○ *Jun–Sep: daily.*

Norman lighthouse at Hook Head, on the tip of the Hook Peninsula

New Ross ㉓

Co Wexford. 🚶 *6,000.* ▣ ⓘ *mid-Jun–Aug: The Quay (051 421857).* 🛒 *Tue.* **Galley Cruising Restaurants** *The Quay (051 421723).*

LYING ON the banks of the River Barrow, New Ross is one of the oldest towns in the county. Its importance, now as in the past, stems from its status as a port. In summer there is much activity on the river. Cruises run by Galley Cruising Restaurants ply both the Barrow and Nore rivers. Traditional shopfronts line the streets, which rise steeply

Castle ruins and harbour at Slade on the Hook Peninsula

from the quayside. The **Tholsel**, now the town hall but originally a tollhouse, was occupied by the British during the 1798 rebellion *(see pp44–5)*. Opposite, a monument to a Wexford pikeman commemorates the bravery of the Irish rebels who faced the British cannons.

Nearby is **St Mary's** which, when founded in the 13th century, was the largest parish church in Ireland. A modern church occupies the site, but the original (now roofless) south transept remains, as do many medieval tombstones.

ENVIRONS: A popular trip up the meandering Barrow goes 16 km (10 miles) north to **Graiguenamanagh**. The main attraction of this market town is **Duiske Abbey**, the largest Cistercian church in Ireland. Founded in 1207, it has been extensively restored and now acts as the parish church. The most striking features include a Romanesque door in the south transept, the great oak roof and traces of a medieval pavement below floor level. There is also a cross-legged statue of the Knight of Duiske, which is one of the finest medieval effigies in Ireland. Outside are two 9th-century granite High Crosses.

Trips along the Nore take you to **Inistioge**. Lying in a deep, wooded valley, this is an idyllic village, with neat 18th-century houses, a square planted with lime trees and a ten-arched bridge spanning the Nore. On a rock above the river stands a ruined Norman fort, a popular place for picnics.

From Inistioge you can walk along the river or up to **Woodstock House Demesne**, a national park. Among the beech woods stands an 18th-century mansion, reduced to a ruin by a fire in 1922.

On a hill 12 km (7.5 miles) south of New Ross, a large area of woodland is enclosed within the **John F Kennedy Park and Arboretum**. Founded in 1968, near the late president's ancestral home in Dunganstown, the park boasts more than 4,500 types of tree and provides splendid panoramic views. There are marked paths and nature trails, and it is also possible to go horse riding.

View over Enniscorthy and St Aidan's cathedral from Vinegar Hill

🛡 **Duiske Abbey**
Graiguenamanagh, Co Kilkenny.
📞 *0503 24238.* ⬜ *daily.* ♿
🌿 **John F Kennedy Park and Arboretum**
New Ross, Co Wexford. 📞 *051 388171.* ⬜ *daily.* ⬤ *Good Fri & 25 Dec.* 📷 ♿

Enniscorthy ㉔

Co Wexford. 🚹 *5,000.* 🚌 🚆 ℹ️
The Castle (054 34699).

T‍HE STREETS of Enniscorthy, on the banks of the River Slaney, are full of character and redolent of the town's turbulent past. In 1798, Enniscorthy witnessed the last stand of the Wexford pikemen, when a fierce battle was fought against a British force of 20,000 on nearby **Vinegar Hill**. The events of that year are told in full at the excellent County Museum inside **Enniscorthy Castle** – an imposing presence in the town, founded by the Normans but altered in the 16th century. Enniscorthy's other main sight is the Neo-Gothic **St Aidan's Cathedral**, designed in the 1840s by AWN Pugin (1812–52), who is most famous for his work on the Houses of Parliament in London.

Granaries and mills overlook the Slaney, along with several potteries for which the town is famous. Carley's Bridge was founded in 1654 and is still producing terracotta pots.

Enniscorthy's historic pubs are another big attraction. They include the Antique Tavern, a half-timbered building which is hung with pikes used during the Battle of Vinegar Hill in 1798.

⛪ **Enniscorthy Castle**
Castle Hill. 📞 *054 35926.*
⬜ *daily (Oct–Dec: pm only).*
📷 ♿ *limited.*

The inland port of New Ross seen from the west bank of the River Barrow

View across the harbour to Wexford town

Irish National Heritage Park 25

Ferrycarrig, Co Wexford. 🚌 *from Wexford in summer.* 📞 *053 20733.* ◯ *Mar–Oct: daily.* 📷 ✉ ♿

BUILT ON former marshland near Ferrycarrig, just north of Wexford, the Irish National Heritage Park is a bold open-air museum. Trails lead visitors through woods to replicas of homesteads, places of worship and burial sites. These provide a good introduction to the country's ancient history *(see pp36–7)*, and the section which deals with the Celtic period is particularly interesting. Other highlights include the Viking boatyard, complete with raiding ship, and a 7th-century horizontal watermill.

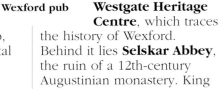

Sign of a popular Wexford pub

Wexford 26

Co Wexford. 🚶 *17,000.* 🚌 🚆 ℹ️ *Crescent Quay (053 23111).*

WEXFORD'S name derives from *Waesfjord*, a Norse word meaning "estuary of the mud flats". It thrived as a port for centuries but the silting of the harbour in the Victorian era put an end to most sea traffic. Wexford's quays, from where ships once sailed to Bristol, Tenby and Liverpool, are now used mainly by a fleet of humble mussel dredgers.

Wexford is a vibrant place, packed with fine pubs and boasting a varied arts scene.

The town's singular style is often linked to its linguistic heritage. The *yola* dialect, which was spoken by early settlers, survives in the local pronunciation of certain words.

Wexford retains few traces of its past, but the Viking fishbone street pattern still exists, with narrow alleys fanning off the meandering Main Street. Keyser's Lane, linking South Main Street with the lively Commodore pub on Paul Quay, is a tiny tunnel-like Viking alley which once led to the Norse waterfront. The Normans were responsible for Wexford's town walls, remnants of which include one of the original gateways. This houses the **Westgate Heritage Centre**, which traces the history of Wexford. Behind it lies **Selskar Abbey**, the ruin of a 12th-century Augustinian monastery. King Henry II is said to have done penance here for ordering the murder of Thomas à Becket in 1170.

Wexford also has several handsome buildings dating from a later period, including the 18th-century market house, known as the **Cornmarket**, on Main Street. The nearby square, the **Bull Ring**, is notable only for its history: it was used for bull-baiting in Norman times and was the scene of a cruel massacre by Cromwell's men in 1649.

Wexford Opera Festival, held in October, is the leading operatic event in the country. Aficionados praise it for its intimate atmosphere – both

during performances and afterwards, when artists and audience mingle together in the pubs: the Centenary Stores off Main Street is a favourite, though the Wren's Nest, on Custom House Quay, is better for traditional music.

🏛 **Westgate Heritage Centre**
Westgate. 📞 *053 46506.* ◯ *Mon–Sat (Sat am only).* ● *25 & 26 Dec.* 📷 ♿

ENVIRONS: Skirting the shore just east of the town is the **Wexford Wildfowl Reserve**. It covers 100 ha (250 acres) of reclaimed land and is noted in particular for its geese: over a third of the world's entire population of Greenland whitefronted geese winter here between October and April.

The mudflats also attract large numbers of swans and waders, and provide a rich hunting ground for birds of prey. The birds can be viewed from a number of hides and an observation tower.

🐦 **Wexford Wildfowl Reserve**
Wexford. 📞 *053 23129.* ◯ *daily.* 🚗 *at weekends.*

Johnstown Castle 27

Co Wexford. 📞 *053 42888.* 🚌 🚆 *to Wexford.* **Gardens** ◯ *daily.* ● *24 & 25 Dec.* 📷

Façade of Johnstown Castle

JOHNSTOWN CASTLE, a splendid Gothic Revival mansion, lies amid ornamental gardens and mature woodland 6 km (4 miles) southwest of Wexford. In state hands since 1945, the house now functions as an

Vast crescent of sand and shingle beach at Rosslare

agricultural research centre. It is not open to the public, but it is possible to visit the **Irish Agriculture Museum**, housed in the castle's farm buildings. Reconstructions illustrate the work of a wheelwright and other traditional trades.

The real glory of Johnstown Castle are the grounds, from the sunken Italian garden and ornamental lakes to the woodlands and shrubberies. Azaleas and camellias flourish alongside an impressive array of trees including Japanese cedars, redwoods and Scots pine.

Hidden among the dense woods west of the house lurk the ruins of **Rathlannon Castle**, a medieval tower house.

🏛 Irish Agriculture Museum
Johnstown Castle. ◯ *Apr–mid-Nov: daily (Sat & Sun pm only); mid-Nov–Mar: Mon–Fri.* 🖾 ♿ *limited.*

Saltee Islands ㉘

Co Wexford. 🚌 *from Wexford to Kilmore Quay: Wed & Sat.* ⛴ *from Kilmore Quay: Apr–Sep (weather permitting).* 📞 *053 29684.*

THESE ISLANDS off the south coast of Wexford are a haven for sea birds. Great and Little Saltee together form Ireland's largest bird sanctuary, nurturing an impressive array of birds, from gannets and gulls to puffins and Manx shearwaters. Great Saltee particularly is famous for its colonies of cormorants. It also

has more than 1,000 pairs of guillemots and is a popular stopping-off place for spring and autumn migrations. A bird-monitoring and research programme is in progress, and a close watch is also kept on the colony of grey seals.

The two uninhabited islands are privately owned, but visitors are welcome. Boat trips are run in fine weather from **Kilmore Quay**. These leave in late morning and return mid-afternoon.

Kilmore Quay is a small fishing village built on rare Precambrian gneiss rock – the oldest rock in Ireland. Pretty thatched cottages nestle above a fine sandy beach and the harbour, where a moored lightship houses a **Maritime Museum**. The boat's original fittings are just as interesting as the exhibits.

🏛 Maritime Museum
Kilmore Quay. 📞 *053 29655.* ◯ *Jun–Oct: daily (pm only); Nov–May: by appt.* 🖾

Rosslare ㉙

Co Wexford. 🚶 *1,200.* 🚇 🚌 ℹ *Kilrane, Rosslare Harbour (053 33623).*

ROSSLARE REPLACED Wexford as the area's main port after the decline of the original Viking city harbour. The port is so active today that people tend to associate the name Rosslare more with the ferry terminal for France and Wales than with the town lying 8 km (5 miles) further north.

Rosslare town is one of the sunniest spots in Ireland and draws many holidaymakers. It boasts a fine beach stretching for 9.5 km (6 miles), lively pubs and an excellent golf course fringed by sand dunes. There are good walks north to Rosslare Point.

ENVIRONS: At Tagoat, 6 km (4 miles) south of Rosslare, **Yola Farmstead** displays traditional crafts such as thatching, glass-blowing and bread-and butter-making.

🏛 Yola Farmstead
Tagoat. 📞 *053 31177.* ◯ *Mar, Apr & Nov: Mon–Fri; May–Oct: daily.* 🖾 ♿

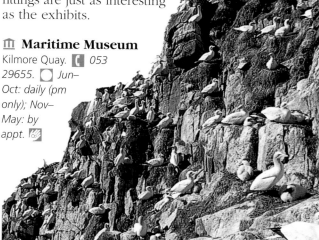

Colony of gannets nesting on the cliffs of Great Saltee Island

Eye-catching façades in the Great Island town of Cobh ▷

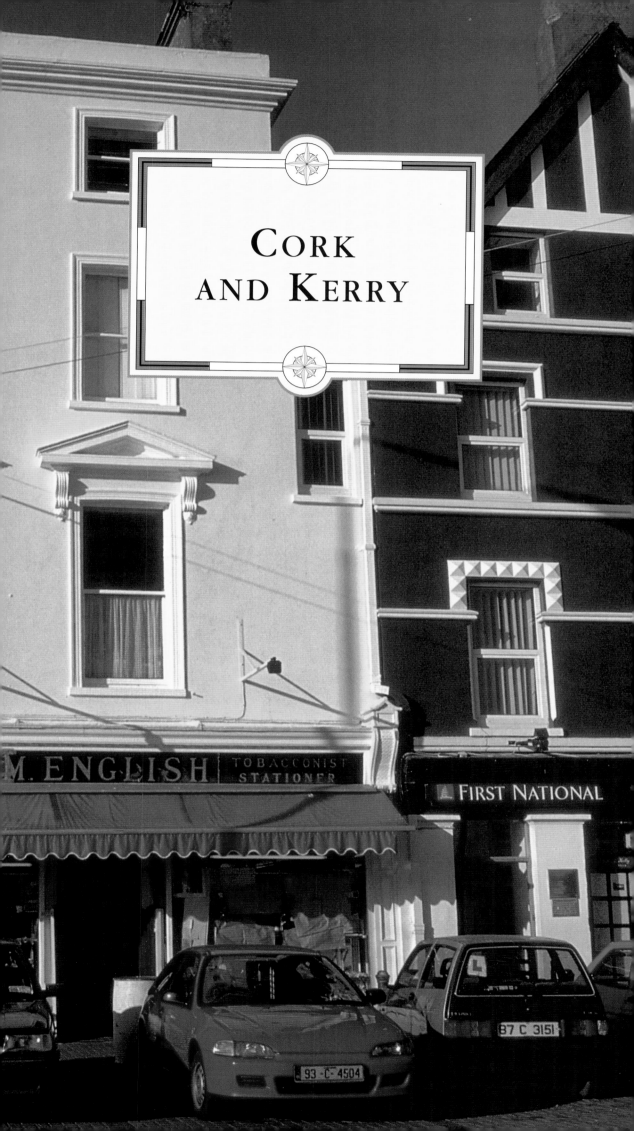

CORK
AND KERRY

CORK AND KERRY

CORK · KERRY

THE MAGNIFICENCE *of this region's scenery has long attracted visitors. Rocky headlands jut dramatically out into the Atlantic and colourful fishing villages nestle in the shelter of the bays. County Kerry offers stunning landscapes and a wealth of prehistoric and early Christian sites, whereas County Cork's gentle charm has seduced many a casual visitor into becoming a permanent resident.*

This region is one of the most popular in Ireland and features some of its most famous attractions. Hundreds of people each day kiss the Blarney Stone at Blarney Castle, just a few miles north of Cork city, and the whole region has very fine scenery. Killarney, with its romantic lakes and stunning Muckross House, is a magnet for tourists, as are the beautiful coastal towns and villages, the lush, verdant valleys and the rich agricultural land of Cork, Ireland's largest county. Kerry is wilder and more mountainous, but by no means less beautiful.

Although visitors to Cork and Kerry tend to concentrate on the coastline, inland areas such as Gougane Barra, where mountains overlook valleys and woodlands, will certainly repay exploration. A further attraction is the strong Gaelic culture and long tradition of arts and crafts which flourish throughout the region.

This corner of Ireland used to be the main point of contact with continental Europe. In the 17th century, in response to the threat of French and Spanish invasions, the English built forts along the Cork coast, including Charles Fort at Kinsale. The town had been the scene of a battle in 1601 in which the defeat of the Irish and their Spanish allies re-established English rule in the area. Descendants of the English 1st Earl of Bantry still live in Bantry House at the head of Bantry Bay. Kinsale's continental influence endures: the restaurants around its harbour are presided over by some of Europe's top chefs.

In the 19th century, the city of Cork became a departure point for people fleeing the Famine, with Cobh serving as the main port for emigrants hoping for a better life the New World.

Extreme poverty and proud temperament combined to cultivate a vigorous Republican spirit all over southwest Ireland.

Puffins on the island of Skellig Michael off the rugged coast of Kerry

◁ **Beach at Barley Cove near Mizen Head, County Cork**

Street life in Casement Square, Cobh

fronted Georgian buildings, down the colourful side streets or along the quays of the River Lee that flows through the centre of town. The river was not damned until the early 19th century, and many of modern Cork's main streets were actually under water until that time. Though its sights can be seen in a day, the nightlife, the people and the atmosphere certainly make it worth a longer stay.

West of town, the river meanders through the woods and farmland of the Lee Valley from its source in Gougane Barra, Ireland's first designated forest park. St Finbarr, founder and patron saint of Cork city, lived on the island in the middle of the lake and there is now a chapel here.

Killarney National Park, ho **of the three Lakes of Killarr**

Local people were very much involved in guerrilla activity in the Irish War of Independence and in the subsequent bloody Civil War.

Cork's status as a port has diminished but it is still the Republic's second city, and Corkonians are known for their canny business sense and prosperity. The lively arts scene and the creative and intellectual energy surrounding one of the country's main universities have given this city a cultural sophistication that rivals Dublin. Cork is vibrant but not hectic and is ideal for strolling – along the main artery of St Patrick street with its bow-

The smooth Caha Mountains form the backbone of the Beara and mark the county line between Cork and Kerry. A tiny road winds up the mountainside to the Healy Pass where there are wonderful views over both counties. Inland, the "tunnel" road crosses the mountains between Glengarriff and the delightful town of Kenmare, which is situated between the Beara Peninsula and the Ring of Kerry, and is a good base for exploration. The River Blackwater flows east from Kerry through a

The mining town of Allihies on the remote Beara Peninsula

wooded valley and offers excellent trout fishing. It then turns south to reach the sea at the historic town of Youghal on the eastern Cork border.

The southwest coast is made up of a string of rocky peninsulas jutting into the Atlantic to create some stunning seascapes. On stormy days, with the waves

A rustic scene on the winding road of the Caha mountains

crashing against the shore, the scenery is dramatic, rivalling the more famous Ring of Kerry to the northwest. Allow plenty of time to explore these headlands as the roads do become progressively narrower and rougher, but the effort is repaid with some spectacular views, such as those from the lighthouse at Mizen Head or from the tip of the Beara Peninsula. Along the way there are many villages, for example Baltimore, Schull and Clonakilty, which are market towns and yachting centres.

Kerry is known as "the Kingdom" because of its tradition of independence and disregard for Dublin rule, and all Irish people are well aware of the distinctive Kerry character, with its boisterous *joie de vivre*.

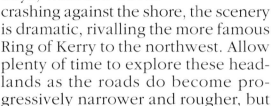
A typical Irish pub in Dingle, Kerry

Navigator, who may have been the first European to reach the New World. The ruins of the cathedral at Ardfert still stand on the site of his 6th-century monastery. There is a stunning drive between the mountains and the sea to the mainland's most westerly point at Dunmore Head, with the Blasket Islands just offshore. The western half of the peninsula is a Gaeltacht area rich in Gaelic culture, and Dingle is famous for its traditional music. Cork and Kerry both mount festivals, including Bantry's Oyster Festival and Killorglin's Puck Fair. The Rose of Tralee festival, held in Kerry's capital, has developed from being a local beauty pageant into an event of international renown. The area also has a strong sporting tradition, with Kerrymen being generally regarded as the country's finest Gaelic footballers.

Ross Castle, Killarney

The Ring of Kerry draws visitors with its mountains and coastal scenery, and although the islands off the Kerry coast appear bleak and inhospitable, many were once inhabited. Rocky Skellig Michael was the site of a 6th-century Christian monastery. The region also offers much earlier remains, such as Staigue Fort, one of Ireland's best preserved Iron Age forts. The Dingle Peninsula is especially rich in archaeology, from the promontory fort at Dunbeg to the early Christian Gallarus Oratory. A son of this area was St Brendan the

Waves blasting against Sybil Head on the stunning Dingle Peninsula

The Irish and the Sea

Galway Bay oyster

IRELAND HAS A HISTORY, and a character, shaped by the sea. An island at the westernmost edge of Europe, it has from its earliest days been open to outside influences from marine traders and invaders. Its people have learned to contend with the Atlantic swell, while for explorers and emigrants the ocean was the passage to a New World. The economy has reaped the benefits of the sea through fishing, leisure and tourism.

Tattered by Atlantic waves and gales, *the western coastline presents scenery that is as varied as it is stunning.*

The threat of invasion by Napoleon in the 18th century prompted the construction of Martello Towers on the south coast. Unlike the Celts, Vikings and Anglo-Normans, he never arrived.

Atlantic gales proved fatal to the defeated Spanish Armada, sent by Philip II of Spain to invade England in 1588. This ship's bell is one of many relics and treasures recovered from the vessels wrecked off the west coast of Ireland.

The sighting of whales is one of the saga's authentic details

THE VOYAGE OF SAINT BRENDAN

The most astonishing sea voyage ever undertaken by Irishmen was that of St Brendan and his fellow monks early in the 6th century, searching the Atlantic for the legendary Island of the Blessed. Descriptions of encounters with whales, ice floes and volcanic islands, if fancifully embellished, were immortalized in a saga which, translated into Latin, became popular all over medieval Christian Europe.

BOATS ANCIENT AND MODERN

The narrow currach (the Celtic word for a coracle), its width determined by the hides that originally covered the frame, is still very much in use as a working boat. Rosslare cots, built from planks of wood and flat-bottomed to negotiate the muddy Wexford estuary, and Galway hookers (traditional wooden sailing boats) are now used solely for pleasure. Passenger and freight ferries are vital modes of transport for tourism and commerce.

Detailed model of a Rosslare cot

Primitive, circular coracle or 'currach

Fishing has always been an important element in the Irish economy and the heavily laden trawler returning from a trip out to sea is still a common sight in many coastal villages. Meanwhile, fish-farming of salmon and shellfish is increasing in the estuaries and bays.

One month's supply of food and drink was carried on board the boat.

All the rules of monastic life were strictly observed by the monks during voyages.

The tall prow of the currach was designed to withstand the Atlantic swell.

The hull was constructed by stretching 49 oxhides taut over a frame of ash wood, with willow or hazel supporting rods.

Yacht racing is a popular tradition in Cork. In the 19th and early 20th centuries the harbour was a busy port of call for transatlantic liners. It was also the principal departure point for the hundreds of thousands of emigrants to America.

GBR9019

Tim Severin's currach, Brendan

THE EPIC RE-CREATED

In 1977 Tim Severin and crew set out across the Atlantic in this sea-going currach, aiming to re-create St Brendan's voyage. Severin made the boat using only materials that would have been available to the monks. Like them, he set sail from Fenit, Co. Kerry, and he reached Newfoundland. His journal, *The Brendan Voyage*, tells how he and his crew witnessed many sights described in the *Navigatio Sancti Brendani Abbatis*.

Currach: canvas now replaces hides

Galway hooker

Island ferry: vital link to the mainland

Exploring Cork and Kerry

KILLARNEY IS A POPULAR BASE with tourists for exploring Cork and Kerry, especially for touring the Ring of Kerry and the archaeological remains of the Dingle Peninsula. Despite the changeable weather, the region attracts many visitors who come to see its dramatic scenery and lush vegetation. As you pass through quiet fishing villages and genteel towns, such as Kenmare, you will always encounter a friendly welcome from the locals. For the adventurous there are plenty of opportunities to go riding, hiking or cycling. Cork city offers a more cosmopolitan atmosphere, with its art galleries and craft shops.

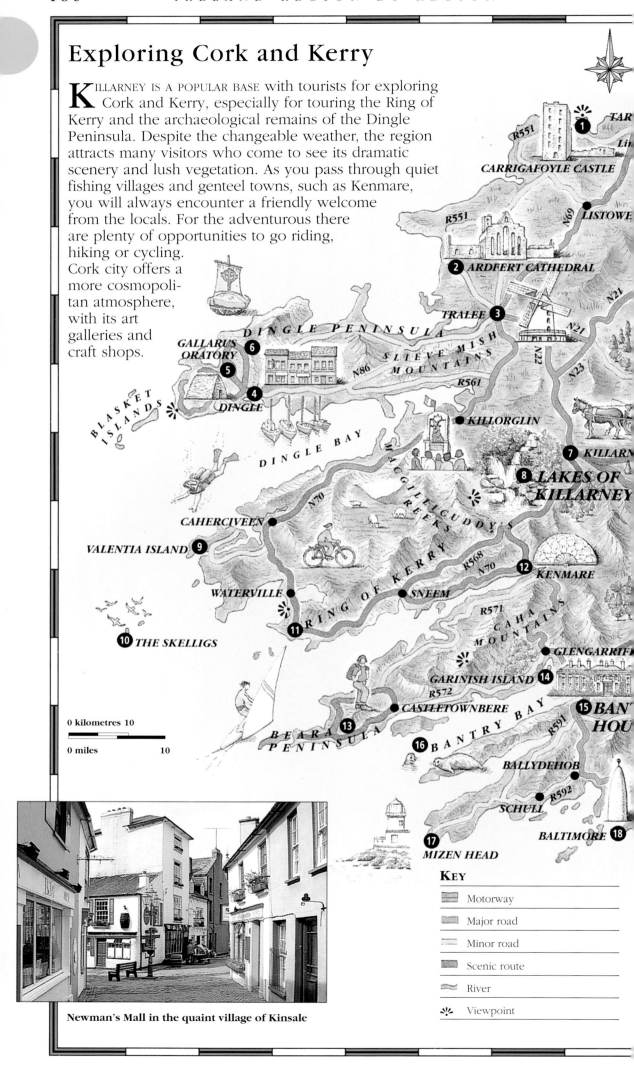

1 CARRIGAFOYLE CASTLE

R551

R551   N69   LISTOWE

2 ARDFERT CATHEDRAL

TRALEE **3**

N21

N21

N22

N23

DINGLE PENINSULA

GALLARUS ORATORY **6**

5

4 DINGLE

SLIEVE MISH MOUNTAINS

N86

R561

BLASKET ISLANDS

KILLORGLIN

DINGLE BAY

MACGILLICUDDY'S REEKS

7 KILLARN

8 LAKES OF KILLARNEY

CAHERCIVEEN

N70

VALENTIA ISLAND **9**

RING OF KERRY

WATERVILLE

11

SNEEM

R568

N70

12 KENMARE

R571

CAHA MOUNTAINS

10 THE SKELLIGS

GLENGARRIF

GARINISH ISLAND **14**

R572

CASTLETOWNBERE

13

BEARA PENINSULA

16 BANTRY BAY

R591

15 BAN HOU

BALLYDEHOB

SCHULL   R592

BALTIMORE **18**

17 MIZEN HEAD

0 kilometres 10

0 miles   10

KEY

▦	Motorway
▦	Major road
▦	Minor road
▦	Scenic route
≈	River
☀	Viewpoint

Newman's Mall in the quaint village of Kinsale

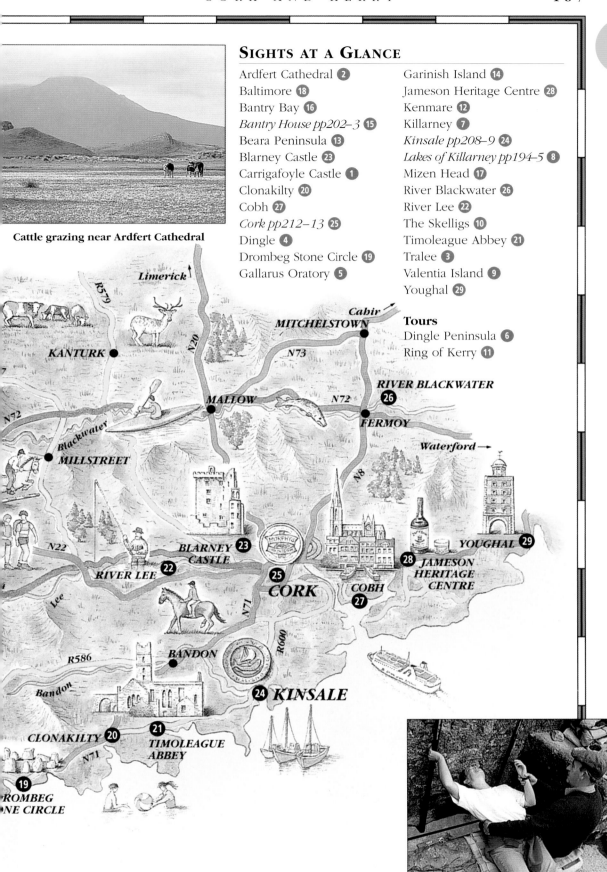

Cattle grazing near Ardfert Cathedral

SIGHTS AT A GLANCE

Ardfert Cathedral **2**
Baltimore **18**
Bantry Bay **16**
Bantry House pp202–3 **15**
Beara Peninsula **13**
Blarney Castle **23**
Carrigafoyle Castle **1**
Clonakilty **20**
Cobh **27**
Cork pp212–13 **25**
Dingle **4**
Drombeg Stone Circle **19**
Gallarus Oratory **5**

Garinish Island **14**
Jameson Heritage Centre **28**
Kenmare **12**
Killarney **7**
Kinsale pp208–9 **24**
Lakes of Killarney pp194–5 **8**
Mizen Head **17**
River Blackwater **26**
River Lee **22**
The Skelligs **10**
Timoleague Abbey **21**
Tralee **3**
Valentia Island **9**
Youghal **29**

Tours
Dingle Peninsula **6**
Ring of Kerry **11**

Kissing the Blarney Stone at
Blarney Castle near Cork

GETTING AROUND

To explore the region a car is essential. The N22 connects Cork, Killarney and Tralee while the N71 follows the coastline via Clonakilty, Bantry and on to Killarney. In the more remote parts the road signs may only be written in Irish. Killarney is the base for organized coach tours of the area. The train service from Cork to Dublin is efficient, and trains also connect Killarney with Dublin and Cork, but you may have to change trains en route. Buses run throughout the region, but services to the smaller sights may be infrequent.

Ardfert Cathedral and the ruins of Teampall na Hoe and Teampall na Griffin

Carrigafoyle Castle ❶

Co Kerry. 🚌 to Listowel.

Ruined keep of Carrigafoyle Castle

HIGH ABOVE the Shannon estuary, just west of Ballylongford, this 15th-century castle belonged to the O'Connor clan, who ruled much of northern Kerry. The English besieged or sacked it repeatedly but the body blow was delivered in 1649 by Cromwellian forces *(see p43)*. The ruins include a keep and walled courtyard, with romantic views of the estuary from the top of the tower.

Ardfert Cathedral ❷

Co Kerry. 🚌 to Ardfert. 📞 066 34711. ◯ May–mid Sep: daily; rest of year on request. 🖐 ♿

THIS COMPLEX of churches is linked to the cult of St Brendan the Navigator *(see p275)*, who was born nearby

in 484 and founded a monastery here. The ruined cathedral dates back to the 12th century and retains a delicate Romanesque doorway and blind arcading. Inside, an effigy of a 14th-century bishop occupies a niche in the northwestern corner. In the graveyard stand the remains of a Romanesque nave-and-chancel church, Teampall na Hoe, and a late Gothic chapel, Teampall na Griffin. The latter is named after the curious griffins carved beside an interior window.

A short walk away are the ruins of a Franciscan friary. It was founded by Thomas Fitzmaurice in 1253, but the cloisters and south chapel date from the 15th century.

ENVIRONS: Just northwest of Ardfert is **Banna Strand**. Irish patriot Roger Casement landed here in 1916 on a German U-boat, bringing in rifles for the Easter Rising *(see pp48–9)*. He was arrested as soon as he landed and a memorial stands

on the site of his capture. This beach was also used for the filming of David Lean's *Ryan's Daughter* (1970).

Tralee ❸

Co Kerry. 👥 22,000. 🚌 🚊 ℹ Ashe Memorial Hall, Denny St (066 21288). 🛒 Thu.

HOST TO the renowned Rose of Tralee International Festival *(see p53)*, Tralee has made great strides in promoting its cultural and leisure facilities. The town's main attraction is **Kerry County Museum** with its theme park, "Kerry the Kingdom". It offers three exhibitions: an audio-visual show on Kerry scenery; a display of archaeological finds and interactive models; and a "time travel experience" through Anglo-Norman Tralee, complete with medieval smells.

Also based in Tralee is the **Siamsa Tíre** folklore theatre, an internationally celebrated

Steam train on the narrow gauge railway between Tralee and Blennerville, with Blennerville Windmill in the background

ambassador for Irish culture. Traditional song and dance performances take place here throughout the summer.

Just outside Tralee is the authentic **Blennerville Windmill**. Built in 1800, it is Ireland's largest working mill and one of Tralee's most popular attractions. The **Steam Railway** connects Blennerville with Tralee along a narrow gauge track. There are trips on the train with multilingual commentary, from Ballyard Station to the windmill.

Kerry County Museum
Ashe Memorial Hall, Denny St.
066 27777. mid-Mar–Dec: daily. 25 & 26 Dec.

Siamsa Tire
Town Park. *066 23055.* for performances only May–Sep.

Blennerville Windmill
066 21064. Apr–Oct: daily.

Steam Railway
Ballyard Station. *066 21064.* May–early Oct: daily.

Dingle ❹

Co Kerry. 1,500. Mar–Nov: Main St (066 51188). Sat.

THIS ONCE REMOTE Irish-speaking town has become a thriving fishing port and an increasingly popular tourist centre. Brightly painted craft shops and cafés abound, often with slightly hippy overtones.

Dingle Bay is attractive with a somewhat ramshackle harbour lined with fishing trawlers. Along the quayside are lively bars offering music and seafood. The harbour is home to Dingle's biggest star: Fungie, the dolphin, who has been a permanent resident since 1983 and can be visited by boat or on swimming trips.

Although Dingle has few architectural attractions, it makes an engaging base for exploring the archaeological remains on the Dingle Penin-sula *(see pp190–91)*.

Gallarus Oratory, a dry-stone early Christian church

Gallarus Oratory ❺

Co Kerry. to Dingle.

SHAPED LIKE an upturned boat, this miniature church overlooks Smerwick harbour. Gallarus was built some time between the 6th and 9th centuries and is the best preserved early Christian church in Ireland. It represents the apogee of dry-stone corbelling, using techniques first developed by Neolithic tomb-makers. The stones were laid at a slight angle, lower on the outside than the inside, allowing water to run off.

Fishing trawlers moored alongside the quay at Dingle

A Tour of the Dingle Peninsula ⑥

GUINNESS
Mar is gnách

Pub sign,
Ballyferriter

THE DINGLE PENINSULA offers some of Ireland's most beautiful scenery. To the north rises the towering Brandon Mountain, while the west coast has some spectacular seascapes. A drive around the area, which takes at least half a day, reveals fascinating antiquities ranging from Iron Age stone forts to inscribed stones, early Christian oratories and beehive huts. These are sometimes found on private land, so you may be asked for a small fee by the farmer to see them. Some parts of the peninsula – especially the more remote areas – are still Gaelic speaking, so many road signs are written only in Irish.

View from Clogher Head

Riasc (An Riasc) ⑦
This excavated monastic settlement dates from the 7th century. The enclosure contains the remains of an oratory, several crosses and an inscribed pillar stone *(see p325)*.

**Ballyferriter
(Baile an Fheirtéaraigh) ⑥**
The attractions of this friendly village include the pastel-coloured cottages, Louis Mulcahy's pottery and a museum featuring the cultural heritage of the area.

**Blasket Centre
(Ionad an Bhlascaoid) ⑤**
Overlooking Blasket Sound, the centre explains the literature, language and way of life of the inhabitants of the Blasket Islands. The islanders moved to the mainland in 1953.

*Dunquin
(Dún Chaoin)*

*Mount
Eagle*

R559

BLASKET ISLANDS

Blasket Sound

Clogher Head

DINGLE BA

**Dunmore Head
(Ceann an Dúin Mhóir) ④**
Mainland Ireland's most westerly point offers dramatic views of the Blaskets.

**Slea Head
(Ceann Sléibe) ③**
As you round the Slea Head promontory, the Blasket Islands come into full view. The sculpture of the Crucifixion beside the road is known locally as the Cross *(An Cros)*.

KEY

▬▬	Tour route
═══	Other roads
☀	Viewpoint

0 kilometres   2

0 miles   1

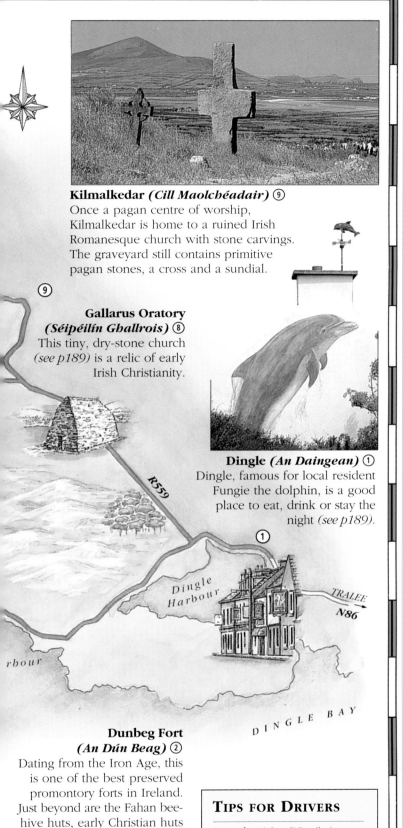

Kilmalkedar *(Cill Maolchéadair)* ⑨

Once a pagan centre of worship, Kilmalkedar is home to a ruined Irish Romanesque church with stone carvings. The graveyard still contains primitive pagan stones, a cross and a sundial.

Gallarus Oratory *(Séipéilín Ghallrois)* ⑧

This tiny, dry-stone church *(see p189)* is a relic of early Irish Christianity.

Dingle *(An Daingean)* ①

Dingle, famous for local resident Fungie the dolphin, is a good place to eat, drink or stay the night *(see p189)*.

Dunbeg Fort *(An Dún Beag)* ②

Dating from the Iron Age, this is one of the best preserved promontory forts in Ireland. Just beyond are the Fahan bee-hive huts, early Christian huts thought to have been built for pilgrims visiting the area.

TIPS FOR DRIVERS

Length: 40 km (25 miles).
Stopping-off points: Most villages on the route, for example Dunquin and Ballyferriter, have friendly bars offering pub meals. There are also many opportunities to stop for a picnic. On the winding coast road around Slea Head stop only at the safe and clearly marked coastal viewing points.

Jaunting cars waiting to take visitors to sights around Killarney

Killarney ❼

Co Kerry. 👥 *9,500.* 🚉 🚌 ℹ️ *Beech Road (064 31633).*

KILLARNEY is commonly derided as "a tourist town" but this has not dented the town's open, cheerful atmosphere. The infectious Kerry humour is personified by the wise-cracking jarveys whose families have run jaunting cars (pony and trap rides) here for generations. The town does get crowded in summer but has much to offer, with shops open until 10pm in summer, several excellent restaurants, and a sprinkling of prestigious hotels around the lake and the heights. From the town visitors can explore the sights around the Lakes of Killarney *(see pp194–5)* and the surrounding heather-covered hills.

ENVIRONS: Overlooking the lakes and a short drive from Killarney is **Muckross House**. This imposing Victorian mansion was built in 1843 in Elizabethan style. Inside, the elegant rooms are decorated with period furnishings. There is also a museum of Kerry Life, with displays on the history of southwest Ireland, and a craft centre with numerous workshops. The landscaped gardens are especially beautiful in spring when the rhododendrons and azaleas are in bloom. A short walk away is Muckross Farm – a working farm which still uses traditional farming techniques.

🏛 **Muckross House**
4 km (2.5 miles) S of Killarney.
📞 *064 31440.* ◯ *daily.* ● *10 days at Christmas.* 🎨 📷 ♿ ✍️

Stunning mountain scenery near Moll's Gap on the Ring of Kerry ▷

Lakes of Killarney 8

Fruit of the strawberry tree

Renowned for its splendid scenery, the area is one of Ireland's most popular tourist attractions. The three lakes are contained within Killarney National Park. Although the landscape is dotted with ruined castles and abbeys, the lakes are the focus of attention: the moody watery scenery is subject to subtle shifts of light and colour. The area has entranced many artists and writers including Thackeray, who praised "a precipice covered with a thousand trees ... and other mountains rising as far as we could see". In autumn, the bright red fruits of the strawberry tree colour the shores of the lakes.

Meeting of the Waters
This beauty spot, best seen from Dinis Island, is where the waters from the Upper Lake meet Muckross Lake and Lough Leane. At the Old Weir Bridge, boats shoot the rapids.

Long Range River

Torc Waterfall
The Owengarriff River cascades through the wooded Friars' Glen into Muckross Lake. A pretty path winds up to the top of this 18-m (60-ft) high waterfall, revealing views of Torc Mountain.

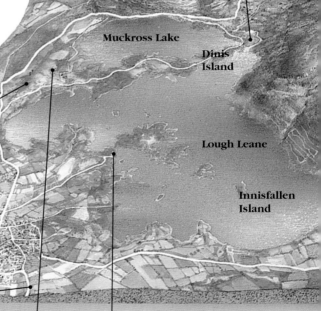

Muckross Lake

Dinis Island

Lough Leane

Innisfallen Island

Muckross Abbey was founded by the Franciscans in 1448, but was burnt down by Cromwellian forces in 1653.

Killarney *(see p191)* is the main town from which tourists visit the sights around the lakes.

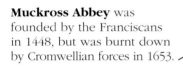

N22 to Tralee *(see pp188–9)*

Ross Castle, built around 1420, was the last stronghold under Irish control to be taken by Cromwellian forces in 1653.

★ **Muckross House**
The 19th-century manor (see p191) enjoys a lovely location overlooking the lakes. Visit the wildlife centre for an introduction to the flora and fauna of the National Park.

Upper Lake
This narrow lake is the smallest of the three lakes. It flows into the Long Range River to the Meeting of the Waters.

VISITORS' CHECKLIST

Killarney, Co Kerry. ✈ *Kerry (066 64644).* 🚌 🚏 **National Park** ◯ *9am–6pm (6:30pm Jun–Aug) daily (for access by car).* ℹ *Killarney (064 31633).* **Muckross House** 📞 *064 31440.* ◯ *9am–6pm (5:30pm Nov–Mar) daily.* ⬤ *25 Dec–1 Jan.* 🎫 📷 🍴 🎪 **Ross Castle** 📞 *064 35851.* ◯ *Mar–Apr: 11am–6pm Tue–Sun; May–Sep: 9am–6pm daily; Oct: 9am–5pm daily.* 🎫 🎫 *obligatory.* ⛴ *from Ross Castle:* **Destination Killarney** *(064 32638): daily (weather permitting);* **The Lily of Killarney** *(064 31068): Mar–Oct.* **Kate Kearney's Cottage** 📞 *064 44146.* ◯ *Easter–Sep: 9am–midnight daily; Oct–Easter: 9:30am–6pm.* 🍴 🎪

Ladies' View gets its name from the delight it gave Queen Victoria's ladies-in-waiting when they visited the spot in 1861.

N71 to Moll's Gap and Kenmare *(pp196–200)*

Upper Lake

Purple Mountain, 832 m (2,730 ft)

★ **Gap of Dunloe**
Glaciers carved this dramatic mountain pass which is popular with walkers, cyclists and horse riders. The route through the gap offers fabulous views of the boulder-strewn gorge and three small lakes.

Tomies Mountain, 735 m (2,411 ft)

Kate Kearney's Cottage was home to a local beauty who ran an illegal drinking house for passing travellers in the mid-19th century.

R562 to Killorglin *(see pp196–7)*

0 kilometres   2

0 miles   1

STAR SIGHTS

★ **Muckross House**

★ **Gap of Dunloe**

Lough Leane
The largest lake is dotted with un-inhabited islands and fringed with wooded slopes. Boat trips run between Ross Castle and Innisfallen.

Valentia Island ⑨

Co Kerry. 🚌 *to Caherciveen.* ℹ️
Caherciveen (066 72589).

ALTHOUGH it feels like the mainland, Valentia is an island, albeit linked by a causeway to Portmagee. It is 11 km (7 miles) long and noted for its water sports, seascapes and views

Stairway leading to Skellig Michael monastery

from Geokaun Mountain. Valentia is also popular for its proximity to the Skellig Islands which lie around 15 km (10 miles) southwest of the Iveragh Peninsula.

The **Skellig Experience Centre**, near the causeway linking Valentia to the mainland, houses an audiovisual display about the construction and history of the monastery on Skellig Michael, the largest of the Skellig Islands. Other subjects covered include sea birds and the marine life around the islands, a reminder that the Skellig cliffs lie underwater for a depth of 50 m (165 ft), providing a habitat for giant basking sharks, dolphins and turtles. The centre also operates cruises around the islands.

The main village on Valentia is **Knightstown**, which offers accommodation and lively pubs with music and dancing.

The first transatlantic cable was laid from the southwest point of the island to Newfoundland, Canada, in 1866.

🏛 **Skellig Experience Centre**
Valentia Island. 📞 *066 76306.*
🕐 *Apr–mid-Nov: daily.* 📷 ♿

The Skelligs ⑩

Co Kerry. 🚢 *Apr– Oct: from Valentia Island.* 📞 *066 77156 (ring two or three days ahead).*

SKELLIG MICHAEL, also known as Great Skellig, is an inhospitable pinnacle of rock rising out of the Atlantic and covering an area of 17 ha (44 acres). Perched on a ledge almost 218 m (714 ft) above sea level and reached by an amazing 1,000-year-old

---

A Tour of the Ring of Kerry ⑪

THIS LONG-ESTABLISHED ROUTE around the Iveragh Peninsula, which can be taken in either direction, is always referred to as the Ring of Kerry. Allow a day to see its captivating mountain and coastal scenery, dotted with slate-roofed fishing villages. Set out early to avoid the mass of coach tours which converge on the towns for lunch and tea. There are interesting detours across the spine of the peninsula.

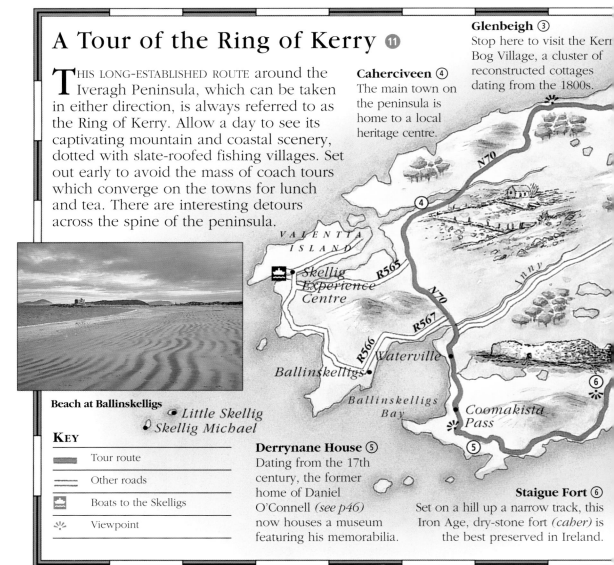

Beach at Ballinskelligs

Glenbeigh ③
Stop here to visit the Kerry Bog Village, a cluster of reconstructed cottages dating from the 1800s.

Caherciveen ④
The main town on the peninsula is home to a local heritage centre.

KEY

▬▬	Tour route
═══	Other roads
🚢	Boats to the Skelligs
☀	Viewpoint

Derrynane House ⑤
Dating from the 17th century, the former home of Daniel O'Connell *(see p46)* now houses a museum featuring his memorabilia.

Staigue Fort ⑥
Set on a hill up a narrow track, this Iron Age, dry-stone fort *(caher)* is the best preserved in Ireland.

stairway is an isolated early Christian monastery. Monks settled for solitude on Skellig Michael during the 6th century, building a cluster of six corbelled beehive cells and two boat-shaped oratories. These dry-stone structures are still standing, despite being raked by storms over the centuries. The monks were totally self-sufficient, trading eggs, feathers and seal meat with passing boats in return for cereals, tools and animal skins. The skins were needed to produce the vellum on which the monks copied their religious manuscripts. They remained on this bleak island until the 12th century, when they retreated to the Augustinian priory at Ballinskelligs on the mainland.

Today the only residents on Skellig Michael are the thousands of sea birds which nest

Gannets flying around the precipitous cliffs of Little Skellig

and breed on the high cliffs, including storm petrels, puffins and Manx shearwaters. The huge breeding colonies are protected from predators by the sea and rocky shores.

Slightly closer to the mainland is Little Skellig. Covering an area of 7 ha (17 acres), the island has steep cliffs. Home to a variety of sea birds, it has one of the largest colonies of gannets (about 22,000 breeding pairs) in the British Isles.

A cruiser from Valentia Island circles the Skelligs but does not dock. Except for a pier on Skellig Michael, there are no proper landing stages on the islands. This is to discourage visitors from disturbing the birdlife, fragile plant cover and archaeological remains.

Atlantic gales permitting, local fishermen may run unofficial trips around the islands from Portmagee or Ballinskelligs, during the summer.

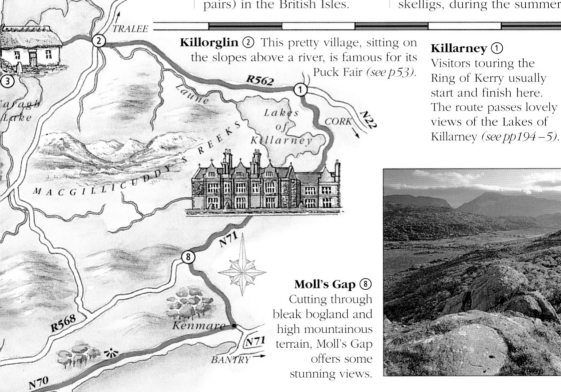

Killorglin ② This pretty village, sitting on the slopes above a river, is famous for its Puck Fair *(see p53)*.

Killarney ①
Visitors touring the Ring of Kerry usually start and finish here. The route passes lovely views of the Lakes of Killarney *(see pp194–5)*.

Moll's Gap ⑧
Cutting through bleak bogland and high mountainous terrain, Moll's Gap offers some stunning views.

Sneem ⑦
Brightly painted cottages line the streets of this charming town which also has a quaint village green.

0 kilometres 10

0 miles 5

TIPS FOR DRIVERS

Length: 180 km (112 miles).
Stopping off points: Many towns such as Killorglin or Caherciveen offer pub snacks. Finish the day in one of the excellent gourmet restaurants in Kenmare.

Lace making at Kenmare

Kenmare ⑫

Co Kerry. 🚶 *1,400.* 🚌 ℹ️ *Apr–Oct: Main St (064 41233).* 🛒 *Wed.*

THIS TOWN, on the mouth of the River Sheen, was founded in 1670 by William Petty, Cromwell's surveyor general. However, Kenmare's appearance owes more to his descendant, the first Marquess of Lansdowne who, in 1775, made it a model landlord's town of neat stone façades with decorative plasterwork.

Today Kenmare is renowned for its traditional lace. During the famine years, nuns from the local convent, St Clare's, introduced lace making to create work for the women and girls. Other attractions include the fine hotels and gourmet restaurants. The town is also an excellent base for exploring the Beara Peninsula and the Ring of Kerry *(see pp196–7)*.

Set in a riverside glade off Market Street is the **Druid's Circle**, a prehistoric ring of 15 stones associated with human sacrifice.

Beara Peninsula ⑬

Co Cork & Co Kerry. 🚌 *to Glengarriff & Castletownbere (Fri only).* ℹ️ *Castletownbere (027 70344).*

DOTTED WITH sparsely populated fishing villages surrounded by bleak moorland, this peninsula is remote. It used to be a refuge for smugglers, with the Irish getting the better deal in their exchange of pilchards for contraband French brandy.

The peninsula offers some spectacular scenery and wonderful walking country. From the **Healy Pass**, which cuts a jagged path across the spine of the Caha Mountains, there are some fine views of Bantry Bay and the rugged landscape of West Cork. To the west of the pass is **Hungry Hill**, the highest mountain in the Caha range and popular with hill walkers.

Encircled by the Caha and Slieve Miskish Mountains is **Castletownbere**, the main town on the peninsula. This sheltered port was once a haven for smugglers, but is now awash with foreign fishing trawlers. McCarthey's Bar on Town Square features an authentic matchmaking booth, where Cork families used to agree marriage terms until a generation ago.

West of Castletownbere stands the shell of **Puxley Mansion**, home of the Puxley family who owned the mines at nearby **Allihies**. Centre of the copper-mining district until the 1930s, it is now a desolate place, with tall Cornish-style chimneys and piles of ochre-coloured spoil; beware of unguarded mine shafts.

From the tip of the peninsula a cable car travels across to **Dursey Island**, with its ruined castle and colonies of sea birds. Licensed to carry three passengers and one cow, the cable car swings across the strait, offering views of Bull, Cow and Calf islands.

From the headland the R757 road back to Kenmare passes through the pretty villages of **Eyeries**, noted for its brightly painted cottages and crafts, and **Ardgroom**, which is a centre for mussel farming and a base for exploring the scenic glacial valley around **Glenbeg Lough**.

Garinish Island ⑭

Co Cork. ⛴️ *from Glengarriff.* **Gardens** 📞 *027 63040.* ⭕ *Mar–Oct: daily.* 📷 ♿ *limited.*

ALSO KNOWN as Ilnacullin, this small island was turned into an exotic garden in 1910 by Harold Peto for Annan Bryce, a Belfast businessman.

View of Caha Mountains from the Healy Pass, Beara Peninsula

◁ **Stunning mountain scenery near Moll's Gap on the Ring of Kerry**

Italianate garden with lily pool and folly on Garinish Island

Framed by views of Bantry Bay, the gardens are landscaped with Neo-Classical follies and planted with rich subtropical flora. The microclimate and peaty soil provide the damp, warm conditions needed for these ornamental plants to flourish.

Exotic shrubberies abound especially during the summer months. Throughout May and June, visitors can admire the beautiful camellia beds, azaleas and rhododendrons. There is also a New Zealand fernery and a Japanese rockery, as well as a rare collection of Bonsai trees. A Martello tower crowns the island and among the follies are a clock tower and a Grecian temple.

The centrepiece is a colonnaded Italianate garden, with a Classical folly and ornamental lily pool. Much of its charm resides in the contrast between the cultivated lushness of the garden and the glimpses of wild seascape and barren mountains beyond. An added attraction of the boat trip across to this Gulf Stream paradise is the chance to see cavorting seals in Bantry Bay.

Bantry House ⓯

See pp202–203.

Bantry Bay ⓰

Co Cork. 🚌 *to Bantry and Glengarriff.* ℹ️ *Jun–Sep: The Square, Bantry (027 50229).*

BANTRY BAY ENCOMPASSES the resorts of **Bantry** and **Glengarriff**. It is also a springboard for trips to Mizen Head and the Beara Peninsula.

Bantry nestles beneath the hills which run down to the bay. Just offshore you can see **Whiddy Island**, the original home of the White family, who moved to Bantry House in the early 18th century. Further along is **Bere Island**, a British base until World War II which still boasts Martello towers on its southern side.

Glengarriff at the head the bay, exudes an air of Victorian gentility with its neatly painted shopfronts and craft shops. On the coast is the Eccles Hotel, a haunt of Queen Victoria and where George Bernard Shaw supposedly wrote *Saint Joan*.

The wooded hinterland to the north of Glengarriff is set in a bowl of the Caha Mountains. There are some pleasant walks leading to waterfalls.

Mizen Head ⓱

Co Cork. 🚌 *to Goleen.* ℹ️ *Town Hall, North St, Skibbereen (028 21766).*

MIZEN HEAD, the most southwesterly tip of Ireland, has steep cliffs, which are often lashed by storms. Here, a lighthouse and new visitors' centre, **Mizen Vision**, are reached by a bridge across a rocky chasm. From the car park, a fine headland walk takes in views of vertiginous cliffs and Atlantic breakers. The sandy beaches of nearby **Barley Cove** attract bathers and walkers alike, and to the east is **Crookhaven**, a pretty yachting harbour. From here, a walk to Brow Head offers views of the lighthouse.

Mizen Head can be reached either from Bantry via Durrus or from the market town of **Skibbereen**, on the R592, via the charming crafts centre of **Ballydehob** and the village of **Schull**. Trips to Clear Island *(see p162)* leave from Schull.

🏛 **Mizen Vision**
Mizen Head. 📞 *028 35115.* ⬜ *Apr–Oct: daily; Nov–Mar: Sat & Sun.* 📷

Rocky cliffs at Mizen Head

Bantry House ⑮

BANTRY HOUSE has been the home of the White family, formerly Earls of Bantry, since 1739. The original house was built in 1720, but the north façade overlooking the bay was a later addition. Inside there is an eclectic collection of art and furnishings brought from all over Europe by the 2nd Earl of Bantry. In the carriage house and stable block behind the house is the French Armada Centre, which explains the events surrounding Wolfe Tone's attempted invasion in 1796.

William and Mary clock in anteroom

North façade

The anteroom contains family mementoes, china and a collection of 18th-century prints.

Loggia

To car park

Gobelins Room
The subject of this 18th-century Gobelins tapestry is The Bath of Cupid and Psyche. *The room also contains an early 19th-century piano.*

The Rose Garden, laid out in the early 18th century, is, in the words of the 1st Earl of Bantry, "a parterre after the English manner".

Tearoom and shop

1ST EARL OF BANTRY (1767–1851)

Richard White, 1st Earl of Bantry, played a leading role in defending Ireland against an attempted invasion by Wolfe Tone and the United Irishmen *(see pp44–5)*. On 16 December 1796, Tone sailed from Brest in Brittany with a fleet of 43 French ships bound for Ireland. White chose strategic spots around Bantry Bay and mustered volunteers to fight. His efforts proved unnecessary as the French fleet was forced back by bad weather. Nonetheless, White was rewarded with a peerage by George III for his "spirited conduct and important services". In 1801 he was made Viscount Bantry, becoming Earl of Bantry in 1816.

★ Dining Room
This room is dominated by portraits of King George III and Queen Charlotte by court painter, Allan Ramsay. The Spanish chandelier is decorated with Meissen china flowers.

Entrance hall

★ **Rose Room**
The rose-coloured tapestries (c. 1770) hanging in this room are thought to have been made for Marie Antoinette on her marriage to the Dauphin of France.

Statue of Diana (1840)

South façade

To 1796 French Armada Centre

Library

★ **View of House and Bantry Bay**
Bantry House enjoys a magnificent location overlooking Bantry Bay. This lovely view, from the terraces above the house, shows the harbour with Whiddy Island and the Caha Mountains beyond.

VISITORS' CHECKLIST

Bantry, Co Cork. 027 50047. from Cork to Bantry (Mon–Sat). late Mar–late Oct: 9am–6pm daily. 25 Dec. limited. **Concerts** (summer only). **1796 French Armada Centre** 027 51796. Apr–Sep: 10am–6pm daily (last adm: 5:40pm). limited. Joint tickets for entrance to the House and the Armada Centre are available.

STAR FEATURES

★ **View of House and Bantry Bay**

★ **Rose Room**

★ **Dining Room**

The steps, known as the "Staircase to the Sky", lead to a series of terraces with fabulous views over the house and across the bay.

Italian Garden
Inspired by the Boboli Gardens in Florence, this garden encircles a pool decorated in Classical Grotesque style. It was designed in the early 1850s by the 2nd Earl.

Baltimore ⑱

Co Cork. 👥 *220.* 🚌 ⛴ *to Sherkin Island (028 20125); to Clear Island (028 39159).*

BALTIMORE'S most bizarre claim to fame dates back to 1631 when more than 100 citizens were carried off as slaves by Algerian pirates. Now that the threat of being kidnapped has gone, this village appeals to the yachting fraternity and island-hoppers. Like neighbouring Schull and Castletownshend, the town bustles with summer festivals.

Overlooking the harbour is a ruined 15th-century castle, once the stronghold of the O'Driscoll clan. Also worth a visit are the seafood pubs, including Bushe's Bar, an atmospheric inn hung with nautical memorabilia. Behind the village, cliff walks lead to splendid views of Carbery's Hundred Isles – mere specks on Roaringwater Bay. Baltimore Beacon is an important marker for boats in the bay.

A short ferry ride away is **Sherkin Island** with its sandy beaches in the west, a ruined 15th-century abbey, marine station and pubs. The ferry ride to **Clear Island** is more dramatic, as the boat weaves between sharp black rocks to this remote, Irish-speaking island, noted for its bird observatory in the North Harbour. There are some spectacular views of the mainland from Clear Island.

Distinctive white beacon for boats approaching Baltimore

Drombeg Stone Circle, erected around the 2nd century BC

Drombeg Stone Circle ⑲

Co Cork. 🚌 *to Skibbereen or Clonakilty.*

SITUATED ON the Glandore road 16 km (10 miles) west of Clonakilty, Drombeg is the finest of the many stone circles in County Cork. Dating back to about 150 BC, this circle of 17 standing stones is 9 m (30 ft) in diameter. At the winter solstice, the rays of the setting sun fall on the flat altar stone which faces the entrance to the circle, marked by two upright stones.

Nearby is a small stream with a Stone Age cooking pit (*fulacht fiadh*), similar to one at Craggaunowen (*see p238*). A fire was made in the hearth and hot stones from the fire were dropped into the cooking pit to heat the water. Once the water boiled, the meat, usually venison, was added.

Clonakilty ⑳

Co Cork. 👥 *3,000.* 🚌 ℹ️ *Jun–Sep: Astna Street (023 33226) .*

FOUNDED as an English outpost around 1588, this market town has a typically hearty West Cork atmosphere. The **West Cork Regional Museum**, housed in an old schoolhouse, pays tribute to the town's industrial heritage. A number of the quayside buildings, linked to the town's

Sign for Clonakilty black pudding

industrial past, have been restored. Particularly pleasant is the neat Georgian nucleus of Emmet Square.

Until the 19th century Clonakilty was a noted centre of linen production. Today, however, it is renowned for its rich black puddings, hand-painted Irish signs and traditional music pubs. A short walk from the town centre is a model village exhibition, depicting Clonakilty as it was during the 1940s. Just east of town is the reconstructed **Lisnagun Ring Fort**, with earthworks, huts and souterrains (*see p24*). A causeway links Clonakilty to **Inchydoney** beach.

🏛 **West Cork Regional Museum**
Western Road. ⃝ *Mon–Sat.* 🚫 ♿

Timoleague Abbey ㉑

Co Cork. 🚌 *to Clonakilty or Courtmacsherry.* ⃝ *daily.*

TIMOLEAGUE ABBEY enjoys a waterside setting overlooking an inlet where the Argideen estuary opens into Courtmacsherry Bay. Founded around the late 13th century, the abbey is a ruined Franciscan friary. The buildings have been extended at various times. The earliest section is the chancel of the Gothic church. The most recent addition, the 16th-

◁ **Looking across the bay from Bantry House**

century tower, was added by the Franciscan Bishop of Ross. The friary was ransacked by the English in 1642 but much of significance remains, including the church, infirmary, fine lancet windows, refectory and a walled court-yard in the west. There are also sections of cloisters and wine cellars. In keeping with Franciscan tradition, the complex is plain to the point of austerity. Yet such restraint belied the friars' penchant for high living: the friary prospered on trade in Spanish wines, easily delivered thanks to its position on the then navigable creek.

Lancet window in ruined church at Timoleague Abbey

River Lee ㉒

Co Cork. 🚌 🚍 *to Cork.* ℹ️ *Cork (021 273251).*

CARVING A COURSE through farm- and woodland to Cork city *(see pp212–15)*, the River Lee begins its journey in the lake of the enchanting **Gougane Barra Park**. The shores of the lake are linked by a causeway to **Holy Island**, where St Finbarr, the patron saint of Cork, founded a monastery. The Feast of St Finbarr, on 25 September,

signals celebrations that climax in a pilgrimage to the island on the following Sunday.

The Lee flows through several Irish-speaking market towns and villages. Some, such as **Ballingeary**, with its fine lake-side views, have good angling. The town is also noted for its Irish language college. Further east, near the town of Inchigeela, stand the ruins of **Carrignacurra Castle**. Further downstream lies the Gearagh, an alluvial stretch of marsh and woods which has been designated a wildlife sanctuary.

The river then passes through the Sullane valley, home of the thriving market town of **Macroom**. The hulk of a medieval castle, with its restored entrance, lies just off the main square. In 1654, Cromwell granted the castle to Sir William Penn. His son, who was to found the American state of Pennsylvania, also lived there for a time.

Between Macroom and Cork, the Lee Valley passes through a hydroelectric power scheme surrounded by artificial lakes, water meadows and wooded banks. Just outside Cork, on the south bank of the river is **Ballincollig**, home to the fascinating Royal Gunpowder Mills museum *(see p215)*.

Blarney Castle ㉓

Blarney, Co Cork. 📞 *021 385252.* 🚌 *to Cork.* 🚌 *to Blarney.* ⬜ *daily.* ⬤ *24 & 25 Dec.* 📷 ♿

VISITORS from all over the world flock to this ruined castle to see the legeNndary Blarney Stone. Kissing the stone is a long-standing tradition which is intended to confer a magical eloquence. The stone is set in the wall below the castle battlements and, in order to kiss it, the visitor is grasped by the feet and suspended backwards under the parapet. Little remains of the castle today except the keep, built in 1446 by Dermot McCarthy. Its design is typical of a 15th-century tower house *(see p24)*. The vaulted first floor was once the Great Hall. To reach the battlements you need to climb the 127 steps to the top of the keep.

The castle grounds offer some attractive walks, including a grove of ancient yew trees and limstone rock formations at Rock Close. **Blarney House**, a Scottish baronial mansion and the residence of the Colthurst family since the 18th century, is not open to the public.

Just a short walk from the castle, Blarney also has a pretty village green with welcoming pubs and a number of craft shops. The **Blarney Woollen Mills,** selling quality garments and souvenirs, is well worth a visit.

Battlemented keep and ruined towers of Blarney Castle

Street-by-Street: Kinsale ㉔

Old office sign in Kinsale

FOR MANY VISITORS to Ireland, Kinsale heads the list of places to see. One of the prettiest small towns in Ireland, it has had a long and chequered history. The defeat of the Irish forces and their Spanish allies in the Battle of Kinsale in 1601 signified the end of the old Gaelic order. An important naval base in the 17th and 18th centuries, Kinsale today is a popular yachting centre. It is also famous for the quality of its cuisine – the town's annual Gourmet Festival attracts food lovers from far and wide. As well as its many wonderful restaurants, the town has pubs and wine bars to cater for all tastes.

Desmond Castle was built around 1500. It is known locally as the "French Prison".

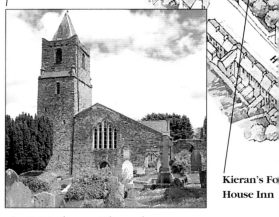

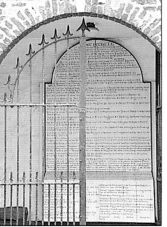

★ **Old Courthouse**
The courthouse, now the regional museum, has a toll board listing the local taxes in 1788.

Market Square

Kieran's Fo House Inn

CHARLES FORT

The star-shaped fort is 3 km (2 miles) east of town in Summercove, but can be reached by taking the signposted coastal walk from the quayside, past the village of Scilly. The fort was built in the 1670s by the English to protect Kinsale harbour against foreign naval forces but, because of its vulnerability to land attack, was taken during the siege of 1690 by William of Orange's army. Nonetheless, it remained in service until 1922 when the British forces left the town and handed it over to the Irish Government. Charles Fort remains one of the finest remaining examples of a star-shaped bastion fort in Europe.

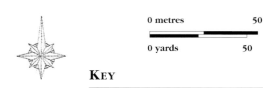

★ **St Multose Church**
This much-altered Norman church is named after an obscure 6th-century saint and marks the centre of the medieval town.

Walls and bastions of Charles Fort

| 0 metres | 50 |
| 0 yards | 50 |

KEY

🅿 Parking

ℹ Tourist information

– – – Suggested route

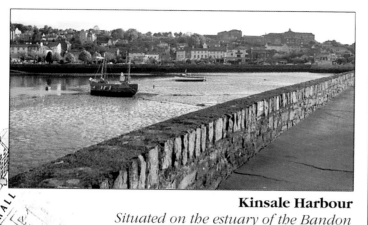

Kinsale Harbour
Situated on the estuary of the Bandon River, this is one of Ireland's most scenic harbours. Kinsale is host to a number of international sailing events throughout the year.

VISITORS' CHECKLIST

Co Cork. 2,000. Pier Road (021 772234). Annual Regatta (Aug); Kinsale Fringe Jazz Festival (Oct); Gourmet Festival (Oct). **Old Courthouse** 021 772044. May–Sep: daily; Oct–May: by appt. **St Multose Church** 021 772220. Jun–Sep: daily; Oct–May: by appt. **Desmond Castle and Wine Museum** 021 774855. Apr–Oct: daily; Nov–Mar by appt. **Charles Fort** 021 772263. Mar–Oct: daily; Nov–Feb: Sat & Sun.

Mother Hubbard's, one of Kinsale's most popular cafés, is situated in the heart of town on Market Street.

To Charles Fort

The Blue Haven, easily identified by the ornate clock above the entrance, is one of Kinsale's finest seafood restaurants.

To Kinsale Harbour, Denis Quay and Compass Hill

To Bandon

STAR SIGHTS

★ **Old Courthouse**

★ **Main Street**

★ **St Multose Church**

★ **Main Street**
Many of Kinsale's best eating and drinking places can be found on this picturesque street.

Cork ㉕

Sign outside a Cork pub

CORK CITY derives its name from the marshy land on the banks of the River Lee – its Irish name *Corcaigh* means marsh – on which St Finbarr founded a monastery around AD 650. The narrow alleys, waterways and Georgian architecture gives the city a Continental feel. Since the 19th century, when Cork was a base for the National Fenian movement *(see p47)*, the city has had a reputation for political rebelliousness. Today this mood is reflected in the city's attitude to the arts and its bohemian spirit, much in evidence at the lively October jazz festival.

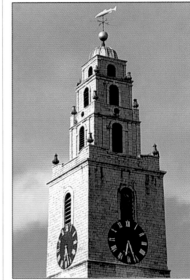

Clock tower and weather vane of St Ann's Shandon

⛪ St Ann's Shandon

Church St. ☎ *021 505906.*
◻ *Mon–Sat.* ● *25 Dec.* 🎫
This famous Cork landmark stands on the hilly slopes of the city, north of the River Lee. Built in 1722, the church has a façade made of limestone on two sides, and of red sandstone on the other two. The steeple is topped by a weather vane in the shape of a salmon. The clock face is known by the locals as the "four-faced liar" because, up until 1986 when it was repaired, each face showed slightly different times. Visitors can climb the tower and, for a small fee, ring the famous Shandon bells.

⛲ Butter Exchange

John Redman St. ◻ *daily.*
Just a short walk away from St Ann's Shandon is the Butter Exchange. Opened in 1770, it was where butter was graded before it was exported to the rest of the world. It also supplied butter to the British navy. By 1892 the exchange was exporting around 500,000 casks of butter a year, bringing prosperity to the city. The exchange closed in 1924.

Part of the building was re-opened in the 1980s to house the Shandon Craft Centre. Here visitors can watch artists and craft workers, such as crystal cutters and weavers, at work.

🏛 Crawford Art Gallery

Emmet Place. ☎ *021 273377.*
◻ *Mon–Sat.* ● *public hols.* ♿
The red brick and limestone building that houses Cork's major art gallery dates back to 1724. Built as the city's original custom house, it became a school of design in 1850. In 1884, art patron William Horatio Crawford extended the building to accommodate studios, and sculpture and picture galleries. It served as a school and art gallery until the school moved in 1979. The gallery houses some fine examples of late 19th- and early 20th-century Irish art including paintings by Jack Yeats.

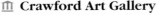

Detail of stained-glass window *The Meeting of St Brendan and the Unhappy Judas* (1911) by Harry Clarke, Crawford Art Gallery

◁ **Fishing boats in Castletown Bearhaven**

SIGHTS AT A GLANCE

There are also three excellent windows by Ireland's foremost stained-glass artist, Harry Clarke (1889–1931), including *The Meeting of St Brendan and the Unhappy Judas* (1911). Another attraction is the small collection by British artists and international works by artists such as Miró and Rouault.

The gallery is well known for its excellent restaurant which is run by the Ballymaloe cookery school, the exponents of authentic Irish cooking with a modern twist.

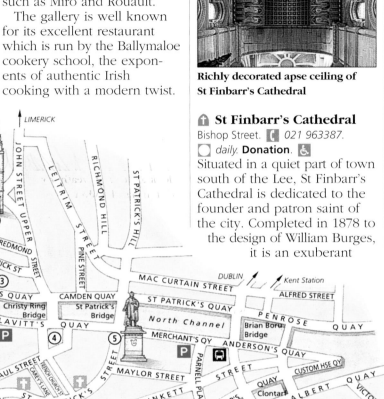

Richly decorated apse ceiling of St Finbarr's Cathedral

↑ St Finbarr's Cathedral

Bishop Street. ☏ 021 963387.
○ *daily.* **Donation.** ♿
Situated in a quiet part of town south of the Lee, St Finbarr's Cathedral is dedicated to the founder and patron saint of the city. Completed in 1878 to the design of William Burges, it is an exuberant triple-spired edifice built in Gothic Revival style, and decorated with stone tracery. Inside, the painted and gilded apse ceiling shows Christ in Glory surrounded by angels. The stained-glass windows below tell the story of Christ's life.

⛫ Cork City Gaol

Convent Avenue, Sunday's Well.
☏ 021 305022. ○ *daily.* ♿
A pretty, 20-minute walk west of the city centre leads to the restored City Gaol, complete with its furnished cells. The exhibition and audiovisual display trace the lives of individual inmates imprisoned here during the 19th and 20th centuries. Conditions were miserable and, for punishment, prisoners were made to run on a human treadmill that was used to grind grain.

There is also a café in the gaol which employs an amusing gimmick: visitors can choose between sampling the Victorian prisoners' fare or the prison governor's menu.

VISITORS' CHECKLIST

Co Cork. 👥 136,000. ✈ 6 km (4 miles) S of Cork. 🚉 Kent Station (021 506766). 🚍 Parnell Place (021 508188). ℹ Tourist House, Grand Parade (021 273251). 🎭 Cork International Choral Festival (May); Cork Jazz Festival (Oct); Cork Film Festival (Oct).

KEY

🚍	Coach station
🅿	Parking
ℹ	Tourist information
⛪	Church

0 metres   250

0 yards   250

South Channel of the River Lee, looking towards Parliament Bridge

Exploring Cork

ONE OF CORK'S great attractions is that it is a city built on water. Its heart lies on an island between two arms of the River Lee, and many of today's streets were in fact once waterways lined with warehouses and merchants' residences. Although the Dutch canalside appearance has faded, picturesque quays and bridges remain. Steep lanes rise to the north and south of the central island to the city's 19th-century suburbs, offering wonderful views of the city and its fine buildings.

The Quays

Although the river now plays only a minor part in the city's economy, much of Cork's commercial activity still takes place around the Quays (pronounced "kays" in the Cork accent). The South Mall, which covers an arm of the River Lee, was a waterway until the late 18th century. Boats were once moored at the foot of a series of stone steps, some of which are still intact today. These led to merchants' domestic quarters above. The arches below led to warehouses where goods were unloaded.

Near South Mall is **Parliament Bridge**, built in 1806 to commemorate the Act of Union *(see p46)*. Walk across the bridge to George's Quay to see Fitzpatrick's second-hand shop, with its bizarre display of bicycles, cartwheels, farm implements and other assorted bric-a-brac on its façade. A short walk away, on Sullivan's Quay, is the Quay Co-Op, a popular restaurant and meeting place. From Sullivan's Quay an elegant footbridge, built in 1985, crosses the river to the south end of Grand Parade.

Grand Parade and St Patrick's Street

On Grand Parade, also once a waterway, stands the grandiose **National Monument**, recalling the Irish patriots who died between 1798 and 1867. Bishop Lucey Park, off Grand Parade, has a section of city walls and a fine gateway from the old corn-market. Between St Patrick's Street and Grand Parade is the well-restored **English Market**, a covered fruit and vegetable market established in 1610. Bustling St Patrick's Street, the backbone of the city, was a waterway until 1800 when boats were moored under the steps of gracious houses such as the Chateau Bar. A landmark at the top of the street, near Patrick Bridge, is the **Father Mathew Statue**, which is a monument to the founder the Temperance Movement.

National Monument, Grand Parade

Fitzpatrick's second-hand shop on George's Quay

Paul Street

Noted for its ethnic restaurants, chic bars, bookshops and trendy boutiques, Paul Street is the hub of the liveliest district in town. Just off Paul Street are the busy backstreets of Carey's Lane and French Church Street. In the early 18th century, Huguenots (French Protestants) settled in these streets and set themselves up as butter exporters, brewers and wholesale merchants. This area is Cork's equivalent to Dublin's Temple Bar *(see p90)*.

Shandon Quarter

Crossing the Christy Ring Bridge to Pope's Quay, you will see on your left **St Mary's Dominican Church**, with its portico of Ionic columns topped by a huge pediment. John Redmond Street leads to the northern slopes of Cork, dominated by the spire of St Ann's Shandon *(see p212)* with its fine views of the city. To the northeast lies the lofty Montenotte district, once the epitome of Victorian gentility.

St Finbarr's Quarter

South of the river, rising above the city, this area's distinctive landmark is St Finbarr's Cathedral *(see p213)*. Nearby is the ivy-clad **Elizabeth Fort**, a 16th-century structure which was converted into a prison in 1835 and later a *Garda* (police) station. A short walk to the east lies the **Red Abbey**, a 13th-century relic from an Augustinian abbey – the oldest building in Cork.

Selling fruit and vegetables at the English Market

ENVIRONS: Some beautiful countryside surrounds the city of Cork, especially along the lush valley of the River Lee *(see p207)*. The landscape of East Cork is much gentler than the wild, rocky coastline of West Cork and County Kerry, and the land is much more fertile. Many local attractions make good day trips and there are also plenty of opportunities for outdoor activities such as walking, riding and fishing.

Blackrock Castle

Blackrock. *to the public.*
On the banks of the River Lee 1.5 km (1 mile) downstream from the city centre stands Blackrock Castle. Originally built in 1582 by Lord Mountjoy as a harbour fortification, the castle was destroyed by fire in 1827. It was rebuilt in 1830 to the design of architects J and GR Pain. The castle was recently bought by a private company and is no longer open to the public. A little further south at Carrigtuohill, near Fota Wildlife Park *(see pp216–17)*, is the 13th-century Barryscourt Castle, with its two intact towers.

Blackrock Castle standing on the banks of the River Lee

Dunkathel House

Glanmire. *021 821014.*
May–mid-Oct: Wed–Sun (pm only or by appt). *ground floor.*
Standing just outside the village of Glanmire, 6 km (3.5 miles) northeast of Cork, is this gracious Neo-Classical country house. The building was totally remodelled around 1785 for Abraham Morris, a wealthy Cork merchant, but retains a few features from an earlier

Copy of *The Three Graces* by Antonio Canova, Dunkathel House

house, including some Italianate stuccowork. The interior is decorated with Adam fireplaces and a fine collection of Irish furniture. In the spacious entrance hall is an elegant Bath stone staircase with an iron balustrade. On the half landing stands a plaster copy of Canova's *The Three Graces,* thought to have been cast in the early 19th century. The drawing room, hung with Victorian watercolours, offers lovely views of the wooded banks of the River Glanmire. Charming parkland surrounds the house.

Royal Gunpowder Mills

Ballincollig. *021 874430.*
mid-Mar–mid-Apr: Sat & Sun; mid-Apr–Sep: daily.
This unusual museum is 10 km (6 miles) west of Cork. Covering 320 ha (130 acres) of landscaped grounds, it is an impressive heritage project featuring canals, weirs, sluice gates, mills and workers' cottages. The mills were established in 1794 and flourished during the Napoleonic Wars, when they were also used as a British military base. By the 1850s, gunpowder production had become one of Cork's foremost industries. The mills finally closed in 1903, at the end of the Boer War. A guided tour covers the production of gunpowder in the main mills, and visitors are free to explore the rest of the complex.

River Blackwater 26

Co Cork. *to Mallow.* *to Fermoy, Mallow or Kanturk.*

THE SECOND LONGEST RIVER in Ireland after the Shannon *(see p229)*, the Blackwater rises in high bogland in County Kerry. It then flows eastwards through County Cork until it reaches Cappoquin, County Waterford, where it changes course south through wooded sandstone gorges to the sea at Youghal *(see p217)*. Much of the valley is wooded, a reminder that the entire area was completely covered by forests until the 17th century. The river passes some magnificent country houses and pastoral views. However, the region is best known for its fishing – the Blackwater's tributaries are filled with fine brown trout.

The best way to see the valley is to take the scenic Blackwater Valley Drive from Youghal to Mallow. The route passes through **Fermoy**, a town founded by Scottish merchant John Anderson in 1789. Angling is the town's main appeal, especially for roach, rudd, perch and pike. Further west is **Mallow**, a prosperous town noted for its fishing, golf and horse racing, and a good base for tours of the area. Detours along the tributaries include **Kanturk**, a pleasant market town with a castle, on the River Allow.

Weirs and bridge at Fermoy on the River Blackwater

Cobh ㉗

Co Cork. 🚶 10,000. 🚉 ℹ️ *Old Yacht Club (021 813301).*

COBH (pronounced "cove") lies on Great Island, one of the three islands in Cork harbour which are now linked by causeways. The Victorian seafront has rows of steeply terraced houses overlooked by **St Colman's**, an imposing Gothic Revival cathedral.

Following a visit by Queen Victoria in 1849, Cobh was renamed Queenstown but reverted to its original name in 1921. The town commands one of the world's largest natural harbours – the reason for its rise to prominence as a naval base in the 18th century. It was also a major port for merchant shipping and the main port from which Irish emigrants left for America.

Cobh was also a port of call for luxury passenger liners. In 1838, the *Sirius* made the first transatlantic crossing under steam power from here. Cobh was also the last stop for the *Titanic*, before its doomed Atlantic crossing in 1912. Three years later, the *Lusitania* was torpedoed and sunk by a German submarine just off Kinsale *(see pp208–9)*, south-west of Cobh. A memorial on the promenade is dedicated to all those who died in the attack.

IRISH EMIGRATION

Between 1848 and 1950 almost six million people emigrated from Ireland – two and a half million of them leaving from Cobh. The famine years of 1844–8 *(see p281)* triggered mass emigration as the impoverished made horrific transatlantic journeys in cramped, insanitary conditions. Many headed for the United States and Canada, and a few risked the long journey to Australia. Up until the early 20th century, emigrants waiting to board the ships were a familiar sight in Cobh. However, by the 1930s world recession and immigration restrictions in the United States and Canada led to a fall in the numbers leaving Ireland.

19th-century engraving of emigrants gathering in Cobh harbour

🏛 The Queenstown Story

Cobh Heritage Centre. 📞 *021 813591.* ⭕ *daily.* ♿ ♿

Housed in a Victorian railway station, *The Queenstown Story* is an exhibition detailing the town's marine history. Exhibits and audiovisual displays recall the part Cobh played in Irish emigration and the transportation of convicts. Between 1791 and 1853, 40,000 convicts were sent to Australian penal colonies in notorious "coffin ships"; many prisoners were also kept in floating jails in Cork Harbour.

On a happier note, the exhibition also documents Cobh's role as a port of call for glamorous transatlantic liners.

ENVIRONS: North of Cobh is the 280-ha (700-acre) Fota Estate. Surrounding the Regency mansion is the **Fota Wildlife Park and Arboretum**, which concentrates on breeding and reintroducing animals to their natural habitat. The white-tailed sea eagle is one native species that has been saved from extinction in Ireland. The landscaped park boasts

Cobh harbour with the steeple of St Colman's rising above the town

over 70 species of animal, including giraffes, flamingoes, and zebras. Only the cheetahs, subject to a long-term breeding programme, are restricted in enclosures. A train links the various sections of the park.

The arboretum has rare trees and shrubs from Japan, China, South America, the Himalayas and North America.

🦌 Fota Wildlife Park and Arboretum

Carrigtuohill. ☎ 021 812678. ○ Apr–Oct: daily. 🎟 ♿

Jameson Heritage Centre 28

Distillery Walk, Midleton, Co Cork. ☎ 021 613594. 🚌 to Midleton. ○ daily. 🎟 ♿ 🎧

A SENSITIVELY RESTORED 18th-century distillery, Jameson Heritage Centre is part of the vast Irish Distillers group at Midleton. Bushmills (*see p360*) is the oldest distillery in Ireland but Midleton is the largest. It comprises a series of separate distilleries each producing a different Irish whiskey, including Jameson and Tullamore Dew.

The story of Irish whiskey is presented through audiovisual displays, working models and authentic machinery. A tour of the old distillery takes in the mills, maltings, still-houses, kilns, granaries and ware-houses. Visitors can take part in whiskey tasting and try to distinguish between various brands of Irish whiskey and Scotch. Highlights of the visit include the world's largest pot still, with a capacity of over 30,000 gallons, and the water wheel, which is still in good working order.

Clock tower on the main street of Youghal

Youghal 29

Co Cork. 🏘 9,300. 🚌 🛈 *Market House, Market Square (024 92390).*

Y OUGHAL (which is pronounced "yawl") is a historic walled town and thriving fishing port. The town was granted to Sir Walter Raleigh by Queen Elizabeth I but later sold to the Earl of Cork. In Cromwellian times, Youghal became a closed borough – an English Protestant garrison town.

The picturesque, four-storey **Clock tower** was originally the city gate, but was recast as a prison. Steep steps beside the tower lead up to a well-preserved section of the medieval town wall and fine views across the Blackwater estuary. Through the tower, in the sombre North Main Street, is the **Red House**. This authentic Dutch mansion was built in 1710. Virtually next door are some forbidding Elizabethan almshouses and, on the far side of the road, a 15th-century tower, known as **Tynte's Castle**.

Nestling in the town walls opposite is **Myrtle Grove**, one of the few unfortified Tudor manor houses to survive in Ireland. It has a triple-gabled façade and exquisite interior oak panelling. Just uphill is the Gothic **Church of St Mary**. Inside are tomb effigies and stained-glass windows depicting the coats of arms of local families.

Grain truck (c. 1940) at the Jameson Heritage Centre

Bunratty Castle, imperious over the Ratty river ▷

THE LOWER
SHANNON

THE LOWER SHANNON

CLARE · LIMERICK · TIPPERARY

I N THE THREE COUNTIES *which flank the lower reaches of the Shannon, Ireland's longest river, the scenery ranges from the rolling farmland of Tipperary to the eerie limestone plateau of the Burren. The Shannon's bustling riverside resorts draw many visitors, and there are medieval strongholds and atmospheric towns of great historic interest. The region also boasts a vibrant music scene.*

The River Shannon stretches 170 miles (274 km) from its source into a long, wide estuary that forms the dividing line between counties Limerick and Clare. This waterway has long made the area attractive to settlers. It provided transport far into the interior, and early farming communities thrived thanks to the fertile topsoil deposited along its banks by glaciers at the end of the Ice Age. There are several important Stone Age sites, including a settlement near Lough Gur which has an impressive stone circle and a wedge tomb. At Craggaunowen in County Clare, prehistoric life is re-created in authentic dwellings that include a crannog and a ring fort. Tens of thousands of these circular enclosed homesteads once existed throughout the country, but the Clare ring forts were unique in that they were built of stone rather than wood. The remains of more than 2,000 such structures have survived. Verdant grassland, which has turned the Lower Shannon into prime dairy country, covers the area, and the fertile pastures have also made it a centre for horse-breeding. Off the main roads, this is a region of pretty country lanes woven through acres of rich farmland that gives way to glens and mountains, such as the Galty range in southern Tipperary. From those and other nearby ranges such as the Silvermines (where mining for zinc and silver still takes place), the plains of the Golden Vale surrounding the county town of Tipperary and the Glen of Aherlow are visible. This

Ruins of Dysert O'Dea monastery in County Clare with an outstanding 12th-century High Cross

◁ **Traditional musicians playing at Feakle in County Clare**

The beautiful pleasure port of Killaloe, by Lough Derg

is splendid country for indulging in such outdoor pursuits as hiking, biking and horseback riding.

In the early Christian period, monasteries proliferated in the fertile countryside, but the Vikings penetrated the Shannon in the 10th century, pillaging many of its religious centres. Although the Gaelic clans put up stern resistance, the Norsemen managed to found a colony at the head of the estuary which became the city of Limerick.

During the Norman period, Irish clans such as the Thomonds retained control of significant parts of the region, building Bunratty Castle and other fortresses that rivalled the strongholds that were being erected by the Anglo-Irish dynasties. Foremost among the latter families were the Butlers, the Earls of Ormonde, who held much land in Tipperary, and the Fitzgeralds, the main landowners in the Limerick area. Cahir Castle, located on a small island in the middle of the River Suir, was a Butler fortress, as was Ormond Castle at Carrick-on-Suir. Clonmel, with its striking Franciscan friary, was another Anglo-Saxon stronghold. The 12th-century cathedral at Kilnefora in the Burren is known for its graveyard's fine high crosses.

The monastic ruins that survive were built mainly during the medieval period.

Remains include Athassel Priory, once the largest in Ireland, and the Cistercian abbeys of Holy Cross near Thurles and Hore outside Cashel. This atmosphere of this era is re-created at the banquets staged at Bunratty and Knappogue castles.

The Shannon region is often called "Castle Country" as hundreds of castles and abbeys were built here in the 16th century as part of the campaign by Elizabeth I to subdue the province of Munster. The countryside is still dotted with their remains, and many crumbling towers are visible through the forest trees.

Limerick was often the focus of events in the Lower Shannon. In 1691, William of Orange lay seige to the city, bringing about the Treaty of Limerick, which effectively trig-

Bunratty Castle, Clare

gered the Catholic nobility's precipitous departure for Europe, the so-called "Flight of the Wild Geese".

In more recent times, the Republic's fourth-largest city tended to be overlooked, but the construction of

A recreated prehistoric crannog, part of the reconstruction project at Craggaunowen in County Clare

Shannon International Airport has transformed Limerick into the gateway to western Ireland.

The city also has literary associations: it gave its name to the nonsense verses that were first created by poets in the county in the 18th century. The publication in 1997 of Frank McCourt's best-selling novel *Angela's Ashes* has sparked much interest in the city. Many Limerick natives were far from happy with the author's rather bleak representation of their home, and first-time visitors who have read the book may be pleasantly surprised to find a modern town centre and streets lined with some beautifully renovated Georgian buildings.

The breathtaking face of the Cliffs of Moher, County Clare

The wide estuary of the Shannon flows away from Limerick through a landscape of rolling hills to the sea. The mudflats here are a haven for wildlife. In this area is one of Ireland's top golf courses, Ballybunion. The road that runs along the Shannon's banks goes through Foynes, which has a celebrated Flying Boat Museum, and then through Glin, with its elegantly restored castle. To the south is one of Ireland's most popular villages, Adare, which is widely known for its quaint antique shops and beautiful thatched cottages.

An informal music-making session

Northeast of Limerick is the largest of the Shannon lakes, Lough Derg. Among its port towns are Killaloe, with its fine Romanesque cathedral, and Mountshannon, just across the lake from Holy Island. Landlubbers enjoy the beautiful views on the scenic route that encircles the lake.

The region's most dramatic scenery is found along the coast of County Clare. Here the lush and fertile fields of the Shannon give way to the amazing limestone plateau known as the Burren. Its vast expanses of grey pavement are broken by deep fissures, and in spring and summer delicate wildflowers brighten its surface. The area also has a series of underground caves, prehistoric dolmens and wedge tombs, as well as a Victorian spa town.

Clare enjoys a thriving traditional music scene. Its county town, Ennis, has several atmospheric pubs where nightly sing-alongs are *de rigeur*. The town also holds a major music festival, and local villages such as Doolin are renowned for their musicians.

The austere limestone plateau of the Burren in northwest County Clare

Irish Forts and Castles

THE IRISH LANDSCAPE IS INDELIBLY marked with forts and castles. They range from the ruins of crude Iron Age enclosures to restored luxury 19th-century homes and tell the island's tale of fortified settlement, conquest and internal strife. The Celts left a legacy of stone, often in the form of circular fortifications; the conquering Anglo-Normans introduced the motte and bailey, later replacing timber palisades with stone tower and walls, creating the classic medieval castle. The 15th and 16th centuries saw the proliferation of the Irish tower house. Medieval tower houses and castles were later converted into grand family homes.

Iron Age promontory forts *combined natural cliff defences with ditches, banks and ramparts. Dunbeg, on the Dingle Peninsula, is one of many on Ireland's coast.*

The early Norman motte and bailey*, such as that at Knockgraffon, above, was a mound of earth (the motte) topped with a timber palisade and surrounded by a ditch. A bridge led to an enclosed compound (the bailey).*

THE IRISH TOWER HOUSE

By the 15th century the sphere of Anglo-Norman influence had shrunk to the area around Dublin known as the "Pale". To protect these domains, Henry VI offered a £10 subsidy towards the building of a castle or tower to specified dimensions. The tower house became popular, and by the mid-1600s Ireland was peppered with them. Pictured right is Dunguaire Castle, County Galway, a restored tower house.

The ground floor was used as a store.

County Antrim's Dunluce Castle *was built by the MacDonnell family in the 13th century. Perched on an isolated rock stack, it is one of Ireland's most spectacular coastal fortifications.*

Cahir Castle *was the stronghold of the Butlers – the Earls of Ormonde. Its portcullis, crenellated walls and square keep are likely to have been built to keep out rival Anglo-Norman families, rather than native Irish attackers.*

The castle in Limerick, *built on the site of earlier fortifications in 1197, is a splendid example of Anglo-Norman military architecture. The massive drum towers and the curtain walls, originally constructed to withstand siege engines, were lowered in the 17th century to take cannons.*

The living area was on the top floor, where it was safer to have big windows.

Malahide, near Dublin, *was occupied for 800 years by one family, the Talbots. In the 18th century, during a period of peace and prosperity, there was no longer any need for the property to be defensive. The Talbots transformed the original, medieval castle into a gracious family home but chose to retain its 14th-century tower and 15th-century Great Hall.*

Leamaneagh Castle is an example of how Irish families in the 17th century extended their existing tower houses by adding an English-style building. Not long after it was built, the castle was ruined by Cromwell's invaders.

Bawn walls were built around the tower to keep cattle in at night.

Ormonde Castle *at Carrick-on-Suir is Ireland's grandest Elizabethan manor house, dating to the mid-1500s. Like Leamaneagh (above), it was built as an addition to a medieval castle. Following the English fashion of the day, it has a gabled roof and mullioned windows, and is noted for its magnificent Long Gallery and elaborate plasterwork.*

Exploring the Lower Shannon

THE CENTRAL LOCATION of Limerick city makes it a
natural focus for visitors to the region. However,
there are many charming towns that make pleasanter
bases, such as Adare, Cashel and also Killaloe, which is
well placed for exploring the River Shannon. Most places
of interest in Tipperary lie in the southern part of the
county, where historic towns such as Clonmel and Cahir
overlook the River Suir. By contrast, County Clare has
few towns of any size, though it boasts the
major attraction of Bunratty Castle. Beyond
Ennis, the landscape becomes steadily
bleaker until you reach the Burren.

**Looking up at the
Cliffs of Moher**

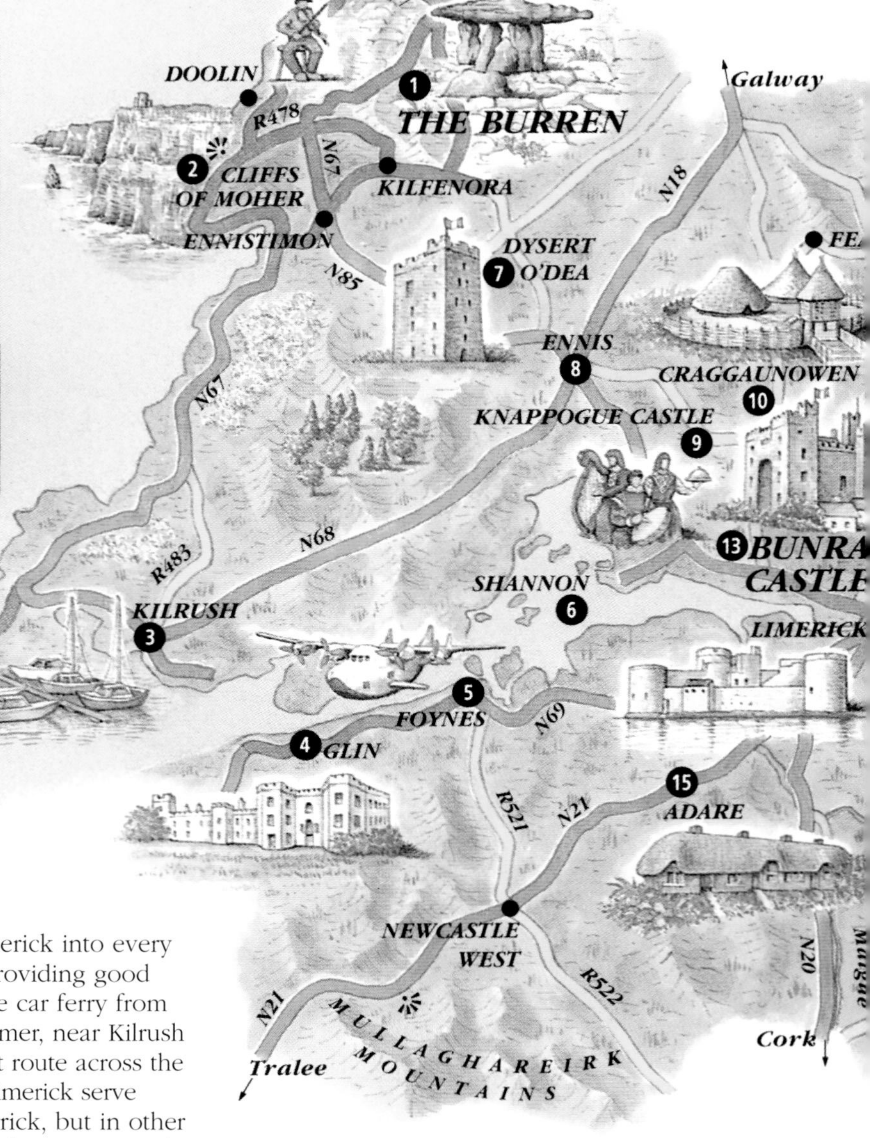

GETTING AROUND

Roads extend from Limerick into every
corner of the region, providing good
access for motorists; the car ferry from
Tarbert in Kerry to Killimer, near Kilrush
in Clare, is a convenient route across the
Shannon. Trains from Limerick serve
Cahir, Clonmel and Carrick, but in other
areas you must rely on the bus network.
This is rather limited, especially in County
Clare, although buses to the Burren
from Limerick pass the Cliffs of Moher.
Some of the most popular sights, such
as Bunratty Castle and the Burren, can
be reached on bus tours from Limerick.

0 kilometres   25

0 miles   25

KEY

Major road

Minor road

Scenic route

River

Viewpoint

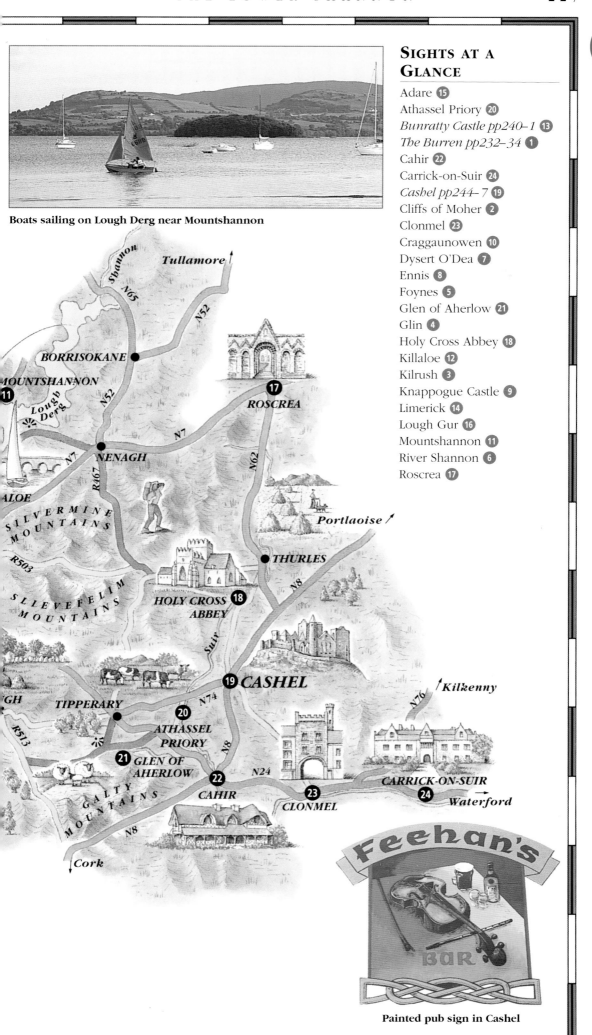

Boats sailing on Lough Derg near Mountshannon

Painted pub sign in Cashel

Looking south along the Cliffs of Moher, one of the most dramatic stretches of Ireland's west coast

The Burren ❶

See pp232–3.

Cliffs of Moher ❷

Co Clare. 🚌 *from Ennis & Limerick.*
Visitors' Centre 📞 *065 81171.*
○ *Easter–Sep: daily.* **O'Brien's Tower**
📞 *065 81171.* ○ *Mar–Oct: daily.*
📷

EVEN WHEN SHROUDED in mist
or buffeted by Atlantic
gales, the Cliffs of Moher are
breathtaking, rising to a height
of 200 m (650 ft) out of the
sea and extending for 8 km (5
miles). The sheer rock face,
with its layers of black shale
and sandstone, provides sheltered ledges where guillemots
and other sea birds nest.
   Well-worn paths lead along
the cliffs. From the **Visitors'
Centre**, 5 km (3 miles) northwest of Liscannor, you can
walk south to **Hag's Head** in
an hour. To the north, a good
alternative is the three-hour
walk along the coast between
O'Brien's Tower – a viewing
point built for the benefit of
Victorian tourists – and Fisher-
street near **Doolin** *(see p234).*

Kilrush ❸

Co Clare. 🏘 *2,800.* 🚌 ℹ️ *Heritage
Centre, Market House (065 51577).*
○ *May–Sep.*

WITH A NEW MARINA and the
promotion of Kilrush as
a heritage town, the fortunes
of this 18th-century estate town
have been greatly revived. It
now has a **Heritage Centre**,
where an exhibition covers the
Great Famine *(see p281)* and
the landlord evictions of 1888

(see pp46–7). A well-marked
walking trail around the town's
historic sights also starts here.

ENVIRONS: From Kilrush, boats
take visitors dolphin-spotting
or to nearby **Scattery Island**,
site of a medieval monastery.
The ruins include five churches
and one of the tallest round
towers in the country.
   The **Loop Head Drive** is a
27-km (17-mile) route which
begins at the resort of Kilkee,
west of Kilrush. It winds south
past dramatic coastal scenery
to Loop Head, from where you
can enjoy superb views.

Glin ❹

Co Limerick. 🏘 *600.* 🚌 *from
Limerick.*

THIS CHARMING village on the
banks of the Shannon is
the seat of the Knights of Glin,
a branch of the Fitzgeralds
who have lived in the district
for seven centuries. Their first
medieval castle is a ruin, but
west of the village you can see

**Rare 18th-century double "flying"
staircase in Glin Castle**

their newer ancestral home,
Glin Castle. Originally built
in 1780, the Georgian manor
succumbed to the vogue for
Gothic romance in the 1820s,
when it acquired battlements
and gingerbread lodges. There
is some fine stuccowork and
18th-century furniture inside.

🏰 **Glin Castle**
📞 *068 34173.* ○ *May–Jun: daily.*
📷 🎥 *obligatory.*

Foynes ❺

Co Limerick. 🏘 *650.* 🚌 *from
Limerick.*

FOYNES ENJOYED short-lived
fame in the 1930s and 1940s
as the eastern terminus of the
first airline passenger route
across the Atlantic. **Foynes
Flying Boat Museum** presents
a detailed history of the sea-
plane service. The original
Radio and Weather Room and
a 1940s-style tea room are particularly evocative of the era.

🏛 **Foynes Flying Boat
Museum**
Aras Ide, Foynes. 📞 *069 65416.*
○ *Apr–Oct: daily.* 📷 ♿

ENVIRONS: The historic town
of **Askeaton**, 11 km (7 miles)
east of Foynes, has a castle
and Franciscan friary founded
by the Fitzgeralds. The friary
is particularly interesting, with
a 15th-century cloister of black
marble. In Rathkeale, 8 km
(5 miles) south, **Castle Matrix**
is a restored 15th-century tower
house renowned for the fine
library in the Great Hall.

🏰 **Castle Matrix**
Rathkeale. 📞 *069 64284.*
○ *May–Sep: Sat–Thu.* 📷

Fishing on Lough Derg, the largest of the lakes on the Shannon

River Shannon ⑥

🚆 to Limerick or Athlone. 🚌 to Carrick-on-Shannon, Athlone or Limerick. 🛈 Arthur's Quay, Limerick (061 317522).

T HE SHANNON IS the longest river in Ireland, rising in County Cavan and meandering down to the Atlantic. Flowing through the heart of the island, it has traditionally marked the border between the provinces of Leinster and Connaught. In medieval times, castles guarded the major fords from Limerick to Portumna, and numerous monasteries were built along the riverbanks, including the celebrated Clonmacnoise *(see pp336–7)*. Work began on the Shannon navigation system in the 1750s, but it fell into disuse with the advent of the railways. It has since been revived, with an additional boost given by the recent restoration of the Shannon-Erne Waterway *(see p309)*.

There are subtle changes of landscape along the length of the river. South of **Lough Allen**, the countryside is covered with the drumlins or low hills typical of the northern Midlands. Towards **Lough Ree**, islands stud the river in an area of ecological importance which is home to otters, geese, grey herons and whooper swans. Continuing south beyond **Athlone** *(see p333)*, the river flows through flood plains and bog before reaching **Lough**

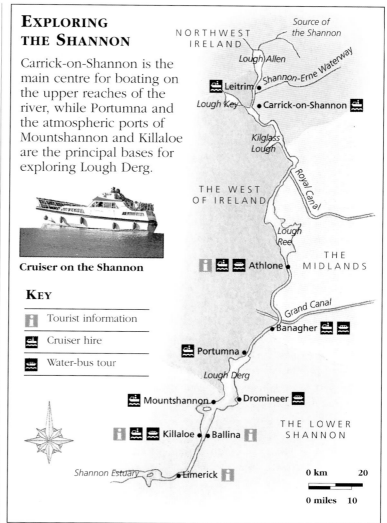

EXPLORING THE SHANNON

Carrick-on-Shannon is the main centre for boating on the upper reaches of the river, while Portumna and the atmospheric ports of Mountshannon and Killaloe are the principal bases for exploring Lough Derg.

Cruiser on the Shannon

KEY

🛈 Tourist information

⛴ Cruiser hire

🚢 Water-bus tour

Grey heron on the Shannon

Derg, the biggest of the lakes on the Shannon. The scenery is more dramatic here, with the lough's southern end edged by wooded mountains. From **Killaloe** *(see p238)*, the river gains speed on its rush towards **Limerick** *(see p239)* and the sea. The mudflats of the Shannon estuary attract a great variety of birdlife. The port of **Carrick-on-Shannon** *(see p309)* is the cruising centre of Ireland, but there are bases all along the river – especially

around Lough Derg, which is the lake most geared to boating. Water-buses connect most ports south of Athlone. If you hire a cruiser, enquire about the weather conditions before setting out, particularly on Loughs Ree and Derg, which are very exposed. The calm stretch from **Portumna** *(see p275)* to Athlone is easier for inexperienced sailors.

Walkers can enjoy the Lough Derg Way, a signposted route around the lake. The woods by **Lough Key** *(see p281)* also provide good walking territory.

Athlone and the southern reaches of Lough Ree

The limestone pavements of the Burren's rocky plateau ▷

The Burren ①

THE WORD BURREN derives from *boireann*, which means "rocky land" in Gaelic – an apt name for this vast limestone plateau in northwest County Clare. In the 1640s, Cromwell's surveyor described it as "a savage land, yielding neither water enough to drown a man, nor tree to hang him, nor soil enough to bury". Few trees manage to grow in this desolate place, yet other plants thrive. The Burren is a unique botanical environment in which Mediterranean and alpine plants rare to Ireland grow side by side. From May to August, an astonishing array of flowers adds splashes of colour to the austere landscape. These plants grow most abundantly around the region's shallow lakes and pastures, but they also take root in the crevices of the limestone pavements which are the most striking geological feature of the rocky plateau. In the southern part of the Burren, limestone gives way to the black shale and sandstone that form the dramatic Cliffs of Moher *(see p228)*.

Dark red helleborine

Grazing in the Burren
A quirk in the local climate means that, in winter, the hills are warmer than the valleys – hence the unusual practice in the Burren of letting cattle graze on high ground in winter.

FAUNA OF THE BURREN

The Burren is one of the best places in Ireland for butterflies, with 28 species found in the area. The birdlife is also varied. Skylarks and cuckoos are common on the hills and in the meadows, while the coast is a good place for razorbills, guillemots, puffins and other sea birds. Mammals are harder to spot. Badgers, foxes and stoats live here, but you are much more likely to see a herd of shaggy-coated wild goats or an Irish hare.

The pearl-bordered fritillary, *one of a number of fritillaries found in the Burren, can be seen in no other part of Ireland.*

An Irish hare's *white and brown winter coat turns to reddish-brown in the summer.*

Whooper swans *from Iceland flock to the wetlands of the Burren in winter.*

The hooded crow *is easily identified by its grey and black plumage.*

Turloughs are shallow lakes which are dry in summer but flood in winter, when they attract wildfowl and waders.

Spring gentian

Bloody Cranesbill
This striking plant, common in the Burren, is a member of the geranium family. It flowers in June.

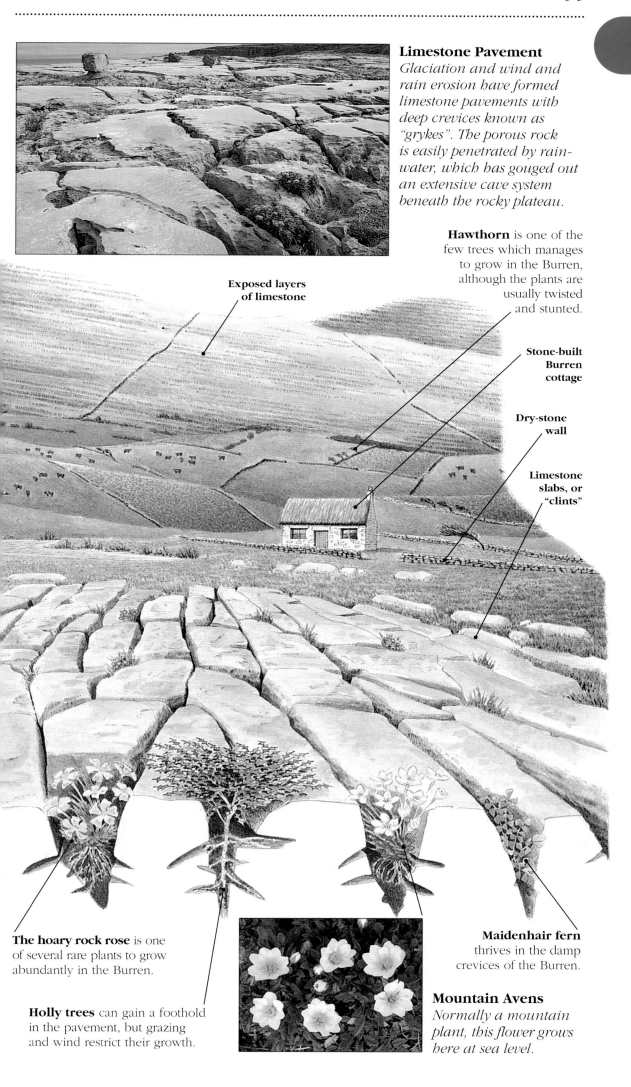

Limestone Pavement
Glaciation and wind and rain erosion have formed limestone pavements with deep crevices known as "grykes". The porous rock is easily penetrated by rain-water, which has gouged out an extensive cave system beneath the rocky plateau.

Hawthorn is one of the few trees which manages to grow in the Burren, although the plants are usually twisted and stunted.

Exposed layers of limestone

Stone-built Burren cottage

Dry-stone wall

Limestone slabs, or "clints"

The hoary rock rose is one of several rare plants to grow abundantly in the Burren.

Holly trees can gain a foothold in the pavement, but grazing and wind restrict their growth.

Maidenhair fern thrives in the damp crevices of the Burren.

Mountain Avens
Normally a mountain plant, this flower grows here at sea level.

Exploring the Burren

If you are interested in the unique geology and natural history of the Burren, head for **Mullaghmore**, to the southeast of the area. This is one of the wildest parts of the plateau and reaches a height of 191 m (626 ft), with some of the best limestone pavements in the area.

A good place to begin a tour of the more accessible parts of the Burren is at the **Cliffs of Moher** *(see p228)*. From here it is a short drive north to **Doolin**, near the port for the Aran Islands *(see pp276–7)*. This rather spread-out village is renowned for its traditional music; Gus O'Connor's pub acts as a focus for music-lovers in the area. The coastal road runs north from Doolin to a desolate limestone outcrop at **Black Head**, while turning inland you will reach **Lisdoonvarna**. The Victorians developed the town as a spa, but it is now most renowned for its colourful pubs and its matchmaking festival *(see p54)*.

Music shop in Doolin

Poulnabrone Dolmen in the heart of the Burren's limestone plateau

To the north along the N67 lies **Ballyvaughan**, a fishing village dotted with slate-roofed cottages and busy with tourists in summer. It is well placed for reaching a number of sights. Nearby **Bishop's Quarter** has a sheltered beach with glorious views across a lagoon towards Galway Bay. **Aillwee Cave**, to the south, is just one of thousands of caves in the Burren, but is the only one open to the public. It consists of a tunnel which opens into a series of caverns. In the first, known as Bear Haven, the remains of hibernation pits used by bears are still visible.

Ruined forts and castles and numerous prehistoric sites dot the landscape. Just west of Aillwee Cave is **Cahermore Stone Fort**, with a lintelled doorway, and to the south

Gleninsheen Wedge Tomb, a style of grave which marks the transition between Stone and Bronze Age cultures. The more famous **Poulnabrone Dolmen** nearby is a striking portal tomb dating back to 2500–2000 BC. Continuing south you reach the ghostly shell of **Leamaneagh Castle**, a 17th-century mansion that incorporates an earlier tower house built by the O'Briens.

On the southern fringe of the Burren lies **Kilfenora**, a Catholic diocese which, by a curious historical quirk, has the Pope for its bishop. The village's modest cathedral, one of many 12th-century churches in the Burren, has a roofless chancel with finely sculpted capitals. Kilfenora, however, is more famous for its High Crosses, of which there are several in the graveyard.

Carved capital in Kilfenora Cathedral

Best preserved is the Doorty Cross, with a carving of a bishop and two other clerics on the east face. Next door, the **Burren Centre** offers an excellent introduction to the geology and flora of the region, as well as to man's impact on the landscape. The displays include a model of the limestone plateau.

🗻 **Aillwee Cave**
Ballyvaughan. 📞 *065 77036.*
⭕ *daily.* ♿ 📷
🏛 **Burren Centre**
Kilfenora. 📞 *065 88030.* ⭕ *Mar–Oct: daily.* ♿

THE BURREN REGION

KEY

⬜	Exposed limestone
=	Minor roads
▬	Major roads
ℹ	Tourist information
🔆	Viewpoint

0 kilometres   10

0 miles   5

Black Head

Bishop's Quarter Beach

N67

Ballyvaughan

SLIEVECARRAN

R477

Cahermore Stone Fort

Aillwee Cave

SLIEVE ELVA

Gleninsheen Wedge Tomb

N67

Poulnabrone Dolmen

R480

Lisdoonvarna

R478

R476

Doolin

R481

MULLAGHMORE

Leamaneagh Castle

R466

Cliffs of Moher

R67

Kilfenora

R476

Dysert O'Dea ⑦

Corrofin, Co Clare. 🚌 *from Ennis.*
Archaeology Centre 📞 *065 37722.*
⭕ *May–Sep: daily.*

DYSERT O'DEA CASTLE stands on a rocky outcrop 9 km (6 miles) north of Ennis. This tower house, erected in the 15th century, is home to the **Archaeology Centre**, which includes a small museum and also marks the start of a trail around nearby historic sights. A map of the path, designed for both walkers and cyclists, is available from the tea room.

Across a field from the castle is a monastic site said to have been founded by the obscure St Tola in the 8th century. The ruins are overgrown and rather worn, but the Romanesque carving above one doorway is still clear, and there is also an impressive 12th-century High Cross, with a bishop sculpted on the east side *(see p325).*

Further south, the trail leads past the remains of two stone forts, a ruined castle and the site of a 14th-century battle.

Ennis ⑧

Co Clare. 🏙 *18,000.* 🚌 🛈 *Clare Rd (065 28366).*

CLARE'S COUNTY TOWN, on the banks of the River Fergus, is a charming place. Narrow, winding lanes are particularly characteristic and recall Ennis's medieval beginnings. The town is also renowned for its painted shopfronts and folk music festivals (known as *fleadh* in Gaelic). It abounds in "singing" pubs and traditional music shops.

Colourful exterior of Michael Kerins pub in Ennis

Ennis can trace its origins to the 13th century and to the O'Briens, Kings of Thomond, who were the area's feudal overlords in the Middle Ages. The Franciscan friary that they founded here in the 1240s is now the town's main attraction. Dating largely from the 14th and 15th centuries, the ruined **Ennis Friary** is famous for its rich carvings and decorated tombs in the chancel – above all the 15th-century MacMahon tomb, whose carved alabaster panels have been incorporated into the later Creagh tomb.

Next door to the friary is a delightful 17th-century house, now Cruise's restaurant, and on the corner of nearby Francis Street stands the Queen's Hotel – featured in James Joyce's *Ulysses.* To the south, O'Connell Square has a monument to Daniel O'Connell *(see p46),* who was elected MP for Clare in 1828. He also gave his name to the town's main street, where, among the pubs and shops, you can spot a medieval tower, a Jacobean chimney stack and an 18th-century arch.

🏛 **Ennis Friary**
Abbey St. 📞 *065 29100.* ⭕ *May–Sep: daily.* 📷 ♿

ENVIRONS: The area around Ennis is rich in monastic ruins. Just 3 km (2 miles) south of the town is **Clare Abbey**, an Augustinian foundation set up by the O'Briens in 1189 but dating mainly from the 1400s.

Quin Franciscan Friary, set in meadows 13 km (8 miles) southeast of Ennis, was also built in the 15th century, and incorporates the romantic ruins of a Norman castle. The well-preserved cloister is one of the finest of its kind in Ireland.

Knappogue Castle ⑨

Quin, Co Clare. 📞 *061 360788.* 🚌 *to Ennis.* ⭕ *Apr–Oct: daily.* 📷 ♿

A POWERFUL LOCAL CLAN called the MacNamaras erected Knappogue Castle in 1467. Apart from a ten-year spell in Cromwellian times, it stayed in their hands until 1815. During the War of Independence *(see pp48–9),* the castle was used by the revolutionary forces.

Knappogue, now owned by Texans, has been restored with meticulous care and attention to detail and is one of the country's most charmingly furnished castles. The central tower house is original, but the rest is Neo-Gothic. Inside are fine Elizabethan fireplaces and linenfold wood panelling.

Medieval banquets are staged in the castle, with storytelling and singing forming part of the entertainment.

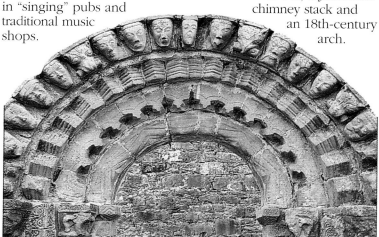
Finely carved Romanesque doorway at Dysert O'Dea

Abandoned farmhouse in the desolate Burren ▷

Craggaunowen ⑩

Kilmurry, Co Clare. 🚌 🚃 to Ennis.
📞 061 360788. ◯ Apr–Oct: daily.
♻ ♿

A woman in peasant costume spinning wool at Craggaunowen

T HE CRAGGAUNOWEN PROJECT, known as "Craggaunowen: the Living Past" and designed to bring Bronze Age and Celtic culture to life, is a shining example of a recreated pre-historic site. The centre was created in the grounds of Craggaunowen Castle in the 1960s by John Hunt, a noted archaeologist who had been inspired by his excavations at Lough Gur *(see p244)*. The castle's tower house contains bronzes and other objects from Hunt's archaeological collection, the rest of which can be seen in Limerick.

At Craggaunowen, people in costume act out particular trades, such as spinning or potting, or serve as guides. A French slave describes how communities lived in the ring fort, a typical early Christian homestead. You can also see meat being prepared in the *fulacht fiadh*, a traditional hunter's cooking hole.

The complex includes part of a *togher*, an original Iron Age timber road that was dis-covered in Longford. The most eye-catching sight, however, is the crannog *(see p37)*, a man-made island enclosing wattle and daub houses – a style of defensive homestead that survived until around 1600.

Another interesting exhibit is a leather-hulled boat built in the 1970s by the explorer, Tim Severin. He used it to retrace the route which legend says St Brendan took in a similar vessel across the Atlantic in the 6th century *(see p31)*.

Mountshannon ⑪

Co Clare. 👥 240.

T HIS PRETTY VILLAGE on the banks of Lough Derg *(see p229)* seems to have its back turned to the lake but is never-theless a major angling centre. Solid 18th-century stone houses and churches cluster around the harbour, together with some good pubs: Madden's is a prime venue for Irish music.

Mountshannon is well placed for exploring the lake's western shores, with plenty of scope for walks and bicycle rides. Fishing boats are available for hire, and in summer you can go by boat to **Holy Island**, the site of a monastery founded in the 7th century. The ruins include four chapels and a graveyard of medieval tombs.

Killaloe ⑫

Co Clare. 👥 950. 🚌 ℹ *May–Sep: Heritage Centre, The Bridge (061 376866).*

K ILLALOE, which enjoys a beautiful setting close to where the Shannon emerges from Lough Derg, is the lake's most prosperous pleasure port. An attractive 17th-century stone bridge divides Killaloe in two, with its twin town of Ballina lying on the opposite bank in Tipperary. Ballina has better pubs, including Goosers on the waterfront, but Killaloe is the main boating centre and also has more to offer of historical interest.

Killaloe's grandest site is **St Flannan's Cathedral**, founded in around 1182. Though a rather plain, solid church, it has a richly carved Romanesque doorway, which was rescued from an earlier chapel. The church also has an ancient Ogham Stone *(see p38)*, un-usual because the inscription is in both Nordic runes and Ogham. Outside stands St Flannan's Oratory, built around the same time as the cathedral.

The Heritage Centre, in a converted boathouse on the bridge, contains an exhibition about the Shannon and Lough Derg, and is the starting point for a marked walk along sections of the old Killaloe Canal. It is also possible to arrange for local fishermen to take you out on the lake.

Bunratty Castle ⑬

See pp240–1.

Bicycle hire and boat trips at Mountshannon

Limerick ⑭

Co Limerick. 🏛 90,000. ✈ Shannon.
🚉 🚌 ℹ Arthur's Quay (061
317522). 🛥 Fri & Sat.

THE THIRD LARGEST CITY in the
Republic, Limerick was
founded by the Vikings. Given
its strategic point on the River
Shannon, it thrived under the
Normans, but later bore the
brunt of English oppression.
After the Battle of the Boyne
(see p326), the rump of the
defeated Jacobite army with-
drew here. The siege which
followed has entered Irish
folklore as a heroic defeat,
sealed by the Treaty
of Limerick in 1691.
English treachery
in reneging on
most of the terms
of the treaty still
rankles. It is no
coincidence that
Catholicism and
nationalism are
strong in the city.

Limerick has a
reputation for high
unemployment,
crime and general
neglect. However, it is fast
acquiring a new image as a
commercial city, revitalized by
new industries and laudable
restoration projects. Even so,
visitors may still have to dig a
little to appreciate its charm.

The city centre consists of
three historic districts. King's
Island was the first area to be
settled by the Vikings and was
later the heart of the medieval
city, when it was known as
Englishtown. The island boasts
Limerick's two main landmarks,
King John's Castle and St Mary's
Cathedral. The old Irishtown,
south of the Abbey River, has
its fair share of drab houses
and shops, but also has its own
historic buildings and a pocket

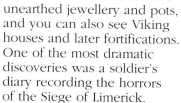

**Carved misericord in
St Mary's Cathedral**

of Georgian elegance in St
John's Square. Near here is
Limerick's most conspicuous
sight, St John's Cathedral, built
in 1861. Its 85-m (280-ft) spire
is the tallest in the country.

The most pleasant part of
Limerick in which to stroll is
Newtown Pery – a grid of
gracious Georgian terraces
focused on O'Connell Street.

⚓ King John's Castle
Nicholas St. ☎ 061 411201.
◯ Apr–Oct: daily. 🎫 ♿
Supposedly founded by King
John in 1200, not long after the
Normans arrived, this castle is
an imposing sight with five
drum towers and
solid curtain
walls. Architec-
turally, the castle
is less interesting
inside, but it
houses a good
exhibition on the
history of the
city. Replicas of
siege machinery
are based on finds
from the castle.
Ongoing
excavations have
unearthed jewellery and pots,
and you can also see Viking
houses and later fortifications.
One of the most dramatic
discoveries was a soldier's
diary recording the horrors
of the Siege of Limerick.

Across the nearby Thomond
Bridge, the Treaty Stone marks
the spot where the Treaty of
Limerick was signed in 1691.

🛕 St Mary's Cathedral
Bridge Street. ☎ 061 416238.
◯ Jun–Aug: 9am–5pm Mon–Sat;
Sep–May: 9am–1pm Mon–Sat.
Built in 1172, this is the oldest
structure in the city. Except for
a fine Romanesque doorway
and the nave, however, little
remains of the early church.

**Characteristic Georgian doorway
in St John's Square**

The 15th-century misericords
in the choir stalls are the pride
of St Mary's, with superb
carvings in black oak of angels,
griffins and other creatures
both real and imaginary.

Nearby, George's Quay is a
pleasant street with restaurants
and outdoor cafés and good
views across the river.

🏛 Hunt Museum
Rutland St. ☎ 061 312833. ◯ daily
(Sun pm only). 🎫 ♿
Located in the Old Customs
House, this museum has one
of the greatest collections of
antiquities in Ireland, gathered
by the archaeologist, John
Hunt. The best exhibits, dating
from the Bronze Age, include
gold jewellery, weapons and
a magnificent shield. Among
the other artifacts are Celtic
brooches and the Antrim
Cross, a masterpiece of 9th-
century metalwork.

🏛 Limerick Museum
Nicholas St. ☎ 061 417826. ◯ Tue–
Sat. ● 7 days at Christmas. ♿
A 19th-century granary building provides the setting for the
city museum. Its displays cover
Limerick's history, its traditions
and passions, from silver- and
lace-making to rugby.

View of Limerick showing Thomond Bridge across the Shannon and King John's Castle

Bunratty Castle ⑬

T HIS FORMIDABLE CASTLE, built in the 15th century, is one of Ireland's major tourist attractions. Its most important residents were the O'Briens, Earls of Thomond, who lived here from around 1500 until the 1640s. The present interior looks much as it did under the so-called "Great Earl", who died in 1624. Abandoned last century, the castle was derelict when Lord Gort bought it in the 1950s, but it has been beautifully restored to its original state. The adjacent Folk Park and mock medieval banquets held in the castle attract many coach parties, giving Bunratty a rather commercialized atmosphere, but it is still well worth visiting.

The chimney is a replica in wood of the stone original. It provided a vent for the smoke given off by the fire in the centre of the Great Hall.

★ **North Solar**
This 17th-century German chandelier is the most curious feature in the Great Earl's private apartments. The term "solar" was used during the Middle Ages to describe an upper chamber.

The Murder Hole was designed for pouring boiling water or pitch on to the heads of attackers.

North Front
Bunratty Castle is unusual for the high arches on both the north and south sides of the keep. However, the first-floor entrance, designed to deter invaders, was typical of castles of the period.

Entrance

The basement, with walls 3 m (10 ft) thick, was probably used for storage or as a stable.

STAR FEATURES

★ **Great Hall**

★ **Main Guard**

★ **North Solar**

VISITORS' CHECKLIST

Bunratty, Co Clare. 061 360788. Shannon. from Ennis, Limerick, Shannon. **Castle** 9:30am–4:45pm (Jun–Sep: 9am) daily. **Folk Park** 9:30am–5:30pm (Jun–Sep: 9am–6:30pm) daily. 23–26 Dec. to Folk Park. **Banquets** see p330.

★ **Main Guard**

Now used for medieval-style banquets, this was the room where Bunratty's soldiers ate, slept and relaxed. Music was played to them from the Minstrels' Gallery, and a gate in one corner gave instant access to the dungeons.

Anteroom

The Robing Room
was where the earls put on their gowns before an audience in the Great Hall. They also used it for private interviews.

South Solar
These guest apartments have fine linenfold wood panelling, a form of decoration popular during the Tudor period. The elaborate fan-vaulted ceiling is partly a reconstruction.

A spiral staircase is found in each of the four towers.

★ **Great Hall**
This Tudor standard was among the many furnishings that Lord Gort brought to the castle. It stands in the Great Hall, once the banqueting hall and audience chamber, and still Bunratty's grandest room.

BUNRATTY FOLK PARK

A meticulous recreation of rural life in Ireland at the turn of the century, this Folk Park began with the reconstruction of a farmhouse which was saved during the building of nearby Shannon Airport. It now consists of a complete village, incorporating shops and a whole range of domestic architecture from a labourer's cottage to an elegant Georgian house. Other buildings include a farmhouse typical of the Moher region in the Burren *(see p228)* and a working corn mill. During the main summer season, people in authentic costume wander through the streets and demonstrate traditional crafts and trades from weaving to butter-making.

Main street of Bunratty Folk Park village

The countryside of the Lower Shannon, County Clare ▷

Typical thatched cottage in the village of Adare

Adare ⑮

Co Limerick. 🏘 *850.* 🚌 ℹ️
Heritage Centre, Main St
(061 396255). ◯ *Mar–Dec: daily.*

ADARE IS BILLED as Ireland's prettiest village. Cynics call it the prettiest "English" village since its manicured perfection is at odds with normal notions of national beauty. Originally a fief of the Fitzgeralds, the Earls of Kildare, Adare owes its present appearance more to the Earls of Dunraven, who restored the estate village in the 1820s and 1830s. The long, thin village is a picture of neat stonework and thatched roofs punctuated by picturesque ruins, all in a woodland setting.

The tourist office is at the new Heritage Centre, which includes a good exhibition on Adare's monastic history. Next door is the **Trinitarian Priory**, founded by the Fitzgeralds in 1230 and over-restored by the first Earl of Dunraven; it is now a Catholic church and convent. Opposite, by a stone-arched bridge, is the Washing Pool, a restored wash-house site.

By the main bridge, on the Limerick road, is the **Augustinian Priory** which was founded by the Fitzgeralds in 1315. Also known as Black Abbey, this well-restored priory has a central tower, subtle carvings, delightful cloisters and a graceful sedilia – a carved triple seat. Just over the bridge, from where it is best viewed, is **Desmond Castle**, a 13th-century feudal castle set on the banks of the River Maigue.

Nearby stands the main gate to **Adare Manor**, a luxury hotel and golf course. Within its 900 ha (365 acres) of parkland lie two evocative ruins. The **St Nicholas Church** and **Chantry Chapel** date back to the 12th century; both are accessible by path. The graceful 15th-century **Franciscan Abbey**, however, is surrounded by the golf course, though it can be seen clearly from the pathway.

In the heart of the village is the elegant Dunraven Arms Hotel from where the local hunt rides to hounds. Some of the nearby cottages, originally built by the Earl of Dunraven in 1828 for his estate workers, have been converted into restaurants, including the cosy Inn-Between.

Lough Gur ⑯

Co Limerick. 🚌 **Visitors' Centre**
📞 *061 385186.* ◯ *May–Sep: daily.*
♿ &.

THIS STONE AGE settlement, 26 km (16 miles) south of Limerick, was extensively inhabited in 3000 BC. Today the horseshoe-shaped lough and surrounding hills enclose an intriguing if rather inscrutable archaeological park. All around Lough Gur are standing stones and burial mounds, including megalithic tombs. One of the most impressive sights is the 4,000-year-old **Great Stone Circle**, just outside the park, by the Limerick–Kilmallock road. Excavations in the 1970s unearthed rectangular, oval and rounded Stone Age huts with stone foundations. The

Colourfully painted shopfronts on Main Street in Adare

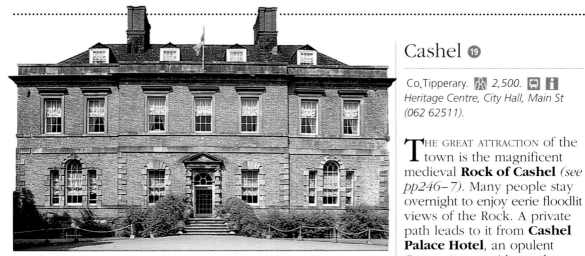

Façade of Cashel Palace Hotel

interpretive centre, which is housed in mock Stone Age huts on the site of the original settlement, offers a range of audiovisual displays, models of stone circles, burial chambers and tools and weapons.

As well as the various prehistoric sights scattered all over the Knockadoon Peninsula, there are two castle ruins from more recent times beside the lough – the 15th-century **Bourchier's Castle** and **Black Castle**, a 13th-century seat of the Earls of Desmond.

Roscrea ⑰

Co Tipperary. 👥 5,500. 🚆 🚌 ℹ️
Heritage Centre, Castle St (0505 21850). ◯ *Jun–Sep: daily.*

THIS MONASTIC TOWN situated on the banks of the River Bunnow, though marred by heavy through traffic, has an interesting historic centre. The 13th-century Anglo-Norman **Roscrea Castle** consists of a gate tower, curtain walls and two corner towers. In the courtyard stands Damer House, a Queen Anne-style residence with a magnificent staircase and Georgian garden. Just over the river lies **St Cronan's Monastery** which has a High Cross, Romanesque church gable and a truncated round tower. There are remains of a 15th-century **Franciscan Friary** on Abbey Street and nearby in St Cronan's churchyard is **Roscrea Pillar** which is an enigmatic early Christian stone.

⛪ **Roscrea Castle**
Castle Street. 📞 *0505 21850.* ◯ *Jun–Sep: daily.* 📷

Holy Cross Abbey ⑱

Thurles, Co Tipperary. 📞 *0504 43241.* 🚆 🚌 *to Thurles.* ◯ *May–Sep: daily; Oct–Apr: Sun.* 📷 📹 ♿

FOUNDED IN 1169 by the Benedictines, Holy Cross was supposedly endowed with a splinter from the True Cross, hence its name. Now it has been completely restored, and the church has become once again a popular place of worship and pilgrimage. Most of the present structure dates from the 15th century. It was built by the Cistercians, who took over the abbey in 1180. This gracious cruciform church, embellished with mullioned windows and sculpted pillars, is one of the finest examples of late Gothic architecture in Ireland.

The chancel has fine ribbed vaulting and, in the south wall, an exquisitely carved sedilia, which is rather oddly called "the tomb of the Good Woman's son". The abbey complex, set in charming gardens, also houses an old-fashioned pub.

Crucifixion carving at Holy Cross Abbey

Cashel ⑲

Co Tipperary. 👥 2,500. 🚌 ℹ️
Heritage Centre, City Hall, Main St (062 62511).

THE GREAT ATTRACTION of the town is the magnificent medieval **Rock of Cashel** *(see pp246–7).* Many people stay overnight to enjoy eerie floodlit views of the Rock. A private path leads to it from **Cashel Palace Hotel**, an opulent Queen Anne residence that was once the Bishop's Palace. Nearby, the remnant of a 12th-century castle has been turned into Kearney Castle Hotel. In the evening you can sample traditional Irish culture at the **Brú Ború Heritage Centre**. Named after Brian Boru, the 10th-century king of Munster *(see pp38–9),* the centre offers folk theatre, traditional music, banquets, and a craft shop.

At the foot of the Rock is the 13th-century **Dominican Friary**. This austere sandstone church has a fine west door, a 15th-century tower and lancet windows. On farmland outside Cashel lie the scant remains of **Hore Abbey**, a 13th-century Cistercian foundation. The abbey was largely remodelled and a tower added in the 15th century, but the barrel-vaulted sacristy, the nave, choir and chapter house are all original.

🎭 **Brú Ború Heritage Centre**
Cashel. 📞 *062 61122.* ◯ *Jun–Sep: daily; Oct–May: phone for details.* ♿
⛪ **Dominican Friary**
Dominic Street. ♿ *limited.*

Ruins of Hore Abbey (1272) with the Rock of Cashel in the background

Rock of Cashel

THIS ROCKY STRONGHOLD, which rises dramatically out of the Tipperary plain, was a symbol of royal and priestly power for more than a millennium. From the 5th century it was the seat of the Kings of Munster, whose kingdom extended over much of southern Ireland. In 1101, they handed Cashel over to the Church, and it flourished as a religious centre until a siege by a Cromwellian army in 1647 culminated in the massacre of its 3,000 occupants. The abbey was finally abandoned in the late 18th century.

Two hundred years on, the Rock of Cashel is besieged by visitors. A good proportion of the medieval complex is still standing, and Cormac's Chapel is one of the most outstanding examples of Romanesque architecture in the country.

★ St Patrick's Cross
The carving on the east face of this cross is said to be of St Patrick, who visited Cashel in 450. The cross is a copy of the original which stood here until 1982 and is now in the museum.

Hall of the Vicars' Choral
This hall was built in the 15th century for Cashel's most privileged choristers. The ceiling, a modern reconstruction based on medieval designs, features several decorative corbels including this painted angel.

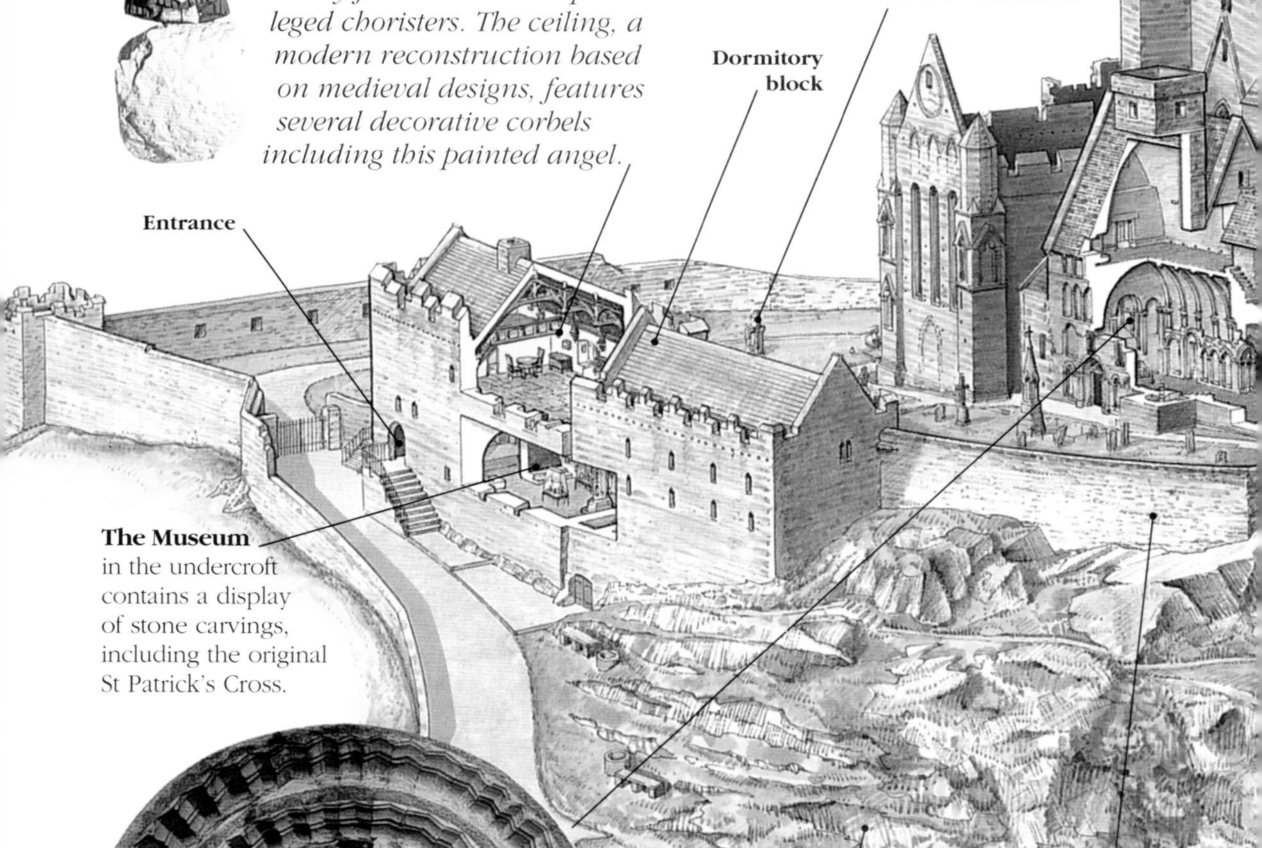

Dormitory block

Entrance

The Museum
in the undercroft contains a display of stone carvings, including the original St Patrick's Cross.

Outer wall

Limestone rock

★ Cormac's Chapel
Superb Romanesque carving adorns this chapel – the jewel of Cashel. The tympanum over the north door shows a centaur in a helmet aiming his bow and arrow at a lion.

STAR FEATURES

★ Cormac's Chapel

★ St Patrick's Cross

★ Cathedral

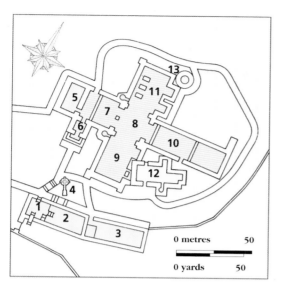

KEY

12th Century
4 St Patrick's Cross (replica)
12 Cormac's Chapel
13 Round tower

13th Century
6 Cathedral porch
7 Nave
8 Crossing
9 South transept
10 Choir
11 North transept

15th Century
1 Ticket office
2 Hall of the Vicars' Choral (museum)
3 Dormitory
5 Castle

0 metres 50
0 yards 50

VISITORS' CHECKLIST

Cashel. 062 61437. to Thurles. to Cashel. mid-Jun–mid-Sep: 9am–7:30pm: daily; mid-Sep–mid-Mar: 9:30am–4:30pm; mid-Mar–mid-Jun: 9:30am–5:30pm. 24–28 Dec.

The Rock
The 28-m (92-ft) round tower, the oldest and tallest building on the rock, enabled Cashel's inhabitants to scour the surrounding plain for potential attackers.

Round tower

Crossing

The Choir contains the 17th-century tomb of Miler Magrath, who caused a scandal by being both a Protestant and Catholic archbishop at the same time.

Graveyard

The O'Scully Monument, an ornate memorial erected in 1870 by a local landowning family, was damaged during a storm in 1976.

North Transept
Panels from three 16th-century tombs in the north transept are decorated with remarkably fresh and intricate carvings. This one, against the north wall, features a vine-leaf design and strange stylized beasts.

★ Cathedral
The roofless Gothic cathedral has thick walls riddled with hidden passages; in the north transept these are seen emerging at the base of the windows.

Athassel Priory ⑳

8 km (5 miles) W of Cashel, Co Tipperary. 🚌 *to Tipperary.* 🕐 *daily.*

THIS RUINED Augustinian priory is situated on the west bank of the River Suir. The tomb of William de Burgh, the Norman founder of the priory, lies in the church. Athassel was established in 1192 and is believed to have been the largest medieval priory in Ireland until it burned down in 1447. The scattered monastic site conveys a tranquil atmosphere, from the gatehouse and church to the remains of the cloisters and chapter house. The church has a fine west doorway, nave and chancel walls, as well as a 15th-century central tower.

The ruins of Athassel Priory, on the banks of the River Suir

Glen of Aherlow ㉑

Co Tipperary. 🚌 *to Bansha or Tipperary.* ℹ️ *Coach Road Inn, on R663 8 km (5 miles) E of Galbally (062 56331).*

THE LUSH VALLEY of the River Aherlow runs between the Galty Mountains and the wooded ridge of Slievenamuck. Bounded by the villages of **Galbally** and **Bansha**, the glen was historically an important pass between Limerick and Tipperary and a notorious hideout for outlaws.

Today there are opportunities for riding, cycling, rambling and fishing. Lowland walks follow the trout-filled river along the valley floor. More adventurous walkers will be tempted by the Galty range, which offers more rugged hill-walking, past wooded foothills, mountain streams, tiny corrie lakes and splendid sandstone peaks.

Cahir ㉒

Co Tipperary. 🏠 *2,100.* 🚊 🚌 ℹ️ *May–Sep: Castle Street (052 41453).* 🏪 *Fri.*

ONCE A GARRISON and mill town, Cahir is today a busy market town. The pub-lined Castle Street is the most appealing area. It leads to the Suir River, Cahir Castle and the well-signposted rural walk to the Swiss Cottage.

On the edge of town lies the ruined **Cahir Abbey**, a 13th-century Augustinian priory. Its fine windows are decorated with carved heads.

🏰 Cahir Castle

Castle Street. ☎ *052 41011.* 🕐 *daily.* 📷 🎫 ♿ *limited.*
Built on a rocky island in the River Suir, Cahir is one of the most formidable castles in Ireland and a popular film set. This well-preserved fortress dates from the 13th century but is inextricably linked to its later owners, the Butlers. A powerful family in Ireland since the Anglo-Norman invasion, they were considered trusty lieges of the English crown and were granted the Cahir barony in 1375. Under their command, the castle was renovated and extended throughout the 15th and 16th centuries. It remained in the Butler family until 1964.

The castle is divided into outer, middle and inner wards, with a barbican at the outer entrance. The inner ward is on the site of the original Norman castle; the foundations are 13th century, as are the curtain walls and keep. The restored interior includes the striking great hall, which dates largely from the 1840s, though one of the walls is original and the windows are 15th century. From the ramparts there are views over the river and millrace.

🏛 Swiss Cottage

Ardfinnan Road, Cahir. ☎ *052 41144.* 🕐 *May–Sep: daily; Mar–Apr & Oct–Nov: Tue–Sun.* 📷 *obligatory.*
The Swiss Cottage is a superb example of a *cottage orné*, a rustic folly. It was designed for the Butlers by the Regency architect John Nash in 1810. Here, Lord and Lady Cahir played at bucolic bliss, enjoying picnics dressed as peasants. Fashion dictated a *cottage orné* should blend in with the

View across the unspoilt Glen of Aherlow

countryside and all designs should be drawn from nature with nothing matching, so the windows and sloping eaves are all of different sizes and design. The enchantingly furnished cottage contains a tea room, gracious music room and two bedrooms, all beautifully restored.

Clonmel ❷❸

Co Tipperary. 🚶 15,500. 🚌 🚋 ℹ️
6 Sarsfield St (052 22960).

SET ON THE RIVER SUIR and framed by the Comeragh Mountains, Clonmel is Tipperary's main town. This Anglo-Norman stronghold was a fief of the Desmonds and eventually of the Butlers. Its prosperity was founded on milling and brewing, and attractive mills still line the quays. Today, Clonmel is a bustling, brash town with quirky architecture and lively nightlife.

The **Franciscan Friary** by the quays was remodelled in Early English style in Victorian times but retains a 15th-century tower and houses 16th-century Butler tomb effigies. Nearby is O'Connell Street, Clonmel's main shopping street, which is straddled by the West Gate, built in 1831. Visitors to **Hearn's**

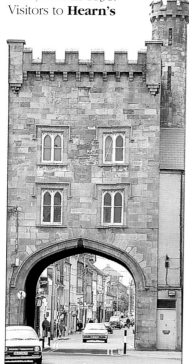
Clonmel's mock Tudor West Gate, spanning O'Connell Street

The Swiss Cottage at Cahir, beautifully restored to its original state

Hotel on Parnell Street can see memorabilia of Charles Bianconi (1786 –1875), including pictures of the horse-drawn coach service he established between Clonmel and Cahir. Eventually this developed into a nationwide passenger service.

Carrick-on-Suir ❷❹

Co Tipperary. 🚶 5,100. 🚌 ℹ️
Heritage Centre (051 640200).

THIS SLEEPY MARKET TOWN has a distinctly old-fashioned air. In the 15th century, it was a strategic site commanding access west to Clonmel and southeast to Waterford, but after Tudor times the town sank into oblivion. Apart from Ormond Castle, there are few specific sights. However, you can stroll by the old waterside warehouses or shop for Tipperary Crystal.

⛪ Ormond Castle

Castle Park. 📞 051 640787.
◯ Jun–Sep: daily. 📷 🚻 limited.
Although once a fortress, Ormond Castle is the finest surviving Tudor manor house in Ireland. It was built by the powerful Butler family, the Earls of Ormonde, who were given their title by the English crown in 1328. The castle has a gracious Elizabethan façade overlaying the medieval original; the battlemented towers on the south side sit rather oddly with the gabled façade and its mullioned and oriel windows.

The finest room is the Long Gallery, which has a stuccoed ceiling studded with heraldic crests, and two ornately carved fireplaces. The Elizabethan section was added by

Black Tom Butler, the 10th Earl of Ormonde and a loyal subject to Elizabeth Tudor. On his death, the Ormondes abandoned Carrick for Kilkenny (see pp166 –8).

Intricate wood carving on a four-poster bed at Ormond Castle

ENVIRONS: In the churchyard at **Ahenny**, about 10 km (6 miles) north of Carrick, stand two magnificent High Crosses (see p325). Both are crowned by "caps" or "bishops' mitres" and have intricate cable, spiral and fret patterns.

At **Kilkieran**, 5 km (3 miles) north of Carrick, are three other interesting High Crosses, dating from the 9th century. The Plain Cross is unadorned but capped; the West Cross is profusely ornamented though weathered; the Long Shaft Cross has an odd design of stumpy arms on a long shaft.

Peat bog with Bog Cotton flowers, Connemara, County Galway ▷

THE WEST
OF IRELAND

THE WEST OF IRELAND

MAYO · GALWAY · ROSCOMMON

THIS IS THE HEART OF CONNAUGHT, *Ireland's historic western province. The West lives up to its image as a traditional, rural, sparsely populated land, with windswept mountains and countryside speckled with low stone walls and peat bogs. Yet it also encompasses Galway, a fast-growing university town whose youthful population brings life to the medieval streets and snug pubs.*

The West of Ireland contains some of the country's most impressive scenery. The variety of landscapes on display make travelling here a visual feast as well as an adventure. The bracken browns and soft violets of Connemara in the west of Galway and the fertile farmland and placid lakes of County Roscommon are in striking contrast to the extensive boglands of County Mayo. Piles of turf, cut by hand in the time-honoured way and left to dry in the sun, are a familiar sight throughout the region.

The rugged Atlantic coastline of the West has been occupied for over 5,000 years. It is rich in prehistoric sites such as the land enclosures of Céide Fields and the ring forts on the Aran Islands. Evidence of the monastic period can be seen in the mysterious and beautiful remains at Kilmacduagh, with its tilting round tower; also from this era came Clonfert cathedral, founded by St Brendan the Navigator in the 6th century, and the Cistercian abbey at Boyle.

In medieval times, the city of Galway was an Anglo-Norman stronghold, surrounded by warring Gaelic clans. After the Cromwellian victories of the 1640s, many Irish were dispossessed of their fertile lands and dispatched 'to hell or Connacht'. Landlords made their mark in the 17th and 18th centuries, building impressive country houses at Clonalis, Strokestown Park and Westport. During the Great Famine, the West, especially County Mayo, lost a great deal of its already sparse population through famine and emigration. In spite of this, strong Gaelic traditions have survived in County Galway.

Galway is Ireland's second-largest county, but apart from its burgeoning county city, it has, like the rest of the region, a relatively small number of inhabitants; certain areas of the West seem frozen in times gone by.

Swans by the quayside of the Claddagh area of Galway

◁ **Typical Connemara landscape dominated by the peaks of the Twelve Bens**

Reconstructed neolithic farm dwellings at the National Heritage Park, County Galway

Two routes heading west from Galway travel through the Connemara. The southern road leads along Galway Bay into the heart of the Irish-speaking region, where timeless fishing villages are set along the shores of rocky bays which cut deep inland. Narrow causeways built of the local stone connect countless little islands scattered offshore. On a fine day, this is a tempting place to explore. Further west are picturesque villages such as Roundstone, which

Detail from an altar tomb, Clare Island, County Mayo

cater for a quiet tourist trade with good pubs and local crafts. A second main road runs north-west along Lough Corrib, the largest lake in the Republic. Fishing boats and pleasure craft cruise these island-studded waters, where there are the remains of early Christian monasteries and, according to legend, a witch's castle. On the north shore of the lake is the village of Cong, with its attractive abbey ruins. Both routes lead round to Connemara National Park, which boasts some of the most splendid vistas in Ireland, notably the four peaks of the Twelve Bens, a majestic range that forms the backdrop to much of the region. Hiking trails lead through a surrounding landscape of heath and bog, grassland and lakes. Here, the small but sturdy Connemara ponies graze contentedly. Clifden is popular, with its superb setting between the mountains and the sea and its proximity to Kylemore Abbey and Dan O'Hara's Homestead.

Although Galway city is one of the country's fastest-growing urban areas, its town centre is small and retains its medieval flavour with compact, pedestrianized streets lined with some colourful shop fronts and pubs. Its atmosphere is lively: Galway is home to a university as well as artists and writers, and it is a centre for music and theatre.

In southern County Galway are the delightful village of Kinvarra, with its storefront murals, and Thoor Ballylee, retreat of WB Yeats. Summer in the county is very much a time for festivities: there are the Galway Races in July, traditional sailing ship races off Kinvarra in August and the Galway Oyster Festival in September. All are lively, sociable events that attract locals and a stream of visitors.

The remote bogland landscape of County Mayo

View across the calm waters of Lough Furnace in County Mayo

Roscommon was originally established as a result of westward expansion in the 13th century, its urban development taking place gradually around the area of the Anglo-Norman Roscommon Castle. Geologically, the county belongs to the central limestone plain, with a relatively flat landscape covered in fields, pastures or bogland, broken by patches of woodland, heather and lakes. Its rather soulless busy county town is certainly not representative of the rest of the county, parts of which have a simple and almost ineffably remote beauty.

County Mayo has a most distinct identity. Its landscapes, its remoteness and its people seem in a way to be so far removed from areas in the south of the country as to be part of a completely different nation. Throughout history, potential

Ancient stone cliff-top construction at Rosmuck, County Galway

invaders were deterred by some of the most desolate bogland country in Ireland. Even before the years of famine, locals looked to emigrate to more promising areas. Yet Mayo is a fascinating environment: thousands of years ago, when the climate was warmer and drier, this region was completely covered in forest, an intriguing notional contrast to the boglands of today. Those who venture across it now will reach coastal cliffs and remote headlands.

The splendours of the West also include the starkly magnificent cliff scenery of the remote islands off the coast. Achill Island, with its fine beaches and stunning scenic drive, is a popular holiday destination. Clare Island was, along with Inishbofin, a stronghold of Grace O'Malley, the famous Pirate Queen. Most celebrated are the Aran Islands, where traditional Irish culture and occupations have endured in isolated communities.

In fact, the whole of the West has a long-standing craft tradition. Galway in particular is strong on local crafts, from traditional Claddagh rings to knitted sweaters, woven goods and even musical instruments. The An Ceardlann craft centre at Spiddal is an excellent place at which to observe craftspeople at their work.

Although the West of Ireland is often shrouded in a misty drizzle or battered by Atlantic winds and accompanying heavy downpours, the climate is mild. In the hedgerows of Connemara and along the coast, lush red fuchsia and purple rhododendra grow in profusion. When sunshine illuminates the landscape, transforming the lakes into sapphire jewels, the boglands to tawny gold and the stone-wall fences to glinting threads of silver, the region produces vistas that are nothing short of magical.

Textiles in Ireland

IRELAND HAS A LONG TRADITION of hard-wearing textiles designed to withstand its damp, often windy weather. The functional garments made from them have become very popular overseas, where fashion, not practicality, fuels demand. The Aran sweater, now sold all over the world, originated on three tiny, exposed islands 30 miles out in Galway Bay. One of the country's traditional sheep-rearing areas gave birth to the much sought-after Donegal tweed, and the arrival of Huguenot weavers in the late 17th century made Ulster the place where the famous linen industry first flourished.

The rugged landscape of the Aran Islands: influential on the nature of its textiles

WEAVING: CONTINUING THE TRADITION

The production of tweed (the word is derived from "tweel", Scottish for twill) has been big business in Ireland since the 18th century. The cloth is now mostly woven on power looms, but handloom weaving demonstrations are often given in craft workshops. Originally the tweed was made using undyed wool, in shades of grey, cream and brown. Now yarns are dyed in a range of colours.

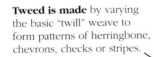

Tweed is made by varying the basic "twill" weave to form patterns of herringbone, chevrons, checks or stripes.

Linen has been made in Ireland since the Bronze Age, but it was when the Huguenot workers from France arrived in Lisburn in 1698 that the industry began to flourish. As it is strong, warm, hard-wearing, and absorbs and releases moisture quickly, linen was traditionally used for working clothes. It has long been highly valued as a textile for household items, too.

ARAN KNITTING PATTERNS

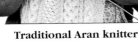

The intricate patterns used in the traditional Aran sweater were developed and handed down within families, some clans inventing their own distinct designs. The origins of the patterns are uncertain, but they may reflect life on the islands, with some of the stitches named after fishermen's ropes, the mesh of their nets, and rocks and waves. Other stitches may have religious significance, such as the three-in-one, one-in-three "trinity" stitch and the tree of life.

Traditional Aran knitter

Eight-stitch cable

Aran knitwear is now a commercialized industry. Patterns have been adapted so that they can easily be made up in different sizes, and while the traditional creamy-coloured wool, or "bainín", is still very popular, other colours and yarns are also used in items that range from cardigans, hats and scarves to cushion covers.

Hardy, rough-textured traditional tweeds

"Donegal tweed" is synonymous with the warm, weather-resistant, hard-wearing cloth used originally by working people in the west of Ireland. It is now used in classic jackets, skirts and suits, and increasingly by fashion designers.

FISHERMEN'S SHIRTS

Aran sweater

Aran fishing "shirts" (or sweaters) were originally developed as protection for the men who were out fishing in currachs, in all types of perilous weather and in treacherous seas off the stormy west coast. The hardy island sheep produced the perfect naturally waterproof wool, while the close stitching of the design traps air and thus provides insulation. The patterning was designed to give elasticity and ease of movement.

Trellis with moss stitch

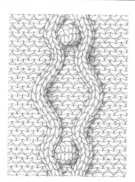

Bobble and wave

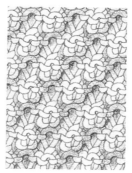

Trinity stitch

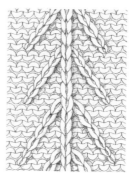

Tree of life

Exploring the West of Ireland

Galway city, Clifden and Westport make the best bases for exploring the region, with cosy pubs, good walks and access to the scenic islands. Connemara and the wilds of County Mayo attract nature lovers, while the islands of Achill, Aran, Clare and Inishbofin appeal to water-sports enthusiasts and ramblers. The lakes of County Roscommon are popular with anglers, and Lough Corrib and Lough Key offer relaxing cruises.

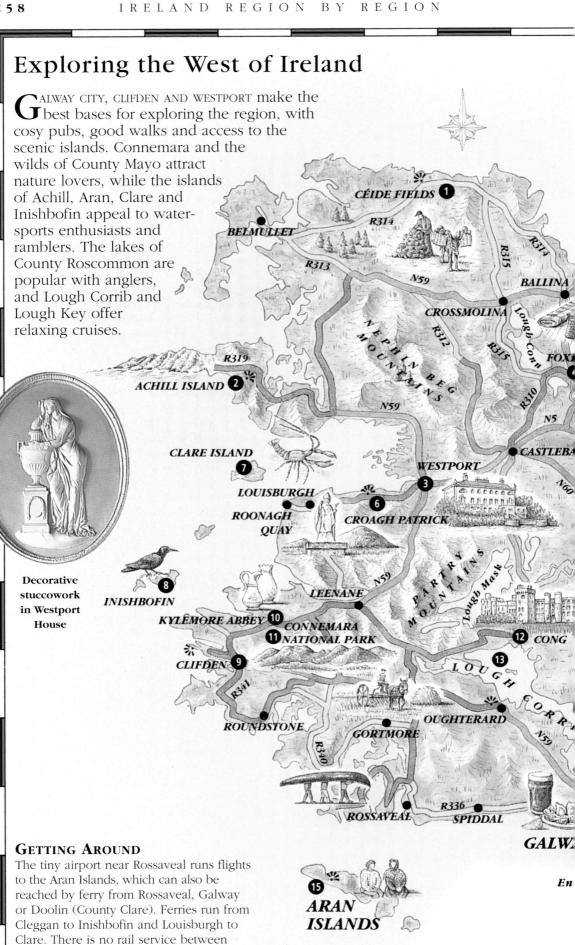

Decorative
stuccowork
in Westport
House

CÉIDE FIELDS 1
BELMULLET
R314
R313
N59
BALLINA
CROSSMOLINA
R312
Lough Conn
R315
FOX
NEPHIN BEG MOUNTAINS
N59
N5
R319
ACHILL ISLAND 2
N59
CASTLEBA
CLARE ISLAND 7
WESTPORT
N60
LOUISBURGH
ROONAGH QUAY
6
3
CROAGH PATRICK
N59
PARTRY MOUNTAINS
Lough Mask
INISHBOFIN
8
LEENANE
KYLEMORE ABBEY 10
CONNEMARA
11 NATIONAL PARK
12 CONG
CLIFDEN 9
13
LOUGH CORR
R341
ROUNDSTONE
OUGHTERARD
GORTMORE
N59
R340
ROSSAVEAL
R336
SPIDDAL
GALW

Getting Around

The tiny airport near Rossaveal runs flights to the Aran Islands, which can also be reached by ferry from Rossaveal, Galway or Doolin (County Clare). Ferries run from Cleggan to Inishbofin and Louisburgh to Clare. There is no rail service between Galway and Westport but the towns are linked by reliable (if slow) buses. Connemara is reached by Bus Éireann services from Galway and Clifden (via Oughterard or Cong) or can be explored on day-long minibus tours also from Galway or Clifden.

15
ARAN
ISLANDS

En

0 kilometres		20
0 miles		10

River valley at Delphi in northern Connemara

Sligo

Lough Key

BOYLE ㉕

KNOCK

CLONALIS ㉓ CASTLEREA
HOUSE

STROKESTOWN PARK HOUSE ㉔

N60

TUAM

ROSCOMMON ㉒

Lough Ree

Suck

N63

Dublin

Shannon

BALLINASLOE

HENRY R348
AUGHRIM

TUROE STONE ㉑

N6

CLONFERT ⑳
CATHEDRAL

N66

N65

ARRA

THOOR ⑱
BALLYLEE R353

GORT

PORTUMNA ⑲ Limerick

Lough Derg

CDUAGH

**Colourful shopfronts lining
Quay Street, Galway**

KEY

▬	Major road
▭	Minor road
▬	Scenic route
〰	River
☀	Viewpoint

Bogwood centrepiece in Céide Fields interpretative centre

Céide Fields ❶

8 km (5 miles) W of Ballycastle, Co Mayo. 📞 096 43325. 🚌 from Ballycastle. 🔵 mid-Mar–Nov: daily. 🅿 ♿ ground floor.

SURROUNDED by heather-clad moorlands and mountains along a bleak, dramatic stretch of north Mayo coastline is Europe's largest Stone Age land enclosure. Over 10 sq km (4 sq miles) were enclosed by walls to make fields suitable for growing wheat and barley, and grazing cattle. Remains of farm buildings indicate that it was an extensive community. The fields were slowly buried below the creeping bog formation, where they have been preserved for 5,000 years.

Part of the bog has been cut away to reveal the collapsed stone walls of the ancient fields. The remains are simple rather than spectacular, but excellent guides help visitors to find and recognize key features. Stone Age pottery and a primitive plough have been found in recent excavations. The striking, pyramid-shaped interpretative centre has a viewing platform overlooking the site, audiovisual presentations and displays on local geology and botany.

ENVIRONS: Scattered around the wilderness of the spectacular north Mayo coast from Ballina to the end of the Mullet peninsula is a series of sculptures forming the **North Mayo Sculpture Trail**. Created by 12 sculptors from three continents, the 15 works, often on a huge scale, are made from earth, stone and other natural materials; additional sculptures are planned. They aim to highlight the coast's grandeur and enduring nature.

Achill Island ❷

Co Mayo. 🚌 from Westport. 🛈 Jun–Sep: The Sound (098 45384).

IRELAND's largest island, 22 km (13.5 miles) long and 19 km (12 miles) wide, is reached by a road bridge that can be raised for boats to pass through. Achill offers the more intrepid visitor moorland, mountains, rugged cliffs and beautiful long beaches, and is a very popular spot for angling and water sports.

For motorists, the best introduction is the **Atlantic Coast Drive**, a circular, signposted route from Achill Sound, by the bridge. The road goes to the island's southern tip, then north around the rest of Achill. Between Doeega and Keel in the southwest, run the dramatic Minaun Cliffs and Cathedral Rocks. In the north is Slievemore, a mountain overlooking the village of Slievemore, which was abandoned during the Great Famine (see p281). Sharks can be spotted off Keem Bay in the west.

Westport ❸

Co Mayo. 🏃 4,500. 🚉 🚌 🛈 The Mall (098 25711). 🛒 Thu.

The *Angel of Welcome* above the marble staircase at Westport House

WESTPORT is a neat landlord town and has a bustling, prosperous air. In the 1770s, architect James Wyatt laid out the wide, tree-lined streets, including North and South Mall on either side of Carrowbeg River. The town traded in yarn, cloth, beer and slate, but industrialization and the Great Famine (see p281) brought decline until the 1950s when new industry and visitors were attracted to the area.

Beyond the South Mall is Bridge Street, lined with cafés and pubs; the most appealing is Matt Molloy's, named after and owned by the flautist from The Chieftains.

🏛 **Westport House**
Off Louisburgh Rd. 📞 098 27766. 🔵 Easter & May: Sat–Sun; Jun–Sep: daily. 🅿
Just west of the town is the Carrowbeg estuary and Clew Bay. At the head of the bay

The deserted village of Slievemore on Achill Island

Statue of St Patrick at the foot of Croagh Patrick, looking out to Clew Bay

stands Westport House, the seat of the Earls of Altamont, descendants of the Browne family, who were Tudor settlers. The town of Westport itself was started in the 1750s by John Browne, first Lord Altamont, to complement the house. Designed in 1732 by Richard Castle, and completed by James Wyatt in 1778, the limestone mansion stands on the site of an O'Malley castle. Its imposing interior includes a sweeping marble staircase and an elegant James Wyatt dining room and is adorned with family portraits, antique Waterford chandeliers and 18th-century Chinese wallpaper. The estate includes a small boating lake, miniature railway, children's zoo, an amusement arcade and several shops.

Bog oak and silver bowl from Westport House

Foxford ④

Road map B3. Co Mayo. 👥 *1,000.* 🚌 *from Galway.* ℹ️ *Westport (098 25711).*

THIS TRANQUIL market town is known for good angling in nearby Lough Conn and for its woven rugs and tweeds. In the town centre is **Foxford Woollen Mills**, founded in 1892 by an Irish nun, Mother Arsenius (originally named Agnes). The thriving mill now supplies top fashion houses. An audiovisual tour traces the mill's history, and visitors can see craftspeople at work.

🏭 Foxford Woollen Mills and Visitor Centre

St Joseph's Place. 📞 *094 56756.* 🕐 *daily.* 🔴 *Good Fri, 24–26 Dec.*

Knock ⑤

Co Mayo. 👥 *440.* ✈️ *15 km (9 miles) N of Knock.* 🚌 ℹ️ *May–Sep: Knock (094 88193).*

IN 1879, two local women saw an apparition of the Virgin, St Joseph and St John the Evangelist by the gable of the Church of St John the Baptist. It was witnessed by 13 more onlookers and validated by the Catholic Church amid claims of miracle cures. Every year, a million and a half believers make the pilgrimage to the shrine, including Pope John Paul II in 1979 and Mother Teresa in 1993. Its focal point is the gable where the apparition was seen, which is now covered over to form a chapel. Nearby is the Basilica of Our Lady, a modern basilica and Marian

Bottles of holy water for sale at the shrine in Knock

shrine. **Knock Folk Museum,** beside the basilica, portrays life in 19th-century rural Ireland with reconstructions of a cottage and schoolroom. An Apparition section covers the background to the miracle.

🏛️ Knock Shrine and Folk Museum

📞 *094 88100.* 🕐 *May–Oct: daily; Nov–Apr: by appt.*

Croagh Patrick ⑥

Murrisk, Co Mayo. 🚌 *from Westport.*

IRELAND'S holy mountain, named after the national saint *(see p377),* is one of Mayo's best-known landmarks. From the bottom it seems cone-shaped, an impression dispelled by climbing to its flat peak. This quartzite, scree-clad mountain has a history of pagan worship from 3000 BC. However, in AD 441, St Patrick is said to have spent 40 days on the mountain fasting and praying for the Irish.

Since then, penitents, often barefoot, have made the pilgrimage to the summit in his honour, especially on Reek or Garland Sunday, the last in July. From the start of the trail at Campbell's Pub in Murrisk, where there is huge statue of the saint, it is about a two-hour climb to the top, at 765 m (2,510 ft). Mass is celebrated there in the modern chapel. There are also panoramic views over Clew Bay. Recently, there have been proposals to mine for gold and bauxite on the mountain.

Fishing nets on a harbour wall in the Aran Islands ▷

Clare Island ⑦

Co Mayo. 👥 180. ⛴ from Roonagh Quay, 6.5 km (4 miles) W of Louisburgh. ℹ️ Westport.

Cᴌᴀʀᴇ ɪsʟᴀɴᴅ, set in Clew Bay, is dominated by two hills, and a square 15th-century castle commands the headland and harbour. In the 16th century the island was the stronghold of Grace O'Malley, pirate queen and patriot, who held sway over the western coast. Although, according to Tudor state papers, she was received at Queen Elizabeth I's court, she stood out against English rule until her death in her seventies in 1603. She is buried here in a tiny Cistercian abbey decorated with medieval murals and inscribed with her motto: "Invincible on land and sea".

The island is dotted with Iron Age huts and field systems as well as promontory forts and Bronze Age cooking sites *(see p206)*. Clare is rich in bog flora and fauna, making it popular with walkers. Animal lovers come to see the seals, dolphins, falcons and otters.

Eɴᴠɪʀᴏɴs: The mainland coastal village of **Louisburgh** offers rugged Atlantic landscape, sheltered coves, sea angling

The ferry to Inishbofin leaving Cleggan Harbour

and water sports. It is also home to the **Granuaile Centre** which celebrates the exploits of Grace O'Malley (*Granuaile* in Gaelic) and has displays on Mayo folklore and archaeology.

🏛 **Granuaile Centre**
St Catherine's Church, Louisburgh.
📞 *098 66195.* ⭕ *May–Oct: daily.*

Inishbofin ⑧

Co Galway. 👥 200. ⛴ from Cleggan.
ℹ️ Clifden.

Tʜᴇ ɴᴀᴍᴇ Inishbofin means "island of the white cow". This mysterious, often mist-swathed island was chosen for its remoteness by the exiled 7th-century St Colman, English Abbot of Lindisfarne. On the site of his original monastery is a late medieval church, graveyard and holy well. At the sheltered harbour

entrance lies a ruined castle, occupied in the 16th century by Spanish pirate Don Bosco in alliance with Grace O'Malley. In 1653 it was captured by Cromwellian forces and used as a prison for Catholic priests. Inishbofin was later owned by a succession of absentee landlords and now survives on farming and lobster-fishing.

Surrounded by reefs and islets, the island's landscape is characterized by stone walls, small abandoned cottages, reed-fringed lakes and hay meadows, where the corn-crake *(see p22)* can be seen, or heard. Inishbofin's beaches offer bracing walks.

Clifden ⑨

Co Galway. 👥 800. 🚌 ℹ️ Apr–Sep: Market St (095 21163). 🛒 Tue.

Fʀᴀᴍᴇᴅ by the grandeur of the Twelve Bens mountain range and with a striking skyline dominated by two church spires, this early 19th-century market town passes for the capital of the Connemara region and is a good base for exploring. Clifden was founded in 1812 by John d'Arcy, a local landowner and High Sheriff of Galway, to create a pocket of respectability within the lawlessness of Connemara. Unfortunately, the family eventually went bankrupt trying to bring prosperity and order to the town. The Protestant church contains a copy of the Cross of Cong *(see p77)*.

Today craft shops have taken over much of the town. In the centre is the Square, a place for lively pubs such as EJ Kings. Nearby is O'Grady's Seafood Restaurant which is one of the finest in Galway. Connemara is noted for its *sean-nos* (unaccompanied

Clifden against a backdrop of the Twelve Bens mountains

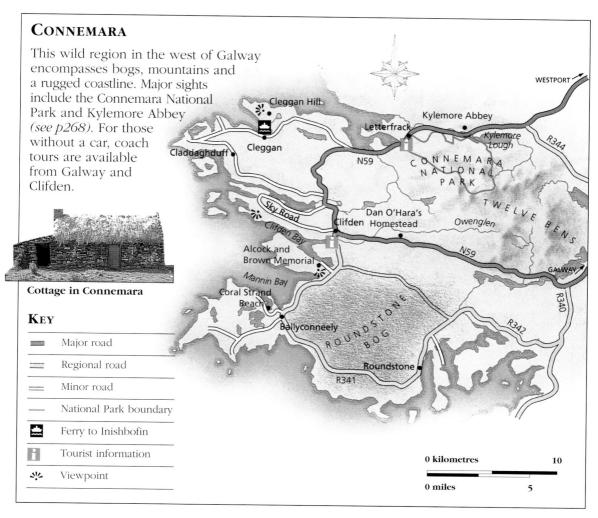

CONNEMARA

This wild region in the west of Galway encompasses bogs, mountains and a rugged coastline. Major sights include the Connemara National Park and Kylemore Abbey *(see p268)*. For those without a car, coach tours are available from Galway and Clifden.

Cottage in Connemara

KEY

▬▬	Major road
═	Regional road
═	Minor road
—	National Park boundary
⛴	Ferry to Inishbofin
ℹ	Tourist information
☀	Viewpoint

0 kilometres   10
0 miles   5

---

singing), but in Clifden, general traditional music is more common.

Jutting out into **Clifden Bay** is a sand spit and beach, sign-posted from Clifden Square. South of Clifden, at the start of the Roundstone Road, is Owenglen Cascade where, in May, salmon leap on their way to spawn upstream.

ENVIRONS: The **Sky Road** is an 11-km (7-mile) circular route with stunning ocean views. The road goes northwest from Clifden and passes desolate scenery and the narrow inlet of Clifden Bay. Clifden Castle, John d'Arcy's Gothic Revival ruin, lies just off the Sky Road, as do several beaches.

The coastal road north from Clifden to **Cleggan**, via Claddaghduff, is spectacular, passing former smuggling coves. Cleggan, an attractive fishing village, nestles into the head of Cleggan Bay. From here boats leave for Inishbofin and Inishturk. **Cleggan Hill** has a ruined Napoleonic Martello tower at the top and a megalithic tomb at the foot.

To the south of Clifden, the coastal route to Roundstone skirts a mass of bogland pitted with tiny lakes. The **Alcock and Brown Memorial** over-looks the bog landing site of the first transatlantic flight made by Alcock and Brown in 1919. Nearby is Marconi's wireless station, which exchanged the first transatlantic radio mes-sages with Nova Scotia in 1907. The **Ballyconneely** area has craggy islands and the beautiful **Coral Strand Beach**. The village of **Round-stone** is best seen during the summer regatta of traditional Galway hookers *(see p271)*.

A short drive to the east of Clifden is **Dan O'Hara's Homestead**. In a wild, rocky setting, this organic farm recreates the tough conditions of life in Connemara before the 1840s. The folksy air of Connemara is accentuated by pony and trap rides and traditional music.

🏛 **Dan O'Hara's Homestead**
Heritage Centre, Lettershea, off N59.
📞 *095 21246.* ⭕ *Apr–end Oct: daily.*
♿

View of the coast from the Sky Road

The misty Maumturk Mountains, Connemara, County Galway ▷

The imposing Kylemore Abbey on the shores of Kylemore Lough

Kylemore Abbey ⑩

Connemara, Co Galway. 📞 095 41146. 🚌 from Galway and Clifden. ○ daily. 🖼 ♿ limited.

SHELTERED BY THE SLOPES of the Twelve Bens, this lakeside castle is a romantic, battlemented Gothic Revival fantasy. It was built as a present for his wife by Mitchell Henry (1826–1911), who was a Manchester tycoon and later Galway MP. The Henrys also purchased a huge area of moorland, drained the boggy hillside and planted thousands of trees as a windbreak for their new orchards and exotic walled gardens. After the sudden deaths of his wife and daughter, Henry left Kylemore and the castle was sold.

It became an abbey when Benedictine nuns fleeing from Ypres in Belgium during World War I, sought refuge here. The nuns now run the abbey as a select girls' boarding school. Visitors are restricted to the grounds, restaurant and craft shop where they can watch the abbey pottery being hand-decorated and fired. The cream earthenware pottery is painted with a fuchsia motif.

In 1999 a 2.5 ha (6-acre) restored Victorian walled garden opened in the grounds of the abbey, featuring the longest double herbaceous borders in Ireland, a nuttery and a meandering stream-side walk.

Connemara National Park ⑪

Letterfrack, Connemara, Co Galway. 📞 095 41054. **Visitors' Centre** ○ May–Sep: daily. 🖼 ♿

A COMBINATION of bogland, lakes and mountains makes up this National Park in the heart of Connemara. Within its more than 2,000 ha (5,000 acres) are four of the Twelve Bens, including Benbaun, the highest mountain in the range at 730 m (2,400 ft), and the peak of Diamond Hill. At the centre is the valley of Glanmore with the Polladirk River flowing through it.

Visitors come for some of the most spectacular landscape in the region and to glimpse the famous Connemara ponies.

Part of the land originally belonged to the Kylemore Abbey estate. In 1980 it became a National Park. There are traces of the land's previous uses all over the park: megalithic tombs, up to 4,000 years old, can be seen as well as old ridges marking former grazing areas and arable fields.

The park is open all year, while the Visitors' Centre near the entrance, just outside Letterfrack, is open only in the summer months. It has displays on how the landscape developed and was used and on local flora and fauna. There is also an audiovisual theatre and an indoor picnic area. Two signposted walks start from the Visitors' Centre. In summer there are guided walks, some led by botanists, and various children's activities. Climbing the Twelve Bens should be attempted only by experienced walkers equipped for all weather conditions.

CONNEMARA WILDLIFE

The blanket bogs and moorlands of Connemara are a botanist's paradise, especially for unusual bog and heathland plants. Birdlife is also varied with hooded crows, which can be recognized by their grey and black plumage, stonechats, peregrines and merlins – the smallest falcons in the British Isles. Red deer have been successfully reintroduced into the area and a herd can be seen in the National Park. Badgers, foxes, stoats and otters may also be spotted, as well as grey seals along the rocky coast.

***The merlin** nests in old clumps of heather and feeds mainly on small birds.*

***St Dabeoc's heath**, a pretty heather, grows nowhere else in Ireland or Great Britain.*

Cong ⑫

Co Mayo. 👥 *200*. 🚌 ℹ️ *Galway (091 563081)*.

Tᴴɪꜱ ᴘɪᴄᴛᴜʀᴇꜱQᴜᴇ ᴠɪʟʟᴀɢᴇ lies on the shores of Lough Corrib, just within County Mayo. Cong means isthmus – the village lies on the strip of land between Lough Corrib and Lough Mask. During the 1840s, as a famine relief project, a canal was built linking the two lakes, but the water drained through the porous limestone bed. Stone bridges and stone-clad locks are still in place along the dry canal.

Cong Abbey lies close to the main street. The Augustinian abbey was founded in the early 12th century by Turlough O'Connor, King of Connaught and High King of Ireland, on the site of a 6th-century monastery established by St Fechin. The abbey has doorways in a style transitional between Romanesque and Gothic, stone carvings and restored cloisters. The Cross of Cong, an ornate processional cross intended for the abbey, is now in Dublin's National Museum

Carved 12th-century doorway of Cong Abbey

(see pp76–7). The most fascinating remains are the Gothic chapter house, stone bridges and the monks' fishing-house overhanging the river – the monks devised a system so that a bell rang in the kitchen when a fish took the bait.

Just south of Cong is **Ashford Castle**, rebuilt in Gothic Revival style in 1870 by Lord Ardilaun of the Guinness family. One of Ireland's best hotels, its grounds can be visited by boat from Galway and Oughterard. Cong was the setting for *The Quiet Man*, the 1950s' film starring John Wayne. "Quiet Man" tours cover locations near the castle.

Lough Corrib ⑬

Co Galway. 🚌 *from Galway and Cong.* 🚢 *from Oughterard and Wood Quay, Galway.* ℹ️ *Oughterard (091 552808)*.

Aɴ ᴀɴɢʟᴇʀ'ꜱ ᴘᴀʀᴀᴅɪꜱᴇ, Lough Corrib offers the chance to fish with local fishermen for brown trout, salmon, pike, perch and eels. Despite its proximity to Galway, the lake is a haven of tranquillity, dotted with uninhabited islands and framed by meadows, reed-beds and wooded shores. The water-side is home to swans and coots. On **Inchagoill**, one of the largest islands, stand the ruins of an early Christian monastic settlement and a Romanesque church.

The lake's atmosphere is best appreciated on a cruise. From Galway, the standard short cruise winds through the marshes to the site of an Iron Age fort, limestone

View over Lough Corrib from the shore northwest of Oughterard

quarries and the battlemented Menlo Castle. Longer cruises continue to Cong or include picnics on the islands.

Eɴᴠɪʀᴏɴꜱ: On the banks of Lough Corrib, **Oughterard** is known as "the gateway to Connemara". The village has craft shops, thatched cottages and friendly pubs. It is also an important centre for golf, angling, hiking and pony trekking. Other country pursuits include riverside walks, a stroll to a waterfall west of the village and cycle rides.

About 4 km (2.5 miles) southeast of Oughterard (off the N59) is **Aughnanure Castle**. This well-restored six-storey tower house clings to a rocky island on the River Drimneen. The present castle, built by the O'Flaherty clan, is on the site of one dating from 1256. The clan controlled West Connaught from Lough Corrib to Galway and the coast in the 13th to 16th centuries. From this castle the feuding O'Flaherty chieftains held out against the British in the 16th century. In 1545 Donal O'Flaherty married the pirate Grace O'Malley *(see p264)*. The tower house has an unusual double bawn *(see p24)* and a murder hole from which missiles could be dropped on invaders.

⚓ **Aughnanure Castle**
Oughterard. 📞 *091 522214.*
🕐 *mid-Jun–mid-Sep: daily.* 📷
♿ *limited.*

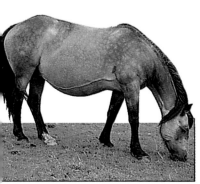

Connemara ponies *roam semi-wild and are fabled to be from Arab stock that came ashore from Spanish Armada wrecks.*

Fuchsias *grow profusely in the hedgerows of Connemara, thriving in the mild climate.*

Galway ⑭

Inside The Quays seafood
restaurant and pub

**Sign with Claddagh
ring design**

GALWAY IS BOTH THE CENTRE for the
Irish-speaking regions in the West
and a lively university city. Under the
Anglo-Normans, it flourished as a
trading post. In 1396 it gained a Royal
Charter and, for the next two centuries,
was controlled by 14 merchant families,
or "tribes". The city prospered under
English influence, but this allegiance to
the Crown cost Galway dear when, in 1652, Cromwell's
forces wreaked havoc. After the Battle of the Boyne (see
p326), Galway fell into decline, unable to compete with
east-coast trade. In recent years, as a developing centre
for high-tech industry, the city's profile has been revived.

Houses on the banks of the Corrib

Exploring Galway
The centre of the city lies on
the banks of the River Corrib,
which flows down from Lough
Corrib (see p269) widening
out as it reaches Galway Bay.
Urban renewal since the 1970s
has led to extensive restoration of the narrow, winding
streets of this once-walled
city. Due to its compact size,
Galway is easy to explore on
foot, and a leisurely pace
provides plenty of opportunity
to stop off at its shops, pubs
and historic sights.

Eyre Square
The square encloses a pleasant
park lined with imposing,
mainly 19th-century, buildings.
On the northwest of the square
is the **Browne Doorway**, a
17th-century entrance from a
mansion in Abbeygate Street
Lower. Beside it are two cannons from the Crimean War
and a fountain adorned
with a sculpture of a
Galway hooker boat.
The **Eyre Square
Centre**, overlooking
the park, is a modern
shopping mall built
to incorporate sec-
tions of the historic
city walls. Walkways
link Shoemakers and
Penrice towers, two of the
wall towers that used to ring
the city in the 17th century.

Latin Quarter
From Eyre Square, William
Street and Shop Street are the
main routes into the bustling
"Latin Quarter". On the corner
of Abbeygate Street Upper
and Shop Street stands
Lynch's Castle, now a bank,
but still the grandest 16th-
century town house in Galway.
It was owned by the Lynch
family, one of the 14 "tribes".
A side street leads to the
**Collegiate Church of St
Nicholas**, Galway's finest
medieval building. The
church, founded in
1320, was extended
in the 15th and
16th centuries, but
then damaged by
the Cromwellians,
who used it to stable
horses. The west
porch is from the
15th century and
there are some finely carved
gargoyles under the parapet.
Quay Street is lined with
restaurants and pubs, including
The Quays. Tí Neachtain is a
town house which belonged
to "Humanity Dick", an 18th-
century MP who promoted
laws against cruelty to
animals. Today, it too is a
restaurant and pub. Nearby
are the Taibhdhearc and
Druid theatres.

**Lynch family crest on
Lynch's Castle**

North Galway
The **Cathedral of St Nicholas**
(1965), made from local limestone and Connemara marble,
stands on the west bank. From
here you can see Wood Quay,
where Lough Corrib cruises
start (see p269). **University
College Galway**, further west,

Outside dining at one of the cosmopolitan cafés in Shop Street

GALWAY HOOKERS

Galway's traditional wooden sailing boats, featured on the city's coat of arms, were known as *pucans* and *gleotogs* – hookers in English. They have broad black hulls, thick masts and white or rust-coloured sails. Once common in the Claddagh district, they were also used along the Atlantic coast to ferry peat, cattle and beer. Hookers can be seen in action at the Cruinniú na mBád festival in Kinvarra *(see p274)*.

Small Galway hooker sailing by the old quays and Spanish Arch

VISITORS' CHECKLIST

Co Galway. 🏘 *56,000.* ✈ Carnmore, 11 km (7 miles) NE of Galway. 🚃 Ceannt Station (091 564222). 🚌 Ceannt Station (091 562000). ℹ Victoria Place, Eyre Square (091 563081). 🏬 Sat. 🎭 Galway Arts Festival (late Jul); Galway Races (late Jul); Galway Oyster Festival (late Sep).

is a sprawling campus with a 1849 Gothic Revival quad. Salmon Weir Bridge links the two banks. Shoals of salmon rest under the bridge on their way upstream to spawn.

The Old Quays

The **Spanish Arch**, where the river opens out, was built in 1584 to protect the harbour, which was then outside the city walls. Here, Spanish traders unloaded their ships. The old quays are a tranquil spot for a stroll down the Long Walk to the docks.

The Claddagh

Beyond the Spanish Arch, on the west bank of the Corrib, lies the Claddagh. The name comes from *An Cladach*, meaning "flat, stony shore". From medieval times, this fiercely independent fishing community beyond the city walls was governed by a "king" or "mayor", the last of whom died in 1954. The only remnants of this once close-knit, Gaelic-speaking community

are friendly pubs and Claddagh rings, betrothal rings traditionally handed down from mother to daughter.

ENVIRONS: Just west of the city is **Salthill**, Galway's seaside resort. The beaches at Palmer's Rock and Grattan Road are particularly popular with families in summer. A bracing walk along the promenade is still a Galway tradition.

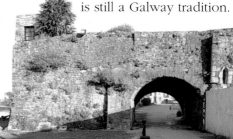

Spanish Arch on the site of the former docks

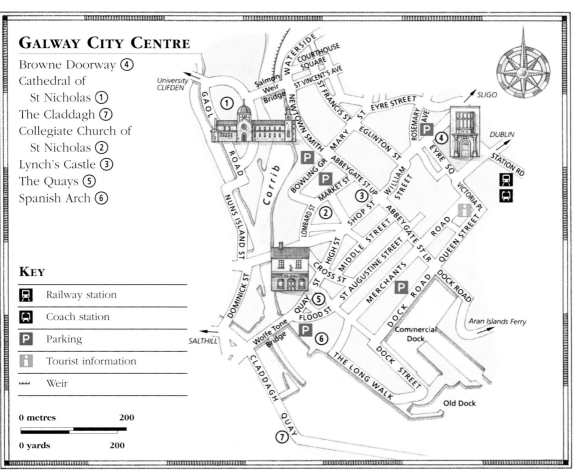

GALWAY CITY CENTRE

Browne Doorway ④
Cathedral of
  St Nicholas ①
The Claddagh ⑦
Collegiate Church of
  St Nicholas ②
Lynch's Castle ③
The Quays ⑤
Spanish Arch ⑥

KEY

🚃	Railway station
🚌	Coach station
🅿	Parking
ℹ	Tourist information
⌣	Weir

0 metres   200

0 yards   200

Shop-front mural on the quay at Kinvarra, County Galway ▷

FISHING
TACKLE
HOOKS
NETS
ROPES
LAMPS
FISHING
RODS
REELS

SIOP

Mural in the centre of Kinvarra depicting a shopfront

Aran Islands 15

See pp276–7.

Kinvarra 16

Co Galway. 550. 🚌 ℹ️ *Galway (091 563081).*

ONE OF the most charming fishing villages on Galway Bay, Kinvarra's appeal lies in its sheltered, seaweed-clad harbour and traditional seafaring atmosphere. From medieval times, its fortunes were closely linked to Kilmacduagh, the powerful monastery and bishopric upon which the village depended.

The pier is bordered by a row of fishermen's cottages. Kinvarra remains a popular port of call for sailors of traditional Galway hookers *(see p271)* and is known for the Cruinniú na mBád (gathering of the boats) festival in August. Rambles include historical and nature trails. Bird-watchers may spot teal, curlews and oystercatchers by the shore.

ENVIRONS: North of Kinvarra, on a promontory on the shore of Galway Bay, lies **Dunguaire Castle**. It is perched just beyond some quaint thatched cottages and a stone bridge. The castle is named after the 7th-century King Guaire of Connaught, whose court here was renowned as the haunt of bards and balladeers. Although the medieval earthworks survive, the present castle was built in the 16th century, a quintessential tower house *(see p24)* with sophisticated machicolations. The banqueting hall is still used for "medieval banquets" with Celtic harp music and the poetry of Yeats.

⚐ Dunguaire Castle
📞 *091 37108.* ○ *mid-Apr–Sep: daily.* 📷

Kilmacduagh 17

Outside Gort on Corofin Rd, Co Galway. 🚌 *to Gort.* ○ *daily.*

THIS MONASTIC SETTLEMENT is in a remote location on the borders of Counties Clare and Galway, roughly 5 km (3 miles) southwest of Gort. The sense of isolation is accentuated by the stony moonscape of the Burren to the west *(see pp232–34)*. Reputedly founded by St Colman MacDuagh in the early 7th century, Kilmacduagh owes more to the monastic revival which led to rebuilding from the 11th century onwards.

The centrepiece of the extensive site is a large, slightly leaning 11th- or 12th-century round tower and a roofless church, known as the cathedral or Teampall. The cathedral is a pre-Norman structure, which was later remodelled in Gothic style, with flamboyant tracery and fine tomb carvings. In the surrounding fields lie the remains of several other churches that once depended on the monastery. To the northeast of the Teampall is the late medieval Glebe or Abbot's House, a variant of a 14th- or 15th-century tower house *(see p24)*.

Thoor Ballylee 18

Gort, Co Galway. 📞 *091 631436.* 🚌 *to Gort.* ○ *Apr–Oct: daily.* 📷 ♿ *limited.*

FOR MUCH of the 1920s, this beguiling tower house was a summer home to the poet WB Yeats *(see pp26–7)*. Yeats was a regular visitor to nearby Coole Park, the home of his friend Lady Gregory (1852–1932), a cofounder of the Abbey Theatre *(see p104)*.

On one visit Yeats came upon Ballylee Castle, a 14th-century de Burgo tower adjoining a cosy cottage with a walled garden and stream. In 1902, both the tower and the cottage became part of the Gregory estate and Yeats bought them in 1916. From 1919 onwards, his family divided their time between

Round tower and cathedral, the most impressive monastic remains at Kilmacduagh

Dublin and their Galway tower. Yeats used the name Thoor Ballylee as the address, using the Irish word for tower to "keep people from suspecting us of modern gothic and a deer park". His collection, *The Tower* (1928), includes several poems inspired by Thoor Ballylee.

Today, the audiovisual tour includes readings from Yeats's poetry, but the charm of a visit lies in the tower itself, with its spiral stone steps and views from the battlements over forest and farmland.

ENVIRONS: Just to the north of Gort is **Coole Park**, once the home of Lady Gregory. Although the house was demolished in the 1950s, the estate farm has been restored and the fine gardens survive. In particular, there is the "autograph tree", a spreading copper beech carved with the initials of George Bernard Shaw, JM Synge *(see pp26–7)*, Jack Yeats *(see p80)* and other famous visitors. In the farm buildings is an audiovisual display. The emphasis of the visitors' centre is on natural history: it is the start of two signposted walks, one around the gardens and the other through beech, hazel, birch and ash woodland to Coole Lake.

Coole Park

3 km (2 miles) NE of Gort. ⬛ *091 631804*. **Visitors' centre** ⬭ *mid-Apr–mid-Jun: Tue–Sun; mid-Jun–Sep: daily; park open all year.* 🅿 ♿ *limited.*

Thoor Ballylee tower house, the summer home of WB Yeats

Gentle hills and woodland by Coole Lake in Coole Park

Portumna ⑲

Co Galway. 🚶 *1,000.* 🚌 ℹ️ *Galway (091 563081).* 🚢 *Fri.*

PORTUMNA is a historic market town with scattered sights, many of which are newly restored. Situated on Lough Derg, it is a convenient base for cruising the River Shannon *(see p229)* and has a modern marina. **Portumna Castle**, built in the early 17th century, was the main seat of the de Burgo family. Now partially restored, it has a symmetrical façade and some elaborate interior stonework. The façade surveys formal gardens. Near the castle is **Portumna Priory**. Most of the remains date from around 1414 when the priory was founded by the Dominicans, but traces can also be found of the Cistercian abbey that was previously on the site. The large de Burgo estate to the west of the town now forms **Portumna Forest Park**, with picnic sites and signposted woodland trails leading to Lough Derg.

Clonfert Cathedral ⑳

Clonfert, Co Galway. ⬭ *daily.* ♿

SITUATED near a bleak stretch of the Shannon bordering the boglands of the Midlands, Clonfert undoubtedly is one of the great jewels of Irish-Romanesque architecture.

Human heads carved on the tympanum at Clonfert Cathedral

The tiny cathedral occupies the site of a monastery, which was founded by St Brendan in AD 563, and is believed to be the burial place of the saint.

Although a great scholar and enthusiastic founder of monasteries, St Brendan is best known as the "great navigator". His journeys are recounted in *Navigatio Sancti Brendani*, written in about 1050, which survives in medieval manuscripts in several languages including Flemish, Norse and French. The account seems to describe a voyage to Wales, the Orkneys, Iceland and conceivably the east coast of North America. His voyage and his boat *(see p238)*, have been recreated by modern explorers in an attempt to prove that St Brendan may have preceded Columbus by about 900 years.

The highlight of Clonfert is its intricately sculpted sandstone doorway. The round arch above the door is decorated with animal and human heads, geometrical shapes, foliage and symbolic motifs. The carvings on the triangular tympanum above the arch are of strange human heads. In the chancel, the 13th-century east windows are fine examples of late Irish-Romanesque art. The 15th-century chancel arch is adorned with sculptures of angels and a mermaid. Although Clonfert was built over several centuries and altered in the 17th century, the church has a profound sense of unity.

Aran Islands ⑮

Jaunting car on Inishmore

INISHMORE, INISHMAAN and Inisheer, the three Aran Islands, are formed from a limestone ridge. The largest, Inishmore, is 13 km (8 miles) long and 3 km (2 miles) wide. The attractions of these islands include the austere landscape crisscrossed with dry-stone walls, stunning coastal views and several large prehistoric stone forts. In the 5th century, St Enda brought Christianity to the islands, starting a long monastic tradition. Protected for centuries by their isolated position, the islands today are a bastion of traditional Irish culture. Farming, fishing and tourism are the main occupations of the islanders.

Looking over the cliff edge at Dún Aonghasa

Clochán na Carraige is a large, well-preserved beehive hut *(see p25)*, probably built by early Christian settlers on the islands.

The Seven Churches
(Na Seacht dTeampaill)

Clochán na Carraige

Dún Eoghanachta

Dún Eoghanachta is a 1st-century BC circular stone fort with a single wall terraced on the inside.

Dun Aengus
(Dún Aonghasa)

KILMURVY
(Cill Mhuirbh

I N I S H M O R E

Na Seacht dTeampaill
The so-called Seven Churches make up a monastic settlement dedicated to St Brecan. Built between the 9th and 15th centuries, some are probably domestic buildings.

★ Dún Aonghasa
This Iron or Bronze Age promontory fort (see p24), has four concentric stone walls. It is also protected by a chevaux de frise, *a ring of razor-sharp, pointed stone stakes.*

ARAN TRADITIONS

Colourful Aran costume

The islands are famous for their distinctive knitwear and for the traditional Aran costume that is still worn: for women this consists of a red flannel skirt and crocheted shawl; for men it includes a sleeveless tweed jacket and a colourful knitted belt. From time to time you also see a *currach* or low rowing boat, the principal form of transport for centuries. Land-making, the ancient and arduous process of creating soil by covering bare rock with sand and seaweed, continues to this day.

Currach **made from canvas coated in tar**

FERRY ROUTES TO THE ARAN ISLANDS

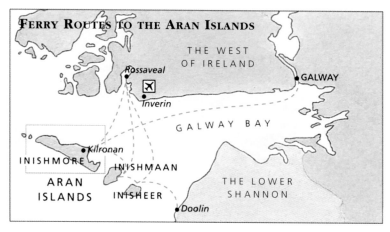

THE WEST OF IRELAND

Rossaveal

GALWAY

Inverin

GALWAY BAY

Kilronan

INISHMORE

INISHMAAN

ARAN ISLANDS

INISHEER

THE LOWER SHANNON

Doolin

Kilmurvy Beach

The attractive sandy beach east of Kilmurvy offers safe swimming in a sheltered cove. The town itself is a quiet place to stay near a number of the island's most important sights.

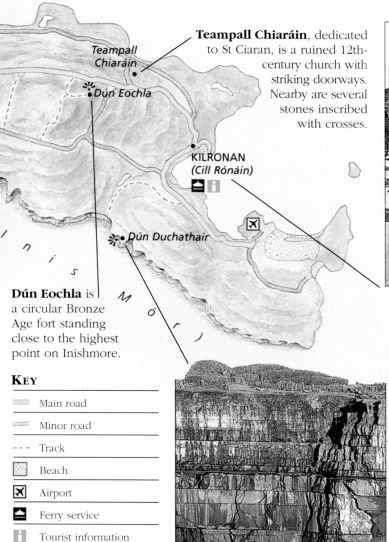

Teampall Chiaráin

Dún Eochla

Teampall Chiaráin, dedicated to St Ciaran, is a ruined 12th-century church with striking doorways. Nearby are several stones inscribed with crosses.

KILRONAN
(Cill Rónáin)

Dún Duchathair

I n i s h M ó r

Dún Eochla is a circular Bronze Age fort standing close to the highest point on Inishmore.

KEY

	Main road
	Minor road
- - -	Track
	Beach
✕	Airport
	Ferry service
i	Tourist information
☀	Viewpoint

0 kilometres   2

0 miles   1

★ Kilronan

The Aran Islands' main port is a busy place, with jaunting cars (ponies and traps) and minibuses waiting by the pier to give island tours; bicycles can also be hired. Nearby, the fascinating Aran Heritage Centre is dedicated to the disappearing Aran way of life.

★ Dún Duchathair

Built on a headland, this Iron Age construction is known as the Black Fort. It has dry-stone ramparts.

STAR SIGHTS

★ **Kilronan**

★ **Dún Aonghasa**

★ **Dún Duchathair**

East wall and gatehouse at Roscommon Castle

Turoe Stone ㉑

Turoe, Bullaun, Loughrea, Co Galway.
📞 091 841580. ○ Apr–Oct: daily;
Nov–Mar: groups by appt. 🔲 ♿ 🖥

THE TUROE STONE stands at the centre of a large area of parkland, the Turoe Pet Farm and Leisure Park, near the village of Bullaun (on the R350). The white granite boulder, which stands about 1 m (3 ft) high, dates back to the 3rd or 2nd century BC. Its top half is carved with curvi-linear designs in a graceful Celtic style, known as La Tène, which is also found in Celtic parts of Europe, particularly Brittany. The lower half has a smooth section and a band of step-pattern carving. The stone was originally discovered at an Iron Age ring fort nearby, and is thought to have been used there in fertility rituals.

The park around the Turoe Stone is designed mainly for children. The Pet Farm has some small fields containing farm animals and a pond with several varieties of ducks and geese. There is also a wooded

The Celtic Turoe Stone carved with graceful swirling patterns

riverside walk (wear heavy shoes or walking boots as it's often muddy), a picnic area, tea rooms and a playground.

Roscommon ㉒

Co Roscommon. 🚶 3,500. 🚆 🚌
ℹ Jun–Sep: Harrison Hall (0903 26342). 🅿 Fri.

THE COUNTY CAPITAL is a busy market town with scattered sights. In Main Street is the former gaol, celebrated for having a woman as its last ex-ecutioner. "Lady Betty", as she came to be known, was sen-tenced to death for the murder of her son in 1780, but nego-tiated a pardon by agreeing to become a hangwoman. She continued for 30 years.

South of the town centre, just off Abbey Street, is the **Dominican Friary**, founded in 1253 by Felim O'Conor, King of Connaught. Set in the north wall of the choir is a late 13th-century effigy of the founder.

Roscommon Castle, an Anglo-Norman fortress north of the town, was built in 1269 by Robert d'Ufford, Lord Justice of Ireland, and rebuilt 11 years later after being des-troyed by the Irish led by Hugh O'Conor, King of Connaught. The rectangular castle has 16th-century mullioned windows.

Clonalis House ㉓

Castlerea, Co Roscommon. 📞 0907 20014. ○ Jun–mid-Sep: Tue–Sun.
🔲 ♿ ground floor.

THIS VICTORIAN manor just outside Castlerea is the ancestral home of the O'Conors, the last High Kings of Ireland and Kings of

Connaught. This ancient Gaelic family can trace its heritage back 1,500 years. The ruins of their gabled 17th-century home are visible in the grounds. On the lawn lies the O'Conor inauguration stone, dating from 90 BC.

The interior includes a Venetian hallway, a library of many books and documents recording Irish history, a tiny private chapel and a gallery of family portraits spanning 500 years. In the billiard room is the harp once played by Turlough O'Carolan (1670–1738), blind harpist and last of the Gaelic bards (see p28).

Strokestown Park House ㉔

Strokestown, Co Roscommon. 🚌
House and Museum 📞 078 33013.
○ Apr–Oct: daily; Nov–Mar: by appt.
🔲 ♿ museum only.

STROKESTOWN PARK HOUSE, the greatest Palladian mansion in County Roscommon, was built in the 1730s for Thomas Mahon, an MP whose family was granted the lands by Charles II after the Restoration. It incorporates an earlier 17th-century tower house (see p24). The design of the new house owes most to Richard Castle, architect of Russborough (see p154). The galleried kitchen, panelled stairwell and groin-vaulted stables are undoubtedly his work, tailoring Palladian principles to the requirements of the Anglo-Irish gentry.

The house stayed in the family's hands until 1979, when major restoration began. In its heyday, the estate included ornamental parkland, a deer park, folly, mausoleum and the town of

Roscommon itself. By 1979, the estate's original 12,000 ha (30,000 acres) had dwindled to 120 ha (300 acres), but recent replanting restores a sense of spaciousness. The original decor and furnishings of the house are intact.

Set in the stable yards, the **Famine Museum** commemorates the 1840s Famine. During the crisis, landlords divided into two camps: the charitable, some of whom started up Famine Relief schemes, and the callous, like the Mahons of Strokestown. Major Denis Mahon, landlord in the 1840s, was murdered after forcing two-thirds of the starving peasantry off his land by a combination of eviction and assisted passages in "coffin ships" to North America. The exhibition uses the Strokestown archives to tell the story of tenants and landlords during the Famine. A section deals with continuing famine and malnutrition worldwide.

Boyle 25

Co Roscommon. 🏘 *2,200.* 🚌 ℹ *May–Sep: King House (079 62145).* 🛒 *Fri.*

COUNTY ROSCOMMON'S most charming town, Boyle is blessed with fine Georgian and medieval architecture. **Boyle Abbey** is a well-preserved Cistercian abbey founded in 1161 as a sister house to Mellifont in County Louth *(see p327)*. It survived raids by Anglo-Norman barons and Irish chieftains, as well as the 1539 suppression of the monasteries. In 1659 it was turned into a castle. The abbey is still remarkably intact, with a church, cloisters, cellars, sacristy and even kitchens. The nave of the church has both Romanesque and Gothic arches and there are well-preserved 12th-century capitals. The visitors' centre in the old gatehouse has exhibits on the abbey's history.

King House, a Palladian mansion near the centre of town, is the ancestral home of the Anglo-Irish King family, later Earls of Kingston. Inside is a contemporary art gallery, as well as displays covering various subjects, such as Georgian architecture and the mansion's restoration, the history of the surrounding area and the Connaught chieftains.

THE GREAT FAMINE

The failure of the Irish potato crop in 1845, 1846 and 1848, due to potato blight, had disastrous consequences for the people of Ireland, many of whom relied on this staple crop. More than a million died of starvation and disease, and by 1856 over two and a half million had been forced to emigrate. The crisis was worsened by unsympathetic landlords who often continued collecting rents. The Famine had far-reaching effects: mass emigration became a way of life *(see pp46–7)* and many rural communities, particularly in the far west, were decimated.

Peasants queuing for soup during the Famine (1847)

🏛 **Boyle Abbey**
📞 *079 62604.* ⬭ *Apr–Oct: daily.* 📷
🏛 **King House**
Main St. 📞 *079 63242.* ⬭ *May–Sep: daily; Apr & Oct: Sat & Sun; Nov–Mar: by appt.* 📷

ENVIRONS: Lough Key is often called the loveliest lake in Ireland. The island-studded lake and surrounding woodland make a glorious setting for the **Lough Key Forest Park**. The 320-ha (790-acre) park formed part of the Rockingham estate until 1957, when Rockingham House, a John Nash design, burnt down. The extensive woods were added by 18th-century landlords. Other features of the park include nature trails, an observation tower, a 17th-century ice house, a deer enclosure and, by the lake, a 17th-century gazebo known as the Temple. The park also has several ring forts *(see p24)*. From the jetty, cruisers ply the Boyle River. A river bus visits Church and Trinity Islands, which both contain medieval ruins, and Castle Island, which has a 19th-century folly.

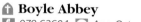

Carved capital in the nave at Boyle Abbey

🏞 **Lough Key Forest Park**
N4 8 km (5 miles) E of Boyle.
⬭ *daily.* 📷 *Easter–Sep.* ♿

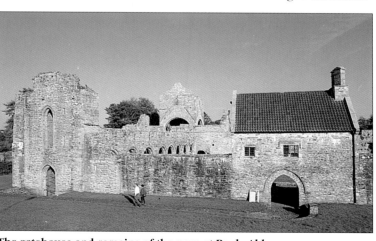

The gatehouse and remains of the nave at Boyle Abbey

Portsalon on the Fanad Peninsula, County Donegal ▷

NORTHWEST
IRELAND

NORTHWEST IRELAND

DONEGAL · SLIGO · LEITRIM

Towering cliffs, *deserted golden beaches and rocky headlands abound along the rugged coast of Donegal, which incorporates some of Ireland's wildest scenery. To the south, Sligo is steeped in prehistory and Celtic myth, with its legacy of ancient monuments and natural beauty enriched by associations with the poet, WB Yeats. By contrast, Leitrim is a quiet county of unruffled lakes and waterways.*

In Celtic mythology, Sligo was the power base of the warrior Queen Maeve of Connaught. Its rich legacy of prehistoric sites confirms that it was quite heavily populated in Celtic times. Carrowmore, the country's largest Neolithic cemetery, contains megalithic tombs older than those at Newgrange. Further south, at Lough Arrow, is the location of Carrowkeel Passage Tomb Cemetery, another major site of archaeological interest.

Intriguingly for an area of such prehistoric importance, the dearth of archaeological evidence suggests that County Sligo was little affected by subsequent phases in the rest of Ireland's historical development. Even though outside influences appear barely to have impinged on the county, one event in this region changed the entire course of Irish history: from a castle at the village of Dromohair on Lough Gill, Dermot MacMurrough, king of Leinster, eloped with the wife of the local king, Tiernan O'Rourke, and their feud led to the Normans landing on Irish shores. Even then, the Normans barely disturbed the rule of the local clans.

What it lacks in recorded history, Sligo makes up for in natural beauty. Its finest landscapes are found inland, around Lough Gill, and among the sparsely populated Bricklieve Mountains. Vistas are dominated by the county's striking sculpted mountains. Flat-topped

The 19th-century interior of Hargadon's bar in Sligo town, with its original counter and stout jars

◁ **View across to Falcarragh from Bloody Foreland in County Donegal**

Looking north to Ben Bulben from the mountain of Knockarea, County Sligo

Ben Bulben (said to be the site of the grave of Queen Maeve) looms imperiously above the plain to Knocknarea. Though the outskirts of Sligo Town have spread to the edges of Lough Gill, this popular lake seems naturally to resist the restraints of urban expansion, becoming ever more wild as it moves towards its eastern end. The many places of great interest in the area of its shores include the Tobernalt Holy Well, a superb viewpoint at Dooney Rock and Parke's Castle. Lough Arrow, to the south, is an excellent spot for fishing and boating.

Sligo Town, with its art galleries and poetry readings, is an enclave of culture in a region otherwise oriented towards outdoor recreation. This was the childhood retreat of two of Ireland's greatest artistic luminaries, the poet WB Yeats and his brother, the painter Jack B Yeats. So influential were the brothers in their respective spheres, and so dominant was the region in their work that the area around Sligo and Lough Gill is widely known as 'Yeats Country'.

County Donegal has little in common with its neighbours in the Republic. It is one of the most remote parts of Ireland, and it is no coincidence that it boasts the country's largest number of Gaelic speakers. Unlike Sligo and Leitrim, Donegal has a long tradition of historical importance. It was part of Ulster until 1921 and played an active role in that province's history. From the 5th to 12th centuries, Ulster's high kings, the O'Neills, ruled their lands from an impressive Iron Age fort, the Grianán of Aileach. Another influential local family, the O'Donnells, ruled most of Donegal in the Middle Ages, but they fled to Europe in 1607 after their ill-fated stand alongside the O'Neills against the English.

Although Protestant settlers moved onto land confiscated from the two clans, they left much of Donegal and its poor soil to the Irish, who lived in isolation from the rest of Ulster. This remote corner of the province remained Catholic and, at the time of Partition in 1921, was left out of Protestant Northern Ireland.

The northwest's most dramatic scenery is in Donegal. Coastal roads run high above the sea, which has now fashioned tiny inlets all along the shore. On the northern coast, Horn Head Drive opens out onto fabulous

Garden statue from Glenveagh castle

Pillar stone in County Donegal

views of the broad beach at Dunfanaghy set far below. The Atlantic Drive circles the clifftops of the Rosguill Peninsula. To the east are routes round the Fanad and remote Inishowen peninsulas. On the west coast, the rocky headland of the Rosses, splattered with dozens of small lakes, looks out to Aranmore, County Donegal's largest island.

The northern inland region is dominated by the lofty Derryveagh Mountains. The finest scenery in this region lies within Glenveagh National Park, and in the gardens of Glenveagh Castle. Southern Donegal has some equally stunning landscapes. The road west from Donegal Town has superb vistas over Donegal Bay, leading through the fishing harbour of Killybegs to the Slieve League mountains, the beginning of the heady ascent to the Bunglass Cliffs, Europe's highest cliff face. Across the wild Glengesh Pass, the village of Ardara is famous for its woven goods. Donegal's population is largely rural and, until recently, economic prospects here were among the poorest in the nation. Today, however, Letterkenny is one of the fastest-growing towns in Ireland, and Donegal Town is now a bustling tourist hub. Ballyshannon, with its handsome Georgian houses rising up the hill above the River Erne, holds an annual traditional music festival which encourages tourism, and there are also thriving resorts such as those at Rossnowlagh, Bundoran and beautiful Rosses Point.

The tranquil splendour of the rugged Fanad Peninsula, County Donegal

Leitrim stretches to Donegal in the north, and is split in two by Lough Allen. As with Sligo, the county is somewhat short of real historical interest. Leitrim does, however, possess great natural beauty. It boasts scenic glens, which lie north of the main road between Sligo Town and Manorhamilton. Glencar, with its beautiful lough and waterfall, is a favourite hiking place. The mighty River Shannon also features here as a major Leitrim recreation spot. The Shannon-Erne Waterway, which links the county with Upper Lough Erne in Fermanagh, Northern Ireland, is awash with memorable vistas. The attractive town of Carrick-on-Shannon serves as a boating and tourist centre, and the nearby Lough Rynn Estate is of interest for its extensive grounds with tasteful ornamental gardens and trees.

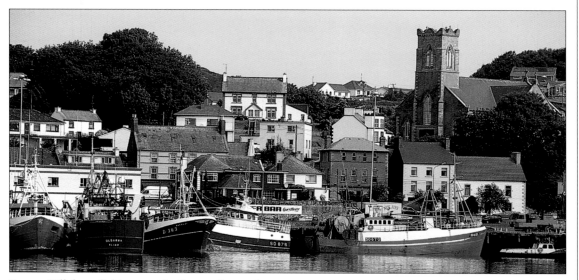
Serene Killybegs fishing port in County Donegal

Music and Entertainment

Two aspects of the national character are typified in Irish music. Much impromptu instrumental music and dance is performed for the fun of it (the *craic*) at informal pub sessions, expressing the exuberance of the Irish nature. The other musical tradition of old-style balladry links the love of story-telling with an acknowledgement of the turbulence of Irish history and has often led artists to explore socio-political issues. The vibrancy of these two traditions is reflected in the success of contemporary performers who still draw on them for inspiration.

Traditional music being played in a pub

The bodhran *is a traditional instrument whose name appropriately translates as "deafener". This goatskin drum can be hit with either a stick or the back of the hand.*

HIT STAGE SHOWS

Productions such as *Lord of the Dance* and *Riverdance* merged the old and the new. The latter, a vivid mixture of innovative choreography and thundering music, enjoyed huge success both in the West End and on Broadway. An allegory for the history of Ireland, with up to 70 performers on stage at one time, it featured a stunning international cast incorporating flamenco, Russian ballet and American gospel artists.

Step dancing *is inextricably linked to the music tradition and includes vigorous jigs and hornpipes for men and light-footed reels for women. Solo dances are an art form in themselves. They require great skill and are usually danced in an atmosphere of fierce competition at fleadhs (festivals). Ceilidhs are formal venues for social dances, where a strict dress code of green clothing, black stockings and white apron is observed by female participants.*

MUSIC FOR CHANGE

From the times when performers risked death by singing nationalistic songs, the Irish have never been afraid to give vent to socio-political feelings. The spirit of old rebel songs has influenced works by the Boomtown Rats and U2, and Irish musicians have taken it upon themselves to bring about change on an international scale. In 1985 Bob Geldof set up Live Aid to provide famine relief, and U2 have lent their name to Greenpeace activities and to the Jubilee 2000 campaign to cancel Third World debt.

U2 taking part in Live Aid at Wembley in 1985

Modern folk artists such as Enya, Clannad and Altan cross the border between traditional and contemporary music, singing in both Gaelic and Irish to great commercial acclaim. Their haunting vocal style closely echoes the bardic tradition.

Temple Bar Blues Festival in Dublin plays host to international stars every July. There is a link between Irish music and the blues, the music of the underdog.

Irish pop and rock artists from Van Morrison's Them and Phil Lynott's Thin Lizzy to The Undertones, Stiff Little Fingers, The Pogues, U2, Sinead O'Connor and the Cranberries have enjoyed huge international success. The eclectic mix of Irish and more international musical styles such as rock, punk and soul gives Irish bands a unique sound. Recent popular outfits such as Boyzone, B*witched and the Corrs have incorporated large sections of traditional rhythms and melodies into their songs.

The Corrs at the Brit awards in 1999

Van Morrison

Exploring Northwest Ireland

THE SUPREME APPEAL of Donegal lies in the natural beauty of its coast, with windswept peninsulas, precipitous cliffs and a host of golden beaches. There is a scattering of small seaside resorts which make good bases, and Donegal town is well placed for exploring the southern part of the county. The cultural heartland of the Northwest lies in and around Sligo, the only size-able town in the region, from where you can reach several prehistoric remains and other historic sights. Further south, lovely scenery surrounds Lough Gill and the more remote Lough Arrow. In Leitrim, a county of lakes and rivers, the main centre of activity is the lively boating resort of Carrick-on-Shannon.

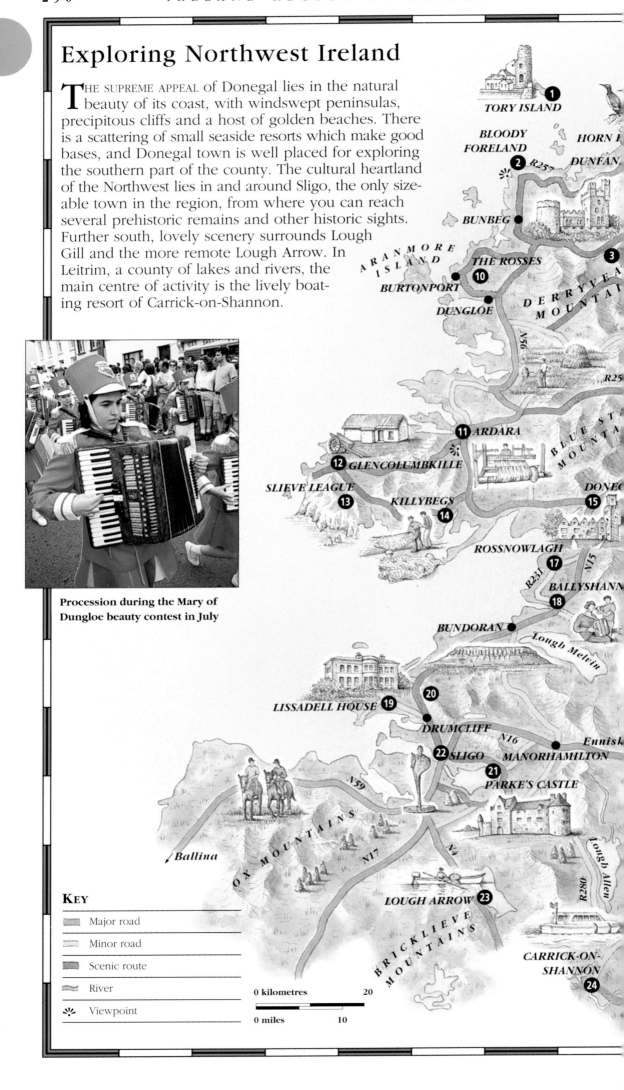

Procession during the Mary of Dungloe beauty contest in July

TORY ISLAND 1

BLOODY FORELAND 2   R257   HORN F   DUNFAN.

BUNBEG

ARANMORE ISLAND   THE ROSSES   3   10   BURTONPORT   DERRYVEA MOUNTAI   DUNGLOE   N56   R25

ARDARA 11   BLUE ST MOUNTA   GLENCOLUMBKILLE 12   DONE   SLIEVE LEAGUE 13   KILLYBEGS 14   15

ROSSNOWLAGH 17   N15   R231   BALLYSHANN 18

BUNDORAN   Lough Melvin

LISSADELL HOUSE 19   20   DRUMCLIFF   N16   Ennisk   22 SLIGO   MANORHAMILTON   21   PARKE'S CASTLE

Ballina   OX MOUNTAINS   N59   N17   N4   Lough Allen   LOUGH ARROW 23   R280   BRICKLIEVE MOUNTAINS   CARRICK-ON-SHANNON 24

KEY

▬ Major road

▭ Minor road

▬ Scenic route

〜 River

☀ Viewpoint

0 kilometres   20

0 miles   10

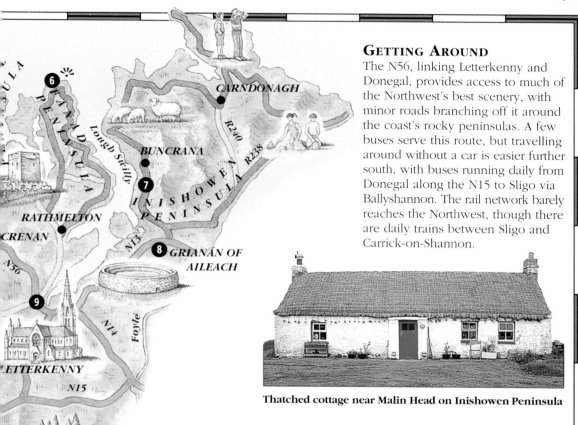

GETTING AROUND

The N56, linking Letterkenny and Donegal, provides access to much of the Northwest's best scenery, with minor roads branching off it around the coast's rocky peninsulas. A few buses serve this route, but travelling around without a car is easier further south, with buses running daily from Donegal along the N15 to Sligo via Ballyshannon. The rail network barely reaches the Northwest, though there are daily trains between Sligo and Carrick-on-Shannon.

Thatched cottage near Malin Head on Inishowen Peninsula

SIGHTS AT A GLANCE

Ardara ⑪
Ballyshannon ⑱
Bloody Foreland ②
Carrick-on-Shannon ㉔
Derryveagh Mountains ③
Donegal ⑮
Fanad Peninsula ⑥
Glencolumbkille ⑫
Grianán of Aileach ⑧
Horn Head ④
Killybegs ⑭
Letterkenny ⑨
Lissadell House ⑲
Lough Arrow ㉓

Lough Derg ⑯
Lough Rynn Estate ㉕
Parke's Castle ㉑
Rosguill Peninsula ⑤
The Rosses ⑩
Rossnowlagh ⑰
Slieve League ⑬
Sligo ㉒
Tory Island ①

Tours
Inishowen Peninsula ⑦
Yeats Country ⑳

View from Carrowkeel Bronze Age cemetery above Lough Arrow

Quartzite cone of Errigal, the highest of the Derryveagh Mountains

Tory Island ①

Co Donegal. 140. from Magheraroarty Pier near Gortahork (074 35061) and Bunbeg (075 31991): daily in summer, weather permitting in winter.

THE TURBULENT Tory Sound separates this windswept island from the northwestern corner of mainland Donegal. Given that rough weather can cut off the tiny island for days, it is not surprising that Tory's inhabitants have developed a strong sense of independence. Most of the islanders speak Gaelic and they even have their own monarch: the powers of this non-hereditary position are minimal, but the current incumbent is heavily involved in promoting the interests of his "subjects" and in attracting visitors to the island.

During the 1970s, the Irish government tried to resettle most of the islanders on the mainland, but they refused to move. Their campaign of resistance was led by Tory's school of Primitive artists. This emerged after 1968, inspired by a local man called James Dixon who claimed he could do better than a visiting English painter, Derek Hill. Since then, the school of artists has drawn a growing number of tourists; the new **Dixon Gallery** opened recently in the main village of West Town.

There are ruins of a monastery founded by St Columba (see p38) nearby, or else you can explore the island's dramatic cliffs and seabird rookeries.

🏛 Dixon Gallery
West Town. 074 35011.
◯ Easter–Sep: daily.

Bloody Foreland ②

Co Donegal. to Bunbeg from Letterkenny or Dungloe.

BLOODY FORELAND, which gets its name from the rubescent glow of the rocks at sunset, boasts magnificent scenery. The R257 road skirts the coast around the headland, providing lovely views. The most scenic viewpoint is on the north coast and looks across to the cliffs of nearby offshore islands, including Tory. A short distance further south, the tiny village of **Bunbeg** has a pretty harbour, but elsewhere the rocky landscape is spoilt by a blanket of holiday bungalows.

Derryveagh Mountains ③

Co Donegal.

THE WILD BEAUTY of these mountains provides one of the high spots of a visit to Donegal. Errigal Mountain, the range's tallest peak at 751 m (2,466 ft), attracts keen hikers, but the cream of the mountain scenery lies within **Glenveagh National Park**. Covering nearly 16,500 ha (40,000 acres), this takes in the beautiful valley occupied by Lough Veagh, and Poisoned Glen, a marshy valley enclosed by dramatic cliffs. The park also protects the largest herd of red deer in the country.

Glenveagh Castle stands on the southern shores of Lough Veagh, near the visitors' centre. This splendid granite building was constructed in 1870 by John Adair, notorious for his eviction of many families from the area after the Famine (see p281). The castle was given to the nation in the 1970s by its last owner, a wealthy art dealer from Pennsylvania.

Minibuses whisk you up the private road to the castle from the visitors' centre. You can go on a guided tour of the sumptuous interior or just stroll

Glenveagh Castle overlooking Lough Veagh

Looking across to Dunfanaghy, gateway to the Horn Head peninsula

through the formal gardens and rhododendron woods. Trails weave all around the castle grounds; one path climbs steeply to reward you with a lovely view over Lough Veagh.

Glebe House and Gallery overlooks Lough Gartan 6 km (4 miles) south of the visitors' centre. This modest Regency mansion was the home of the painter, Derek Hill, who was also a keen collector. The house reveals his varied tastes, with William Morris wallpapers, Islamic ceramics and paintings by Tory Island artists. The gallery contains works by Picasso, Renoir and Jack B Yeats among others.

Fountain at Glenveagh

The **Colmcille Heritage Centre**, a short distance south, uses stained glass and illuminated manuscripts to trace the life of St Columba (Colmcille in Gaelic), who was born in nearby Church Hill in AD 521 (*see p38*). A flagstone in the village is said to mark the site of the saint's birthplace.

🌸 **Glenveagh National Park and Castle**
Off R251, 16 km (10 miles) N of Church Hill. ☎ *074 37090.* **Park** *and* **Castle** ◯ *Mar–Nov: daily.* 🚫 📷 ♿ *limited.*

🏛 **Glebe House and Gallery**
☎ *074 37071.* ◯ *Easter & May–Sep: Sat–Thu.* 🚫 ♿ *limited.*

🏛 **Colmcille Heritage Centre**
☎ *074 37306.* ◯ *Easter & May–Sep: daily.* 🚫

Horn Head ④

Co Donegal. 🚌 *to Dunfanaghy from Letterkenny.* ℹ️ *The Workhouse, Dunfanaghy (074 36540).*

CARPETED IN HEATHER and rich in birdlife, Horn Head is the most scenic of the northern Donegal headlands. It rises 180 m (600 ft) straight out of the Atlantic and gives lovely views out to sea and inland towards the mountains. The appeal of the area is enhanced by **Dunfanaghy**, a delightful town with an air of affluence and Presbyterianism which is unusual in this area. The local beach, **Killahoey Strand**, offers excellent swimming.

Rosguill Peninsula ⑤

Co Donegal.

ROSGUILL PENINSULA juts out into the Atlantic Ocean between Sheephaven and Mulroy bays. The simplest way to see it is to follow the 11-km (7-mile) Atlantic Drive, a circular route which skirts the clifftops at the tip of the headland.

Doe Castle, 5 km (3 miles) north of Creeslough village, is worth a visit as much for its setting on a promontory overlooking Sheephaven Bay as for its architectural or historical interest. Even so, it is still a substantial ruin – the remains of a castle erected in the 16th century by the MacSweeneys, a family of Scottish mercenaries.

Fanad Peninsula ⑥

Co Donegal. 🚌 *to Rathmelton & Portsalon from Letterkenny.*

A PANORAMIC ROUTE winds its way between the hilly spine and rugged coast of this tranquil peninsula. The eastern side is by far the most enjoyable and begins at **Rathmelton**, a charming Plantation town founded in the 17th century. Elegant Georgian homes and handsome old warehouses flank its tree-lined Main Street.

Further north, **Portsalon** offers safe bathing and great views from nearby Saldanha Head. Near **Doaghbeg**, on the way to Fanad Head in the far north, the cliffs have been eroded into arches and other dramatic shapes.

Doe Castle on Rosguill Peninsula, with its 16th-century battlements

Tory Island, County Donegal ▷

A Tour of the Inishowen Peninsula ⑦

INISHOWEN, THE LARGEST of Donegal's northern peninsulas, is an area laden with history, from early Christian relics to strategically positioned castles and forts. The most rugged scenery lies in the west and north, around the the steep rock-strewn landscape of the Gap of Mamore and the spectacular cape of Malin Head, the northern-most point in Ireland. Numerous beaches dot the coastline and cater for all tastes, from the remote Isle of Doagh to the busy family resort of Buncrana. From the shores, there are views to Donegal's Derryveagh Mountains in the west and the Northern Ireland coast in the east. The Inishowen Peninsula can be explored by car as a leisurely day trip.

Tower on Banba's Crown, Malin Head

Carndonagh Cross ④
This 7th-century early Christian cross is carved with human figures and inter-lacing lines.

Gap of Mamore ③
The road between Mamore Hill and the Urris Hills is 250 m (820 ft) above sea level and offers panoramic views.

Dunree Head ②
On the headland, Dunree Fort overlooks Lough Swilly. It was built in 1798 to counter the threat of French invasion. Since 1986, it has been a military museum.

Buncrana ①
Buncrana has 5 km (3 miles) of sandy beaches and two castles. Buncrana Castle was rebuilt in 1718 and the intact keep of O'Doherty Castle dates from Norman times.

KEY

▬▬	Tour route
═══	Other roads
☀	Viewpoint

Grianán of Ailigh ⑦
At the neck of the Inishowen Peninsula, perched on a hilltop, stands this formidable circular stone fort. The solid structure that can be seen today is the result of extensive restoration in the 1870s.

Shores of Lough Swilly near Dunree Fort

TIPS FOR DRIVERS

Tour length: 157 km (98 miles).
Stopping-off points: Malin,
Greencastle and Carndonagh all
have pubs and eating places;
picnic sites are dotted around the
coast. The Guns of Dunree
Military Museum has a café.
There is a 3 km (1.5 mile) scenic
walk between Moville and
Greencastle.

Malin Head ⑤
This traditional cottage makes
a good stop for tea after
enjoying the superb Atlantic
views from Malin Head. At
the highest point, Banba's
Crown, stands a tower built
in 1805 to monitor shipping.

Greencastle ⑥
A resort and fishing port,
Greencastle is named after
the overgrown castle ruins
just outside town. Built in
1305 by Richard de Burgo,
Earl of Ulster, the castle
guarded the entrance to
Lough Foyle.

0 kilometres   5

0 miles   5

Enjoying the views from the ramparts of the Grianán of Aileach

Grianán of Ailigh ⑧

Co Donegal. 🚌 *from Letterkenny or
Londonderry.* ℹ️ *Burt (077 68512).*

DONEGAL'S most impressive
and intriguing ancient
monument stands just 10 km
(6 miles) west of Londonderry
(see pp350–51) at the entrance
to the Inishowen Peninsula.
Overlooking Lough Swilly
and Lough Foyle, the circular
stone structure, measuring
23 m (77 ft) in diameter, is
believed to have been built as
a pagan temple around the
5th century BC, although the
site was probably a place of
worship before this date. Later,
Christians adopted the fort:
St Patrick is thought to have
baptized Owen, founder of
the O'Neill dynasty, here in
AD 450. The fort became the
royal residence of the O'Neills,
but was badly damaged in the
12th century by the army of
Murtagh O'Brien, King of
Munster.

The fort was restored in the
1870s. Two doorways lead
from the outside through 4-m
(13-ft) thick defences into a
grassy arena ringed by three
terraces. The most memorable
feature of the fort, however, is
its magnificent vantage point,
which affords stunning views
in every direction.

At the foot of the hill stands
an attractive church, dedicated
to St Aengus and built in 1967.
Its circular design echoes that
of the Grianán.

Letterkenny ⑨

Co Donegal. 👥 *7,100.* 🚌 ℹ️ *Derry
Rd (074 21160).*

STRADDLING the river Swilly,
with the Sperrin Mountains
to the east and the Derryveagh
Mountains *(see pp292–93)*
to the west, Letterkenny is
Donegal's largest town. It is
also the region's main business
centre, a role it took over from
Londonderry after partition in
1921. The likeable town makes
a good base from which to
explore the northern coast of
Donegal and, for anglers, is
well placed for access to the
waters of Lough Swilly.

Letterkenny has one of the
longest main streets in Ireland,
which is dominated by the
65-m (215-ft) steeple of **St
Eunan's Cathedral**. A Neo-
Gothic creation built in the
late 19th century, it contains
Celtic-style stonework, a rich
marble altar and vivid stained-
glass windows. The **County
Museum** is small but has
informative displays on local
history and a collection of
archaeological artifacts found
in Donegal, some of them
dating from the Iron Age.

Every August, the centre of
Letterkenny is taken over for
four days by the International
Folk Festival, when traditional
and folk musicians play in the
bars and hotels, and dancing
competitions are held.

🏛 **County Museum**
High Rd. 📞 *074 24613.* ⏰ *Mon–
Sat.* ⚫ *10 days at Christmas and
public hols.* ♿

The imposing spire of St Eunan's
Cathedral in Letterkenny

Isolated cottage near Burtonport in the Rosses

The Rosses ⑩

Co Donegal. 🚌 *to Dungloe or Burtonport from Letterkenny.* ℹ️ *Jun–Sep: Main St, Dungloe (075 21297).* ⛴️ *to Aranmore from Burtonport (075 20532).*

A ROCKY HEADLAND dotted with more than 100 lakes, the Rosses is one of the most picturesque and unspoilt corners of Donegal. It is also a strong Gaeltacht area, with many people speaking Gaelic.

The hub of the Rosses, at the southern end of the headland, is **Dungloe**, a bustling market town and major angling centre.

ENVIRONS: There is a glorious sheltered beach 8 km (5 miles) west of Dungloe at **Maghery Bay**. From here you can also walk to nearby **Crohy Head**, known for its caves, arches and unusual cliff formations. From Burtonport, 8 km (5 miles)

north of Dungloe, car ferries sail daily to Donegal's largest island, **Aranmore**. The rugged northwest coast is ideal for clifftop walks, and from the south coast you can enjoy fine views across to the Rosses. Most of Aranmore's population of 1,000 lives in Leabgarrow. The village's thriving pub culture is due partly to the granting of 24-hour licences, for the benefit of fishermen returning from sea.

Ardara ⑪

Co Donegal. 👥 *700.* 🚌 *from Killybegs or Donegal.* ℹ️ *Easter–Sep: Heritage Centre, The Diamond (075 41704).*

THE TOWN of Ardara is the weaving capital of Donegal and proliferates in shops selling locally made tweeds and hand-knitted sweaters.

Some larger stores put on displays of hand-loom weaving. Ardara is also worth a stop for its pubs, which are much loved for their fiddle sessions.

ENVIRONS: There is superb scenery between Ardara and **Loughros Point**, 10 km (6 miles) west of the town: the drive along the narrow peninsula provides dramatic coastal views. Another picturesque route runs southwest from Ardara to Glencolumbkille, going over **Glengesh Pass**, a series of bends through a wild, deserted landscape.

Hand-loom worker in Ardara

Glencolumbkille ⑫

Co Donegal. 👥 *260.* 🚌 *from Killybegs.* ℹ️ *Cashel St (073 30116) or Donegal (073 21148).*

GLENCOLUMBKILLE, a quiet, grassy valley scattered with brightly coloured cottages, feels very much like a backwater, in spite of the sizeable number of visitors who come here.

The "Glen of St Colmcille" is a popular place of pilgrimage due to its associations with the saint more commonly known as St Columba. Just north of the valley's main village of Cashel, on the way to Glen Head, there is a tiny church where St Columba worshipped: it is said that between prayers the saint slept on the two stone slabs still visible in one corner.

Another attraction here is the **Folk Village Museum**, which depicts rural Donegal lifestyles through the ages. It was started in the 1950s by a local priest called Father James

Old irons at the Folk Village Museum in Glencolumbkille

Slieve League, the highest sea cliffs in Europe

MacDyer. Concerned about the high rate of emigration from this poor region, he sought to provide jobs and a sense of regional pride, partly by encouraging people to set up craft cooperatives. The Folk Village shop sells local wares, and has a good stock of wine – made of anything from seaweed to fuchsias.

There is plenty to explore in the valley, which is littered with cairns, dolmens and other ancient monuments. The nearby coast is lovely too, the best walks taking you west across the grassy foreland of **Malinbeg**. Beyond the small resort of Malin More, steps drop down to an idyllic sandy cove hemmed in by cliffs.

🏛 **Folk Village Museum**
Cashel. 📞 073 30017. 🕐 Easter & May–Sep: daily. 🚫 🎫

Slieve League ⑬

Co Donegal. 🚌 to Carrick from Glencolumbkille or Killybegs.

THE HIGHEST cliff face in Europe, Slieve League is spectacular not just for its sheer elevation but also for its colour: at sunset the rock is streaked with changing shades of red, amber and ochre. The 8-km (5-mile) drive to the eastern end of Slieve League from **Carrick** is bumpy but certainly well worth enduring. Beyond Teelin, the road becomes a series of alarming switchbacks before reaching **Bunglass Point** and Amharc Mor, the "good view". From here, you can see the whole of Slieve League, its sheer cliffs rising dramatically out of the ocean.

Only experienced hikers should attempt the treacherous ledges of **One Man's Pass**. This is part of a trail which climbs westwards out of Teelin and up to the highest point of Slieve League – from where you can admire the Atlantic Ocean shimmering 598 m (1,972 ft) below. The path then continues on to Malinbeg, 16 km (10 miles) west. During the summer, for a less strenuous but safer and equally rewarding excursion, pay a boat-owner from Teelin to take you out to see Slieve League from the sea.

Killybegs ⑭

Co Donegal. 🏃 1,700. 🚌 from Donegal. 🛈 Donegal (073 21148).

NARROW WINDING streets give Killybegs an attractive timeless feel, in stark contrast with the industriousness of this small town. The sense of prosperity stems in part from the manufacture of the Donegal carpets for which the town is famous, and which adorn Dublin Castle (see pp88–9) and other palaces around the world.

Killybegs is one of Ireland's busiest fishing ports and the quays are well worth seeing when the trawlers arrive to off-load their catch: gulls squawk overhead and the smell of fish fills the air. Trawlermen come from far and wide – so do not be surprised if you hear Eastern European voices as you wander around the town.

Trawler crew in Killybegs relaxing after unloading their catch

THE IRISH GAELTACHTS

The term "Gaeltacht" refers to Gaelic-speaking areas of Ireland. Up to the 16th century, virtually the entire population spoke the native tongue. British rule, however, undermined Irish culture, and the Famine (see p281) drained the country of many of its Gaelic-speakers. The use of the local language has fallen steadily since. Even so, in the Gaeltachts 75 per cent of the people still speak it, and road signs are exclusively in Irish – unlike in most other parts of Ireland.

Gaelic pub sign in Gaeltacht region

The Donegal Gaeltacht stretches almost unbroken along the coast from Fanad Head to Slieve League and boasts the largest number of Irish-speakers in the country. Ireland's other principal Gaeltachts are in Galway and Kerry.

Donegal town, overlooked by the ruins of its 15th-century castle

Donegal ⑮

Co Donegal. 🚶 *2,300.* 🚌 ℹ️ *Quay St (073 21148).*

DONEGAL MEANS "Fort of the Foreigners", after the Vikings who built a garrison here. However, it was under the O'Donnells that the town began to take shape. The ruins of **Donegal Castle** in the town centre incorporate the gabled tower of a fortified house built by the family in the 15th century. The adjoining house and most other features are Jacobean – added by Sir Basil Brooke, who moved in after the O'Donnells were ousted by the English in 1607 *(see pp42–3)*. The castle has recently been partly restored.

Brooke was also responsible for laying out the market square, which is known as the **Diamond**. An obelisk in the centre commemorates four Franciscans who wrote the *Annals of the Four Masters* in the 1630s. This manuscript traces the history of the Gaelic people from 40 days before the Great Flood up to the end of the 16th century. Part of it was written at **Donegal Abbey**, south of the market square along the River Eske. Built in 1474, little now remains of the abbey but a few Gothic windows and cloister arches. About 1.5 km (1 mile) further on is **Donegal Craft Village**, a showcase for the work of local craftspeople.

While there is not a huge amount to explore in Donegal town, it has some pleasant hotels and makes a good base for exploring the southern part of the county.

🏰 **Donegal Castle**
Tirchonaill St. 📞 *073 22405.* ⭕ *mid-Mar–Oct: daily.* 📷 ♿ *limited.*
🏠 **Donegal Craft Village**
Ballyshannon Rd. 📞 *073 22053.* ⭕ *May–Sep: daily.* ♿ *limited.*

Lough Derg ⑯

Co Donegal. 🚢 *Jun–mid-Aug (pilgrims only).* 🚌 *to Pettigo from Donegal.*

PILGRIMS HAVE made their way to Lough Derg ever since St Patrick spent 40 days praying on one of the lake's islands in an attempt to rid Ireland of all evil spirits. The Pilgrimage of St Patrick's Purgatory began in around 1150 and still attracts thousands of Catholics every summer. Their destination is the tiny **Station Island**, close to Lough Derg's southern shore and reached by boat from a jetty 8 km (5 miles) north of the border village of Pettigo. The island is completely covered by a religious complex, which includes a basilica, built in 1921, and hostels for pilgrims.

The pilgrimage season runs from June to mid-August. People spend three days on the island, eating just one meal of dry bread and black tea per day. Although only pilgrims can visit Station Island, it is interesting to go to the jetty to savour the atmosphere and get a good view of the basilica near the shore.

Rossnowlagh ⑰

Co Donegal. 🚶 *55.* 🚌 *from Bundoran & Donegal.* ℹ️ *Apr–Oct: Main St, Bundoran (072 41350).*

Holiday-makers enjoying the fine sandy beach at Rossnowlagh

AT ROSSNOWLAGH, Atlantic waves break on to one of Ireland's finest beaches, drawing crowds of both bathers and surfers to this tiny place. Even so, the village remains far more peaceful than the resort of Bundoran, 14 km (9 miles) south. In addition, the cliffs at Rossnowlagh provide scope for exhilarating coastal walks. Away from the sea, you can visit the **Donegal Historical Society Museum**, housed in a striking Franciscan friary

Basilica on Station Island viewed from the shores of Lough Derg

Lissadell House dining room with Gore-Booth family portraits

built in the 1950s. The tiny but fascinating collection includes displays of Stone Age flints, Irish musical instruments and other local artifacts.

Rossnowlagh never fails to make the news on 12 July, when it hosts the only parade to take place in the Republic by the Protestant organization, the Orange Order *(see p53)*.

Donegal Historical Society Museum
072 51267. daily. 25 Dec.

Ballyshannon 18

Co Donegal. 2,600. from Bundoran & Donegal.

IN BALLYSHANNON, well-kept Georgian homes jostle for space along hilly streets on the banks of the River Erne, near where it flows into Donegal Bay. This is a bustling town, full of character and off the main tourist track – though it gets packed during August's festival of traditional music, which is one of the best of its kind in the country.

The festival apart, Ballyshannon is most famous as the birthplace of poet William Allingham (1824–89), who recalled his home town in the lines "Adieu to Ballyshanny and the winding banks of the Erne". He lies buried in the graveyard of St Anne's Church, off Main Street. There is a fine view over the river from here: you can see the small island of **Inis Saimer** where, according to legend, Greeks founded the first colony in Ireland after the Great Flood. Beyond, you can glimpse a large Irish Army base: Ballyshannon's position on a steeply rising bluff overlooking the River Erne has always made the town a strategic military site.

Mural of the family dog in Lissadell's dining room

About 1.5 km (1 mile) northwest of town lie the scant ruins of **Assaroe Abbey**, founded by Cistercians in 1184. A graveyard with some ancient burial slabs and headstones remains. Nearby, two water wheels installed by the monks have been restored and incorporated into an interpretive centre called the **Water Wheels**. One wheel now drives a generator.

Water Wheels
Assaroe Abbey. 072 51580.
Jun–Aug: daily; mid-Feb–May & Sep: Sun pm; Oct–mid-Feb: by appt.

Lissadell House 19

Carney, Co Sligo. 071 63150. or to Sligo. Jun–Sep: Mon–Sat.

A LATE GEORGIAN mansion built in the 1830s, Lissadell is famous more for its occupants than its architecture. It was once the home of the Gore-Booths who, unlike some of the Anglo-Irish gentry, contributed much to the region. During the Famine *(see p281)*, Sir Robert mortgaged the house to help feed his employees.

The most famous member of the Gore-Booth family was Sir Robert's granddaughter, Constance Markievicz (1868–1927). She was a leading revolutionary who took part in the 1916 Rising *(see pp48–9)* and was the first woman to be elected to the British House of Commons. WB Yeats, a regular visitor to the house, immortalized Constance and her sister, Eva, in one of his poems, describing them as "Two girls in silk kimonos, both beautiful, one a gazelle". The house is still in the hands of the Gore-Booth family.

Built in grey limestone, the exterior of Lissadell House is rather austere. The interior, on the other hand, has an appealing atmosphere of faded grandeur, with peeling paintwork and copious memorabilia of the building's former occupants. The finest rooms are the gallery (previously the music room) and the dining room, which is decorated with extraordinary full-length murals of the Gore-Booth family, their servants and their dog. Painted directly on to the wall, they were the work of Constance's husband, Count Casimir Markievicz.

Both the house and the overgrown estate are slowly being restored. There are plans, for example, to open up the woodland vistas to recreate the sweeping views down to the sea. You can already explore along paths skirting the lakeshore, and there is also a wildlife reserve which is a popular winter refuge for barnacle geese.

Colourful fishing boats in Killybegs harbour ▷

A Tour of Yeats Country 20

Yeats tour sign

EVEN FOR PEOPLE unfamiliar with the poetry of WB Yeats, Sligo's engaging landscapes are reason enough to make a pilgrimage. This tour follows a route through varied scenery, taking you past sandy bays and dramatic limestone ridges, through forest and alongside rivers and lakes. The delightful Lough Gill lies at the heart of Yeats country, enclosed by wooded hills crisscrossed by walking trails. In summer, boats ply the length of the lough, or you can head to one of the northwest's best beaches, at Rosses Point.

Ben Bulben ⑤
The eerie silhouette of Ben Bulben rises abruptly out of the plain. You can climb to the top, but go with great care.

Lissadell House ④
Yeats was a close friend of the Gore-Booth sisters who lived at Lissadell. You can see the room where the poet slept as a guest *(see p303)*.

Drumcliff ③
Although he died in France, in 1948 Yeats's body was laid to rest in Drumcliff churchyard. The ruins of an old monastic site include a fine High Cross.

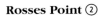

DONEGAL
N15
Carney
Drumcliff Bay
⑤
④
③
Drum
R291
N15
N16
Sligo Harbour
②
①
Garavogue
R287
R284
N4
GALWAY

Rosses Point ②
Yeats and his brother used to spend their summers at this pretty resort. It stands at the entrance to Sligo Bay, and a steady flow of boats passes by.

TIPS FOR DRIVERS

Length: 88 km (55 miles).
Stopping-off points: Outside Sligo, the best choice of eating places is at Rosses Point, although there are good pubs in Drumcliff and Dromahair, and Parke's Castle has a café. Lough Gill provides most choice in terms of picnic spots.
Boat trips: Wild Rose Water Bus (071 64266 or 087 2598869).

KEY

▬	Tour route
═	Other roads
⛴	Boat trips
☀	Viewpoint

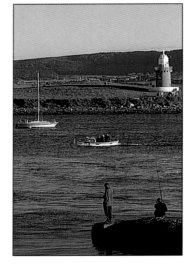

Sligo ①
This town is a good place to begin a tour of Yeats country. It has many connections with the poet and his family, whose literary and artistic legacy has helped to inspire Sligo's thriving arts scene *(see p308)*.

WB YEATS AND SLIGO

WB Yeats
(1865–1939)

As a schoolboy in London, Yeats *(see p27)* longed for his native Sligo, and as an adult he often returned here. He lovingly describes the county in his *Reveries over Childhood and Youth*, and the lake-studded landscape haunts his poetry. "In a sense", Yeats said, "Sligo has always been my home", and it is here that he wished to be buried. His gravestone in Drumcliff bears an epitaph he penned himself: "Cast a cold eye on life, on death. Horseman pass by."

Parke's Castle viewed from across the calm waters of Lough Gill

Parke's Castle ㉑

6 km (4 miles) N of Dromahair, Co Leitrim. 071 64149. or to Sligo. mid-Mar–May: Tue–Sun; Jun–Oct: daily. ground floor only.

THIS FORTIFIED MANOR HOUSE dominates the eastern end of Lough Gill. It was built in 1609 by Captain Robert Parke, an English settler who later became MP for Leitrim. It has been beautifully restored by the Office of Public Works using 17th-century building methods and native Irish oak.

Parke's Castle was erected on the site of a 16th-century tower house belonging to the O'Rourkes, a powerful local clan, and stones from this earlier structure were used in the new building. The original foundations and part of the moat were incorporated, but otherwise Parke's Castle is the epitome of a Plantation manor house *(see p43)*. It is protected by a large enclosure or bawn, whose sturdy wall includes a gatehouse and two turrets as well as the house itself.

Among the most distinctive architectural features of Parke's Castle are the diamond-shaped chimneys, mullioned windows and the parapets. There is also a curious stone hut, known as the "sweathouse", which was an early Irish sauna. Inside, an exhibition and audiovisual display cover Parke's Castle and various historic and prehistoric sites in the area, with photos and archaeological finds. There is also a working forge.

Boat trips around sights on Lough Gill that are associated with the poet, WB Yeats, leave from outside the castle walls.

Glencar Lough ⑥

"There is a waterfall ... that all my childhood counted dear", wrote Yeats of the cataract which tumbles into Glencar Lough. A path leads down to it from the road.

Parke's Castle ⑦

This 17th-century fortified manor house commands a splendid view over the tranquil waters of Lough Gill. It is a starting point for boat trips around the lough.

Isle of Innisfree ⑧

"There midnight's all a glimmer, and noon a purple glow", is how Yeats once described Innisfree. There is not much to see on this tiny island but it is a romantic spot. In summer, a boatman ferries visitors here.

Dooney Rock ⑨

A steep path leads from the road to Dooney Rock, from where glorious views extend over the lough to Ben Bulben. Trails weave through the surrounding woods and by the lake.

0 kilometres 3

0 miles 2

Hargadon's bar, one of Sligo town's most famous watering holes

Sligo ㉒

Co Sligo. 🚶 20,000. 🚌 🚍 🛈
Aras Reddan, Temple St (071 61201).
🚭 *Fri.*

THE PORT of Sligo sits at the mouth of the River Gara-vogue, sandwiched between the Atlantic and Lough Gill. The largest town in the northwest, it rose to prominence under the Normans, being well placed as a gateway between the provinces of Ulster and Connaught. The appearance of Sligo today is mainly the result of growth during the late 18th and 19th centuries.

Sligo is perfectly situated for touring the ravishing countryside nearby, and it is a also a good centre for traditional music. While the town itself can seem rather sombre, the quiet back streets are reason-ably atmospheric.

Sligo's link with the Yeats family is the main source of the town's appeal. WB Yeats (*see pp306–7*), Ireland's best-known poet, was born into a prominent local family. The Pollexfen warehouse, at the western end of Wine Street, has a rooftop turret from which the poet's grandfather would observe his merchant fleet moored in the docks.

The town's sole surviving medieval building is **Sligo Abbey**, founded in 1253. Some original features remain, such as the delicate lancet windows in the choir, but this ruined Dominican friary dates mainly from the 15th century. The best features are a beautifully carved altar and the cloisters.

A short distance west from the abbey is O'Connell Street, with the town's main shops

Bronze statue of WB Yeats

and Hargadon's bar – an old Sligo institution complete with a dark, wooden interior, snugs and a grocery counter. Near the junction with Wine Street, overlooking Hyde Bridge, is the Yeats Memorial Building. This houses the Yeats Society and the **Sligo Art Gallery**, which puts on shows by foreign and Irish artists. The Yeats International Summer School is held here too: Sligo's renown as the arts capital of northwest Ireland rests partly on this annual festival of readings and lectures on the poet's life and work.

The Yeatsian associations continue on the other side of the river. The first thing you see on crossing Hyde Bridge is a statue of the poet, engraved with lines from his own verse. From here, it is just a short walk east to **Sligo County Museum and Art Gallery**. The museum has a small selection of Yeatsian memorabilia, while the gallery includes evocative Sligo land-scapes by WB Yeats's brother, Jack, and several portraits by his father, John B Yeats.

🏰 **Sligo Abbey**
Abbey St. ◯ *daily.* 🎫 🌙 *mid-Jun–Sep.*
🏛 **Sligo Art Gallery**
Hyde Bridge. 🕻 *071 45847.*
◯ *Mon–Sat.*
🏛 **Sligo County Museum and Art Gallery**
Stephen St. 🕻 *071 42212.*
◯ *Tue–Sat (Nov–Mar pm only).*

ENVIRONS: In a most unlikely setting in the suburbs of Sligo, **Carrowmore Megalithic Cemetery** once boasted the country's largest collection of Stone Age tombs. Quarrying destroyed many graves, but about 40 passage tombs (*see pp330–1*) and dolmens (*see p36*) survive among the aban-doned gravel pits, with some in private gardens and even protruding from cottages.

Dwarfing these tombs from atop **Knocknarea** mountain is a huge, unexcavated cairn, which dates back about 5,000 years and is said to contain the tomb of the legendary Queen Maeve of Connaught (*see p30*). You can climb the mountain in about an hour; the path starts 4 km (2.5 miles) west of Carrowmore.

Tobernalt, by Lough Gill 5 km (3 miles) south of Sligo, means "cliff well", after a near-by spring with alleged curative powers. It was a holy site in Celtic times and later became a Christian shrine. Priests came here to celebrate Mass in secret during the 18th century, when Catholic worship was illegal. The Mass rock, next to an altar erected around 1900, remains a place of pilgrimage.

🏕 **Carrowmore Cemetery**
🕻 *071 61534.* ◯ *May–Sep: daily.* 🎫

Altar by the holy well at Tobernalt, overlooking Lough Gill in Sligo

Lough Arrow ㉓

Co Sligo. 🚌 to Ballinafad. ℹ️
May–Oct: Boyle (079 62145).

P EOPLE GO to Lough Arrow to
sail and fish for the local
trout, and also simply to enjoy
the glorious countryside. You
can explore the lake by boat,
but the views from the shore
are the real joy of Lough
Arrow. A full circuit of the
lake is highly recommended,
but for the most breathtaking
views of all head for the
southern end around
Ballinafad. This small town
lies in a gorgeous spot,
enclosed to the north and
south by the Bricklieve and
Curlew Mountains.

The **Carrowkeel Passage
Tomb Cemetery** occupies a
remote and eerie spot in the
Bricklieve Mountains to the
north of Ballinafad. The best
approach is up the single track
road from Castlebaldwin, 5 km
(3 miles) northeast of the site.

The 14 Neolithic passage
graves, which are scattered
around a hilltop overlooking
Lough Arrow, are elaborate
corbelled structures. One is
comparable with Newgrange
(see pp330–1), except that the
burial chamber inside this
cairn is lit by the sun on the
day of the summer solstice
(21 June) as opposed to the
winter solstice. On a nearby
ridge are the remains of Stone
Age huts, presumably those
occupied by the farmers who
buried their dead in the
Carrowkeel passage graves.

Passage tomb in Carrowkeel cemetery above Lough Arrow

Carrick-on-Shannon ㉔

Co Leitrim. 🚶 1,900. 🚌 🚍 ℹ️
Apr–Sep: The Marina (078 20170).

T HE TINY CAPITAL of Leitrim,
which is one of the least
populated counties in Ireland,
stands in a lovely spot on a
tight bend of the River
Shannon.

The town's location by the
river and its proximity to the
Grand Canal were crucial to
Carrick's development. They
are also the main reasons for
its thriving tourist industry.
There is a colourful, modern
marina, which in summer fills
up with private launches and
boats available for hire.

Already a major boating
centre, Carrick has benefited
from the reopening of the
Shannon-Erne Waterway, one
end of which begins 6 km
(4 miles) north at Leitrim. The
channel was restored in a
cross-border joint venture
billed as a symbol of peaceful
cooperation between Northern
Ireland and the Republic.

Away from the bustle of the
marina, Carrick-on-Shannon is
an old-fashioned place, with
19th-century churches and
convents mixed in with more
refined Georgian houses and
shopfronts. The town's most
curious building is the quaint
Costello Chapel on Bridge
Street. One of the smallest of
its kind anywhere in the world,
the chapel was built in 1877
by local a businessman,
Edward Costello, to house the
tombs of himself and his wife.

Lough Rynn Estate ㉕

Mohill, Co Leitrim. 📞 078 31427.
🚌 or 🚍 to Carrick-on-Shannon. ⭘
April–mid-Sep: daily. 🎫 🛍️ ♿

T HIS VAST ESTATE, lying 3 km
(2 miles) south of Mohill,
was the ancestral seat of the
Clements family, Earls of
Leitrim. The baronial-style
house, constructed in 1832
and full of hunting trophies
and grandiose furniture, is of
less interest than the grounds.
These extend across 40 ha
(100 acres) of land and more
than 240 ha (600 acres) of
lakes. There is a lot to explore,
including ornamental gardens,
water meadows, lush wood-
land and an arboretum with
California redwoods and other
exotic trees. The ruins of a
16th-century castle overlook
one of the lakes, and you can
also walk up to the remains
of a Neolithic burial site.

SHANNON-ERNE WATERWAY

This labyrinthine system
of rivers and lakes passes
through unspoilt border
country, linking Leitrim on
the Shannon and Upper
Lough Erne in Fermanagh.
It follows the course of a
canal which was completed
and then abandoned in
the 1860s. The channel
was reopened in 1993,
enabling the public to
enjoy both the Victorian
stonework (including 34
bridges) and the state-of-
the-art technology used to
operate the 16 locks.

**Cruiser negotiating a lock on
the Shannon-Erne Waterway**

Megalithic burial stone, Newgrange, County Meath ▷

THE MIDLANDS

THE MIDLANDS

CAVAN · MONAGHAN · LOUTH · LONGFORD · WESTMEATH
MEATH · OFFALY · LAOIS

THE CRADLE *of Irish civilization and the Celts' spiritual home, the Midlands encompass some of Ireland's most sacred and symbolic sites. Much of the region is ignored, but the ragged landscapes of lush pastures, lakes and bogland reveal ancient Celtic crosses, gracious Norman abbeys and Gothic Revival castles.*

The topography of Ireland is saucer-shaped: mountains form the perimeter and the low-lying Midlands make the bowl. This region covers several counties, encompassing towns such as Meath and Louth, whose populations have grown steadily in recent years, and more tranquil areas such as the Boyne Valley.

Although grassland and bog dotted with lakes are most characteristic of the Midlands, the Slieve Bloom Mountains and the Cooley Peninsula provide good walking country. The latter is reached via the busy town of Dundalk, which once marked the northern edge of the Pale. A better base for exploring is Carlingford, which is magnificently set between the Cooley mountains and the lough. This village, another Pale border town, is said to have once

had 32 castles, and the impressive remnants of King John's Castle are among the remains of many forts.

One of the predominant geological features of the Midlands are tiny lakes, formed by glaciers over 10,000 years ago. Some are set in idyllic countryside and provide a peaceful fishing retreat. A real angler's paradise is the flat central county of Longford, which is replete with lakes and streams. Other loughs, such as Derravaragh, Owel, Ennell and Sheelin in County Westmeath, are local recreation spots, while Lough Ree to the west is part of the Shannon waterway. The Royal Canal and the Grand Canal, which run west from Dublin to the Shannon, also traverse the Midlands, providing a wide range of water-based recreation.

Carlingford village and harbour, with the hills of the Cooley Peninsula rising behind

◁ **Temple Finghin round tower at Clonmacnoise monastery on the banks of the River Shannon**

The remains of St Patrick's friary in County Meath

Water from the melted glaciers has influenced the area's economic profile. The well-watered pastures of Westmeath and Longford form the heart of Ireland's cattle industry, which is a major contributor to the national economy. While the region is largely made up of quiet villages and country roads, there are also several bustling market towns such as Mullingar and Athlone.

As a consequence of the combination of low-lying land and the volume of water, much of the Midlands is covered by bog. The area has its own distinctive type of bog, which is dome-shaped and elevated, in contrast to the thinner, flatter blanket variety found to the west. The vast Bog of Allen stretches across the region, and most of County Offaly is bogland. There is also a large section of unspoiled raised bog in Westmeath. Bogland has been vital to the Irish economy, with peat-cutting providing employment, and the deposit itself being used as fuel and fertilizer.

The Midlands has a most fascinating history. The fertile Boyne Valley in County Meath was settled during the Stone Age and became the most important centre of habitation in the country. The remains of ancient sites from this early

Spiral figure from a stone passage grave

civilization fill the area. Newgrange, probably the finest Neolithic tomb in the country, lies in the area called Brú na Bóinne, meaning 'Palace of the Boyne', along with the sites of Knowth and Dowth. These massive graves, which held great ritual significance, are older than the pyramids of Egypt. In Celtic times, the focus shifted south to the Hill of Tara, the seat of the High Kings of Ireland and the Celts' spiritual and political capital. (Indeed, there is archaeological evidence to suggest that Tara was a major cult centre long before the arrival of the Celts.) Its heyday came in the 3rd century AD, but it retained its dominance for another 200 years, its downfall beginning on the nearby Hill of Slane, where, in the 5th century, St Patrick lit a fire in defiance of the Irish king, heralding the rise of Christianity in Ireland and the demise of the old pagan beliefs. By the end of the 16th century, the area radiating out from the village incorporated nearly all the counties in the Midlands. Tullynally Castle, one of the largest in Ireland, also dates from this time, although its

The ruins of the large Benedictine friary at Fore Abbey in County Westmeath

The delightful setting of Drumlane in County Cavan

impressive façade of turrets and battlements are due to a later Gothic Revival makeover.

Tara never lost its spiritual significance to the Midlanders, and its sons did not accept English rule without a fight. Descendants of the Irish and Norman lords, who were staunchly Catholic, resented the Protestant plantation of Ulster lands to the north by the Crown. In the 1640, they joined the Irish rebels against the settlers. But in 1649, the avenging armies of Oliver Cromwell launched the Siege of Drogheda, one of the most brutal attacks in Irish history; the long campaign also resulted in the destruction of the ancient castle atop the Rock of Dunamase. The Boyne Valley made a dramatic return to prominence in 1690, when the Battle of the Boyne resulted in a decisive Protestant victory. The Midlands' history has left a varied legacy of fascinating places for the modern-day visitor to enjoy. In addition to the ancient sites of Meath, the historical highlights of the region include the monasteries of Fore Abbey, Mellifont and Drumlane, which are surrounded by beautiful countryside. The austere ruins at Monasterboice contain Muiredach's Cross, one of the finest high crosses

Ornate Celtic enamel brooch

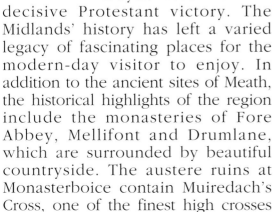

"Unfinished" Cross, Meath

in Ireland. The monks of Kells Monastery, which was founded by St Columba, one of Ireland's patron saints, are thought to have been the creators of one of the country's most beautiful treasures, the illuminated manuscript known as the Book of Kells (now in Trinity College Library). This sumptuous copy of the gospels is, in the intricacy of its ornament and artistic mastery, a quite stunning achievement; and the mystery of its symbolism evokes the obscure fascination which seems to be the hallmark of this historical period. The most famous monastic site in the region is Clonmacnoise, which lies to the west beside the Shannon and ranks among Europe's greatest early Christian centres. The Midlands also contains a considerable number of wonderful stately homes, including Carrigglas Manor and Emo Court.

Monastic site of Clonmacnoise, burial location of the kings of Tara

Irish Christianity

ST PATRICK'S 5TH-CENTURY missionary work laid the foundations for a Church that would develop in isolation from Europe, centred not on bishops with dioceses but on monastic establishments. By the 8th century, Celtic monasteries had become renowned for their scholarship and dazzling works of crafts-manship – the Irish High Crosses date from this period. The 11th and 12th centuries saw a resurgence of Christianity when the Church accepted obedience to Rome, with the flow-ering of Romanesque architecture and the founding of the first Cistercian monasteries.

**Tall Cross,
Monasterboice,
County Louth**

The reliquary of St Patrick's Bell, which dates from c.1100, and is one of many metalwork marvels crafted by Celtic Christians.

THE BOOK OF KELLS

One of a group of illuminated manuscripts created in Ireland between the 7th and 10th centuries, the Book of Kells is unparalleled for the sumptuousness of its decorated pages. Shown here is part of a page devoted to the symbols of the four evangelists. The illuminators – like the sculptors of high crosses – seemed to have been driven to fill every available space with intricate patterns and motifs, many of them symbolic.

Winged man symbolizing St Matthew

Pigments used include woad, indigo and lapis lazuli

St Patrick, Ireland's patron saint, came over from Britain to encourage missionary work and the ascetic life. The image above depicts him entering "St Patrick's Purgatory" on an island in Lough Derg, Donegal, where he spent 40 days praying and fasting.

Ornamental and symbolic motifs, such as interlacing and spirals, have parallels in metalwork and stonecarving.

The stylized initial, a characteristic of the illuminated book, originated in classical times when it was placed out in the margin. Irish scribes integrated it into the text by pulling it in from the margin and gradually decreasing the size of the following letters, as seen here in the Beatus Vir initial page of this 8th-century majuscule psalter.

MONASTIC ASCETICISM

The early monastic movement in Ireland was notable for its asceticism. Some monks organized themselves into small, self-sufficient communities in very remote, inaccessible places. Often these were on islands, and of these the most spectacular was the inhospitable rock stack of Skellig Michael, off the coast of Kerry, on which perched a settlement of six beehive cells and two oratories. In principle and in practice, asceticism was rigorous in its abstention from worldly comforts and pleasures. In the 12th century, it was the severity of the Cistercian rule that attracted so many men in Ireland to turn to monasticism.

Monks going to Skellig by Eamon O'Doherty, in Caherciveen

Jerpoint Abbey was founded in 1180 by the Cistercians. After the arrival of the Continental monastic orders, monastery buildings were grouped around cloisters, unlike the early Irish establishments, which were laid out at random.

Lion symbolizing St Mark

Stylized peacocks are entwined in vines sprouting from a chalice – the meaning of much early medieval religious symbolism is obscure.

Knock has been a major place of pilgrimage since 1879, when a vision of Mary, Joseph and St John by two local women was followed by reports of miracle cures. Pilgrimages take place on saints' days at religious sites across the country.

Exploring the Midlands

D ROGHEDA IS THE OBVIOUS BASE from which to explore the Boyne Valley and neighbouring monastic sites, such as Monasterboice. Trim and Mullingar, to the southwest, are less convenient but make pleasanter places in which to stay. The northern counties of Monaghan, Cavan and Longford are quiet backwaters with a patchwork of lakes that attract many anglers. To the south, Offaly and Laois are dominated by dark expanses of bog, though there is a cluster of sights around the attractive Georgian town of Birr. For a break by the sea, head for the picturesque village of Carlingford on the Cooley Peninsula.

West doorway of Nuns' Church at Clonmacnoise

KEY

▬	Motorway
▬	Major road
▬	Minor road
▬	Scenic route
≈	River
☼	Viewpoint

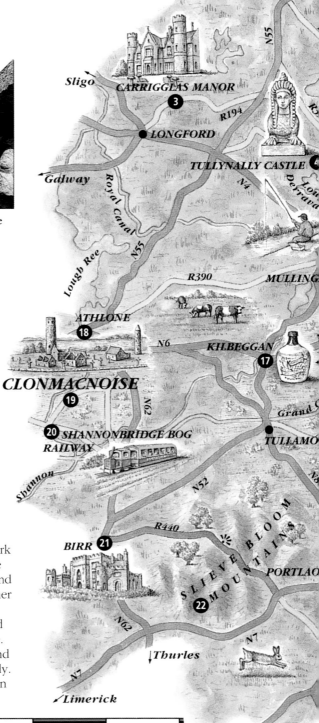

GETTING AROUND

In the Midlands, there is an extensive network of roads and rail lines fanning out across the country from Dublin. As a result, getting around on public transport is easier than in most other areas. The Dublin–Belfast railway serves Dundalk and Drogheda, while Mullingar and Longford town lie on the Dublin–Sligo route. The railway and N7 road between Dublin and Limerick give good access to Laois and Offaly. For motorists, roads in the Midlands are often flat and straight but also potholed.

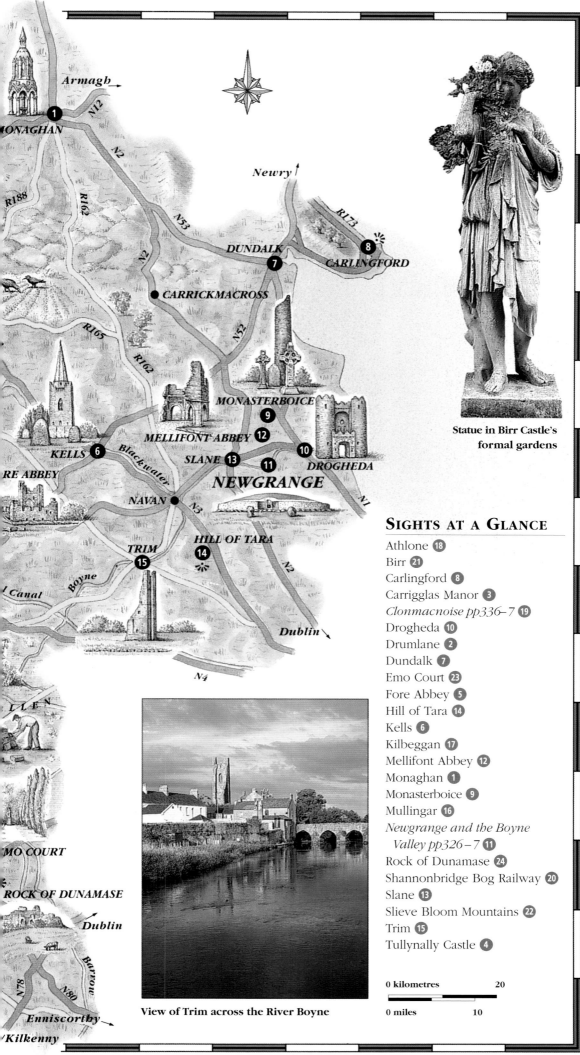

**Statue in Birr Castle's
formal gardens**

Sights at a Glance

View of Trim across the River Boyne

0 kilometres 20

0 miles 10

Rossmore Memorial drinking fountain in Monaghan

Monaghan ❶

Co Monaghan. 🏘 *6,000.* 🚌 ℹ️
*Market House, Market Square (047
81122).*

THE SPRUCE AND THRIVING town
of Monaghan is the urban
highlight of the northern Midlands. Planted by James I in
1613 *(see p43)*, it developed
into a prosperous industrial
centre, thanks mainly to the
local manufacture of linen. A
crannog *(see p37)* off Glen
Road is the sole trace of the
town's Celtic beginnings.

Monaghan centres on three
almost contiguous squares.
The main attraction in Market
Square is the 18th-century
Market House, a squat but
charming building with the
original oak beams still visible.
It is now home to the tourist
office. To the east lies Church
Square, very much the heart of
modern Monaghan and lined
with dignified 19th-century
buildings, such as the Classical-
style courthouse. The third
square, which is known as the
Diamond, was the original
marketplace. It contains the
Rossmore Memorial, a large
Victorian drinking fountain
with an ornate stone canopy
supported by marble columns.

Do not miss the excellent
County Museum, just off
Market Square, which tells the
story of Monaghan's linen and
lace-making industries. The
pride of its historical collection
is the Cross of Clogher, an
ornate bronze altar cross which
dates from around 1400.

The Gothic Revival Cathedral
of St Macartan perches on a
hilltop south of the town, from
where you can enjoy a fine
view over Monaghan.

🏛 County Museum
Hill St. 📞 *047 82928.* ◯ *Tue–Sat.*
⬤ *public hols.* ♿ *limited.*

Drumlane ❷

*1 km (0.5 miles) S of Milltown, Co
Cavan.* 🚌 *to Belturbet.*

STANDING ALONE by the River
Erne, the medieval church
and round tower of Drumlane
merit a visit as much for their
delightful setting as for the
ruins themselves. The abbey
church, founded in the early
13th century but significantly
altered about 200 years later,
features fine Romanesque
carvings. The nearby round
tower has lost its cap but is
unusual for the well-finished
stonework, with carvings of
birds on the north side.

Carrigglas Manor ❸

Co Longford. 📞 *043 45165.* 🚌 *to
Longford.* ◯ *Jun–Aug: Sun–Tue, Thu,
Fri; May & Sep: Mon & Fri.* 🎨 ✍ ♿
limited.

CARRIGGLAS MANOR has been
the seat of the Lefroys, a
family of Huguenot descent,
ever since its construction in
1837. It has changed little in
the intervening years and is a
fine example of the Tudor
Revival style. The Victorian
atmosphere is still very much
alive inside, where the rooms
are decorated with pseudo-

Drawing room in Carrigglas Manor with original 19th-century features

Authentic Victorian kitchen in Tullynally Castle

Gothic panelling and ornate plasterwork ceilings. The stable block, by contrast, is a grand Neo-Classical building by James Gandon, the architect of Dublin's Custom House *(see p86)*. The manor is set in pleasant grounds consisting primarily of woodland.

ENVIRONS: Just 14 km (9 miles) south of Carrigglas Manor, **Ardagh** is considered the most attractive village in Longford, with pretty stone cottages gathered around a green.

Tullynally Castle ❹

Castle Pollard, Co Westmeath. 044 61159. to Mullingar. **Castle** mid-Jun–mid-Aug: daily (pm only). obligatory. **Grounds** May–Sep: daily (pm only). limited.

THIS HUGE STRUCTURE, adorned with numerous turrets and battlements, is one of Ireland's largest castles. The original 17th-century tower house was given a Georgian gloss, but this was all but submerged under later Gothic Revival changes. The Pakenham family have lived at Tullynally since 1655. Thomas Pakenham, son of the present Earl of Longford, now manages the estate.

The imposing great hall leads to a fine panelled dining room hung with family portraits. Of equal interest are the Victorian kitchen and laundry room and the adjacent drying room, complete with its immense boiler.

The 8,000-volume library looks out on to rolling wooded parkland, much of which was landscaped in the 1760s. The grounds include Victorian terraces, walled kitchen and flower gardens, and two small lakes where black swans have recently been introduced.

Fore Abbey ❺

Fore, Castle Pollard, Co Westmeath. to Castle Pollard. daily.

THE RUINS of Fore Abbey lie in glorious rolling countryside about 8 km (5 miles) east of Tullynally Castle. St Fechin established a monastery here in 630, but what you see now are the remains of a large Benedictine priory founded around 1200. Located on the northern border of the Pale *(see p154)*, Fore Abbey was heavily fortified in the 15th century as protection against the native Irish.

The ruined church was part of the original Norman priory, but the cloister and refectory date from the 1400s. On the hill opposite lies St Fechin's Church, a Norman building said to mark the site of the first monastery. The tiny church nearby incorporates a 15th-century anchorite's cell.

Kells ❻

Co Meath. 5,500. *Mill St, Trim (046 37111).*

SIGNPOSTED by its Irish name, Ceanannus Mór, this modest town provides an unlikely backdrop to the monastery for which it is so famous. **Kells Monastery** was set up by St Columba in the 6th century, but its heyday came after 806, when monks fled here from Iona. They may have been the scribes who illuminated the superb *Book of Kells,* now kept at Trinity College, Dublin *(see p72).*

Lying in the west of town, the monastery centres on an 18th-century church. This is a rather gloomy building, but the displays in the gallery that relate to Kells are worth seeing. A decapitated round tower stands guard outside, and you can also see several 9th-century High Crosses; the South Cross is in the best condition.

Just north of the enclosure is **St Columba's House**, a tiny steep-roofed stone oratory, similar to St Kevin's Kitchen at Glendalough *(see p162).*

In Cross Street is the Market Cross, a High Cross that once marked the entrance to the monastery. It was used as a gallows during the uprising in 1798 *(see p45).* The battle scene on the base is a subject rarely used in High Cross art.

Ruins of Fore Abbey, a medieval Benedictine priory

Celtic crosses at Monasterboice cemetery, County Louth ▷

Thatched cottage in Carlingford on the mountainous Cooley Peninsula

Dundalk ❼

Co Louth. 🏠 *30,000.* 🚌 🚆 ℹ️
Jocelyn Street (042 35484). 🚢 *Thu.*

Dundalk once marked the northernmost point of the Pale, the area controlled by the English during the Middle Ages *(see p154).* Now it is the last major town before the border with Northern Ireland, situated midway between Dublin and Belfast.

Dundalk also provides a gateway to the magnificent countryside of the Cooley Peninsula. The **County Museum**, which is housed in an 18th-century distillery in the town, gives an insight into some of Louth's traditional industries such as beer-making.

🏛 **County Museum**
Jocleyn St. ☎ *042 27056.* ⬜ *Mar–Sep: daily; Oct–Feb: Tue–Sun.* ⬤ *25 & 26 Dec & 1 Jan.* 📷 ♿

Carlingford ❽

Co Louth. 🏠 *650.* 🚆 ℹ️ **Holy Trinity Heritage Centre** *Churchyard Rd (042 73454).* **Carlingford Adventure Centre** *Tholsel St (042 73100).*

This is a picturesque fishing village, beautifully located between the mountains of the Cooley Peninsula and the waters of Carlingford Lough. The border with Northern Ireland runs right through the centre of this drowned river valley, and from the village you can look across to the Mountains of Mourne on the Ulster side *(see pp382–3).* Carlingford is an interesting place to explore, with its

pretty whitewashed cottages and ancient buildings clustered along medieval alleyways. The ruins of **King John's Castle**, built by the Normans to protect the entrance to the lough, still dominate the village, and there are other impressive fortified buildings, including the Mint. The **Holy Trinity Heritage Centre**, which is housed in a medieval church, traces the history of the port from Anglo-Norman times.

Carlingford is the country's oyster capital, and its oyster festival in August draws a large crowd. The lough is a popular watersports centre too, and in summer you can go on cruises around the lough from the village quayside.

Carlingford is well placed for hikes around the Cooley Peninsula. The **Carlingford Adventure Centre** provides information for walkers and also organizes its own tours.

ENVIRONS: A scenic route weaves around the **Cooley Peninsula**, skirting the coast and then cutting right through the mountains. The section along the north coast is the most dramatic: just 3 km (1.5 miles) northwest of Carlingford, in the **Slieve Foye Forest Park**, a corkscrew road climbs to give a gorgeous panoramic view over the hills and lough.

The Tain Trail, which you can join at Carlingford, is a 30-km (19-mile) circuit through some of the peninsula's most rugged scenery, with cairns and other prehistoric sites scattered over the moorland. Keen hikers will be able to walk it in a day.

Monasterboice ❾

Co Louth. 🚌 *to Drogheda.* ⬜ *daily.*

Founded in the 5th century by an obscure disciple of St Patrick called St Buite, this monastic settlement is one of the most famous religious sites in the country. The ruins of the medieval monastery are enclosed within a graveyard in a lovely secluded spot north of Drogheda. The site includes a roofless round tower and two churches, but Monasterboice's greatest treasures are its 10th-century High Crosses.

Muiredach's High Cross is the finest of its kind in Ireland, and its sculpted biblical scenes are still remarkably fresh. They depict the life of Christ on the west face, while the east face, described in detail opposite, features mainly Old Testament scenes. The cross is named after an inscription on the base – "A prayer for Muiredach by whom this cross was made" – which is perhaps a reference to the abbot of Monasterboice. The 6.5-m (21-ft) West Cross, also

Detail from a tomb in Monasterboice graveyard

known as the Tall Cross, is one of the largest in Ireland. The carving has not lasted as well as on Muiredach's Cross, but you can make out scenes from the Death of Christ. The North Cross, which is the least notable of the three, features a Crucifixion and a carved spiral pattern.

Round tower and West High Cross at Monasterboice

Ireland's High Crosses

HIGH CROSSES exist in Celtic parts of both Britain and Ireland. Yet in their profusion and craftsmanship, Irish High Crosses are exceptional. The distinctive ringed cross has become a symbol of Irish Christianity and is still imitated today. The beautiful High Crosses associated with medieval monasteries were carved between the 8th and 12th centuries. The early crosses bore only geometric motifs, but in the 9th to 10th centuries a new style emerged when sculpted scenes from the Bible were introduced. Referred to as "sermons in stone", these later versions may have been used to educate the masses. In essence, though, the High Cross was a status symbol for the monastery or a local patron.

Pillar stones inscribed with crosses, like this 6th-century example at Riasc (see p190), were precursors of the High Cross.

Capstone, showing St Anthony and St Paul meeting in the desert

The High Cross at Abenny (see p249) is typical of 8th-century "ornamental" crosses. These were carved with interlacing patterns and spirals similar to those used in Celtic metalwork and jewellery.

Tenon

MUIREDACH'S CROSS

Each face of this 10th-century cross at Monasterboice features scenes from the Bible, including the east face seen here. The 5.5-m (18-ft) cross consists of three blocks of sandstone fitted together by means of tenons and sockets.

The Last Judgment shows Christ in Glory surrounded by a crowd of resurrected souls. The devil stands on his right clutching a pitchfork, ready to chase the damned souls into Hell.

Angle moulding

The ring served a functional as well as a decorative purpose, providing support for the head and arms of the stone cross.

Moses smites the rock to obtain water for the Israelites.

Adoration of the Magi

David struggling with Goliath

The Fall of Man shows Adam and Eve beneath an apple-laden tree, with Cain slaying Abel alongside. Both scenes are frequently depicted on Irish High Crosses.

Socket

Base

Tenon

The Dysert O'Dea Cross (see p235) dates from the 1100s and represents the late phase of High Cross art. It features the figures of Christ and a bishop carved in high relief.

Drogheda ⑩

Co Louth. 🏃 *30,000.* 🚉 🚌 ℹ️
West St (041 37070).
🚌 *Sat.*

I N THE 14TH CENTURY, this historic Norman port near the mouth of the River Boyne was one of Ireland's most important towns. However, the place seems never to have recovered from the trauma of a vicious attack by Cromwell in 1649 *(see p43)*, in which 2,000 citizens were killed. Although it now looks rather dilapidated, the town has retained its original street plan and has a rich medieval heritage.

Little remains of Drogheda's medieval defences but **St Lawrence Gate**, a fine 13th-century barbican, has survived. Nearby, there are two churches called **St Peter's**. The one belonging to the Church of Ireland, built in 1753, is the more striking and has some splendid grave slabs. The Catholic church is worth visiting to see the embalmed head of Oliver Plunkett, an archbishop martyred in 1681.

South of the river you can climb Millmount, a Norman motte topped by a Martello tower. As well as providing a good view, this is the site of the **Millmount Museum**,

Drogheda viewed from Millmount across the River Boyne

which contains an interesting display of historical artifacts, as well as craft workshops.

🏛 Millmount Museum

Millmount Square. 📞 *041 33097.*
⭕ *daily (Sun pm only).* ⬤ *10 days at Christmas.* 📷 🎥 ♿

Newgrange and the Boyne Valley ⑪

Co Meath. 🚌 *to Drogheda.* 🚌 *to Slane or Drogheda.* ℹ️ *Brú na Bóinne Interpretive Centre (041 24488).*

K NOWN AS Brú na Bóinne, the "Palace of the Boyne", this river valley was the cradle of Irish civilization. The fertile soil supported a sophisticated society in Neolithic times. Much evidence survives, in the form of ring forts, passage graves and sacred enclosures.

The most important Neolithic monuments in the valley are three passage graves: supreme among these is **Newgrange** *(see pp330–1)*, but **Dowth** and **Knowth** are significant too. The Boyne Valley also encompasses the Hill of Slane and the Hill of Tara *(see p332)*, both of which are major sites in Celtic mythology. Indeed, this whole region is rich in associations with Ireland's

River Boyne near the site of the Battle of the Boyne

THE BATTLE OF THE BOYNE

In 1688, the Catholic King of England, James II, was deposed from his throne, to be replaced by his Protestant daughter, Mary, and her husband, William of Orange. Determined to win back the crown, James sought the support of Irish Catholics, and challenged William at Oldbridge by the River Boyne west of Drogheda. The Battle of the Boyne took place on 1 July 1690, with James's poorly trained force of 25,000 French and Irish Catholics facing William's hardened army of 36,000 French Huguenots, Dutch, English and Scots. The Protestants triumphed and James fled to France, after a battle that signalled the beginning of total Protestant power over Ireland. It ushered in the confiscation of Catholic lands and the suppression of Catholic interests, sealing the country's fate for the next 300 years.

William of Orange leading his troops at the Battle of the Boyne, 1 July 1690

prehistory. With monuments predating Egypt's pyramids, the Boyne Valley is marketed as the Irish "Valley of the Kings".

Newgrange and Knowth can only be seen on a tour run by **Brú na Bóinne Interpretive Centre** near Newgrange. The centre also has displays on the area's Stone Age heritage and a reconstruction of Newgrange.

⌂ Dowth

Off N51, 3 km (2 miles) E of Newgrange. ⬤ *to the public.*

The passage grave at Dowth was plundered by Victorian souvenir hunters and has not been fully excavated. You cannot approach the tomb, but it can be seen from the road.

⌂ Knowth

1.5 km (1 mile) NW of Newgrange. ⬤ *as Newgrange (see pp238–9).*

Knowth outdoes Newgrange in several respects, above all in the quantity of its treasures, which form the greatest concentration of megalithic art in Europe. Also, the site was occupied for a much longer period – from Neolithic times right up until about 1400.

Unusually, Knowth has two passage tombs, although they are not open to the public. Excavation work, which was begun in 1962, continues on the site. About a third of the site is open and you can see into several of the 17 satellite tombs. Some of the kerbstones, many of them finely carved, are also on display.

Slane Castle in grounds landscaped by Capability Brown

Mellifont Abbey ⑫

Cullen, Co Louth. 📞 *041 26459.* 🚌 *to Drogheda.* 🚌 *to Drogheda or Slane.* ⬤ *May–Oct: daily; Nov–Apr: by appt.* 🎫

ON THE BANKS of the River Mattock, 10 km (6 miles) west of Drogheda, lies the first Cistercian monastery to have been built in Ireland. Mellifont was founded in 1142 on the orders of St Malachy, the Archbishop of Armagh. He was greatly influenced by St Bernard who, based at his monastery at Clairvaux in France, was behind the success of the Cistercian Order in Europe. The archbishop introduced not only Cistercian rigour to Mellifont, but also the formal style of monastic architecture used on the continent. His new monastery became a model for other Cistercian centres built in Ireland, retaining its supremacy over them until 1539, when the abbey was closed and turned into a fortified house. William of Orange used Mellifont as his headquarters during the Battle of the Boyne in 1690. The abbey is now a ruin, but it is still possible to appreciate the scale and ground

Glazed medieval tiles at Mellifont Abbey

plan of the original complex. Not much survives of the abbey church, but to the south of it, enclosed by what remains of the Romanesque cloister, is the most interesting building at Mellifont: a unique 13th-century lavabo where monks came to wash their hands in a fountain before meals. Four of the building's original eight sides survive, each with a graceful Romanesque arch. On the eastern side of the cloister stands the 14th-century chapter house. It has an impressive vaulted ceiling and a floor laid with glazed medieval tiles taken from the abbey church.

Slane ⑬

Co Meath. 🏠 *700.* 🚌

SLANE IS AN ATTRACTIVE estate village, centred on a quartet of Georgian houses. The Boyne flows through it and skirts the grounds of **Slane Castle**, set in glorious gardens laid out in the 18th century by Capability Brown. Sadly, the Gothic Revival castle has been closed since a fire in 1991.

Just to the north rises the **Hill of Slane** where, in 433, St Patrick is said to have lit a Paschal (Easter) fire as a challenge to the pagan High King of Tara (*see p332*). The event is endowed with symbolic importance as the triumph of Christianity over paganism.

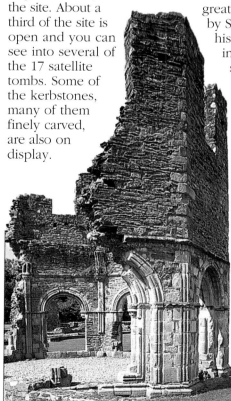

Ruined lavabo at Mellifont Abbey

Detail of 12th-century reliquary of St. Manchan, County Offaly ▷

Newgrange

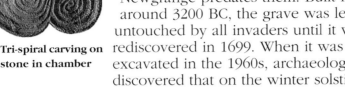

Tri-spiral carving on
stone in chamber

THE ORIGINS of Newgrange, one of the
most important passage graves in
Europe, are steeped in mystery. According
to Celtic lore, the legendary kings of
Tara (see p332) were buried here, but
Newgrange predates them. Built in
around 3200 BC, the grave was left
untouched by all invaders until it was
rediscovered in 1699. When it was
excavated in the 1960s, archaeologists
discovered that on the winter solstice
(21 December), rays of sun enter the tomb and light
up the burial chamber – making it the world's oldest
solar observatory. Newgrange is popular, especially in
summer, but visits are by tour only, so the site itself
does not get too crowded. Tours start at Brú na Bóinne
Interpretive Centre and include nearby Knowth (see
pp326–7).

Basin Stone
*The chiselled stones, found in
each recess, would have once
contained funerary offerings
and the bones of the dead.*

The chamber has three recesses
or side chambers: the north
recess is the one struck by sunlight on the winter solstice.

Chamber Ceiling
*The burial chamber's intricate
corbelled ceiling, which reaches
a height of 6 m (20 ft) above
the floor, has survived intact.
The overlapping slabs form a
conical hollow, topped by a
single capstone.*

CONSTRUCTION OF NEWGRANGE

The tomb at Newgrange was designed by
people with clearly exceptional artistic
and engineering skills, who had use of
neither the wheel nor metal tools. About
200,000 tonnes of loose stones were transported to build the mound, or cairn,
which protects the passage grave. Larger
slabs were used to make the circle around
the cairn (12 out of a probable 35 stones
have survived), the kerb and the tomb
itself. Many of the kerbstones and the
slabs lining the passage, the chamber
and its recesses are decorated with
zigzags, spirals and other geometric
motifs. The grave's corbelled ceiling
consists of smaller, unadorned slabs
and has proved completely waterproof for the last 5,000 years.

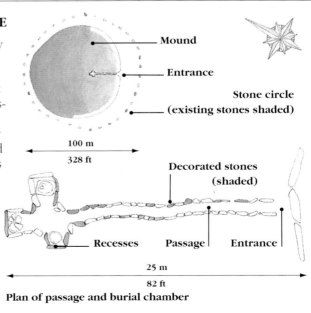

Mound

Entrance

Stone circle
(existing stones shaded)

100 m
328 ft

Decorated stones
(shaded)

Recesses   Passage   Entrance

25 m
82 ft
Plan of passage and burial chamber

VISITORS' CHECKLIST

8 km (5 miles) E of Slane, Co
Meath. 🚌 to Drogheda. 🚌 to
Drogheda or Slane. **Brú na
Bóinne Interpretive Centre** 📞
041 24488. ◯ May–Sep:
9am–6:30pm (Jun–mid-Sep: 7pm)
daily; Oct–Apr: 9:30am–5:30pm
(Nov–Feb: 5pm) daily; last tour: 90
mins before close. ● 24–26 Dec.
📷 🚫 inside tomb. ♿ interpretive centre only. 🎫 obligatory. 🍴

Restoration of Newgrange

Located on a low ridge north of the Boyne, Newgrange took more than 70 years to build. Between 1962 and 1975 the passage grave and mound were restored as closely as possible to their original state.

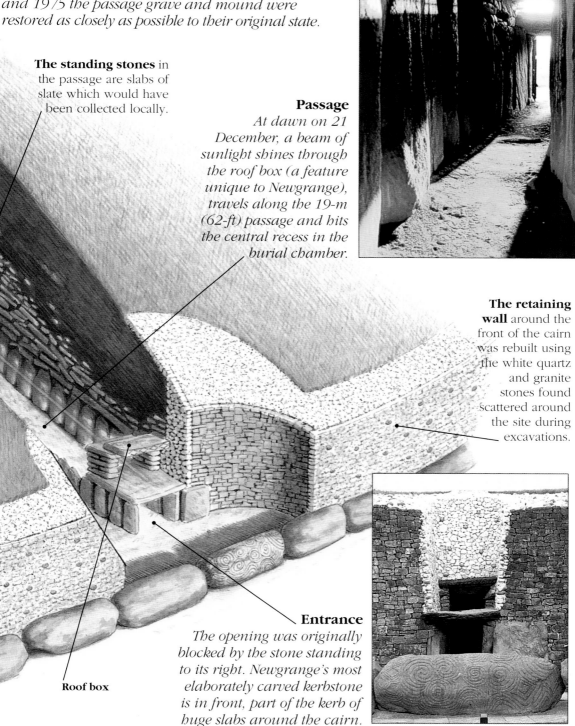

The standing stones in the passage are slabs of slate which would have been collected locally.

Passage
At dawn on 21 December, a beam of sunlight shines through the roof box (a feature unique to Newgrange), travels along the 19-m (62-ft) passage and hits the central recess in the burial chamber.

The retaining wall around the front of the cairn was rebuilt using the white quartz and granite stones found scattered around the site during excavations.

Roof box

Entrance
The opening was originally blocked by the stone standing to its right. Newgrange's most elaborately carved kerbstone is in front, part of the kerb of huge slabs around the cairn.

Trim Castle set in water meadows beside the River Boyne

Hill of Tara ⑭

Nr Killmessan Village, Co Meath. 📞 046 25903 (May– Oct). 🚌 to Navan. ○ daily. 💷 for Interpretative Centre. 📷

A SITE of mythical importance, Tara was the political and spiritual centre of Celtic Ireland and the seat of the High Kings until the 11th century. The spread of Christianity, which eroded the importance of Tara, is marked by a statue of St Patrick. The symbolism of the site was not lost on Daniel O'Connell (see p46), who chose Tara for a rally in 1843, attended by over one million people.

Tours from the Interpretative Centre point out a Stone Age passage grave and Iron Age hill forts, though to the untutored eye, these earthworks look like mere hollows and grassy mounds. Clearest is the Royal Enclosure, an oval fort, in the centre of which is Cormac's House containing the "stone of destiny" (*Lialh Fail*), an ancient fertility symbol and inauguration stone of the High Kings. However, all this is secondary to the poignant atmosphere and views over the Boyne Valley.

Trim ⑮

Co Meath. 👥 4,000. 🚌 ℹ️ Mill St (046 37111). 🛒 Fri.

T RIM IS ONE of the most pleasing Midlands market towns. A Norman stronghold on the River Boyne, it marked a boundary of the Pale (see p154). Trim runs efficient heritage and genealogy centres

while the **Duchas Trim Folk Theatre** provides rousing summer entertainment. (This popular company is at present in search of new premises.) Equally engrossing is the Nun Run, a bizarre summer horse race with nuns as jockeys, which takes place near **Trim Castle**. The castle was founded in 1173 by Hugh de Lacy, a Norman knight, and is one of the largest medieval castles in Ireland. It makes a spectacular backdrop so is often used as a film set, most recently seen in Mel Gibson's *Braveheart* (1995). Over the river is **Talbot Castle**, an Augustinian abbey converted to a manor house in the 15th century. Just north of the abbey, **St Patrick's Cathedral** incorporates part of a medieval church with a 15th-century tower and sections of the original chancel.

Butterstream Gardens, on the edge of town, are the best in the county. A luxuriant herbaceous bed is the centrepiece, but equally pleasing are the exotic woodland, rose and white gardens. The design is enhanced by pergolas, pools and bridges.

🏰 **Trim Castle**
📞 046 37111. ○ daily.
🌿 **Butterstream Gardens**
Kildalkey Rd. 📞 046 36017.
○ Apr–Sep: daily. 📷

Mullingar ⑯

Co Westmeath. 👥 12,500. 🚉 🚌 ℹ️ Market House (044 48650). 🛒 Sat.

T HE COUNTY TOWN of Westmeath is a prosperous but unremarkable market town encircled by the Royal Canal

Aerial view of Iron Age forts on the Hill of Tara

(see p121), which with its 46 locks links Dublin with the River Shannon. The cost of building the canal bankrupted its investors and it was never profitable. Although Mullingar's main appeal is as a base to explore the surrounding area, pubs such as Con's and the cheery Canton Casey's can make a pleasant interlude.

ENVIRONS: Recent restoration of the Dublin to Mullingar stretch of the Royal Canal has created attractive towpaths for walkers, and angling facilities.

Just off the Kilbeggan road from Mullingar stands **Belvedere House**, a romantic Palladian villa overlooking Lough Ennel. The house, built in 1740 by Richard Castle, and decorated with Rococo plasterwork, is being restored, but the wonderful gardens are open.

Shortly after the house was built, the first Earl of Belvedere accused his young wife of having an affair with his brother, and imprisoned her for 31 years in a neighbouring house. In 1755, the Earl built a Gothic folly – the Jealous Wall – to block the view of his second brother's more opulent mansion across the lake. The Jealous Wall remains, as does an octagonal gazebo and other follies.

Charming terraces, framed by urns and yews, descend to the lake; on the other side of the house is a picturesque walled garden, enclosed by an arboretum and rolling parkland.

🏛 Belvedere House
6.5 km (4 miles) S of Mullingar.
📞 *044 42820.* **House and Gardens**
○ *Apr–Oct: daily.* 🖼 ♿

The Jealous Wall at Belvedere House, near Mullingar

Athlone Castle below the towers of the church of St Peter and St Paul

Kilbeggan ⑰

Co Westmeath. 👥 *600.* 🚌

SITUATED BETWEEN Mullingar and Tullamore, this pleasant village has a small harbour on the Grand Canal. However, the main point of interest is **Locke's Distillery**. Founded in 1757, it claims to be the oldest licensed pot still distillery in the world. Unable to compete with Scotch whisky manufacturers, the company went bankrupt in 1954, but the aroma hung in the warehouses for years and was known as "the angel's share". The distillery was reopened as a museum in 1987. The building is authentic, a solid structure complete with water wheel and inside steam engine. A tour traces the process of Irish whiskey-making, from the mash tuns to the vast fermentation vats and creation of wash (rough beer) to the distillation and maturation stages. At the tasting stage, workers would sample the whiskey in the can pit room. Visitors can still taste whiskeys in the bar but, unlike the original workers, cannot bathe in the whiskey vats.

Miniature whiskey bottles at Locke's Distillery in Kilbeggan

🏛 Locke's Distillery
Main Street. 📞 *0506 32134.*
○ *daily.* 🖼

Athlone ⑱

Co Westmeath. 👥 *15,000.* 🚉 🚌
ℹ *Market Square (0902 94630).*
🛒 *Fri.*

THE TOWN owes its historical importance to its position by a natural ford on the River Shannon. **Athlone Castle** is a much altered 13th-century fortress, which was badly damaged in the Jacobite Wars *(see pp42–3)*. It lies in the shadow of the 19th-century church of St Peter and St Paul. The neighbouring streets offer several good pubs. Across the river from the castle, boats depart for Clonmacnoise *(see pp336–7)* or Lough Ree.

⛪ Athlone Castle
Visitors' Centre 📞 *0902 92912.*
○ *May–Oct: daily; Nov–Apr: by appt.* 🖼 ♿ *limited.*

ENVIRONS: The **Lough Ree Trail** starts 8 km (5 miles) northeast of Athlone, at Glasson. The route passes picturesque views and unspoilt countryside. The trail is a popular cycling tour.

Birr Castle, County Offaly, seat of the Earls of Rosse ▷

Clonmacnoise ⑲

THIS MEDIEVAL MONASTERY, in a remote spot by the River Shannon, was founded by St Ciaran in 545–548. Clonmacnoise lay at a crossroads of medieval routes, linking all parts of Ireland. Known for its scholarship and piety, it thrived from the 7th to the 12th century. Many kings of Tara and of Connaught were buried here. Plundered by the Vikings and Anglo-Normans, it fell to the English in 1552. Today, a group of stone churches (temples), a cathedral, two round towers and three High Crosses remain.

Detail on a grave slab

Last Circuit of Pilgrims at Clonmacnoise
This painting (1838), by George Petrie, shows pilgrims walking the traditional route three times around the site. Pilgrims still do this every year on 9 September, St Ciaran's Day.

The Pope's Shelter was where John Paul II conducted Mass during his visit in 1979.

Cross of the Scriptures
This copy of the original 9th-century cross (now in the museum) is decorated with biblical scenes, but the identity of most of the figures is uncertain.

VISITING CLONMACNOISE

The Visitors' Centre is housed in three buildings modelled on beehive huts *(see p25)*. The museum section contains early grave slabs and the three remaining High Crosses, replicas of which now stand in their original locations. The Nuns' Church, northeast of the main site, has a Romanesque doorway and chancel arch.

KEY

1 South Cross	**7** Cathedral
2 Temple Dowling	**8** North Cross
3 Temple Hurpan	**9** Cross of the Scriptures
4 Temple Melaghlin	**10** Round Tower
5 Temple Ciaran	**11** Temple Connor
6 Temple Kelly	**12** Temple Finghin

0 metres   50

0 yards   50

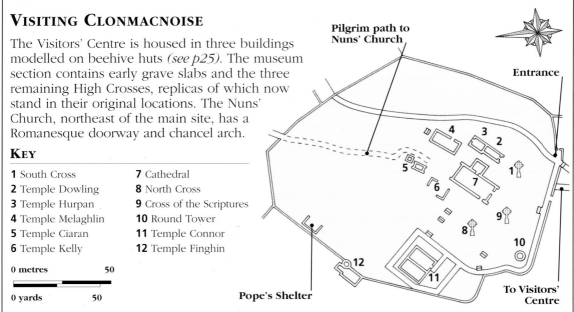

Pilgrim path to Nuns' Church

Entrance

Pope's Shelter

To Visitors' Centre

VISITORS' CHECKLIST

7 km (4 miles) N of
Shannonbridge, Co Offaly. [phone]
0905 74195. [bus] [bus] to Athlone,
then minibus (0905 74 165). [boat]
from Athlone. ◯ Jun–Aug:
9am–7pm daily; Sep–May:
10am–6pm (Nov–Apr: 5:30pm).
● 25 Dec. [icons]

Whispering Door

Above the cathedral's 15th-century north doorway are carvings of saints Francis, Patrick and Dominic. The acoustics of the doorway are such that even a whisper is carried inside the building.

The Shannonbridge Bog Railway passing an area of cut bog

Shannonbridge Bog Railway ⑳

5 km (3 miles) E of Shannonbridge,
Co Offaly. [phone] 0905 74114. [bus] to
Athlone. ◯ Apr–Oct: daily;
Nov–Mar: groups by appt. [icons]

STARTING near Shannonbridge, this guided tour by train is run by the Irish Peat Board (Bord na Móna). The 45-minute tour covers 9 km (6 miles) of bogland and gives a fascinating insight into the history and development of the Blackwater raised bogs – an area of great ecological importance, parts of which are protected.

Tour guides describe the transformation from lake to marshy fen and thence to bog *(see p338)*, and explain that in several hundred years the bog will become fields and woodland. They also point out the area's distinctive flora and fauna, from dragonflies to bog cotton, bog asphodel and sphagnum moss. The small lakes and pools that punctuate the bog provide excellent habitats for wetland birds.

Bog oaks – old trees which have been preserved in the bog – are visible in the places where the peat has been harvested. For centuries, peat has been the main source of fuel in rural Ireland, and visitors can watch peat being cut by hand using the traditional tool known as a "slane". Modern peat-harvesting machines in use nearby supply the power station at Shannonbridge. There is a craft shop and also a machinery museum close to where the train ride begins.

The Round Tower *(see p24)* is over 19 m (62 ft) high with its doorway above ground level.

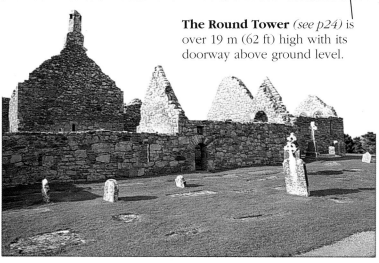

Temples Dowling, Hurpan and Melaghlin

Built as a family crypt, Temple Hurpan was a 17th-century addition to the early Romanesque Temple Dowling. The 13th-century Temple Melaghlin has two fine round-headed windows.

The Raised Bogs of the Midlands

PEATLAND OR BOG, which covers about 15 per cent of the Irish landscape, exists in two principal forms. Most extensive is the thin blanket bog found chiefly in the west, while the dome-shaped raised bogs are more characteristic of the Midlands – notably in an area known as the Bog of Allen.

Four-spotted chaser dragonfly

Although Irish boglands are some of the largest in Europe, the use of peat for domestic fuel and fertilizer has greatly reduced their extent. This has threatened not only the shape of the Irish landscape but also the survival of a unique habitat and the unusual plants and insects it supports.

Unspoilt expanse of the Bog of Allen

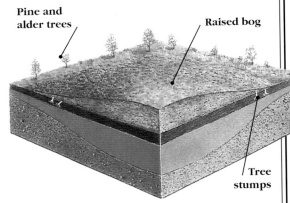

Peat cutters still gather turf (as peat is known locally) by hand in parts of Ireland. It is then set in stacks to dry. Peat makes a good fuel, because it is rich in partially decayed vegetation, laid down over thousands of years.

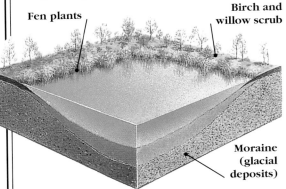

Fen plants

Birch and willow scrub

Moraine (glacial deposits)

8000 BC: *Shallow meltwater lakes that formed after the Ice Age gradually filled with mud. Reeds, sedges and other fen plants began to dominate in the marshy conditions which resulted.*

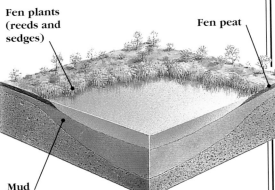

Fen plants (reeds and sedges)

Fen peat

Mud

6000 BC: *As the fen vegetation died, it sank to the lake bed but did not decompose fully in the waterlogged conditions, forming a layer of peat. This slowly built up and also spread outwards.*

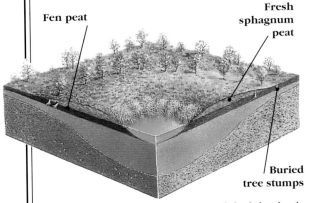

Fen peat

Fresh sphagnum peat

Buried tree stumps

3000 BC: *As the peat built up and the lake slowly disappeared, plant life in the developing bog had to rely almost exclusively on rainwater, which is acid. Fen plants could not survive in these acidic conditions and gave way to bog mosses, mainly species of sphagnum. As these mosses died, they formed a layer of sphagnum peat on the surface of the bog which, over the centuries, attained a distinctive domed shape.*

Pine and alder trees

Raised bog

Tree stumps

Present day: *Few raised bogs are actively growing today. Those that remain contain a fascinating historical record of the landscape. The survival of ancient tree stumps shows how well plants are preserved in peat.*

Sphagnum moss

Birr ㉑

Co Offaly. 4,100.
May–Sep: Rosse Row (0509 20110).

BIRR, A GENTRIFIED estate town, grew up in the shadow of the castle where the Earls of Rosse have resided for almost four centuries. It is famous for its authentic Georgian layout, with houses displaying original fanlights, door panelling and iron railings. Two particularly elegant streets are Oxmantown Mall, designed by the 2nd Earl of Rosse, and John's Mall. Emmet Square may have sold its Georgian soul to commerce, but Dooly's Hotel is still a fine example of an old coaching inn. Foster's bar, in nearby Connaught Street, is one of many traditional shopfronts to have been restored in Birr.

🏛 Birr Castle
Rosse Row. 0509 22154.
Gardens daily. 25 Dec.

Birr Castle was founded in 1620 by the Parsons, later Earls of Rosse, and is still the family seat. They have been most noted for their contribution to astronomy – a telescope, built by the 3rd Earl in 1845, was the largest in the world at the time. The 17-m (56-ft) wooden tube, supported by two walls, can be seen in the grounds and is currently being restored to its original condition.

The castle is closed to the general public, but the true glory of Birr lies in its grounds. First landscaped in the 18th century, these are famous for their 9-m (30-ft) box hedges and for the exotic trees and shrubs that were gathered during foreign expeditions sponsored by the

An alcove in the front hall of Emo Court with a *trompe l'oeil* ceiling

6th Earl. The magnolias and maples are particularly striking. The gardens overlook the meeting of two rivers, and water greatly influenced the planning of the grounds. There is a charming riverside garden and a small suspension bridge.

Slieve Bloom Mountains ㉒

Co Offaly and Co Laois. to Mountmellick. May–Sep: Rosse Row, Birr (0509 20110).

THIS LOW RANGE of mountains rises unexpectedly from the bogs and plains of Offaly and Laois, providing a welcome change in the predominantly flat Midlands. You can walk along the **Slieve Bloom Way**, a 30-km (19-mile) circular trail through an unspoilt landscape of open vistas, deep wooded glens and mountain streams. There are other marked paths too. Good starting points are **Cadamstown**, with an attractive old mill, and the pretty village of **Kinnitty** – both in the northern foothills.

Emo Court ㉓

13 km (8 miles) NE of Portlaoise, Co Laois. 0502 26573. to Monasterevin or Portlaoise. **House** mid-Jun–mid-Sep: Tue–Sun. **Gardens** daily. limited.

EMO COURT, commissioned by the Earl of Portarlington in 1790, represents the only foray into domestic architecture by James Gandon, designer of the Custom House in Dublin (*see p104*). The monumental Neo-Classical mansion has a splendid façade featuring an Ionic portico. Inside are a magnificent gilded rotunda and fine stuccowork ceilings.

Emo Court became the property of the Office of Public Works in 1994 but the previous owner, who restored the house, is still resident and is now working on the grounds. These are adorned with fine statuary and include a lakeside walk.

Rock of Dunamase ㉔

5 km (3 miles) E of Portlaoise, Co Laois. to Portlaoise.

THE ROCK OF DUNAMASE, which looms dramatically above the plains east of Portlaoise, has long been a military site. Originally crowned by an Iron Age ring fort, the 13th-century castle which succeeded it is now more prominent – though it was virtually destroyed by Cromwellian forces in 1650. You can reach the battered keep by climbing up banks and ditches through two gateways and a fortified courtyard.

Rock of Dunamase viewed from Stradbally to the east

The Mountains of Mourne, County Down ▷

NORTHERN
IRELAND

NORTHERN IRELAND

LONDONDERRY · ANTRIM · TYRONE · FERMANAGH
ARMAGH · DOWN

NORTHERN IRELAND has sights from every era of Ireland's history as well as magnificently varied coastal and lakeland scenery. In the past, it has received fewer visitors than the Republic as a result of the "Troubles". Following recent moves towards peace, there seems every chance that it will at last attract the attention it deserves.

The province of Northern Ireland was created after partition of the island in 1921. Its six counties were originally part of Ulster, one of Ireland's four traditional kingdoms. It was most probably here that Christianity first ousted Celtic pagan beliefs, and in 432 St Patrick landed at Saul in County Down, later founding a church at Armagh, still the spiritual capital of Ireland.

The dominant political force in the early Christian period was the Uí Néill clan, and their descendants, the O'Neills, put up fierce resistance to the English in the late 16th century. Hugh O'Neill, Earl of Tyrone, had some successes against Elizabeth I, but in 1607 he was forced to flee to Europe with other Irish lords from Ulster, in what became known as the 'Flight of the Earls'. Their estates became home to English and Scottish Protestants, whose arrival meant that the Irish Catholics were marginalized, sowing the seeds of 400 years of conflict.

In the relative tranquillity of the 18th century, the Anglo-Irish nobility built stately homes, such as Mount Stewart House on the Ards Peninsula and Castle Coole near Enniskillen. Ulster also enjoyed much prosperity in the 19th century through its shipbuilding, linen and ropemaking industries.

Because of its place on the modern-day political frontline, Belfast has perhaps suffered more than most parts of the province in terms of low tourist numbers. This is a shame, for visitors are rarely affected by any violence. Whatever the political events that assail its population, Northern Ireland's scenery is wonderful. Though Belfast is densely populated and industrialized, the region away from the capital is primarily agricultural and has areas of outstanding natural beauty, notably the rugged Antrim

Belfast's City Hall (1906), symbol of the city's civic pride

◁ **Carrick-a-rede Rope Bridge, an unusual tourist attraction on the Causeway Coast**

The astonishing basalt column steps of the Giant's Causeway, County Antrim

coastline around the Giant's Causeway, the Mountains of Mourne in County Down and the Erne lakeland in the west of the region. Belfast's environs hold much of interest. At the entrance to Belfast Lough is the formidable Carrickfergus Castle, built in the mid-12th century by the invading Anglo-Normans. Around the narrows of Strangford Lough is one of Ireland's largest seal colonies, and there are several nature reserves here that attract native and migrating birds. Downpatrick and the surrounding area are noted for their associations with St Patrick, who is said to lie at rest in the churchyard of Down Cathedral. Beyond here is the Lecale Peninsula, drenched in history by its numerous castles, from the handsome Castle Ward estate to ruined tower houses.

One of the country's most scenic areas surrounds the Mountains of Mourne, stretching from Newcastle, with its broad sandy beach, south to Carlingford Lough. There is a fine coastal road that runs between the foothills and the sea, making the region very good hiking country.

The smooth-peaked beauty of the Mountains of Mourne

Northern Ireland's most exciting scenery can be found along the north coast. The Antrim Coast Road is a bracing drive between high mountain walls and the sea. Inland, the Antrim Mountains are split by nine deep valleys, known as the Glens of Antrim. This was once the most remote part of the province, the last stronghold of the old Irish ways and the setting for many Ulster legends. There are several attractive villages set along this coast road, including Carnlough with its sandy beach and Cushendall, the 'capital' of the glens.

The section of the coastline that runs between Ballycastle and Portrush is known as the Causeway. Its vast, spectacular cliffs, rocky inlets, dunes and sullen, windswept headlands have been designated an Area of Outstanding Natural Beauty. The geological highlight of this stunning area is the famous Giant's Causeway, Northern Ireland's most visited attraction. This strange, thousand-fold regiment of basalt columns was formed by the cooling of lava from a volcanic explosion millions of years ago. This is a singular, unmissable phenomenon.

To the east of the Giant's Causeway are found the sandy shores of White Park Bay, the pretty Ballintoy harbour, the massive ruined wall of Dunseverick Castle, built during the 5th century as a launching point for raids on Scotland. A little further east along this coast are the austere ruins of the 16th-century

The popular seaside resort of Portrush, County Londonderry

Kinbane castle, windswept Rathlin Island and the challenging Carrick-a-Rede Rope Bridge. Perched on a rugged clifftop is romantic Dunluce Castle, a spectacular sight when silhouetted against the setting sun. The twin resorts of Portrush, with its championship golf course, and Portstewart, with its long sandy beach, are popular holiday spots.

Straddling the banks of the River Foyle, Londonderry is one of Northern Ireland's most historic cities (it can trace its foundation back to 546, when Columba established a monastery here.) The city centre is surrounded by some of the finest city walls in Europe, built in the early 17th century, and a pleasant stroll around the top of the wide ramparts affords fine views of Londonderry's historic buildings.

Central Ulster is somewhat tamer than its dramatic coastlands, with sleepy villages and an agricultural landscape. The Sperrin Mountains are a scenic area and have the added attraction of being a place where optimists pan for gold. Lough Neagh, near Cookstown, is the largest lake in the British Isles. The ancients explained its magnitude by claiming that a giant created the lake by picking up some turf and tossing it into the sea. The Ardboe Cross, one of the finest in Northern Ireland, stands along its shores, and a little way to the east stands the Wellbrook Beetling Mill, a nod towards the region's once-flourishing linen industry. Just outside Omagh is the inspiring and moving Ulster-American Folk Park, which tells the story of the progress of Ulster's emigrants to the US.

Cascading waterfall, Glenariff

County Fermanagh is one of Ireland's favourite recreation spots, especially the lakeland region around Lower Lough Erne near Enniskillen. Among its many attractions are pagan and early Christian sites, ruined castles, stately homes, the Marble Arch caves and the famous Belleek pottery.

County Down's Castle Ward, the 18th-century Palladian Mansion of Lord and Lady Bangor

Irish Whiskey

The Father Mathew statue is a landmark in Cork City. His anti-alcohol campaign dented domestic consumption in the 19th century.

ITINERANT IRISH MONKS are reputed to have learned the art of distilling from Arab perfumiers in the Dark Ages, but when they returned home they preferred to make *uisce beatha* – whiskey. Countless stills bubbled away over the centuries, and, by the start of the 20th century, whiskey was big business, supporting 25 large distilleries. During the last one hundred years, the industry has contracted to the point where there are only five distilleries, one of which, Cooley, has now started to stimulate the creation of new brands.

Paddy's whiskey

ALLMAN'S IRISH WHISKEY

This historic, colourfully-labelled whiskey was made at the great Bandon Distillery. Irish whiskey differs from Scotch in that it is made from an equal mixture of malted and unmalted barley, triple-distilled to create the Pure Pot Still liquor which is Irish whiskey in its classic form. It is the Pot Still element that gives Irish its nutty, sweet, smooth character.

Delivering barley, whiskey's key ingredient. The fermented mixture of malted and unmalted barley is distilled, giving a colourless liquid which acquires its characteristic tawny complexion only after long maturation in oak casks.

Government officers poured away millions of gallons of illegal alcohol during Prohibition.

Prohibition, introduced in the US by the 18th Amendment in 1920, lasted for 13 years and plunged the Irish whiskey industry deep into a recession, from which it never fully recovered. Political instability at home and a failure to modernize the production process also played their part in the industry's decline.

MAKING POTEEN

Ireland's staple illicit spirit is a fiery whiskey which has barley as its core ingredient, although elements such as potatoes and apples also add to the mix. The origin of its production goes back to Christmas Day 1661, when excise duty was applied to spirits. As taxes rose, many producers took evasive action by heading for the hills. Poteen peaked during the early 19th century – in 1834 alone, the Irish Excise seized over 8,000 illegal stills – but even today, this heady brew, which is dangerous unless it is properly distilled, readily finds producers and consumers.

A practitioner of the art of poteen making

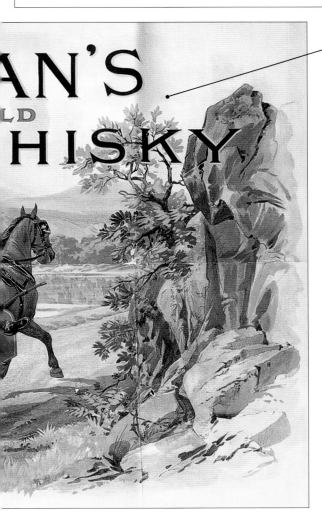

The production and consumption of whiskey is symbolic of many elements of Irish character and culture, such as the outdoor life and *joie de vivre*

Copper pot stills are vital both in the production of classic Irish whiskey and in its development as a classic brand: the element neutralizes impurities in the alcohol and bestows a certain unique smoothness on the product.

LEADING BRANDS

Inishowen and Tyrconnell hailed from Watt's distillery in Derry, once the largest in Ireland. Kilbeggan in County Westmeath was the country's leading pure pot whiskey producer for over two centuries, until its distillery ceased operation in 1958.

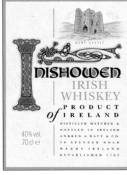

Inishowen

Kilbeggan

Tyrconnell

Exploring Northern Ireland

T HE STARTING POINT for most visitors to the province is
Belfast. The capital has grand Victorian buildings, good
pubs and the excellent Ulster Museum. However, Northern
Ireland's greatest attractions lie along its coast. These range
from the extraordinary volcanic landscape of the Giant's
Causeway to Carrickfergus, Ireland's best preserved Norman
castle. There are also Victorian resorts, like Portstewart, tiny
fishing villages and unspoilt sandy beaches, such as
Benone Strand. Ramblers are drawn to the Mountains
of Mourne, while anglers and boating enthusiasts can
enjoy the lakeland of Lower Lough Erne.

**Harbour and promenade at the seaside
resort of Portstewart**

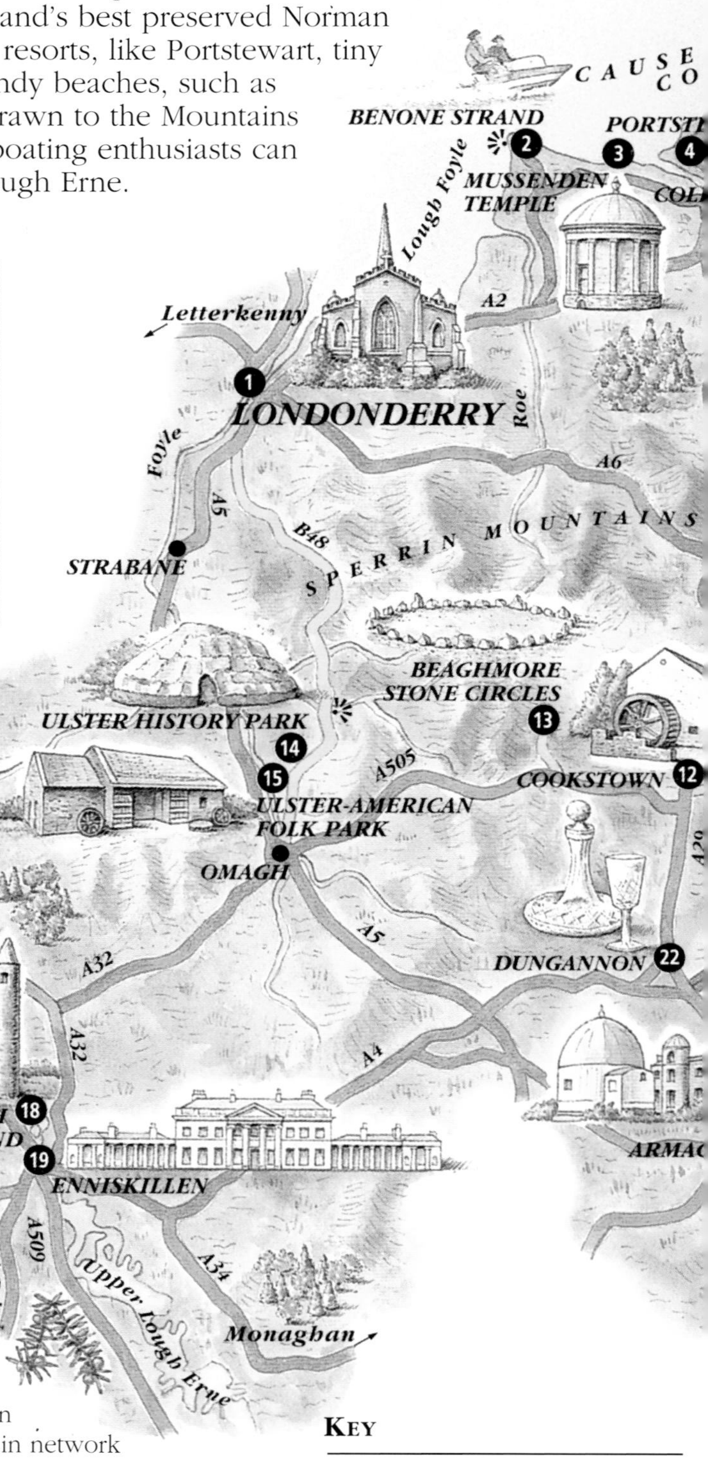

0 kilometres   10

0 miles   5

GETTING AROUND

Belfast is the transport hub of Northern
Ireland. From here the very limited train network
runs northwest to Londonderry and south to
Dublin. In most parts of the province you have to
rely on buses, but fortunately, even in rural areas,
these are fairly frequent and punctual. However, a
car is essential if you want to go off the beaten
track in search of ancient monuments or tour the
coast at leisure. Depending on the security situation,
you may still encounter temporary checkpoints set
up by the army and police.

KEY

	Motorway
	Major road
	Minor road
	Scenic route
	River
	Viewpoint

SIGHTS AT A GLANCE

Ards Peninsula **29**
Armagh **23**
Ballycastle **9**
Beaghmore Stone Circles **13**
Belfast pp372–73 **27**
Belleek Pottery **16**
Benone Strand **2**
Carrickfergus **26**
Castlewellan Forest Park **34**
Causeway Coast **5**
Cookstown **12**
Cushendall **10**
Devenish Island **18**
Downpatrick **32**
Dungannon **22**
Enniskillen **19**

Florence Court **21**
Giant's Causeway pp356–7 **6**
Glenariff Forest Park **11**
Hillsborough **31**
Larne **25**
Lecale Peninsula **33**
Londonderry pp350–51 **1**
Lough Neagh **24**
Marble Arch Caves **20**
Mountains of Mourne **35**
Mount Stewart House pp378–9 **30**
Mussenden Temple **3**
Old Bushmills Distillery **7**
Portstewart **4**
Rathlin Island **8**
Ulster-American Folk Park **15**
Ulster Folk and Transport
    Museum **28**
Ulster History Park **14**

Tours
Lower Lough Erne **17**
Mourne Coast **36**

**Gold Salamander from
Armada wreck at the
Ulster Museum, Belfast**

Dry-stone walls on slopes of the Mountains of Mourne

Londonderry ❶

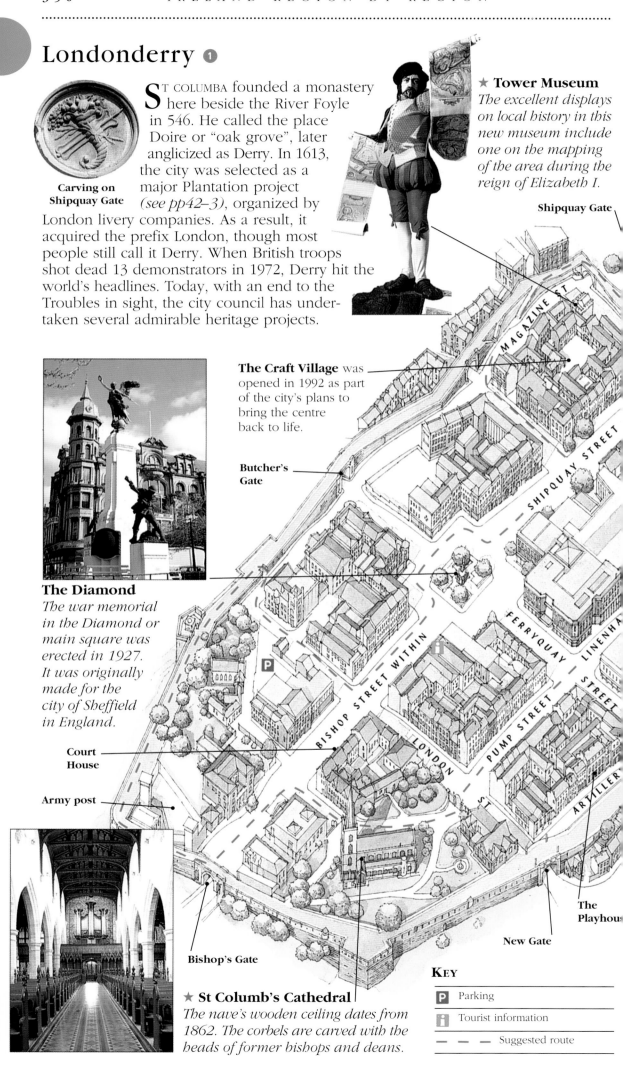

Carving on Shipquay Gate

S T COLUMBA founded a monastery here beside the River Foyle in 546. He called the place Doire or "oak grove", later anglicized as Derry. In 1613, the city was selected as a major Plantation project *(see pp42–3)*, organized by London livery companies. As a result, it acquired the prefix London, though most people still call it Derry. When British troops shot dead 13 demonstrators in 1972, Derry hit the world's headlines. Today, with an end to the Troubles in sight, the city council has undertaken several admirable heritage projects.

★ **Tower Museum**
The excellent displays on local history in this new museum include one on the mapping of the area during the reign of Elizabeth I.

Shipquay Gate

The Craft Village was opened in 1992 as part of the city's plans to bring the centre back to life.

Butcher's Gate

The Diamond
The war memorial in the Diamond or main square was erected in 1927. It was originally made for the city of Sheffield in England.

Court House

Army post

Bishop's Gate

★ **St Columb's Cathedral**
The nave's wooden ceiling dates from 1862. The corbels are carved with the heads of former bishops and deans.

The Playhouse

New Gate

KEY

P	Parking
i	Tourist information
– – – –	Suggested route

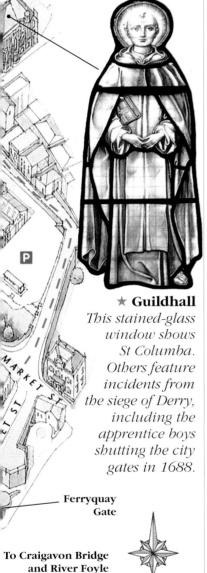

★ **Guildhall**
This stained-glass window shows St Columba. Others feature incidents from the siege of Derry, including the apprentice boys shutting the city gates in 1688.

Ferryquay Gate

To Craigavon Bridge and River Foyle

0 metres 100

0 yards 100

STAR SIGHTS

★ **Tower Museum**

★ **Guildhall**

★ **St Columb's Cathedral**

🛈 St Columb's Cathedral

St Columb's Court. 028 7126 7313. Mon–Sat.
Built between 1628 and 1633, in "Planters' Gothic" style, St Columb's was the first cathedral to be founded in the British Isles after the Reformation. The interior was extensively rebuilt in the 19th century. A small museum in the Chapter House contains relics from the siege of 1689 *(see pp42–3)*, including the 17th-century locks and keys of the city. In the vestibule is a hollow mortar cannonball that was fired into the city by James II's army. It carried terms for capitulation, but the reply of the Protestants within the walls was a defiant "No surrender", a phrase used by Loyalists to this day.

🏛 Tower Museum

Union Hall Place. 028 7137 2411. Jul & Aug: daily; Sep–Jun: Tue–Sat. 17 Mar, Good Fri, 25 & 26 Dec. by arrangement.
Housed in O'Doherty Tower (a replica of the original 16th-century building on this site), the museum traces the history of the city from its foundation to the recent Troubles using multimedia displays. Upstairs, an exhibition about the 1688 Spanish Armada includes artifacts from ships wrecked in nearby Kinnagoe Bay.

⛪ Walls of Derry

Access from Magazine Street.
Among the best preserved city fortifications in Europe, the city walls rise to a height of 8 m (26 ft) and in places are 9 m (30 ft) wide. Completed in 1618 to defend the new

Lock of city gate in St Columb's Cathedral

merchant city from Gaelic chieftains in Donegal, the walls have never been breached, not even during the siege of 1689, when 7,000 out of a population of 20,000 perished from disease or starvation. Extensive restoration work means that it should soon be possible to walk right around the walls for the first time in decades. Just outside the old fortifications, beyond Butcher's Gate, is the Bogside, a Catholic area with a famous mural that announces "You are now entering free Derry".

🏛 Guildhall

Guildhall Square. 028 7137 7335. Mon–Fri.
Standing between the walled city and the River Foyle, this Neo-Gothic building was constructed in 1890, but a fire in 1908 and a bomb in 1972 both necessitated substantial repairs. Stained-glass windows – copies of the originals – recount the history of Derry. To the rear of the Guildhall is Derry Quay, from where Irish emigrants sailed to America in the 18th and 19th centuries.

ENVIRONS: Just off the B194, on the way to Muff, stands a memorial to American aviator Amelia Earhart, the first woman to complete a transatlantic solo flight. She had intended to fly to Paris, but in May 1932 landed in a field outside Derry. A sculpture marks the spot and the nearby **Earhart Centre** contains a small exhibition.

🏛 Earhart Centre

Ballyarnet. 028 7135 4040. Mon–Fri.

The old walled city viewed across the River Foyle

Dunluce Castle, County Antrim ▷

Terraced houses behind the promenade at Portstewart

Benone Strand ❷

Co Londonderry. **ℹ** *Benone Tourist Complex, 53 Benone Ave, Seacoast Rd, Magilligan (028 7775 0555).*

THE WIDE, golden sands of Ireland's longest beach, also known as Magilligan Strand, sweep along the Londonderry coastline for more than 10 km (6 miles). The magnificent beach has been granted EU Blue Flag status for its cleanliness. Marking the western extremity of the beach is **Magilligan Point** where a Martello tower, built during the Napoleonic wars, stands guard over the bottleneck entrance to Lough Foyle. To get to the point, which is renowned for its rare shellfish and sea birds, you have to drive over ramps below the watchtowers and listening devices of a huge army base. The experience is rather unsettling, but well worth the trouble.

Mussenden Temple ❸

Co Londonderry. **📞** *028 7084 8728.* **◯** *Jul–Aug: daily (pm only); Apr–Jun & Sep: Sat, Sun & public hols.* **♿** *limited.*

THE ODDEST SIGHT along the Londonderry coast is this small, domed rotunda perched precariously on a windswept headland outside the family resort of Castlerock. The temple was built in 1785 by Frederick Augustus Hervey, the eccentric Earl of Bristol and Protestant Bishop of Derry, as a memorial to his cousin Mrs Frideswide Mussenden. The design was based on the Temple of Vesta at Tivoli outside Rome.

The walls, made of basalt faced with sandstone, open out at the four points of the compass to three windows and an entrance. Originally designed for use as a library (or, as some stories go, an elaborate boudoir for the bishop's mistress), the structure is now maintained by the National Trust and remains in excellent condition.

The bishop allowed the local priest to say Mass for his Roman Catholic tenants in the basement. Today, this contains artifacts from the bishop's former residence, the nearby Downhill Castle, which was gutted by fire and is now little more than an impressive shell.

The surrounding area offers some good glen and cliff walks and there are some magnificent views of the Londonderry and Antrim coastline. Below the temple is Downhill Strand, where the bishop sponsored horseback races between his clergy.

Portstewart ❹

Co Londonderry. **👥** *5,500.* **🚃** *to Coleraine or Portrush.* **🚌** **ℹ** *Jul & Aug: Town Hall, The Crescent (028 7083 2286).*

A POPULAR HOLIDAY destination for Victorian middle-class families, the resort still emits a sedate, old-fashioned air. Its long, crescent-shaped seafront promenade is sheltered by rocky headlands. Just west of town, and accessible by road or by a cliffside walk, stretches **Portstewart Strand**, a magnificent, long, sandy beach, protected by the National Trust.

On Ramore Head, just to the east, lies **Portrush**, a brasher resort with an abundance of souvenir shops and amusement arcades. The East Strand is backed by sand dunes and runs parallel with the world-class **Royal Portrush Golf Links**. You can stroll along the beach to White Rocks – limestone cliffs carved by the wind and waves into caves and arches.

To the south is the university town of **Coleraine**. The North West 200 (see p32), the world's fastest motorcycle road race, is run between Portstewart, Coleraine and Portrush. The race is held in May in front of 100,000 people.

Mussenden Temple set on a cliff top on the Londonderry coast

Causeway Coast ⑤

Co Antrim. **ℹ** *Giant's Causeway (028 2073 1855).* **Carrick-a-rede Rope Bridge** **☏** *028 2073 1582.* ◯ *Apr–early Sep: daily.* **♿** *for car park.*

The roofless ruins of 13th-century Dunluce Castle

THE RENOWN of the **Giant's Causeway** *(see pp356–7)*, Ireland's only World Heritage Site, overshadows the other attractions of this stretch of North Antrim coast. When visiting the Causeway, it is well worth investigating the sandy bays, craggy headlands and dramatic ruins that punctuate the rest of this inspirational coastline.

Approaching the Causeway from the west, you pass the eerie ruins of **Dunluce Castle** perched vulnerably on a steep crag – a storm once blew its kitchen into the sea. Dating back to the 13th century, it was the main fortress of the MacDonnells, chiefs of Antrim. Although the roof has gone, it is still well preserved, with its twin towers, gateway and some original cobbling intact.

Dunseverick Castle can be reached by road or a lengthy hike from the Causeway. It is a much earlier fortification than Dunluce and only one massive wall remains. Once the capital of the kingdom of Dalriada, it was linked to Tara *(see p332)* by a great road and was the departure point for 5th-century Irish raids on Scotland.

Just past the attractive, sandy **White Park Bay**, a tight switchback road leads down to the picturesque harbour of **Ballintoy**, reminiscent – on a good day – of an Aegean fishing village. **Sheep Island**, a rocky outcrop just offshore, is a cormorant colony. Local boat owners run trips past it in the summer.

Just east of Ballintoy is one of the most unusual and scary tourist attractions in Ireland, the **Carrick-a-rede Rope Bridge**. The bridge hangs 25 m (80 ft) above the sea and wobbles and twists as soon as you stand on it. Made of planks strung between wires, it provides access to the salmon fishery on the tiny island across the 20-m (65-ft) chasm. There are strong handrails and safety nets, but it's definitely not for those with vertigo. Further east along the coast lies **Kinbane Castle**. Little remains of this 16th-century ruin but the views from it are spectacular.

⌂ Dunluce Castle
☏ *028 2073 1938.* ◯ *daily.* **♿** **ℹ**

Fishing boats moored in the shelter of Ballintoy harbour

Carrick-a-rede Rope Bridge

THE NORTH ANTRIM COASTLINE

KEY

═	Minor road	**P**	Parking
▬	Major road	**ℹ**	Tourist information

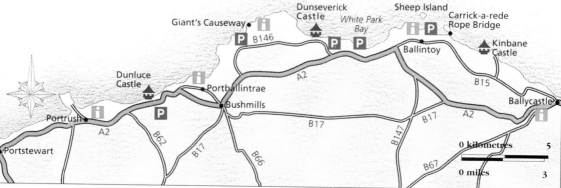

Giant's Causeway ❻

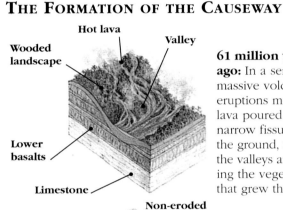

Chimney stacks

THE SHEER STRANGENESS of this place and the bizarre regularity of its basalt columns has made the Giant's Causeway the subject of numerous legends. The most popular tells how the giant, Finn MacCool *(see pp30–1),* laid the causeway to provide a path across the sea to his lady love, who lived on the island of Staffa in Scotland – where similar columns are found. The Giant's Causeway attracts many tourists, who are taken by the busload from the visitors' centre down to the shore. Nothing, however, can destroy the magic of this place, with its looming grey cliffs and shrieking gulls; paths along the coast allow you to escape the crowds.

Aird's Snout
This nose-shaped promontory juts out from the 120-m (395-ft) basalt cliffs that soar above the Giant's Causeway.

THE FORMATION OF THE CAUSEWAY

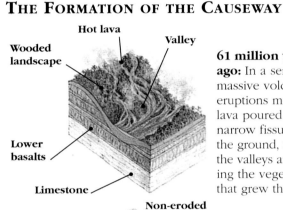

Wooded landscape
Hot lava
Valley
Lower basalts
Limestone

61 million years ago: In a series of massive volcanic eruptions molten lava poured from narrow fissures in the ground, filling in the valleys and burning the vegetation that grew there.

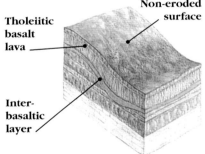

Tholeiitic basalt lava
Non-eroded surface
Inter-basaltic layer

60 million years ago: This layer of tholeiitic basalt lava cooled rapidly. In the process it shrank and cracked evenly into polygonal-shaped blocks, forming columnar jointing beneath the surface.

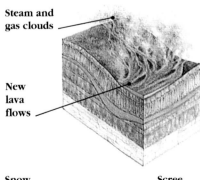

Steam and gas clouds
New lava flows

58 million years ago: New volcanic eruptions produced further lava flows. These had a slightly different chemical composition from earlier flows and, once cool, did not form such well defined columns.

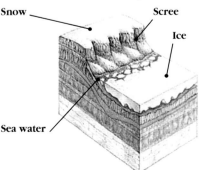

Snow
Scree
Ice
Sea water

15,000 years ago: At the end of the Ice Age, when the land was still frozen, sea ice ground its way slowly past the high basalt cliffs, eroding the foreshore and helping to form the Giant's Causeway.

Inter-basaltic layer

Shape of the Columns
Most columns are hexagonal, but some have four, five, eight or even ten sides. They generally measure about 30 cm (12 in) across.

VISITORS' CHECKLIST

Co Antrim. 🚂 to Portrush. 🚌
from Portrush, Bushmills or
Coleraine. **Visitors' Centre**
Causeway Head, 3 km (2 miles) N
of Bushmills (028 2073 1855).
⬜ Mar–May: 10am–5pm daily;
Jun–Oct: 10am–6pm (Jul & Aug:
7pm); Nov–Feb: 10am–4:30pm.
♿ limited. 🎧 on request. 🖥

Giant's Causeway and the North Antrim Coast

Millions of years of geological activity can be witnessed in the eroded cliffs flanking the Causeway. The striking band of reddish rock is the inter-basaltic layer, which formed during a long period of temperate climatic conditions. The high iron content explains the rock's rich ochre colour.

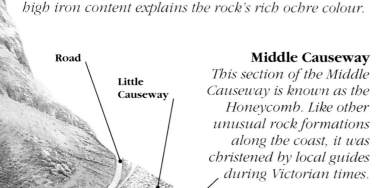

Road

Little
Causeway

Middle Causeway
This section of the Middle Causeway is known as the Honeycomb. Like other unusual rock formations along the coast, it was christened by local guides during Victorian times.

GIANT'S CAUSEWAY TODAY
It has been estimated that 37,000 basalt columns extend from the cliffs down into the sea. Close to the shore, they have been eroded to form the Grand, Middle and Little Causeways.

Plant debris
is trapped
between the
lava flows.

Wishing Chair
Myth has it that this rocky seat was made for Finn MacCool when he was a boy, and that wishes made here will come true.

Lower
basalts

Grand
Causeway

Visitors exploring the Giant's Causeway at low tide ▷

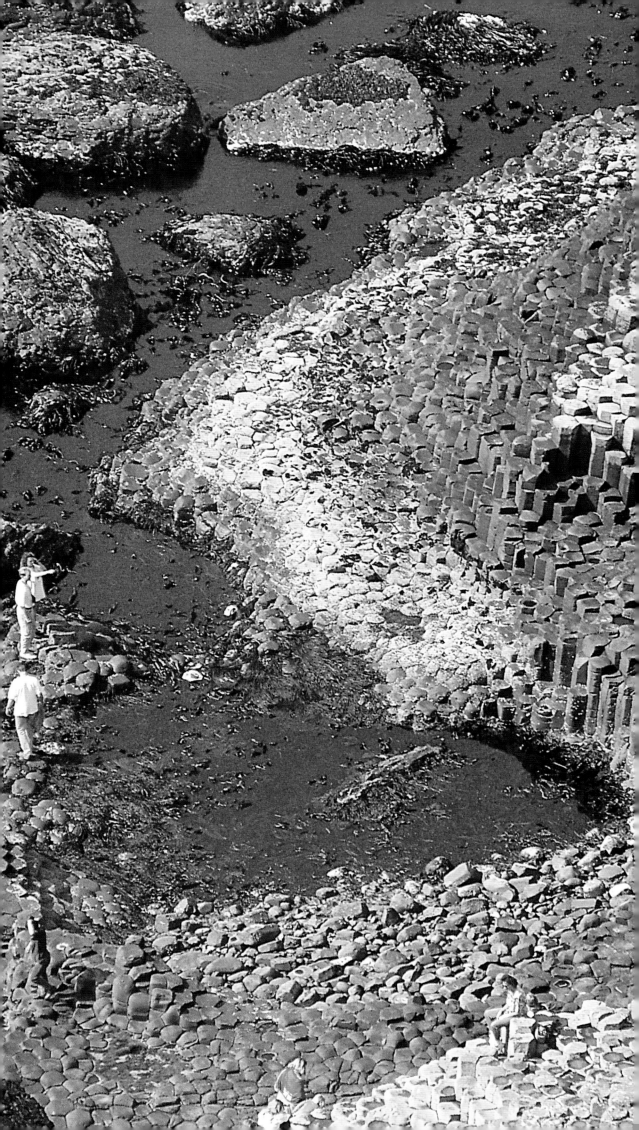

Old Bushmills Distillery ❼

Bushmills, Co Antrim. 📞 *028 2073 1521.* 🚌 *from Giant's Causeway & Coleraine.* ○ *Apr–Oct: daily; Nov–Mar: Mon–Fri.* ● *2 weeks at Christmas.* 📷 🎫 *obligatory.*

THE SMALL TOWN of Bushmills has an attractive square and an excellent river for salmon and trout fishing, but its main claim to fame is its whiskey production. The Old Bushmills plant on the outskirts of the town prides itself on being the oldest distillery in the world. Its Grant to Distil was given in 1608, although the spirit was probably being made here at least 200 years before that.

In 1974 Bushmills joined the Irish Distillers Group based at the Jameson plant *(see p217)* in Midleton, but its products have retained their distinctive character. Most brands are a blend of many different whiskeys; Old Bushmills, in contrast, is made from a blend of a single malt and a single grain.

The tour of the distillery ends with a sampling session in the Potstill Bar in the former malt kilns, which are also home to a mini-museum.

Whiskey barrel at Bushmills Distillery

Murlough Bay, on the coast facing Scotland to the east of Ballycastle

Rathlin Island ❽

Co Antrim. 🚶 *120.* ⛴ *daily from Ballycastle (028 2076 9299).* ℹ️ *Ballycastle (028 2076 2024).*

RATHLIN ISLAND is shaped rather like a boomerang – it is 11 km (7 miles) in length and at no point more than 1.6 km (1 mile) wide. The island is just a 50-minute boat ride from Ballycastle.

About 30 families remain on Rathlin Island, most of them making a living from fishing, farming and a little tourism. Facilities are limited, amounting to just a café, a pub and a guesthouse. The fierce, salty Atlantic winds ensure that the landscape on Rathlin is virtually treeless. High white cliffs encircle much of the island, and at craggy **Bull Point** on the westerly tip, tens of thousands of seabirds, including kittiwakes, puffins and razorbills, make their home. A local minibus service will take visitors to view the birds.

At the opposite end of the island is **Bruce's Cave**, where, in 1306, Robert Bruce, King of Scotland, supposedly watched a spider climbing a thread. The spider's perseverance inspired the dejected Bruce to return and win back his kingdom.

Ballycastle ❾

Co Antrim. 🚶 *4,000.* 🚌 ℹ️ *Sheskburn House, 7 Mary St (028 2076 2024).* 🎪 *Apple Fair (last Tue in Oct).*

A MEDIUM-SIZED resort town, Ballycastle boasts an attractive harbour and a central sandy beach. Near the harbour is a memorial to Guglielmo Marconi, whose assistant sent the first wireless message across water from here to Rathlin Island in 1898.

Ballycastle's annual Oul' Lammas Fair, held in late August, is one of the oldest traditional fairs in Ireland. It features noisy livestock sales and stalls selling yellowman (honeycomb toffee) and dulce (dried, heavily salted seaweed).

On the outskirts of town, the ruined 15th-century **Bonamargy Friary** houses the remains of Sorley Boy MacDonnell, former chieftain of this part of Antrim. Sections of the church, gatehouse and cloisters are well preserved.

Lighthouse on Rathlin Island, County Antrim

ENVIRONS: Off the A2, 5 km (3 miles) east of town, a narrow scenic road starts to wind its way along the coast to Cushendall. First stop is **Fair Head**, where a poorly marked path meanders across heathery marshland to towering cliffs 200 m (650 ft) above the sea. From here there are stunning views of Rathlin and the islands off the Scottish coast.

To the lee side of the headland lies **Murlough Bay**, the prettiest inlet along the coast. This can be reached by road. Further to the southeast stands **Torr Head**, a peninsula that reaches to within 21 km (13 miles) of the Mull of Kintyre making it the closest point in Ireland to Scotland.

Carnlough harbour, a popular stop south of Cushendall

Cushendall ⑩

Co Antrim. 🏠 *1,400.* 🚌 ℹ️ *4b Mill St (028 2177 1180).* ◯ *Jul–Sep: Mon–Sat; Oct–Nov & Feb–Jun: Mon–Fri (am only).*

THREE OF THE NINE Glens of Antrim converge towards Cushendall, earning it the unofficial title of "Capital of the Glens". This attractive village has brightly painted houses and a distinctive edifice known as Curfew Tower, built of local red sandstone in the early 19th century as a lock-up for thieves and idlers.

ENVIRONS: About 1.5 km (1 mile) north of the village stands **Layde Old Church**. It can be reached by a pretty walk along the cliffs. Founded by the Franciscans, it was a parish church from 1306 to 1790 and contains many monuments to the local chieftains, the MacDonnells.

Just over 3 km (2 miles) west of Cushendall, on the slopes of Tievebulliagh mountain, lies **Ossian's Grave**, named after the legendary warrior-poet and son of the giant Finn MacCool *(see pp30–31).*

It is in fact a Neolithic court tomb: the area was a major centre of Stone Age toolmaking and axeheads made of Tievebulliagh's hard porcellanite rock have been found at a wide range of sites all over the British Isles.

Other attractive villages further south along the coast road include **Carnlough**, which has a fine sandy beach and a delightful harbour, and **Ballygally**, whose 1625 castle is now a hotel.

Glenariff Forest Park ⑪

Co Antrim. 📞 *028 2175 8232.* ◯ *daily.* 🚗 *for car park.* ♿ *limited.*

NINE RIVERS have carved deep valleys through the Antrim Mountains to the sea. Celebrated in song and verse, the Glens of Antrim used to be the wildest and most remote part of Ulster. This region was not "planted" with English and Scots settlers in the 17th century and was the last place in Northern Ireland where Gaelic was spoken.

Today the Antrim coast road brings all the glens within easy reach of the tourist. Glenariff Forest Park contains some of the most spectacular scenery. The main scenic path runs through thick woodland and wildflower meadows and round the sheer sides of a gorge, past three waterfalls. There are also other, optional trails to distant mountain viewpoints. William Makepeace Thackeray, the 19th-century English novelist, called the landscape "Switzerland in miniature".

Glenariff Forest Park

Stone circle and stone rows at Beaghmore

Cookstown ⑫

Co Tyrone. 🏘 *11,000.* 🚌 ℹ️
Easter–Oct: 48 Molesworth St (028 8676 6727). 🛒 *Sat; Cattle Market: Mon, Wed, Fri.*

C OOKSTOWN STICKS in the memory for its grand central thoroughfare – 2 km (1.25 miles) long and perfectly straight. The road is about 40 m (130 ft) wide and, as you look to the north, it frames the bulky outline of Slieve Gallion, the highest of the Sperrin Mountains. A 17th-century Plantation town *(see pp42–3)*, Cookstown takes its name from its founder Alan Cook.

Ardboe Cross

ENVIRONS: The countryside around Cookstown is rich in Neolithic and early Christian monuments. To the east, on a desolate stretch of Lough Neagh shoreline, the **Ardboe Cross** stands on the site of a 6th-century monastery. Although eroded, the 10th-century cross is one of the best examples of a High Cross *(see p325)* in Ulster: its 22 sculpted panels depict Old Testament scenes on the east side and New Testament ones on the west. The **Wellbrook Beetling Mill**, west of Cookstown, is a relic of Ulster's old linen industry. "Beetling" was the process of hammering the cloth to give it a sheen. Set amid trees beside the Ballinderry River, the mill dates from 1768 and is now a popular tourist attraction. The National Trust has restored the whitewashed two-storey building and its water wheel. Inside, working displays demonstrate just how loud "beetling" could be. From the mill, there are pleasant walks along the river banks.

ⓗ **Ardboe Cross**
Off B73, 16 km (10 miles) E of Cookstown.
🏚 **Wellbrook Beetling Mill**
Off A505, 6.5 km (4 miles) W of Cookstown. 📞 *028 8675 1735.* ⭕
Jul & Aug: Wed–Mon (pm only); Apr–Jun & Sep: Sat, Sun & public hols. ♿

Beaghmore Stone Circles ⑬

Co Tyrone. Off A505, 14 km (9 miles) NW of Cookstown.

O N A STRETCH of open moorland in the foothills of the Sperrin Mountains lies a vast collection of stone monuments, dating from between 2000 and 1200 BC. There are seven stone circles, several stone rows and a number of less prominent features, possibly collapsed field walls of an earlier period. Their exact purpose remains unknown, though in some cases their alignment correlates with movements of the sun, moon and stars. Three of the rows, for example, are clearly aligned with the point where the sun rises at the summer solstice.

The individual circle stones are small – none is more than 1.20 m (4 ft) in height – but their sheer numbers make them a truly impressive sight. As well as the circles and rows, there are a dozen round cairns (burial mounds). Up until 1945, the whole complex, one of Ulster's major archaeological finds, had lain buried beneath a thick layer of peat.

ULSTER'S HISTORIC LINEN INDUSTRY

The rise in Ulster's importance as a linen producer was spurred on by the arrival from France of refugee Huguenot weavers at the end of the 17th century. Linen remained a flourishing industry for a further two centuries, but today it is produced only in small quantities for the luxury goods market. Hundreds of abandoned mills dot the former "Linen Triangle" bounded by Belfast, Armagh and Dungannon. One of the reasons why the material diminished in popularity was the expensive production process: after cutting, the flax had to be retted, or soaked, in large artificial ponds so that scutching – the separation of the fibres – could begin. After combing, the linen was spun and woven before being bleached in the sun, typically in fields along river banks. The final stage was "beetling", the process whereby the cloth was hammered to give it a sheen.

18th-century print, showing flax being prepared for spinning

Copy of Iron Age Celtic stone head at the Ulster History Park

Ulster History Park 14

Co Tyrone. (028 8264 8188. from Omagh. Apr–Sep: daily; Oct–Mar: Mon–Fri. 1 Jan, 23–29 Dec.

NESTLING AT THE EDGE of the Sperrin Mountains, the Ulster History Park is filled with full-scale models of structures built by successive waves of settlers in Ireland. They range from a Mesolithic hunter/gatherer's hut covered with animal pelts, dating from 7000 BC, to a 17th-century Plantation village (*see pp42–3*). There are also megalithic burial tombs, a crannog (*see p37*) from the early Christian period and a Norman motte and bailey (a wooden fortress built on a high mound). An exhibition centre helps put the exhibits in perspective.

Ulster-American Folk Park 15

Co Tyrone. (028 8224 3292. from Omagh. Easter–Sep: daily; Oct–Easter: Mon–Fri and public hols.

ONE OF THE BEST open-air museums of its kind, the Folk Park grew up around the restored boyhood home of Judge Thomas Mellon (founder of the Pittsburgh banking dynasty). The Park's permanent exhibition, called "Emigrants", examines why two million people left Ulster for America during the 18th and 19th centuries. It also shows what became of them, following stories of both fortune and failure, including the grim lives of indentured servants and the 15,000 Irish vagrants and convicts transported to North America in the mid-18th century.

The park has more than 30 historic buildings, some of them original, some replicas. There are settler homesteads (including that of John Joseph Hughes, the first Catholic Archbishop of New York), churches, a schoolhouse and a forge, some with craft displays, all with costumed interpretative guides. There's also an Ulster streetscape, a reconstructed emigrant ship and a Pennsylvania farmstead,

complete with log barn, corn crib and smokehouse. The six-roomed farmhouse is based on one built by Thomas Mellon and his father in the early years of their new life in America.

A fully stocked library and database allow visitors to trace their family roots. Popular American festivals such as Independence Day and Hallowe'en are celebrated at the park and there is an Appalachian-Bluegrass music festival in early September.

Belleek Pottery 16

Belleek, Co Fermanagh. (028 6865 8501.   Mar–Aug: daily; Sep–Nov: Mon–Sat; Dec–Feb: Mon–Fri. 17 Mar & 10 days at Christmas.

Worker at the Belleek factory making a Parian ware figurine

THE LITTLE BORDER VILLAGE of Belleek would attract few visitors other than anglers were it not for the world-famous Belleek Pottery, founded in 1857. The company's pearly coloured china is known as Parian ware. Developed in the 19th century, it was supposed to resemble the famous Parian marble of Ancient Greece.

Belleek is now best known for its ornamental pieces of fragile lattice work decorated with pastel-coloured flowers. These are especially popular in the USA. Several elaborate showpieces stand on display in the visitors' centre and small museum. There's also a 20-minute video presentation on the company's history, a gift shop and ample parking space for tour buses.

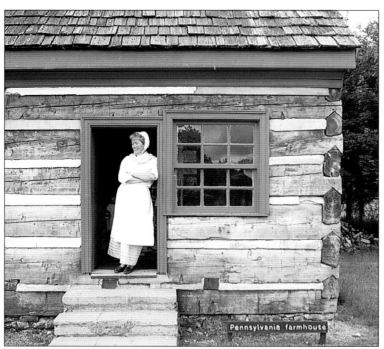

Pennsylvania log farmhouse at the Ulster-American Folk Park

A Tour of Lower Lough Erne ⑰

Kingfisher

THE AREA AROUND Lower Lough Erne boasts a rich combination of both natural and historic sights. From pre-Christian times, settlers sought the security offered by the lough's forests and inlets. Monasteries were founded on several of its many islands in the Middle Ages, and a ring of castles recalls the Plantation era *(see p43)*. The lake is a haven for water birds such as ducks, grebes and kingfishers, and the trout-rich waters attract many anglers. Lough Erne is a delight to explore by land or by boat. In summer, ferries serve several islands, and cruisers are available for hire.

View across Lower Lough Erne

Boa Island ⑤
Two curious double-faced figures stand in Caldragh cemetery, a Christian graveyard on Boa Island. While little is known about the stone idols, they are certainly pre-Christian.

Belleek ⑦
Northern Ireland's most westerly village, Belleek is famous for its pottery *(see p363)*. There is also a new museum, ExplorErne, which covers most aspects of the region.

Castle Caldwell Forest Park ⑥
The park's wooded peninsulas are a sanctuary for birds, and you can watch waterfowl from hides on the shore. You may see great crested grebes, the common scoter duck and perhaps even otters.

Lough Navar Forest Drive ⑧
An 11-km (7-mile) drive through pine forest leads to a viewpoint atop the Cliffs of Magho, with a magnificent panorama over Lough Erne and beyond. Trails weave through the woods.

TIPS FOR DRIVERS

Length: *110 km (68 miles).*
Stopping-off points: *Outside Enniskillen, the best places to eat are the pubs in Kesh and Belleek; in summer, a café opens in Castle Archdale Country Park. There are good picnic places all along the route of this tour, including at the Cliffs of Magho viewpoint.*

KEY

▬▬ Tour route

╌╌ Other roads

🚤 Boats to islands

❊ Viewpoint

Tully Castle ⑨
A delightful 17th-century-st* herb garden has recently been planted alongside th* fortified Plantation house, whose protective enclosur* or bawn, is still visible.

White Island ④

The Romanesque church on White Island has bizarre pagan-looking figures set into one wall. Of uncertain origin, they probably adorned an earlier monastery on this site. Ferries to the island leave from Castle Archdale Marina in summer.

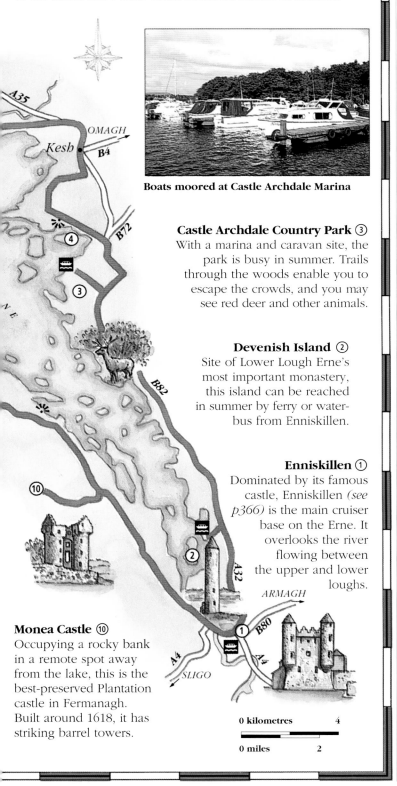

Boats moored at Castle Archdale Marina

Castle Archdale Country Park ③

With a marina and caravan site, the park is busy in summer. Trails through the woods enable you to escape the crowds, and you may see red deer and other animals.

Devenish Island ②

Site of Lower Lough Erne's most important monastery, this island can be reached in summer by ferry or water-bus from Enniskillen.

Enniskillen ①

Dominated by its famous castle, Enniskillen (see p366) is the main cruiser base on the Erne. It overlooks the river flowing between the upper and lower loughs.

Monea Castle ⑩

Occupying a rocky bank in a remote spot away from the lake, this is the best-preserved Plantation castle in Fermanagh. Built around 1618, it has striking barrel towers.

0 kilometres 4

0 miles 2

Beautifully constructed round tower on Devenish Island

Devenish Island ⑱

Co Fermanagh. 🚢 from Trory Point, 5 km (3 miles) N of Enniskillen (028 6632 9656): Apr–Sep: Tue–Sat & Sun pm; from Enniskillen (028 6632 2882): May–Jun: Sun pm; Jul–Aug: daily; Sep: Tue, Sat & Sun. 🎟 for museum and tower.

S T MOLAISE, who had 1,500 scholars under his tutelage, founded a monastery on this tiny windswept island in the 6th century. Although raided by Vikings in the 9th century and burnt in 1157, it remained an important religious centre up to the early 17th century.

Several fine buildings from the medieval monastery have survived, including **Teampall Mor** near the jetty. Built in 1225, this church displays the transition between Roman-esque and Gothic styles. On the highest ground stands **St Mary's Priory**, an Augustinian church that was erected in the 15th century. An intricately carved stone cross close by dates from the same period.

The most spectacular sight on Devenish Island, however, is the 12th-century round tower, which stands some 25 m (82 ft) high. It is perfectly preserved, and the five floors can be reached by internal ladders. Supporting the roof is an elaborate cornice with a human face carved above each of the four windows; this is a unique feature in an Irish round tower. A small museum covers both the history and architecture of the island, and contains a collection of stone carvings and other antiquities discovered at the site.

Enniskillen ⑲

Co Fermanagh. 🏠 *14,000.* 🚌 ℹ️
Wellington Road (028 6632 3110).
🛒 *Thu.*

THE BUSY tourist centre of Enniskillen occupies an island between Upper and Lower Lough Erne. The town gained fame for the wrong reason in 1987, when 11 people died in an IRA bomb attack, but it deserves a visit for its setting and sights.

At the west end of town stands **Enniskillen Castle**, which dates back to the 15th century. It houses a heritage centre and the Inniskilling Regimental Museum. Its most stunning feature, however, is the Watergate, a fairy-tale twin-turreted tower, best admired from the far bank of the river. Further west, **Portora Royal School**, founded in 1618, counts among its old boys the playwrights Oscar Wilde and Samuel Beckett *(see pp26–27)*.

The **Cole Monument** stands on a little hill in a pretty Victorian park on the east side of town. It is a tall Doric column with an internal

Enniskillen Castle seen from across the River Erne

spiral staircase that can be climbed for magnificent views of the lake country.

🏰 **Enniskillen Castle**
📞 *028 6632 5000.* ◯ *Jul & Aug: daily (Sat–Mon pm only); May–Jun & Sep: Mon–Sat; Oct–Apr: Mon–Fri.* 🏷️ 🚫 *1 Jan, 25 & 26 Dec.* ♿ *limited.*

ENVIRONS: Just outside town, set in a park with mature oak woodland overlooking a lake, is **Castle Coole**, one of the finest Neo-Classical homes in Ireland. It has a long Portland stone façade, with a central portico and small pavilions at each end. The stone was shipped from Dorset to Ballyshannon in County Donegal. Many of the fixtures and fittings were also brought from England. The first Earl of Belmore, who commissioned the house in the 1790s, was almost bankrupted by the cost of it. The original design was by Irish architect Richard Johnston, but the Earl then commissioned a second set of drawings by the fashionable English architect James Wyatt. The extravagant Earl died, deep in debt, in 1802 and it was left to his son to complete the decorating and furnishing during the 1820s.

The glory of Castle Coole is that almost all the house's original furniture is still in place. Family portraits from the 18th century line the walls of the dining room. In the lavish State Bedroom there is a bed made specially for King George IV on the occasion of his visit to Ireland in 1821, though in the end he never came here to sleep in it. One of the finest rooms is the oval saloon (or ballroom) at the back of the house. The heavy curtains and richly gilded Regency furniture may not be to everyone's taste, but the spacious oak-floored room produces a magnificent effect of unostentatious luxury.

🏛️ **Castle Coole**
Off A4, 1.6 km (1 mile) SE of Enniskillen. 📞 *028 6632 2690.* ◯ *May–Aug: Fri–Wed (pm only); Apr & Sep: Sat, Sun & public hols (pm only).* 🏷️ ♿

The saloon at Castle Coole, with original Regency furnishings

Marble Arch Caves ⑳

Marlbank Scenic Loop, Florence Court,
Co Fermanagh. 📞 028 6634 8855.
◯ Apr–Sep: daily (phone first as
weather can cause sudden closure).
📷 🎥 obligatory.

T HE CAVES are cut by three
streams which flow down
the slopes of Cuilcagh
Mountain, unite underground
and emerge as the Cladagh
River. Tours lasting 75 minutes
consist of a boat ride into the
depths of the cave complex
and a guided walk that leads
past stalagmites, calcite cascades and other curious limestone formations. The 9-m
(30-ft) "Marble Arch" itself
stands outside the cave system
in the glen where the river
gushes out from below ground.
    The caves are very popular,
so it's best to book ahead. It
is also advisable to ring to
check the local weather conditions before setting out; the
caves may be closed because
of rain. Whatever the weather,
bring a sweater and sensible
walking shoes.

Boat trip through Marble Arch Caves

Florence Court ㉑

Co Fermanagh. 📞 028 6634 8249.
🚌 from Enniskillen (Jul & Aug).
House ◯ Jun–Aug: Wed–Mon (pm
only); Apr–May & Sep: Sat, Sun &
public hols. 📷 ♿ **Grounds** ◯
daily. 📷 for car park.

T HIS THREE-STOREY Palladian
mansion was built for the
Cole family in the mid-18th
century. The arcades and
pavilions, which are of a later
date than the main house,
were probably added around
1770 by William Cole, first
Earl of Enniskillen. The house
features flamboyant Rococo

plasterwork said to be by the
Dublin stuccodore Robert
West. Sadly, however, hardly
any of what you see today is
original as most of the central
block was seriously damaged
by fire in 1955. The furniture
was lost, but the plasterwork
was painstakingly recreated
from photographs. The finest
examples are in the dining
room, the staircase and the
small Venetian room.
    Perhaps more spectacular
are the grounds, which occupy
a natural amphitheatre set
between hills and mountains.
The area is fairly wild and
there are many enjoyable
walks and nature trails around
the house. One woodland
trail leads to the famous
Florence Court yew tree,
whose descendants are to be
found all over Ireland. Closer
to the house is a walled
garden where pink and white
roses make an attractive sight
in early summer.

Dungannon ㉒

Co Tyrone. 👥 10,000. 🚌 ℹ️
Killymaddy Tourist Centre, Ballygawly
Rd, 8 km (5 miles) W of town (028
8776 7259). 🛒 Thu.

D UNGANNON'S HILLY location
made an ideal site for the
seat of government of the
O'Neill dynasty from the 14th
century until Plantation (see
pp42–3), when their castle
was razed. The town's **Royal
School** claims to be the oldest
school in Northern Ireland.
Opened in 1614, it moved to
its present site on Northland
Row in 1789.
    Once a major linen centre,
this busy market town's best-
known factory is now **Tyrone
Crystal**, the largest concern
of its kind in Northern Ireland.
Tours of its modern complex
cover all stages of production,
including glass-blowing.

🏭 **Tyrone Crystal**
Coalisland Road. 📞 028 8772 5335.
◯ Mon–Sat. ● 10 days at
Christmas. 📷 🎥 ♿

Florence Court, the former seat of the Earls of Enniskillen

Victorian interior of the Crown Liquor Saloon, County Antrim ▷

View of Armagh dominated by St Patrick's Roman Catholic Cathedral

Armagh ㉓

Co Armagh. 🚶 *14,400.* 🚌 ℹ️ *40 English St (028 3752 1800).* 🚢 *Tue & Fri.*

ONE OF IRELAND's oldest cities, Armagh dates back to the age of St Patrick *(see p377)* and the advent of Christianity. The narrow streets in the city centre follow the ditches that once ringed the church, founded by the saint in 455. Two cathedrals, both called **St Patrick's**, sit on opposing hills. The more visually striking is the huge Roman Catholic one, a twin-spired Neo-Gothic building with seemingly every inch of wall covered in mosaic. The older Protestant Cathedral dates back to medieval times. It boasts the bones of Brian Boru, the King of Ireland who defeated the Vikings in 1014 *(see pp38–9)*, and an 11th-century High Cross.

Skull of Barbary ape from Navan Fort

Armagh's gorgeous oval, tree-lined Mall, where cricket is played in summer, is surrounded by dignified Georgian buildings. One of these houses the small **Armagh County Museum**, which has a good exhibition on local history. Off the Mall, **St Patrick's Trian** is a heritage centre telling the story of the city. It also has a "Land of Lilliput" fantasy centre for children, based on *Gulliver's Travels* by Jonathan Swift *(see p95)*. Ireland's only planetarium is on College Hill in the **Observatory Grounds**, from where there are splendid views over the city.

🏛 **Armagh County Museum**
The Mall East. 📞 *028 3752 3070.* ⭕ *Mon–Sat.* 🌑 *some public hols.* 📷 *by arrangement.*

🏛 **St Patrick's Trian**
40 English St. 📞 *028 3752 1801.* ⭕ *daily.* 🌑 *25, 26 Dec.* 📷 ♿

🌿 **Observatory Grounds**
College Hill. 📞 *028 3752 2928.* ⭕ *daily.* **Planetarium** 📞 *028 3752 3689.* ⭕ *daily.*

ENVIRONS: To the west of Armagh stands **Navan Fort**, a large earthwork on the summit of a hill. In legend, Navan was Emain Macha, ceremonial and spiritual capital of ancient Ulster, associated with tales of the warrior Cuchulainn *(see p30)*. The site may have been in use as much as 4,000 years ago, but seems to have been most active around 100 BC when a huge timber building, 40 m (130 ft) across, was erected over a giant cairn. The whole thing was then burnt and the remains covered with soil. Archaeological evidence indicates that this was not an act of war, but a solemn ritual performed by the inhabitants of Emain Macha themselves.

Below the fort, the grass-roofed **Navan Centre**, built to blend in with the landscape, interprets the archaeology and mythology of the site through interactive displays and a 25-minute film. The most unexpected exhibit is the skull of a Barbary ape, found in the remains of a Bronze Age house. The animal must have been brought from Spain or North Africa, evidence that by 500 BC Emain Macha had already become an important place with far-flung trading links.

🏛 **Navan Centre**
On A28 4 km (2.5 miles) W of Armagh. 📞 *028 3752 5550.* ⭕ *daily.* 🌑 *5 days at Christmas.* 📷 ♿

Lough Neagh ㉔

Co Armagh, Co Tyrone, Co Londonderry, Co Antrim.

LEGEND HAS IT that the giant Finn MacCool *(see pp30–1)* created Lough Neagh by picking up a piece of turf and hurling it into the Irish Sea, thus forming the Isle of Man in the process. At 400 sq km (153 sq miles), the lake is the largest in Britain. Bordered by sedgy marshland, it has few roads along its shore. The best recreational areas lie in the south: Oxford Island, actually a peninsula, has walking trails, bird lookouts and the informative **Lough Neagh Discovery Centre**. In the southwest corner, a narrow-gauge railway runs through the bogs of **Peatlands Park**. Salmon and trout swim in the

Navan Fort, the site of Emain Macha, legendary capital of Ulster

Hide for birdwatchers at Oxford Island on the southern shore of Lough Neagh

rivers that flow from Lough Neagh. The lake is famous for its eels, with one of the world's largest eel fisheries at **Toome** on the north shore.

🏛 **Lough Neagh Discovery Centre**
Oxford Island. Exit 10 off M1.
📞 028 3832 2205. ◯ Apr–Sep: daily; Oct–Mar: Wed–Sun. ◉ 25, 26 Dec. ⚄ ⬚

❦ **Peatlands Park**
Exit 13 off M1. 📞 028 3885 1102.
Park ◯ daily. ◉ 25 Dec. **Visitors' centre** ◯ Jun–Aug: daily (pm only); Easter–May & Sep: Sat, Sun & public hols (pm only); rest of year by appt.

Larne ㉕

Co Antrim. 👥 18,000. 🚌 🚋 ℹ️
Narrow Gauge Rd (028 2826 0088) & at Ferry Terminal (028 2827 0517).

INDUSTRIAL LARNE is the arrival point for ferries from Scotland. The town is not the finest introduction to Ulster scenery, however, it is situated on the threshold of the magnificent Antrim coastline (*see p361*).

The sheltered waters of Larne Lough have been a landing point since Mesolithic times – flint flakes found here provide some of the earliest evidence of human presence on the island – nearly 9,000 years ago. Since then, Norsemen used the lough as a base in the 10th century, Edward Bruce landed his Scottish troops in the area in 1315, and in 1914 the Ulster Volunteer Force landed a huge cache of German arms here during its campaign against Home Rule (*see pp48–9*).

Carrickfergus ㉖

Co Antrim. 👥 35,500. 🚌 🚋 ℹ️
Antrim St (028 9336 6455). ⬚ Thu.

CARRICKFERGUS grew up around the massive castle begun in 1180 by John de Courcy to guard the entrance to Belfast Lough. De Courcy was the leader of the Anglo-Norman force which invaded Ulster following Strongbow's conquest of Leinster in the south (*see pp40–41*).

Carrickfergus Castle was shaped to fit the crag on which it stands overlooking the harbour. The finest and best-preserved Norman castle in Ireland, it even has its original portcullis (*see pp40–41*). Naturally, many changes and adaptations have been made since the 12th century, including wide ramparts to accommodate the castle's cannons. Arms and armour are on display in the large rectangular keep, while life-size model soldiers are posed along the ramparts.

In continuous use up to 1928, the castle has changed hands several times over the years. The Scots, under Edward Bruce, took it in 1315, holding it for three years. In the 17th century James II's army was in control of the castle from 1688 until General Schomberg took it for William III in 1690. William himself stayed at the castle before the Battle of the Boyne (*see p326*) in July 1690.

The history of the town is recreated in a series of audio-visual displays at **Knight Ride**. The exhibition is literally a ride through history as you are transported from scene to scene in small cable cars. This appeals principally to children, who also enjoy the gorier episodes from the history of Carrickfergus.

⌂ **Carrickfergus Castle**
📞 028 9335 1273. ◯ daily (Sun pm).
◉ 25 Dec. ⚄ ♿
🏛 **Knight Ride**
Antrim St. 📞 028 9336 6455.
◯ daily (Sun pm). ◉ 25 Dec. ⚄

The massive Norman keep of Carrickfergus Castle

Belfast ㉗

BELFAST WAS THE ONLY CITY in Ireland to experience the full force of the Industrial Revolution. Its ship-building, linen, rope-making and tobacco industries caused the population to rise to almost 400,000 by the end of World War I. The wealth it enjoyed is still evident in its imposing banks, churches and other public buildings. The Troubles and the decline of traditional industries have since damaged economic life, but Belfast remains a handsome city and most visitors are agreeably surprised by the genuine friendliness of the "Big Smoke".

Red Hand of Ulster, Linen Hall Library

Mosaic in St Anne's Cathedral, showing St Patrick's journey to Ireland

Interior of the Grand Opera House

🏛 City Hall
Donegall Square. ℂ *028 9032 0202 ext 2618.* ☒ *usually Wed (must be booked in advance).*

Most of Belfast's main streets (and many major bus routes) radiate out from the hub of Donegall Square. In the centre of the square stands the vast rectangular Portland stone bulk of the 1906 City Hall. It has an elaborate tower at each corner and a central copper dome that rises to a height of 53 m (173 ft). Highlight of the tour of the interior is the sumptuous oak-panelled council chamber.

Statues around the building include a glum-looking Queen Victoria outside the main entrance and, on the east side, Sir Edward Harland, founder of the Harland and Wolff shipyard, which built the *Titanic*. A memorial to those who died when the *Titanic* sank in 1912 stands close by.

Detail of *Titanic* Memorial outside City Hall

🎭 Grand Opera House
Great Victoria St. ℂ *028 9024 0411.*

Designed by Frank Matcham, the renowned theatre-architect, this exuberant late-Victorian building opened its doors in 1894. The sumptuous interior, with its gilt, red plush and intricate plasterwork, was restored to its full glory in 1980. On occasions, bombings of the adjacent Europa Hotel disrupted business at the theatre, but it survives as a major venue for plays and concerts. In 1984, Belfast-born singer Van Morrison recorded a famous live album here.

⛪ St Anne's Cathedral
Donegall St. ℂ *028 9032 8332.*

The Neo-Romanesque façade of this Protestant cathedral, consecrated in 1904, fails to make much of an impression. The interior is far more attractive, especially the vast, colourful mosaics executed by the two Misses Martin in the 1920s. The one covering the baptistry ceiling contains over 150,000 pieces. The wide nave is paved with Canadian maple and the aisles with Irish marble. Lord Carson (1854–1935), implacable leader of the campaign against Home Rule (*see p48*), is buried in in the south aisle.

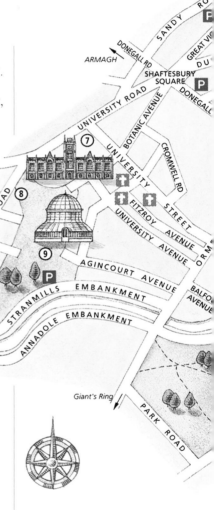

ARMAGH

Giant's Ring

SIGHTS AT A GLANCE
Albert Memorial Clock Tower ⑩
Botanical Gardens ⑨
City Hall ③
Crown Liquor Saloon ②
The Entries ⑤
Grand Opera House ①
Lagan Weir Lookout ⑪
Linen Hall Library ④
Queen's University ⑦
St Anne's Cathedral ⑥
Ulster Museum ⑧

0 metres	500
0 yards	500

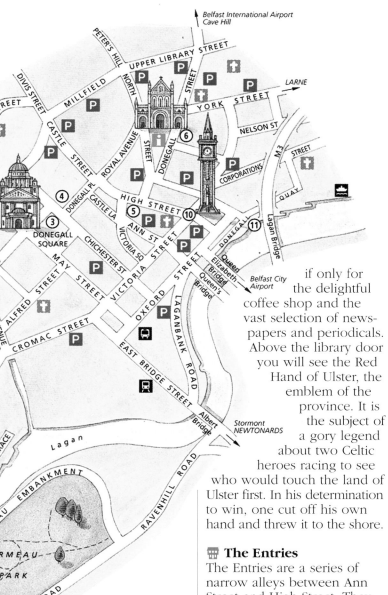

VISITORS' CHECKLIST

Co Antrim. 👥 305,000. ✈ Belfast City Airport, 6.5 km (4 miles) E; Belfast International, 29 km (18 miles) NW. 🚆 Central Station, East Bridge St (028 9089 9411); Great Victoria St Station. 🚌 Europa Buscentre, Great Victoria St & Oxford St (028 9033 3000). ℹ 59 North St (028 9024 6609). 🎭 Royal Ulster Agricultural Show & Lord Mayor's Show (May); Belfast Festival at Queen's (Nov).

if only for the delightful coffee shop and the vast selection of newspapers and periodicals. Above the library door you will see the Red Hand of Ulster, the emblem of the province. It is the subject of a gory legend about two Celtic heroes racing to see who would touch the land of Ulster first. In his determination to win, one cut off his own hand and threw it to the shore.

🍺 The Entries
The Entries are a series of narrow alleys between Ann Street and High Street. They feature some of the best pubs in the city, including White's Tavern, reputedly the oldest bar in Belfast. The Globe in Joy's Entry and the Morning Star on Pottinger's Entry both serve excellent lunches. In 1791, the United Irishmen, a radical movement inspired by the new ideas of the French Revolution, was founded in a tavern on Crown Entry. Its most famous member was Wolfe Tone *(see pp44–5)*.

🍺 Crown Liquor Saloon
Great Victoria St. 📞 028 9024 9476. ⬚ *daily.*
Even teetotallers should make a detour to the multi-coloured tiled façade of this flamboyant Victorian drinking palace. The Crown, which dates back to the 1880s, is the only pub owned by the National Trust. The lovingly restored interior features stained and painted glass, lots of marbling and mosaics and a splendid ceiling with scrolled plasterwork. The wooden snugs facing the long bar have their original gas lamps: the perfect place for a pint of Guinness or Bass and some Strangford Lough oysters.

🍺 Linen Hall Library
17 Donegall Square North.
📞 028 9032 1707. ⬚ *Mon–Sat.*
Founded as the Belfast Society for Promoting Knowledge in 1788, the library has thousands of rare, old books in its dark wooden stacks. There is also extensive documentation of political events in Ireland since 1968 and a vast database of genealogical information. Even if you have no special reason for visiting the library, it is still well worth going inside,

KEY

🚆	Railway station
🚌	Coach station
⛴	Ferry port
🅿	Parking
ℹ	Tourist information
⛪	Church

The ornate Victorian interior of the Crown Liquor Saloon

Exploring Belfast

AWAY FROM THE CITY CENTRE, Belfast has many pleasant suburbs unaffected by the civil strife of recent times. The area around Queen's University to the south of the city has two major attractions in the Ulster Museum and the Botanic Gardens. To the north, there are splendid views to be enjoyed from the heights of Cave Hill, while visitors interested in Belfast's industrial heritage will be keen to see both the old docks and the Harland and Wolff working shipyards.

Interior of the Victorian Palm House at the Botanic Gardens

🏛 Ulster Museum

Botanic Gardens. 📞 *028 9038 3000.*
◯ *daily (Sat & Sun: pm only).*
⬤ *public hols.* 🎫 ♿

This four-floor bunker of a museum covers all aspects of Ulster, from local history, archaeology, antiquities and art to geology, natural history and technology. Especially prized treasures include gold and silver jewellery recovered from the *Girona,* a Spanish Armada ship that sank off the Giant's Causeway in 1588 *(see p349).* One of the most interesting exhibits is of Belfast industry, featuring some crude turn-of-the-century textile machinery.

In the top-floor gallery is a collection of paintings mostly by British and Irish artists, including a large number by Belfast-born Sir John Lavery (1856–1941).

In addition to the Irish collections, there are exhibits ranging from ancient Egyptian mummies to dinosaurs. The museum also mounts frequent temporary exhibitions on a wide variety of themes.

🌿 Botanic Gardens

Stranmillis Rd. 📞 *028 9032 4902.*
◯ *daily.*

Backing on to the university, the Botanic Gardens provide a quiet refuge from the bustle of campus. The 1839 Palm House is a superb example of curvilinear glass and cast-iron work. The Tropical Ravine, or Fernery, is another fine piece of Victorian garden architecture. Visitors can look down from the balcony to a sunken glen of exotic plants.

🏛 Queen's University

University Rd. 📞 *028 9024 5133.*
A 15-minute stroll south from Donegall Square, through the lively entertainment district known as the Golden Mile, leads to Northern Ireland's most prestigious university. The main building, designed in Tudor-style red and yellow brick by Charles Lanyon in 1849, bears similarities to Magdalene College, Oxford. A towered gateway leads to a colonnaded quadrangle.

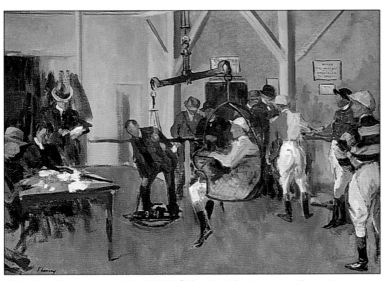

Weighing Room, Hurst Park (1924) by Sir John Lavery, Ulster Museum

---

THE POLITICAL MURALS OF WEST BELFAST

Republican mural in the Falls Road

Ever since the onset of the "Troubles" in 1968, popular art has played a conspicuous role in proclaiming the loyalties of Belfast's two most intransigent working-class communities, on the Protestant Shankill Road and the Catholic Falls Road. The gable walls of dozens of houses in these areas have been decorated with vivid murals expressing local political and paramilitary affiliations. Likewise, kerbstones on certain streets are painted either in the red, white and blue of the United Kingdom or the green, white and gold of Ireland. Even with the successes of the current peace process, many are likely to remain. Some tourists make the journey out to West Belfast just to see the murals. The simplest way to do this is to take a taxi from the centre; cabs that go to the Falls Road leave from Castle Street, while those for the Shankill Road leave from North Street.

Protestant Loyalist mural

☷ Albert Memorial Clock Tower

Queen's Square.

One of Belfast's best-known monuments, the clock tower, was designed by WJ Barre. Prince Albert, Queen Victoria's consort, had no personal connection with Belfast, but memorials to him were built in many British cities in the decade following his death in 1861. Today, the tower arouses most interest for the fact that it leans slightly as a result of subsidence. Beyond it, facing the river, stands the Custom House (1854) by Charles Lanyon, architect of Queen's University.

Belfast cityscape showing the giant cranes, Samson and Goliath

☷ Lagan Weir Lookout

Donegall Quay. ☎ 028 9031 5444. ◯ daily (Sat & Sun: pm only). 📷

Belfast's once thriving harbour area, five minutes' walk from Donegall Square, can best be viewed from the footbridge alongside the new Lagan Weir development. Five computer-controlled steel gates, unveiled in 1994, maintain a fixed water level, getting rid of the smelly mudbanks produced by varying tide levels and creating possibilities for angling and watersports along the river. The Visitors' Centre, on the footbridge, explains how it all works and tells some good tales of modern Belfast folklore. At night, the weir is lit by gas-filter blue light that shimmers across the water.

Unfortunately, the new Cross-Harbour Road and Rail Link bridge partly obscures the view across to the giant yellow cranes – appropriately named Samson and Goliath – of the once-mighty Harland and Wolff shipyards.

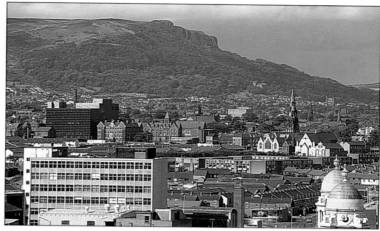

The unmistakeable profile of Cave Hill above the roofs of Belfast

ENVIRONS: The best place for an overall view of Belfast and Belfast Lough is the 360-m (1,118-ft) summit of Cave Hill, the most distinctively shaped of the hills encircling the city.

☷ Cave Hill

Antrim Rd, 6.5 km (4 miles) N of city centre. **Heritage Centre** ☎ 028 9077 6925. ◯ daily. ⬤ 25 Dec. ♿ **Zoo** ☎ 028 9077 4625. ◯ daily. ⬤ 25 Dec. 📷 ♿

It was on Cave Hill, next to the remains of MacArt's Fort (named after an Iron Age chieftain), that Wolfe Tone (see p45) and the northern leaders of the United Irishmen met in 1795 to pledge themselves to rebellion. The five artificial caves near the fort were carved out during the Neolithic period.

On the thickly wooded, eastern slopes of the hill stands the baronial pile of Belfast Castle, built in 1870. Previously home to the Earl of Shaftesbury, the castle now belongs to the city and houses two restaurants and a new heritage centre that interprets the area's history. A little further along the road past the castle is Belfast Zoo, which makes the most of its steep woodland setting.

☷ Giant's Ring

Off B23, 5 km (3 miles) S of city centre. Little is known about this awe-inspiring prehistoric enclosure almost 200 m (660 ft) in diameter. It is surrounded by a grassy bank averaging almost 6 m (20 ft) in width and 4.5 m (15 ft) in height. Bones from a Stone Age burial were found under the dolmen in the centre. During the 18th century the ring was a popular venue for horse races.

☷ Stormont

Newtownards Rd, 8 km (5 miles) SE of city centre. ⬤ to the public. 📷 by arrangement only.

Built between 1928 and 1932, at a cost of £1,250,000, Stormont was designed to house the Northern Ireland Parliament. The huge Anglo-Palladian mass of Portland stone and Mourne granite stands at the end of a majestic avenue, 1.6 km (1 mile) long, bordered by parkland. A statue of Lord Carson (see p48) stands near the front entrance.

Since the parliament was disbanded in 1972, the building has been used as government offices. Its future depends very much on the outcome of the ongoing peace process. The debating chamber was badly damaged in a fire in 1994.

Stormont in its parkland setting outside Belfast

Ulster Folk and Transport Museum 28

Cultra, near Holywood, Co Down.
📞 028 9042 8428. 🚋 🚌 ○ *daily.*
● *24–26 Dec.* 🎫 *(free for the disabled).* ♿

Dozens of old buildings, including flax-, corn- and sawmills, have been plucked from the Ulster countryside and re-erected in this absorbing folk park. Demonstrations of traditional crafts, industries and farming methods are given all year round.

The A2 road splits the folk museum from the transport section. This is dominated by a hangar that houses the Irish Railway Collection. The smaller Transport Gallery exhibits machinery made in Ulster, including a saloon carriage from the tram service that ran from Portrush to Giant's Causeway *(see pp356–7)*. Of particular note is a test model of the spectacularly unsuccessful De Lorean car, made in the early 1980s with a huge government subsidy. There's also a popular exhibit on another ill-fated construction – the *Titanic*. It's best to allow half a day to take in most of the attractions.

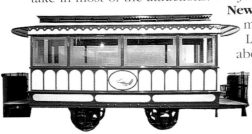

1883 tram carriage at the Ulster Folk and Transport Museum

Ards Peninsula 29

Co Down. 🚋 🚌 *to Bangor.* ℹ *34 Quay St, Bangor (028 9127 0069).*

The peninsula – and some of Northern Ireland's finest scenery – begins east of Belfast at **Bangor**. This resort town has a modern marina and some well-known yacht clubs. A little way south is **Donaghadee**, from where boats sail to the three **Copeland Islands**. These are now populated only by seabirds, as the last human

Scrabo Tower, a prominent landmark of the Ards Peninsula

residents left in the 1940s. **Ballycopeland Windmill** (1784), Northern Ireland's only working windmill, stands on a small hill a little further south, near the town of Millisle.

Just across the peninsula is **Newtownards**, on the even more stunning Strangford Lough side. On a hill above the town is the pleasantly shaded **Scrabo Country Park**. In the park stands **Scrabo Tower**, built in 1857 as a memorial to the third Marquess of Londonderry. The tower's 122 steps lead to a great view of Strangford Lough.

Past the grounds of **Mount Stewart House** *(see pp378–9)* is the hamlet of Greyabbey, with its antique shops and Cistercian abbey ruins. Founded in 1193, **Grey Abbey** was used as a parish church until the 17th century. It is idyllically set in lush meadows by a stream and some of its features, particularly the finely carved west doorway, are well preserved.

On the tip of the peninsula, **Portaferry** overlooks the Strangford Narrows (which is stunning at sunset) across from the Lecale Peninsula *(see p382)*. Portaferry's large aquarium, **Exploris**, displays the surprising diversity of marine life in the Irish Sea and Strangford Lough.

🏚 **Ballycopeland Windmill**
On B172 1.6 km (1 mile) W of Millisle.
📞 028 9186 1413. ○ *Easter–Sep: Tue–Sun & public hols.* 🎫

🏚 **Scrabo Country Park**
Near Newtownards. 📞 028 9181 1491. ○ *daily.* **Tower** ○ *Jun–Oct: Sat–Thu; Nov–May: public hols.*

🏛 **Grey Abbey**
Greyabbey village. 📞 028 4278 8585. ○ *Apr–Sep: Tue–Sun.* 🎫 ♿

🐠 **Exploris**
Castle Street, Portaferry. 📞 028 4272

Ballycopeland Windmill, which dates back to 1784

Mount Stewart House 30

See pp378–9.

Hillsborough 31

Co Down. 🚶 2,600. 🚌 ℹ️ *The Square (028 9268 9717).*

DOTTED WITH antique shops and restaurants, this showpiece Georgian town lies less than 16 km (10 miles) from Belfast. Its most impressive building is the massive **Hillsborough Castle**, where visiting dignitaries to Northern Ireland stay. Though not open to the public, its elaborate wrought-iron gates and coat of arms are worth seeing.

Across from the 18th-century Market House in the town square, and next to the pleasant Forest Park, is **Hillsborough Fort**. An artillery fort dating from 1650, it was remodelled in the 18th century for feasts held by the descendants of Arthur Hill, founder of the town.

⚓ Hillsborough Fort
Access from town square or car park at Forest Park. 📞 *028 9268 3285.* ⏰ *Tue–Sun (pm).*

Downpatrick 32

Co Down. 🚶 10,300. 🚌 ℹ️ *74 Market St (028 4461 2233).* ⛴ *Sat.*

WERE IT NOT for its strong links with St Patrick, Downpatrick would attract few visitors. The Protestant **Down Cathedral**, high on the Hill of Down, dates in its present form from the early 19th century – many previous incarnations have been razed to the ground. In the churchyard is a well-worn 10th-century cross and the reputed burial place of St Patrick, marked by a granite slab (placed here this century) with the simple inscription "Patric". **Down County Museum**, which is housed in the 18th-century Old County Gaol, features refurbished cells and exhibits relating to St Patrick, while close by is the **Mound of Down**, a large Norman motte and bailey.

Terraced houses in the town of Hillsborough

🏛 Down County Museum
The Mall. 📞 *028 4461 5218.* ⏰ *Jun–Aug: daily (Sat & Sun: pm only); Sep–May: Tue–Sat (Sat: pm only).* ⏺ *25 & 26 Dec.*

ENVIRONS: There are several sights associated with St Patrick on the outskirts of Downpatrick. **Struell Wells**, believed to be a former pagan place of worship that the saint blessed, has a ruined church, 17th-century bath houses and good potential for a picnic. Further out and to the north at **Saul**, where St Patrick landed and began his Irish mission in 432, is a small memorial church.

The nearby hill of **Slieve Patrick** is an important place of pilgrimage and has a granite figure of the saint at its summit. An open-air mass is celebrated here every June.

Not far from the banks of the River Quoile is the Cistercian **Inch Abbey**, founded by John de Courcy in about 1180. Its attractive marshland setting is probably more memorable than its scant remains, but it's worth a visit nonetheless.

🏰 Inch Abbey
5 km (3 miles) NW of Downpatrick. ⏰ *Apr–Sep: Tue–Sun.* 📷

THE LIFE OF ST PATRICK

Little hard information is known about St Patrick, the patron saint of Ireland, but he was probably not the first missionary to visit the country – a certain Palladius was sent by Pope Celestine in 431. Most stories tell that Patrick was kidnapped from Britain by pirates and brought to Ireland to tend sheep. From here he escaped to France to study Christianity. In 432, he sailed to Saul in County Down, where he quickly converted the local chieftain. He then travelled throughout the island convincing many other Celtic tribes of the truth of the new religion. The fact that Ireland has no snakes is explained by a legend that St Patrick drove them all into the sea.

19th-century engraving showing St Patrick banishing all snakes from Ireland

Mount Stewart House 30

**Lord Castlereagh
(1769–1822)**

THIS GRAND 19TH-CENTURY HOUSE has a splendid interior, but it is the magnificent gardens which are the main attraction. These were planted only in the 1920s, but the exotic plants and trees have thrived in the area's subtropical microclimate. Now owned by the National Trust, Mount Stewart used to belong to the London-derry family, the most famous of whom was Lord Castlereagh, British Foreign Secretary from 1812 until his death in 1822.

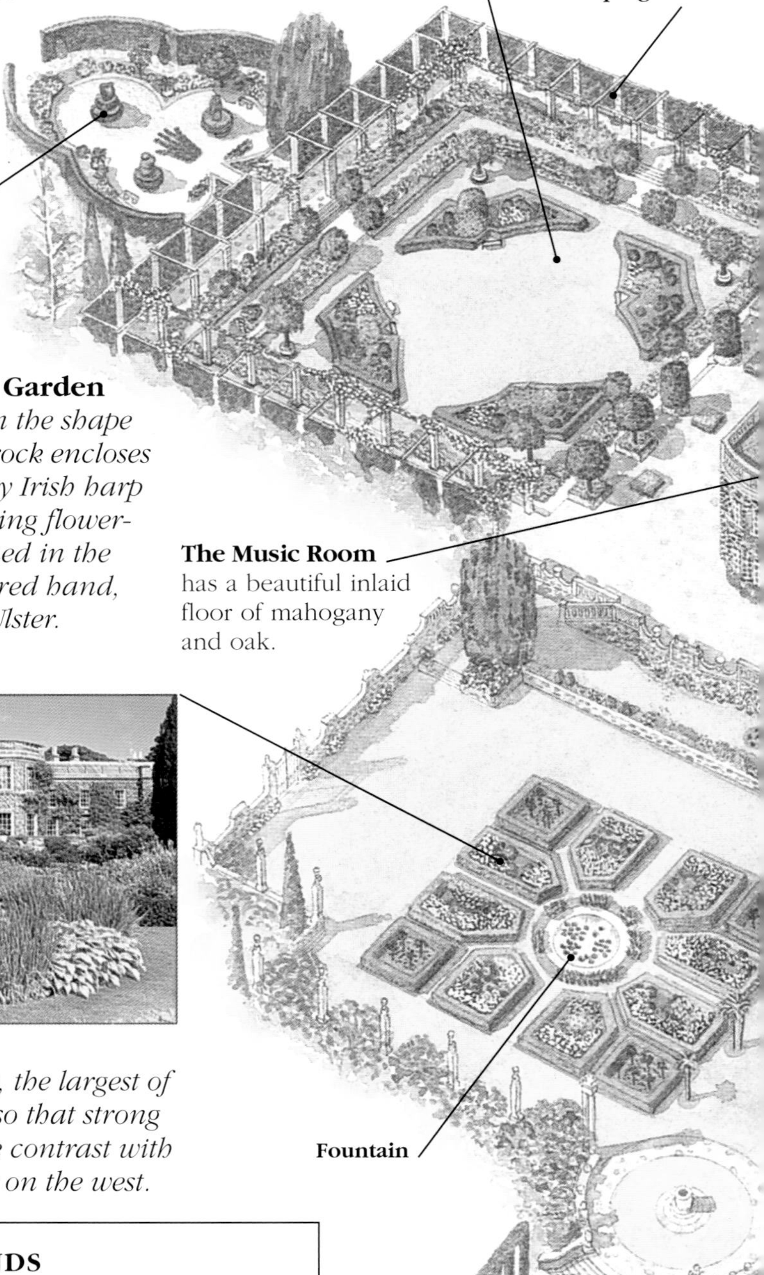

The Sunk Garden comprises symmetrical beds which in summer are full of rich blue, yellow and orange flowers; complemented by purple foliage.

Stone pergola

★ Shamrock Garden
A yew hedge in the shape of a shamrock encloses this topiary Irish harp and a striking flower-bed designed in the form of a red hand, emblem of Ulster.

The Music Room has a beautiful inlaid floor of mahogany and oak.

Italian Garden
The flowers in the Italian Garden, the largest of the formal gardens, are planted so that strong oranges and reds on the east side contrast with the softer pinks, whites and blues on the west.

Fountain

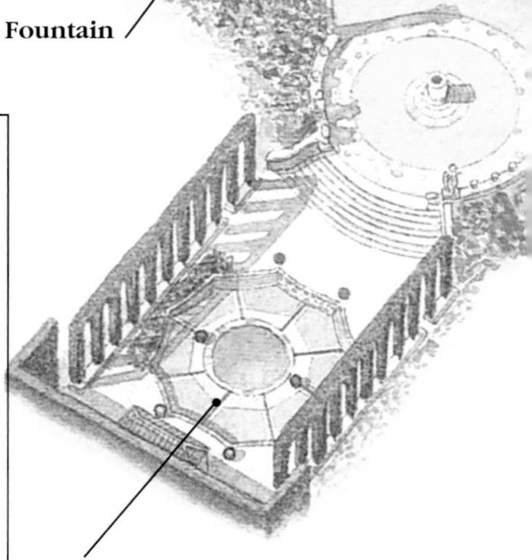

THE TEMPLE OF THE WINDS

This banqueting pavilion looks over Strangford Lough to the east of the house. It was built in 1785 by James "Athenian" Stuart, a renowned pioneer of Neo-Classical architecture, who took his inspiration from the Tower of the Winds in Athens. Restored in the 1960s and now being worked on once more, the building's finest features are the spiral staircase and the upper room's plasterwork ceiling and exquisite inlaid floor.

The Spanish Garden is framed by a neat arcade of clipped cypress trees.

★ **Hambletonian by George Stubbs**
*This picture of the celebrated racehorse at Newmarket,
painted in 1799, hangs halfway up the main staircase.*

VISITORS' CHECKLIST

3 km (2 miles) N of Greyabbey,
Co Down. 📞 *028 4278 8387.*
🚌 *from Belfast.* **House** ◻ *Apr
& Oct: 1–6pm Sat & Sun;
May–Sep: 1–6pm Wed–Mon.*
Temple ◻ *Apr–Oct: 2–5pm Sat
& Sun.* **Gardens** ◻ *Mar: 2–5pm
Sun; Apr–Sep: 11am–6pm daily;
Oct: 11am–6pm Sat & Sun.* 📷
🚫 *in house.* ♿ 🎞 💻

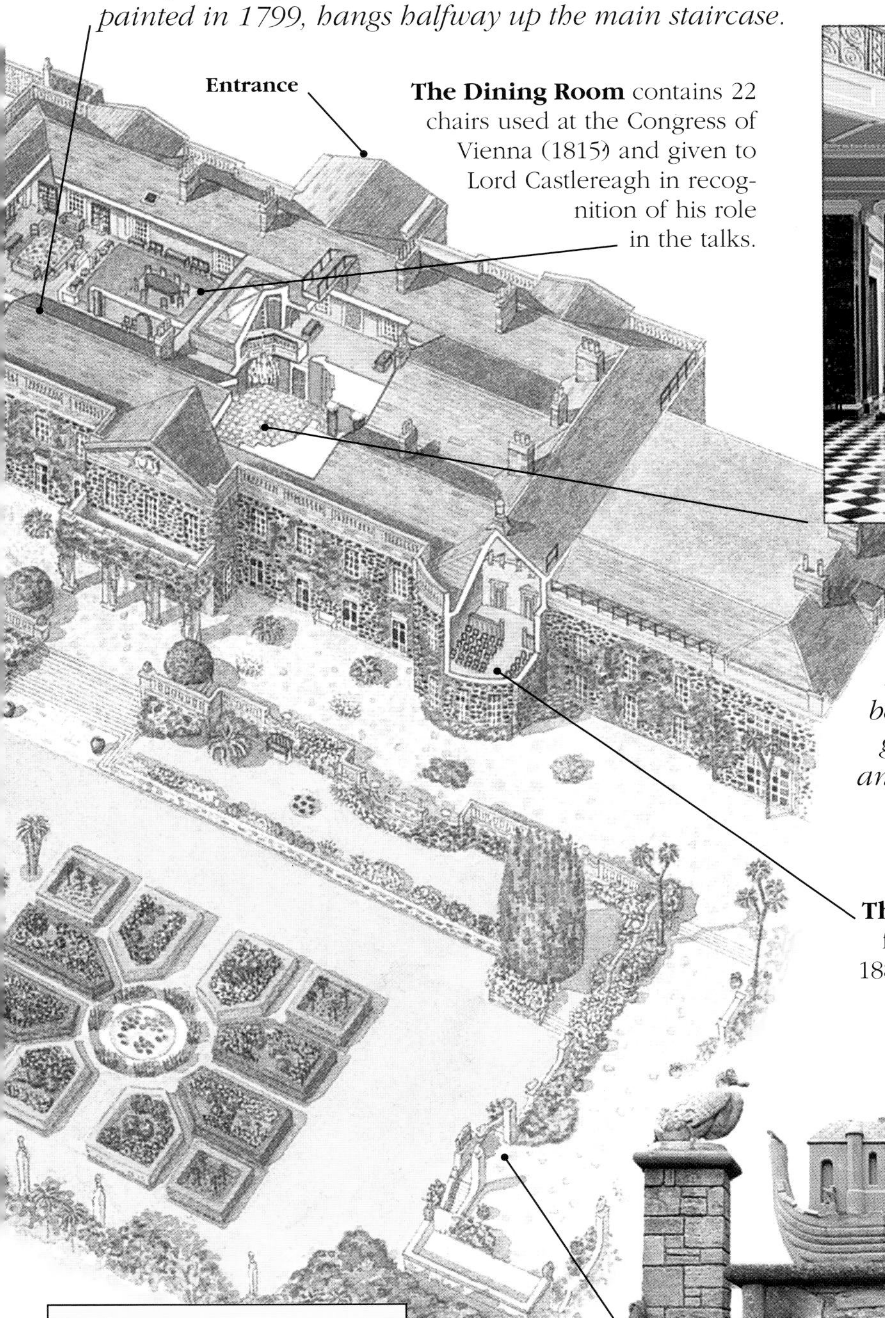

Entrance

The Dining Room contains 22
chairs used at the Congress of
Vienna (1815) and given to
Lord Castlereagh in recog-
nition of his role
in the talks.

Entrance Hall
*The most austere
room in the house,
this hall features Ionic
stone pillars which have
been painted to resemble
green marble. It is lit by
an impressive glass dome.*

The Chapel, converted
from a sitting room in
1884, is still used by the
Londonderry family.

STAR FEATURES

★ **Dodo Terrace**

★ **Shamrock Garden**

★ **Hambletonian by
George Stubbs**

★ **Dodo Terrace**
*The stone dodos and ark on this terrace relate
to the Ark Club, a social circle set up by Lady
Londonderry in London during World War I.
Each member was given an animal nickname.*

The tranquil countryside of County Antrim ▷

Lady Bangor's Gothic boudoir in Castle Ward on the Lecale Peninsula

Lecale Peninsula ③③

Co Down. 🚌 *to Ardglass.* ℹ️
Downpatrick (028 4461 2233).

A GOOD WAY to get to this part
of County Down is to take
the short but scenic car ferry
from Portaferry on the Ards
Peninsula to Strangford. Just
outside this tiny port is **Castle
Ward**, the intriguing estate of
Lord and Lady Bangor, who
seemed to argue about everything – including the design
of their mansion, built in the
1760s. His choice, Palladian,
can be seen at the front, while
her favourite Gothic style
influences the garden façade.
Likewise, the interior is a mix
of Classical and Gothic fantasy.
Look out for Lady Bangor's
cluttered boudoir, with its
extravagant fan-vaulted ceiling
based on Henry VIII's chapel
in Westminster Abbey. Around
the extensive grounds are fine
gardens, gentle walking trails
and a lakeside farmyard with
a working corn mill.
   About 4 km (2.5 miles) south
of Strangford, the A2 passes
Kilclief Castle, which dates
from the 15th century and is
one of the oldest tower
houses *(see p24)* in Ireland.
The road continues to
Ardglass, which is now a
small fishing village but was
once Ulster's busiest harbour.
A cluster of castles was constructed between the 14th and
16th centuries to protect the
port, of which six remain. Only
one of these is open to the

public, **Jordan's Castle**. The
finest view in the area is from
St John's Point, 6 km (3.5
miles) southwest of Ardglass,
which provides a sweeping
panorama over Dundrum Bay.

🏛️ **Castle Ward**
On A25, 2.5 km (1.5 miles) W of
Strangford. 📞 *028 4488 1204.*
House ◯ *May–Aug: Fri–Wed (pm
only); Apr, Sep & Oct: Sat, Sun & public
hols.* 🔲 ♿ **Grounds** ◯ *daily.*
🔲 *for car park.*
⛪ **Jordan's Castle**
Ardglass. ◯ *May–Aug: Tue–Sun.* 🔲

Castlewellan Forest Park ③④

Main St, Castlewellan, Co Down. 📞
028 4477 8664. ◯ *daily.* 🔲 *for car
park.*

T HE OUTSTANDING FEATURE of
Castlewellan Forest Park,
in the foothills of the Mourne
Mountains, is its magnificent
arboretum. This has grown far
beyond the

original walled garden, begun
in 1740, and now comprises
hothouses, dwarf conifer beds
and a rhododendron wood.
   Elsewhere in the park are a
19th-century Scottish baronial-
style castle (now a conference
centre), a lake and pleasant
woodlands; these are at their
most colourful in autumn.

Mountains of Mourne ③⑤

Co Down. 🚆 *to Newry.* 🚌 *to
Newcastle.* ℹ️ *10 Central
Promenade, Newcastle (028 4472
2222).*

T HESE MOUNTAINS occupy just
a small corner of County
Down, with no more than a
dozen peaks surpassing 600 m
(2,000 ft), and yet they attract
thousands of visitors each year.
   Only one road of any size,
the B27 between Kilkeel and
Hilltown, crosses the Mournes,
making this ideal territory for
walkers. A popular but tough
trail runs from **Newcastle**, the
main gateway to the area, up
to the peak of **Slieve Donard**:
at 848 m (2,796 ft), this is the
highest mountain in the range.
Part of the route follows the
Mourne Wall, which was
erected in 1904–22 to enclose
the catchment area of the two
reservoirs in the **Silent Valley**.
   Over 20 other short hikes are
described in the *St Patrick's
Vale Walks* booklet, available
from local tourist offices. These
range from easy strolls around
Rostrevor Forest to rather more
arduous treks up Slieve Muck
and other Mourne peaks.
   Some 35 km (22 miles) north
of Newcastle, the **Legananny
Dolmen** *(see p36)* is one of
the finest and most photographed ancient sights in the
country.

Rounded peaks of the Mountains of Mourne

A Tour of the Mourne Coast 36

NEWCASTLE, where, in the words of the 19th-century songwriter Percy French, "the Mountains of Mourne sweep down to the sea", makes a good base from which to explore this area. Driving up and down the dipping roads of the Mournes is one of the highlights of a trip to Northern Ireland. Along the coast, the road skirts between the foothills and the Irish Sea, providing lovely views and linking a variety of fishing villages and historic castles. Heading inland, you pass through an emptier landscape of moorland, purple with heather. The Silent Valley, with a visitors' centre and well-marked paths, is the only area to have been developed especially for tourists.

Dundrum ②
The town is overlooked by the ruins of a Norman castle, and from the nearby bay you can see the mountains rising in the distance.

Tollymore Forest Park ③
This attractive park is dotted with follies like the Gothic Gate that formed part of the original 18th-century estate.

Spelga Dam ④
There are stunning views north from the Spelga Dam over the Mourne foothills.

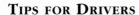

Rostrevor with Slieve Martin behind

Newcastle ①
A popular resort since the early 19th century, Newcastle has a promenade overlooking a sweeping, sandy beach.

Silent Valley ⑦
The valley is closed to traffic, but you can walk to the top of Ben Crom Mountain from the car park, or in summer go by bus.

Rostrevor ⑤
This tranquil and leafy Victorian resort nestles below the peak of Slieve Martin, on the shores of Carlingford Lough.

Green Castle ⑥
Erected in the 13th century, Green Castle lies at the end of a single track road on a rocky outcrop at the entrance to Carlingford Lough.

TIPS FOR DRIVERS

Length: 85 km (53 miles).
Stopping-off points: Newcastle has the biggest choice of pubs and restaurants. Dundrum, Annalong, Kilkeel and Rostrevor all have pubs, and a café opens in the Silent Valley in summer. The Spelga Dam and Tollymore Forest Park are good picnic spots.

0 kilometres   5

0 miles   3

KEY

▬▬	Tour route
-----	Other roads
✹	Viewpoint

Map labels: BELFAST, NEWRY, Slieve Donard, Slieve Muck, MOUNTAINS OF MOURNE, Slieve Martin, Annalong, Kilkeel, Carlingford Lough, B180, B27, B25, A2

Ireland's Golf Courses

IRELAND IS INTERNATIONALLY renowned for its beautiful and well-designed golf courses, in particular the links courses with their views of the Irish coastline. Inland, there are many scenic parkland courses, often built in the grounds of historic buildings. The listings below represent most of the golf courses in Ireland. The prices shown are in Irish punts and are a guideline only. It is advisable to call ahead for full details and to make reservations, especially during the summer season.

DUBLIN

Balbriggan Golf Club

Black Hall, Balbriggan, Co. Dublin. ℂ (01) 841 2229. FAX (01) 841 3927. ◯ Mon, Wed, Thu, Fri. €€ Holes: 18. Par: 71. ¶ ♉ Ⓣ ▨ MC, V.

A championship parkland course with views of the Mourne Mountains and the east coast. Group discounts are available to visitors, by prior arrangement.

Balcarrick Golf Club

Corballis, Donabate, Co. Dublin. ℂ (01) 843 6957. FAX (01) 843 6228. ◯ Daily. €€ Holes: 18. Par: 73. ¶ ♉ ⛫ Ⓣ

Located 15 minutes from Dublin airport, this parkland course has scenic views of Malahide Bay. It also has some extremely challenging holes. Visitors can get a group discount.

Beaverstown Golf Club

Donabate, Co. Dublin. ℂ (01) 843 6721. FAX (01) 843 5059. @ bgc@iol.ie ◯ Mon, Tue, Thu, Fri, Sat. €€ Holes: 18. Par: 71. ¶ ♉ ⛫ Ⓣ

Situated to the north of the county, this parkland course is built on an old orchard overlooking the estuary and offers a testing round of golf. Group discounts are offered.

Blanchardstown Golf Centre

Mulhuddart, Co. Dublin. ℂ (01) 821 3206. FAX (01) 821 7431. ◯ Daily. €€ Holes: 18. Par: 54. ⛳

A parkland course in an idyllic setting 3 km (2 miles) from the town of Mulhuddart, plus a large practice range and pitch and putt.

Castle Golf Club

Woodside Drive, Rathfarnham, Dublin 14. ℂ (01) 490 4207. FAX (01) 492 0264. ◯ Mon–Fri (by appointment). €€€ Holes: 18. Par: 73. ¶ ♉ ⛫ Ⓣ

Located 8 km (5 miles) south of Dublin city centre, this parkland course, designed by Henry Colt nearly a century ago, has wonderful views of the Dublin Mountains and is a bracing place to wield one's irons.

Citywest Hotel & Golf Course

Staggart, Co. Dublin. ℂ (01) 401 0900. FAX (01) 401 0937. @ info@citywest-hotel.iol.ie ◯ Daily. €€€€ Holes: 18. Par: 71. ¶ ♉ ⛫ ⛳ Ⓣ ▨ AE, DC, MC, V.

A parkland course designed by Christy O'Connor Jnr, Ireland's leading designer of golf courses. It played host to the Irish Masters in 1994, and the Ladies Open in 1996. Tuition is available to visitors, and there are discounts for groups.

Clontarf Golf Club

Donnycarney House, Malahide Road, Dublin 3. ℂ (01) 833 1892. FAX (01) 833 1933. ◯ Daily (Mon is Ladies' Day). €€€ Holes: 18. Par: 69. ¶ ♉ ⛫ Ⓣ

This pleasant, well-manicured parkland course is situated 4 km (2.5 miles) from the city centre (the closest golf course to a city centre anywhere in Europe). Tuition is offered to visitors, and group discounts are available on request.

Corballis Golf Links

Corballis, Donabate, Co. Dublin. ℂ (01) 843 6583. @ corballis@golfdublin.com ◯ Daily. €€ Holes: 18. Par: 64. ¶ ⛫ ⛳

This links course with views of the beach was designed by Alan Carroll to championship standard. The greens at this course are thought to be the finest in the country.

Corrstown Golf Club

Corrstown, Killsalaghan, Co. Dublin. ℂ (01) 864 0533. FAX (01) 864 0537. ◯ Mon–Fri. €€ Holes: 9, 18. Par: 35, 71. ¶ ♉ ⛫ ⛳ ▨ AE, DC, MC, V.

Both these courses are parkland, with rivers and orchards and a number of water hazards. The 18th hole is an island green.

Deer Park Hotel & Golf Course

Howth, Co. Dublin. ℂ (01) 832 3487. FAX (01) 839 2405. ◯ Daily. €€ Holes: 9, 9, 18. Par: 36, 35, 72. ¶ ♉ ⛫

Three different courses, all parkland, in the grounds of Howth Castle, with spectacular views of Dublin Bay and the coast.

Dun Laoghaire Golf Club

Eglinton Park, Tivoli Road, Dun Laoghaire, Co. Dublin. ℂ (01) 280 3916. FAX (01) 280 4868. @ dlgc@iol.ie ◯ Mon, Tue, Wed, Fri, Sun. €€€ Holes: 18. Par: 69. ¶ ♉ ⛫ ⛳ Ⓣ ▨ AE, DC, MC, V.

Tuition is offered to visitors at this parkland course 11 km (7 miles) south of Dublin city centre and 1.6 km (1 mile) from the ferry.

Edmondstown Golf Club

Edmondstown Road, Rathfarnham, Dublin 16. ℂ (01) 493 1082. FAX (01) 493 3152. ◯ Mon, Thu, Fri, Sat. €€€ Holes: 18. Par: 70. ¶ ♉ ⛫ ⛳ Ⓣ ▨ AE, DC, MC, V.

This parkland course has a water feature and lies in the foothills of the Dublin mountains, 11 km (7 miles) south of the city centre.

Elmgreen Golf Centre

Castleknock, Dublin 15. ℂ (01) 820 0797. FAX (01) 822 6668. @ elmgreen@golfdublin.com ◯ Daily. €€ Holes: 18. Par: 71. ¶ ♉ ⛫

This is the largest public golf centre within 20 minutes of Dublin city centre. Elmgreen is in fact only 5 minutes from the city.

Glencullen Golf Course

Glencullen, Co. Dublin. ℂ (01) 294 0898. FAX (01) 295 2895. ◯ Mon–Fri (Tue is Ladies Day). €€ Holes: 9. Par: 69. ⛫ Ⓣ

Designed by Des Smyth, this parkland course has fantastic views of Dublin Bay, sand-based greens and two lakes. Tuition is available.

Hollystown Golf

Glencullen, Co. Dublin. ℂ (01) 820 7444. FAX (01) 820 7447. @ info@hollystown.ie ◯ Daily. Holes: 27. Par: 72. ¶ ♉ ⛫ ⛳ Ⓣ ▨ MC, V.

A rich parkland course with stately trees, streams and ponds. The course also has a new pavilion and offers tuition to visitors.

Holywood Lakes Golf Club

Ballyboughal, Co. Dublin. ℂ (01) 843 3407. FAX (01) 843 3002. ◯ Mon–Fri. €€ Holes: 18. Par: 72. ¶ ♉ ⛫ Ⓣ ▨ AE, MC, V.

This parkland course, 15 minutes north of Dublin airport, has magnificent views of the city centre. Do not be fooled by its beauty; it is certainly no push-over. It also boasts the longest par 5 in Ireland. Group discounts are usually available.

Island Golf Club

Corballis, Donabate, Co. Dublin. ℂ (01) 843 6205. FAX (01) 843 6860. @ islandgc@iol.ie ◯ Mon, Tue, Fri. €€€€ Holes: 18. Par: 71. ¶ ♉ ⛫ ⛳ Ⓣ ▨ MC, V.

A friendly welcome is always given at this links course, which has good views of the Fingal area of County Dublin, and was host to the Irish Close Championship in 1998 and the PGA Irish Open in 1999. Tuition and group discounts are available to visitors.

Lutrellstown Castle Golf & Country Club

Castleknock, Dublin 15. ℂ (01) 808 9988. FAX (01) 808 9989. @ golf@luttrellstown.ie ◯ Daily. €€€€ Holes: 18. Par: 72. ¶ ♉ ⛫ ⛳ ▨ AE, DC, MC, V.

Visitor tuition and group discounts are available at this parkland course to the west of Dublin city centre. In a magnificent woodland setting, the course played host to the Guardian Irish Open in 1997 and is renowned for its exceptionally well-kept greens.

Portmarnock Hotel & Golf Links

Strand Road, Portmarnock, Co. Dublin. ℂ (01) 846 1800. FAX (01) 846 1077. ◯ Daily. €€€€ Holes: 18. Par: 72. ¶ ♉ ⛫ ⛳ Ⓣ ▨ AE, MC, V.

Set on the Portmarnock Peninsula, this links course is a real challenge, subject as it is to changeable weather conditions. The championship course, one of the finest in Europe, has a most welcoming clubhouse offering group discounts on request.

St Margaret's Golf & Country Club

St Margaret's, Co. Dublin. ℂ (01) 864 0400. FAX (01) 864 0289. @ sales@stmargarets.com ◯ Daily. €€€€ Holes: 18. Par: 72. ¶ ♉ ⛫ ⛳ Ⓣ ▨ AE, DC, MC, V.

A testing parkland course, the 6th green is very closely based on the 12th green at Augusta in the USA. Located 15 minutes from Dublin city.

SOUTHEAST IRELAND

Bodenstown Golf Club

Sallins, Co. Kildare. (045) 897096. FAX (045) 898126. Mon–Fri. ££ Holes: 18, 18. Par: 72, 72.

A parkland course, just 20 minutes from Newlandscross. The main course is open to visitors on weekdays only, the smaller of the two courses is open every day.

Callan Golf Club

Geraldine, Callan, Co. Kilkenny. (056) 25136. Mon–Sat. ££ Holes: 18. Par: 72.

This parkland course has water features on three holes, and mature spinneys. Situated 1.6 km (1 mile) from Callan town centre, group discounts are available to visitors.

Carlow Golf Club

Deerpark, Carlow, Co. Carlow. (0503) 31695. FAX (0503) 40065. @ carlowgolfclub@tinet.ie Mon–Fri. £££ Holes: 18. Par: 70. MC, V.

Set in a former wild deer park, this parkland course has undulating terrain, elevated tees and is playable all year round. Just north of Carlow, the course offers visitors tuition and group discounts.

Castlecomer Golf Club

Drumgoole, Castlecomer, Co. Kilkenny. (056) 41139. FAX (056) 41139. Mon–Sat. ££ Holes: 9. Par: 71.

This parkland course is one of the longest 9-hole courses in Europe. Known for its friendliness to visitors, Castlecomer is a true test of skill. Group discounts and tuition are offered.

Castlewarden Golf & Country Club

Castlewarden, Straffan, Co. Kildare. (01) 458 9254. FAX (01) 843 6860. Mon, Thu, Fri. ££ Holes: 18. Par: 72.

A very enjoyable and challenging parkland course, with an original walled green that now functions as a putting green. Visitors can have tuition, and group discounts are available on request.

Charlesland Golf Club

Greystones, Co. Wicklow. (01) 287 4350. FAX (01) 287 4360. @ charlesland@tinet.ie Daily. £££ Holes: 18. Par: 72. AE, MC, V.

In the shadow of Sugarloaf Mountain, south of Greystones town, this parkland course is a testing but fair golfing experience. Tuition and group discounts are offered to visitors.

Coolattin Golf Club

Coolattin St, Shillelagh, Co. Wicklow. (055) 29125. FAX (055) 29125. Mon–Fri. ££ Holes: 18. Par: 70.

A parkland course full of mature oaks and redwoods, with Coolattin House, former seat of the Earl of Fitzwilliam, at its centre. Group discount and tuition are available on request.

Courtown Golf Club

Kiltennel, Gorey, Co. Wexford. (055) 25166. FAX (055) 25553. Daily (by appointment). ££ Holes: 18. Par: 71. AE, DC, MC, V.

This is a heavily wooded parkland course with spectacular views of the sea. Situated just 5 km (3 miles) from Gorey, the clubhouse has an excellent bar and restaurant. Tuition and group discounts are available to visitors by arrangement.

Craddockstown Golf Club

Blessington Road, Naas, Co. Kildare. (045) 897610. FAX (045) 896989. Thu, Fri. ££ Holes: 18. Par: 71.

This is a challenging but fun parkland course. Each hole has its own feature and shape to test even the most experienced – and most stoic – of golfers.

Druids Glen Golf Club

Woodstock House, Newtownmountkennedy, Co. Wicklow. (01) 287 3600. FAX (01) 287 3699. @ druids@indigo.ie Daily. £££££ Holes: 18. Par: 71. AE, DC, MC, V.

A championship parkland course that has hosted the Murphy's Irish Open since 1996. Located 32 km (20 miles) south of Dublin, tuition and group discounts are offered.

Dungarvan Golf Club

Knocknagranagh, Dungarvan, Co. Waterford. (058) 43310/41605. FAX (058) 44113. @ dungarvangolf@cablesurf.com Daily. ££ Holes: 18. Par: 72. AE, DC, MC, V.

Designed with 7 lakes and man-made hazards to test all levels of golfer, this championship parkland course is located east of Dungarvan. Tuition and group discounts are available.

Dunmore East Golf Club

Dunmore East, Co. Waterford. (051) 383151. FAX (058) 383151. Daily. ££ Holes: 18. Par: 72. MC, V.

A seaside parkland course with idyllic surroundings, visitors can enjoy a round of stimulating and challenging golf. Group discounts and tuition are available on request.

Enniscorthy Golf Club

Knockmarshall, Enniscorthy, Co. Wexford. (054) 33191. FAX (054) 37637. Mon–Fri. ££ Holes: 18. Par: 72. MC, V.

This is a hidden gem of a course, with breathtaking scenery and testing features. Visitors are offered tuition and group discounts.

The European Club

Brittas Bay, Co. Wicklow. (0404) 47415. FAX (0404) 47449. Daily. ££££ Holes: 18. Par: 71. MC, V.

A links course with difficult rugged dunes, frustratingly deep bunkers and undulating greens, the European Club has wonderful views of the coast.

Faithlegg Golf Club

Faithlegg, Co. Waterford. (051) 382241. FAX (051) 382664. Daily. £££ Holes: 18. Par: 72. MC, V.

Set on the tranquil banks of the River Suir, this parkland course was rated among the top ten courses in Britain and Ireland in 1994. Group discounts and tuition are available on request.

Goldcoast Golf Club

Ballinacourty, Dungarvan, Co. Waterford. (058) 44055. Daily. ££ Holes: 18. Par: 72.

A parkland course bordered by the Atlantic Ocean with unrivalled views of Dungarvan Bay and the Conereagh mountains. It is said to be the most scenic course in southeastern Ireland. Group discounts are available.

The K Club

Straffan, Co. Kildare. (01) 601 7300. FAX (01) 601 7399. @ golf@kclub.ie Daily. £££££ Holes: 18. Par: 72. AE, DC, MC, V.

Home to the Smurfit European Open from 1995 to 1999, this parkland course, designed by the legendary Arnold Palmer, is set in picturesque Kildare woodland. Just 30 minutes from Dublin airport, visitors are offered tuition and group discounts.

Kilcoole Golf Club

Newcastle Road, Kilcoole, Co. Wicklow. (01) 287 2066. FAX (01) 287 1803. Daily (by appointment). ££ Holes: 9. Par: 70.

This parkland course has a superb island green and a tranquil location. Located five minutes south of Greystones. Group discounts are available.

Kilkea Castle Golf Club

Castledermot, Co. Kildare. (0503) 45555. FAX (0503) 45505. @ kilkeagolfclub@aircom.net Mon, Thu. ££ Holes: 18. Par: 71. AE, DC, MC, V.

A cleverly designed, almost playful, parkland course, in the quite magnificent setting of the oldest castle in Ireland. Tuition and group discounts are offered.

Kilkenny Golf Club

Glendine, Kilkenny, Co. Kilkenny. (056) 65400. FAX (056) 23593. Mon–Fri. ££ Holes: 18. Par: 71. MC, V.

A championship parkland course, full of devilish and intriguing nooks and crevices, maintained in excellent tournament condition, just 10 minutes from the city centre. Tuition and group discounts are offered to visitors.

Killeen Golf Club

Kill, Co. Kildare. (045) 866003. FAX (045) 875881. @ admin@killeengc.ie Daily. ££ Holes: 18. Par: 70. MC, V.

Peace, tranquillity and abundant wildlife surround this beautiful and relaxing parkland course just 20 minutes south of Dublin. Almost a holiday in itself.

Knockanally Golf & Country Club

Donadea, North Kildare. (045) 869322. FAX (045) 869322. Daily. £££ Holes: 18. Par: 72.

Home to the Irish Professional Matchplay Championships from 1987 to 1989 and to the Irish Club Professional Championship in 1994, this parkland course is situated on the east coast. Tuition and discounts are available.

Mount Juliet Golf Club

Thomastown, Co. Kilkenny. (056) 73000. FAX (056) 73019. Daily. £££££ Holes: 18. Par: 72. AE, DC, MC, V.

This wonderful parkland course, designed by Jack Nicklaus, played host to the Irish Open from 1993 to 1995. Visitors are offered tuition and group discount is available on request.

Mount Wolseley Golf & Country Club

Tullow, Co. Wicklow. (0503) 51675. FAX (0503) 52123. Daily. £££ Holes: 18. Par: 72. AE, DC, MC, V.

A testing championship parkland course set in the grounds of the Wolseley family's ancestral home and designed by Christy O'Connor Jnr. Tuition and group discounts are available.

New Ross Golf Club

Tinneranny, New Ross, Co. Wexford. (051) 421433. FAX (051) 420098. Mon–Sat. ££ Holes: 18. Par: 71.

This parkland course, 23 km (14 miles) from Waterford, has panoramic views of the surrounding hills and mountains. Group discounts are offered.

Old Conna Golf Club

Ferndale Road, Bray, Co. Wicklow. (01) 282 6055. FAX (01) 282 5611. Mon, Thu, Fri. £££ Holes: 18. Par: 72. AE, DC, MC, V.

A testing parkland course with spectacular views of the Irish Sea and Wicklow Mountains. Tuition is on offer to visitors.

Powerscourt Golf Club

Powerscourt Estate, Enniskerry, Co. Wicklow. (01) 204 6033. FAX (01) 276 1303. @ golfclub@powerscourt.ie Daily. ££££ Holes: 18. Par: 72. AE, MC, V.

This course contains some of Ireland's most beautiful parkland, with stunning views of the coast and Sugarloaf Mountain. Tuition and group discounts are available.

Rathsallagh Golf Club

Dunlavan, Co. Wicklow. (045) 403316. FAX (045) 403295. @ info@rathsallagh.com ◯ Daily. ££££ Holes: 18. Par: 72. MC, V.

An 81 ha (200 acre) lush parkland course, renowned for its magnificent trees and excellent greens. Group discounts and tuition are offered.

St Helen's Bay Golf & Country Club

Rosslare Harbour, Co. Wexford. (053) 33234. FAX (053) 33803. @ sthelens@iol.ie ◯ Daily. ££ Holes: 18. Par: 72. MC, V.

This course combines the best of parkland features with the smartness of a links course. A championship course designed by Philip Walton, it has great views of St Helen's Bay.

Tramore Golf Club

Newtown Hill, Tramore, Co. Waterford. (051) 386170. FAX (051) 390961. @ tragolf@iol.ie ◯ Mon–Fri. £££ Holes: 18. Par: 72. MC, V.

The clubhouse at this championship parkland course, designed by Captain HC Tippet, has a fine view of the Comeragh mountains.

Waterford Castle Golf & Country Club

The Island, Ballinakill, Co. Waterford. (051) 871633. FAX (051) 871634. @ golf@waterfordcastle.com ◯ Daily. £££ Holes: 18. Par: 72. MC, V.

This is Ireland's only true island course. Its mature plantations, sand-based greens and lakes provide a beautiful parkland setting.

CORK AND KERRY

Ardfert Golf Club

Sackville, Ardfert, Co. Kerry. (066) 713 4744. FAX (066) 713 4744. ◯ Daily. ££ Holes: 9. Par: 70.

An undulating parkland course situated in the historic village of Ardfert, north of Tralee. The course is suited to all levels, and tuition and group discounts are available.

Ballybunion Golf Club

Sandhill Road, Ballynunion, Co. Kerry. (068) 27146. FAX (068) 27387. @ bbgolfc@iol.ie ◯ Mon–Fri. ££££ Holes: 18, 18. Par: 71, 72. MC, V.

This famous championship links course is rated among the top ten in the world, with its huge sand dunes and splendid coastline. Tuition is offered to visitors.

Beaufort Golf Club

Churchtown, Beaufort, Killarney, Co. Kerry. (064) 44440. FAX (064) 44752. ◯ Daily. £££ Holes: 18. Par: 71. AE, MC, V.

Part of the Churchtown Estate, this scenic parkland course has an abundance of mature trees along its fairways. Located 11 km (7 miles) west of Killarney, the club offers tuition and group discounts to visitors.

Berehaven Golf Club

Millcove, Castletownbere, Co. Cork. (027) 70700. FAX (027) 70700. @ beara3@tinet.ie ◯ Daily. ££ Holes: 9. Par: 68. MC, V.

An all-year round links course situated on the shores of Bantry Bay, 3 km (2 miles) outside Castletownbere.

Castlegregory Golf & CountryClub

Stradbally, Castlegregory, Co. Kerry. (066) 713 9444. ◯ Daily. ££ Holes: 9. Par: 68.

This is one of the most scenic links golf courses in Ireland, located between Lough Gill and Brandon Bay on the northern side of the Dingle Peninsula. There is an abundance of wildlife around the course and the views from the fairways are breathtaking.

Charleville Golf Club

Smiths Road, Charleville, Co. Cork. (063) 81257. FAX (063) 81274. ◯ Daily. ££ Holes: 9, 18. Par: 72, 71.

There are two parkland courses at Charleville Golf Club – the 18-hole course is flat with many woodland areas, the hilly 9-hole course is more exposed with plenty of bunkers. Group discounts and tuition are available.

Cork Golf Club

Little Island, Co. Cork. (021) 353451. FAX (021) 353410. ◯ Mon, Tue, Wed, Fri. ££££ Holes: 18. Par: 72. AE, DC, MC, V.

This is one of the finest inland parkland courses in Ireland, situated 8 km (5 miles) east of Cork, off the N25 road. Visitors can take private tuition and obtain group discounts.

Dooks Golf Club

Glenbeigh, Co. Kerry. (066) 976 8205. FAX (066) 976 8476. @ office@dooks.com ◯ Mon–Fri. ££ Holes: 18. Par: 70. MC, V.

Opened in 1889, this beautiful links course is set on sand dunes at the head of Dingle Bay, between Killorgin and Glenbeigh. Group discounts are available.

Douglas Golf Club

Douglas, Co. Cork. (021) 895297. FAX (021) 895297. ◯ Mon, Wed, Thu, Fri. £££ Holes: 18. Par: 72.

Designed by Peter McEvoy, this parkland course is the best of its kind in County Cork. Located 5 km (3 miles) from Cork city, the club offers tuition and group discounts to visitors. Soft spikes must be worn.

Dunloe Golf Course

Gap of Dunloe, Killarney, Co. Kerry. (064) 44578. FAX (064) 44733. ◯ Daily. ££ Holes: 9. Par: 34. MC, V.

A parkland course in the Valley of the Gap of Dunloe, with spectacular views of the lakes and mountains of Killarney from the elevated tees and greens. Tuition and group discounts are available.

East Cork Golf Club

Gortacrue, Midleton, Co. Cork. (021) 633667. FAX (021) 613695. ◯ Mon–Fri. ££ Holes: 18. Par: 69.

The River Ownacurragh runs through this tree-lined parkland course, which offers a variety of golfing shots. Visitors can take advantage of private tuition.

Fermoy Golf Club

Corrin, Fermoy, Co. Cork. (025) 32694/31472. FAX (025) 33072. ◯ Daily. ££ Holes: 18. Par: 70.

Experts and novices alike will enjoy this challenging parkland course, located 3 km (2 miles) off the Cork–Dublin road. Tuition and group discounts are available to visitors.

Fota Island Golf Club

Carrigtwohill, Co. Cork. (021) 883700. FAX (021) 883713. @ fotagolfclub@iol.ie ◯ Daily. ££££ Holes: 18. Par: 71. AE, MC, V.

A traditional style parkland course, with pot bunkers and undulating greens, that has played host to three Irish Amateur Opens and the 1997 Smurfit Irish PGA Championship. Tuition and group discounts are offered. Soft spikes must be worn on the course.

Golf Chumann Ceann Sibeal Golf Club

Ballyferriter, Tralee, Co. Kerry. (066) 915 6255. FAX (066) 915 6409. @ dingogc@iol.ie ◯ Daily. £££ Holes: 18. Par: 72. MC, V.

This championship links course, situated 14 km (9 miles) west of Dingle, is the most westerly course in all Europe. Private tuition is available to visitors.

Harbour Point Golf Club

Clash Road, Little Island, Co. Cork. (021) 353094. FAX (021) 354408. ◯ Daily. ££ Holes: 18. Par: 72. MC, V.

A large parkland course with tree-lined fairways and testing greens, 10 km (6 miles) east of Cork city. Tuition and group discounts are offered.

Kanturk Golf Club

Fairyhill, Kanturk, Co. Cork. (029) 50534. FAX (029) 50534/ (087) 221 7510. ◯ Daily. ££ Holes: 18. Par: 72.

This parkland course is located in the picturesque heart of the Dunhallow region, just 1.6 km (1 mile) from Kanturk. The course is well-suited to visiting golfers, as it is rarely overcrowded and the green fees are very reasonable, with discounts available to groups.

Kenmare Golf Club

Kenmare, Co. Kerry. (064) 41291. FAX (064) 42061. ◯ Mon–Fri. ££ Holes: 18. Par: 71. MC, V.

A great golfing experience is to be had on this parkland course on the Cork–Kilgarvan Road, just outside Kenmare. Tuition and group discounts are available.

Killarney Golf Club

Mahoney's Point, Killarney, Co. Kerry. (064) 31034. FAX (064) 33065. @ reservations@killarney/golf.com ◯ Daily. £££ Holes: 18, 18, 18. Par: 72, 72, 73. AE, DC, MC, V.

This lakeside course, on the Ring of Kerry road out of Killarney, has mature woodlands and a backdrop of mountains. The course is flat and easy to walk. Tuition and group discounts are available to visitors.

Killorglin Golf Club

Stealroe, Killorglin, Co. Kerry. (066) 976 1979. FAX (066) 976 1437. @ kilgolf@iol.ie ◯ Daily. ££ Holes: 18. Par: 72. AE, DC, MC, V.

Designed by Eddie Hackett, this spectacular parkland course, located 20 minutes from Killarney, offers an irresistible challenge to all levels of golfer. Tuition and group discounts are offered.

Kinsale Golf Club

Farrangalway, Kinsale, Co. Cork. (021) 774722. FAX (021) 773114. ◯ Daily. £££ Holes: 9, 18. Par: 70, 71.

The 18-hole course at this parkland golf club is set in the lush meadowlands of the Bandon river valley. The challenging, hilly 9-hole course overlooks the Belgody River.

Lee Valley Golf & Country Club

Clashanure, Ovens, Co. Cork. (021) 733 1721. FAX (021) 733 1695. @ leevalleygolfclub@aircom.net ◯ Daily (by appointment). ££ Holes: 18. Par: 72. AE, DC, MC, V.

A championship parkland course in the Lee Valley, with water features and panoramic views of the surrounding countryside. Visitors are offered tuition and group discounts.

Lisselan Golf Course

Lisselan Estate, Clonakilty, Co. Cork. (023) 33249. FAX (023) 34605. ◯ Daily. ££ Holes: 6. Par: 69.

This charming parkland course is located 1.6 km (1 mile) south of Lismore Heritage Town. Group discounts are available.

Macroom Golf Club

Lackaduv, Macroom, Co. Cork. (026) 41072. FAX (026) 41391. ◯ Daily. ££ Holes: 18. Par: 72. MC, V.

Undulating tree-lined fairways and immaculate greens are found at this parkland course situated in the centre of Macroom town. Tuition and group discounts are available to visitors.

Muskerry Golf Club

Carrigohane, Co. Cork. ☎ (021) 385297. FAX (021) 385297. ☐ Thu–Tue. ⓔⓔ Holes: 18. Par: 71. ⓘ ⓟ ⓐ ⓣ ⓥ

Located 3 km (2 miles) from Blarney Castle and 11 km (7 miles) north of Cork city, this parkland course is historically linked with the great golfer, James Bruen, and was founded in 1897 by Sir George Colthurst of Blarney Castle. Tuition and group discounts are available.

Old Head Golf Links

Kinsale, Co. Cork. ☎ (021) 778444. FAX (021) 778022. @ info@oldheadgolf.ie ☐ Daily. ⓔⓔⓔⓔⓔ Holes: 18. Par: 72. ⓘ ⓟ ⓐ ⓒ ⓣ ⓥ AE, DC, MC, V.

This links course is one of the most spectacular courses in the world, set on a cliff-top with dramatic views of the coastline 11 km (7 miles) south of Kinsale. Group discounts and professional tuition are available.

Parknasilla Golf Club

Parknasilla, Co. Kerry. ☎ (064) 45122. FAX (064) 45323. @ ref@parknasilla.gsh.ie ☐ Mon–Fri (by appointment). ⓔⓔ Holes: 9. Par: 70. ⓒ AE, DC, MC, V.

Situated 24 km (15 miles) west of Kenmare, this parkland course has panoramic views across Kenmare Bay. Group discounts offered.

Ring of Kerry Golf & Country Club

Templenoe, Kenmare, Co. Kerry. ☎ (064) 42000. FAX (064) 42533. @ ringofkerrygolf@tinet.ie ☐ Daily. ⓔⓔⓔ Holes: 18. Par: 72. ⓘ ⓟ ⓐ ⓣ ⓒ MC, V.

Macgillicuddy's Reeks provide the backdrop to this parkland course overlooking Kenmare Bay, 6 km (4 miles) west of Kenmare town.

Ross Golf Club

Ross Road, Killarney, Co. Kerry. ☎ (064) 31125. FAX (064) 31860. ☐ Daily. ⓔⓔ Holes: 9. Par: 72. ⓘ ⓐ ⓒ ⓣ ⓒ MC, V.

A championship standard parkland course designed by Roger Jones, to test golfers of all abilities. Ross Castle and the Kerry Mountains provide a picturesque backdrop. Tuition and group discounts are available.

Tralee Golf Club

West Barrow, Ardfert, Co. Kerry. ☎ (066) 713 6379. FAX (066) 713 6008. @ traleegolf@aircom.net ☐ Mon, Tue, Thu, Fri, Sat. ⓔⓔⓔⓔⓔ Holes: 18. Par: 71. ⓘ ⓟ ⓐ ⓒ ⓣ AE, MC, V.

The links course at Tralee, 13 km (8 miles) from Tralee town, provides some of the best golf in the world. Group discounts and tuition are offered to visitors.

Water Rock Golf Course

Water Rock, Midleton, Co. Cork. ☎ (021) 613499. FAX (021) 633150. ☐ Daily (by appointment). ⓔⓔ Holes: 18. Par: 70. ⓘ ⓟ ⓒ ⓣ ⓒ AE, MC, V.

Designed by Paddy Merrigan, this parkland course has spectacular views of the East Cork countryside. The greens are challenging and well-maintained. Group discounts available.

Waterville Golf Club

Waterville, Co. Kerry. ☎ (066) 947 4102. FAX (066) 947 4482. @ wvgolf@iol.ie ☐ Daily. ⓔⓔⓔⓔⓔ Holes: 18. Par: 72. ⓘ ⓟ ⓐ ⓒ ⓣ ⓒ AE, MC, V.

This is one of the top five courses in Ireland, and one of the top 20 links courses in the world. Visitors are offered tuition.

THE LOWER SHANNON

Adare Manor Golf Club

Adare, Co. Limerick. ☎ (061) 396204. FAX (061) 396800. ☐ Mon, Wed, Fri. ⓔⓔ Holes: 18. Par: 69. ⓘ ⓟ ⓐ ⓒ ⓣ ⓒ MC, V.

Established in 1900, the natural beauty of this parkland course is enhanced by historic ruins. The club offers group discounts to visitors.

Ballykisteen Golf & Country Club

Limerick Junction, Tipperary, Co. Tipperary. ☎ (062) 33333. FAX (062) 33711. ☐ Daily. ⓔⓔ Holes: 18. Par: 73. ⓘ ⓟ ⓐ ⓒ ⓣ ⓒ MC, V.

A magnificent championship parkland course in Ireland's "Golden Vale" which provides a challenge for golfers of all abilities. Tuition and group discounts are available to visitors.

Carrick-on-Suir Golf Club

Garravoone, Carrick-on-Suir, Co. Tipperary. ☎ (051) 640047. FAX (051) 640558. ☐ Daily (by appointment). ⓔⓔ Holes: 18. Par: 73. ⓘ ⓒ AE, MC, V.

A parkland course, nestling between the Coneagh Mountains and the Suir Valley, just 3 km (2 miles) from Carrick-on-Suir.

Castletroy Golf Club

Castletroy, Co. Limerick. ☎ (061) 335753. FAX (061) 335373. ☐ Daily. ⓔⓔⓔ Holes: 18. Par: 71. ⓘ ⓟ ⓐ ⓒ ⓣ ⓒ MC, V.

A superbly maintained parkland course with mature trees lining the fairways. The elevated tee at the 13th hole provides panoramic views of the countryside.

County Tipperary Golf & Country Club

Dundrum, Co. Tipperary. ☎ (062) 71717. FAX (062) 71718. ☐ Daily. ⓔⓔⓔ Holes: 18. Par: 72. ⓘ ⓟ ⓐ ⓒ ⓣ ⓒ AE, DC, MC, V.

Designed by Ryder Cup winner Philip Walton, this parkland course makes use of the Multeen river and woodlands to provide testing golf in a beautiful setting.

Dromoland Golf & Country Club

Newmarket-on-Fergus, Co. Clare. ☎ (061) 368444. FAX (061) 368498. @ dromolandgc@aircom.net ☐ Mon–Fri. ⓔⓔⓔ Holes: 18. Par: 71. ⓘ ⓟ ⓐ ⓒ ⓣ ⓒ AE, DC, MC, V.

Situated 8–10 minutes north of Shannon airport is this 167-ha (375-acre) parkland course. Tuition and group discounts are offered to visitors.

East Clare Golf Club

Bodyke, Co. Clare. ☎ (061) 921322. FAX (061) 921717. @ eastclare@tinest.ie ☐ Daily. ⓔⓔ Holes: 18. Par: 71. ⓘ ⓟ ⓣ

Visitors are especially welcome at this popular parkland course located 40 minutes from Shannon airport. Group discounts and tuition are available to visitors.

Ennis Golf Club

Drumbiggle Road, Ennis, Co. Clare. ☎ (065) 682 4074. FAX (065) 684 1848. @ egc@aircom.net ☐ Daily. ⓔⓔ Holes: 18. Par: 70. ⓟ ⓐ ⓒ MC, V.

A mature parkland course, with tree-lined fairways and well-maintained greens, just outside Ennis. Tuition and group discounts are offered.

Kilkee Golf Club

East End, Kilkee, Co. Clare. ☎ (065) 905 6048. FAX (065) 905 6977. ☐ Daily. ⓔⓔ Holes: 18. Par: 69. ⓘ ⓟ ⓐ ⓒ ⓒ MC, V.

Situated on a cliff top in Kilkee this picturesque championship coastal course has magnificent views from its tees and greens.

Killeline Park Golf & Leisure Club

Newcastle West, Co. Limerick. ☎ (069) 61600. FAX (069) 77428. ☐ Daily. ⓔⓔ Holes: 18. Par: 72. ⓘ ⓟ ⓐ ⓒ ⓒ MC, V.

The rolling parkland of this course provides a great variety of golfing shots and scenic views of the countryside.

Kilrush Golf Club

Kilrush, Co. Clare. ☎ (065) 905 1138. FAX (065) 905 2633. @ kelgolf@iol.ie ☐ Daily. ⓔⓔ Holes: 18. Par: 70. ⓘ ⓟ ⓐ ⓒ AE, MC, V.

This golf club is perhaps one of the friendliest in Ireland and visitors are always welcome. The parkland course has excellent greens. Tuition and group discounts are offered.

Lahinch Golf Club

Lahinch, Co. Clare. ☎ (065) 708 1003. FAX (065) 708 1592. @ lgc@iol.ie ☐ Daily. ⓔⓔⓔⓔ Holes: 18, 18. Par: 70, 72. ⓘ ⓟ ⓐ ⓒ ⓣ AE, MC, V.

The rugged terrain of this links course provides a stern test of golfing skills (and the ability to trek cross-country is a distinct advantage). The club was chosen to host the Irish National Championships in 1999. Tuition is available to visitors by arrangement.

Limerick County Golf & Country Club

Ballyneety, Co. Limerick. ☎ (061) 351881. FAX (061) 351384. @ lcgolf@iol.ie ☐ Daily. ⓔⓔ Holes: 18. Par: 72. ⓘ ⓟ ⓐ ⓒ ⓒ AE, DC, MC, V.

This parkland course is built on one of the oldest estates in Ireland, situated 10 km (6 miles) south of Limerick. Tuition and group discounts are offered to visitors.

Newcastle West Golf Club

Ardagh, Co. Limerick. ☎ (069) 76500. FAX (069) 76511. ☐ Mon–Fri. ⓔⓔ Holes: 18. Par: 71. ⓘ ⓟ ⓐ ⓒ MC, V.

This parkland course has 65 ha (160 acres) of rolling countryside, peppered with lakes, trees, streams and man-made bunkers. The club offers tuition and group discounts.

Shannon Golf Course

Shannon, Co. Clare. ☎ (061) 471849. FAX (061) 471507. ☐ Mon–Fri (by appointment). ⓔⓔ Holes: 18. Par: 72. ⓘ ⓟ ⓐ ⓒ ⓣ ⓒ MC, V.

A highly regarded championship parkland course close to Shannon airport. The hazards of bunkers, tree-lined fairways and water features create a stern test for all golfers. Professional tuition is available.

Strandhill Golf Club

Strandhill, Co. Sligo. ☎ (071) 68188. FAX (071) 68811. ☐ Mon–Fri. ⓔⓔ Holes: 18. Par: 69. ⓘ ⓟ ⓐ ⓒ

An attractive links course 8 km (5 miles) from Sligo, with spectacular views of Knocknarea and the Atlantic Ocean. The clubhouse offers a warm welcome and friendly atmosphere to visitors, as well as tuition and group discounts.

Thurles Golf Club

Turtulla, Thurles, Co. Tipperary. ☎ (0504) 21983. FAX (0504) 24647. ☐ Mon, Wed, Thu, Fri, Sat. ⓔⓔ Holes: 18. Par: 72. ⓘ ⓟ ⓐ ⓒ ⓣ ⓒ MC, V.

This well-established parkland course is known for its excellent greens and hazardous bunkers. Tuition and group discounts available.

Tipperary Golf Club

Rathanny, Tipperary Town, Co. Tipperary. ☎ (062) 51119. ☐ Daily. ⓔⓔ Holes: 18. Par: 71. ⓘ ⓟ

This is a very challenging parkland course set in a beautiful location with views of the Galtee Mountains. Group discounts offered.

Woodstock Golf & Country Club

Shanaway Road, Ennis, Co. Clare. ☎ (065) 682 9463. FAX (065) 682 0304. ☐ Daily. ⓔⓔⓔ Holes: 18. Par: 72. ⓘ ⓟ ⓐ ⓒ MC, V.

A technically challenging, championship level parkland course, just 3 km (2 miles) from Ennis. Group discounts are available.

THE WEST OF IRELAND

Ardacong Golf Club

Milltown Road, Tuam, Co. Galway. ☎ (093) 25525. ☐ Daily. ⓔ Holes: 18. Par: 70. ⓒ ⓣ

A 1920s parkland course that has been updated to modern standards to provide a tough but fair golfing challenge.

Athenry Golf Club

Palmerstown, Oranmore, Co. Galway. ☎ (091) 794466. ℻ (091) 794971. ☐ Mon–Sat. ⓔⓔ Holes: 18. Par: 70. 🏠 🌣 🏌 MC, V.

This course is a mixture of parkland and heath, bordered by stone walls and forest. There is a wonderful view of the course from the clubhouse balcony. Tuition and group discounts are available to visitors.

Athlone Golf Club

Hodson Bay, Athlone, Co. Roscommon. ☎ (0902) 92073. ℻ (0902) 94080. ☐ Mon, Wed, Thu, Fri, Sat. ⓔⓔ Holes: 18. Par: 71. 🍴 🌣 🏠 🌣 🌣 🏌 MC, V.

Founded in 1892, this championship parkland course has beautiful views over Lough Ree and offers a stimulating challenge to golfers of all abilities. Visitors are offered tuition and group discounts.

Ballinrobe Golf Club

Cloonacastle, Ballinrobe, Co. Mayo. ☎ (092) 41118. ℻ (092) 41889. @ bgcgolf@iol.ie ☐ Daily. ⓔⓔ Holes: 18. Par: 74. 🌣 🌣 MC, V.

A championship parkland course, set in the mature woodlands of the historic Cloonacastle Estate, incorporating seven man-made lakes. Visitors are offered group discounts.

Bearna Golf & Country Club

Corboley, Bearna, Co. Galway. ☎ (091) 592677. ℻ (091) 592674. @ bearnagc@tinet.ie ☐ Mon–Thu. ⓔⓔⓔ Holes: 18. Par: 72. 🍴 🌣 🏠 🌣 🌣 AE, MC, V.

This moorland course has views of Galway Bay, the Clare hills and Aran Islands. Group discounts are available to visitors.

Connemara Golf Club

Ballyconneely, Clifden, Co. Galway. ☎ (095) 23502. ℻ (095) 23662. @ links@iol.ie ☐ Daily. ⓔⓔⓔ Holes: 27. Par: 73. 🍴 🌣 🏠 🌣 🌣 MC, V.

This is one of Ireland's best and most challenging links courses, enhanced by the breathtaking views of the Atlantic Ocean and the Connemara Mountains. Visitors are offered tuition and group discounts.

Connemara Isles Golf Club

Annaghvane, Bealadaingn, Connemara, Co. Galway. ☎ (091) 572498. ℻ (091) 572214. ☐ Daily. ⓔⓔ Holes: 9. Par: 70. 🍴 🌣 🌣 🌣 MC, V.

An island links course, designed by Craddock and Ruddy, offering some of the finest golf in the country among the beautiful countryside at the heart of Connemara. Group discounts are available to visitors.

Dunmore Demesne Golf Club

Dunmore, Co. Galway. ☎ (093) 38159. ℻ (093) 38632. @ carmel@iol.ie ☐ Mon–Sat. ⓔ Holes: 9. Par: 70. 🌣

This parkland course, with its mature trees and scenic landscape, was designed by Eddie Hackett and built on an old estate. Group discounts are offered.

Galway Bay Golf & Country Club

Renville, Oranmore, Co. Galway. ☎ (091) 790500. ℻ (091) 792510. ☐ Daily. ⓔⓔⓔⓔ Holes: 18. Par: 72. 🍴 🌣 🏠 🌣 🌣 🏌 AE, DC, MC, V.

Designed by Christy O'Connor Jnr, this championship parkland course is surrounded on three sides by the sea. Visitors are offered tuition and group discounts.

Gort Golf Club

Castlequarter, Gort, Co. Galway. ☎ (091) 632244. ℻ (091) 632387. @ gortgolf@tinet.ie ☐ Mon–Sat. ⓔⓔ Holes: 18. Par: 71. 🍴 🌣 🏠 🌣 MC, V.

Set in an area of outstanding beauty, this rugged parkland course is 34 km (21 miles) southwest of Gort and was designed by Christy O'Connor Jnr to championship standards. Group discounts are available.

Mulranny Golf Club

Mulranny, Westport, Co. Mayo. ☎ (098) 36262. ☐ Daily. ⓔⓔ Holes: 9. Par: 71. 🌣

The undulating greens at this links course overlook Clew Bay and Corpatrick, 16 miles (25 km) from Westport. Group discounts offered.

Tuam Golf Club

Barnacurragh, Tuam, Co. Galway. ☎ (093) 28993. ℻ (093) 26003. ☐ Mon–Sat. ⓔⓔ Holes: 18. Par: 72. 🍴 🌣 🏠 🌣 🌣 🏌 MC, V.

A parkland course with mature parkland and a water hazard, providing a fair test for golfers of all capabilities.

Westport Golf Club

Carrowholly, Westport, Co. Mayo. ☎ (098) 28262. ℻ (098) 27217. @ wpgolf@iol.ie ☐ Daily. ⓔⓔ Holes: 18. Par: 73. 🍴 🌣 🏠 🌣 🌣 🏌 MC, V.

Visitors are always welcome at this championship parkland course on the shore of Clew Bay, overlooking Croaghpatrick Mountain. Tuition and group discounts are available.

NORTHWEST IRELAND

Ballybofey & Stranorlar Golf Club

The Glebe, Stranorlar, Co. Donegal. ☎ (074) 31093. ℻ (074) 30158. ☐ Mon–Fri. ⓔⓔ Holes: 18. Par: 68. 🍴 🌣 🏠 🌣

This parkland course, on the shore of Lough Alan, has views of the Donegal Hills and the Finn Valley. Group discounts are offered.

Ballyliffin Golf Club

Ballyliffin, Clonmany, Co. Donegal. ☎ (077) 76119. ℻ (077) 76672. @ ballyliffingolfclub@tinet.ie ☐ Mon–Fri. ⓔⓔⓔ Holes: 18, 18. Par: 71, 72. 🍴 🌣 🏠 🌣 🌣 MC, V.

Ireland's most northerly golf club is a hidden gem, situated 32 km (20 miles) from Londonderry. Both courses are links, one is at championship level. Group discounts offered.

County Sligo Golf Club

Rosses Point, Co. Sligo. ☎ (071) 77134/77186. ℻ (071) 77460. @ cosligo@iol.ie ☐ Daily. ⓔⓔⓔⓔ Holes: 18. Par: 71. 🍴 🌣 🏠 🌣 🌣 🏌 MC, V.

This championship links course is overlooked by Benbulben Mountain and lies adjacent to three beautiful beaches. Tuition and group discounts are offered to visitors.

Donegal Golf Club

Murvagh, Laghey, Co. Donegal. ☎ (073) 34054. ℻ (073) 34377. @ info@donegalgolfclub.ie ☐ Daily. ⓔⓔⓔ Holes: 18. Par: 73. 🍴 🌣 🏠 🏌 MC, V.

A magnificent links course, hidden away on a sandy peninsula and screened by dense woodland. Group discounts are available.

Enniscrone Golf Club

Enniscrone, Co. Sligo. ☎ (096) 36297. ℻ (096) 36657. @ enniscronegolf@tinet.ie ☐ Mon–Sat (by appointment). ⓔⓔⓔ Holes: 18. Par: 72. 🍴 🌣 🏠 🌣 🏌 AE, MC, V.

One of Ireland's great west coast links courses, host to the West of Ireland Championships from 1996. Visitors are offered tuition and group discounts.

Portsalon Golf Club

Portsalon, Fanad, Co. Donegal. ☎ (074) 59459. ℻ (074) 59459. ☐ Mon–Fri (by appointment). ⓔⓔ Holes: 18. Par: 69. 🍴 🌣 🏠

This is a stunning links course, with views of beautiful Ballynastocker Bay, providing a considerable challenge for all golfers.

Rosapenna Golf Links

Rosapenna, Downings, Co. Donegal. ☎ (074) 55301. ℻ (074) 55128. @ rosapenna@aircom.net ☐ Daily. ⓔⓔⓔ Holes: 18. Par: 70. 🍴 🌣 🏠 🌣 🏌 AE, DC, MC, V.

Overlooking Sheephaven Bay on the Roguill Peninsula, this links course, designed by Old Tom Morris, has one of the best golfing sites in the British Isles.

St Patrick's Links

Maheramagorgan, Carrigart, Co. Donegal. ☎ (074) 55114. ℻ (074) 55250. ☐ Daily. ⓔⓔ Holes: 18, 18. Par: 72, 74. 🏌 🌣 DC, MC, V.

This course has a classic links terrain providing some testing golf and spectacular views of Sheephaven Bay and the North Donegal Highlands. Group discounts are offered.

THE MIDLANDS

Ashbourne Golf Club

Ashbourne, Co. Meath. ☎ (01) 835 2005. ℻ (01) 835 2561. @ ashgc@iol.ie ☐ Daily. ⓔⓔ Holes: 18. Par: 72. 🍴 🌣 🏠 🏌

An exciting parkland course offering a great variety of shots. The River Broadmeadows runs through the peaceful countryside of this course, situated just south of Ashbourne. Tuition and group discounts are available.

Castle Barna Golf Club

Daingean, Co. Offaly. ☎ (0506) 53384. ℻ (0506) 53384. @ castlebearna@tinet.ie ☐ Mon–Fri. ⓔⓔ Holes: 18. Par: 72. 🍴 🌣 🏠 🌣

Set on the bank of the Grand Canal, this parkland course has an abundance of streams and mature trees, a lovely environment in which to relax while the course puts golfing prowess to the test.

Clones Golf Club

Hilton Park, Clones, Co. Monaghan. ☎ (047) 56017. ℻ (047) 42333. ☐ Daily. ⓔⓔ Holes: 9. Par: 68. 🌣

This testing parkland course, located 5 km (3 miles) from Clones, boasts superb greens. Visitors can get a group discount.

County Louth Golf Club

Baltray, Drogheda, Co. Louth. ☎ (041) 982 2329. ℻ (041) 982 2969. @ baltray@indigo.ie ☐ Mon, Wed, Thu, Fri. ⓔⓔⓔ Holes: 18. Par: 73. 🍴 🌣 🏠 🌣 🌣 🏌 AE, MC, V.

Located 8 km (5 miles) northeast of Drogheda, this links course is home to the East of Ireland Championship. Visitors are offered tuition and group discounts.

County Meath Golf Club

Newtownmoynagh, Trim, Co. Meath. ☎ (046) 31463. ℻ (046) 37554. ☐ Mon–Fri. ⓔⓔ Holes: 18. Par: 73. 🍴 🌣 🏌

A very attractive but testing parkland course designed by Eddie Hackett, with a large practice area and a warm and welcoming clubhouse.

Delvin Castle Golf Club

Delvin, Co. Westmeath. ☎ (044) 64315. ☐ Daily. ⓔⓔ Holes: 18. Par: 70. 🍴 🌣 🏠 🌣

Visitors are always welcome at this beautiful parkland course, with its many trees, water hazards and mixture of long and short holes. Tuition and group discounts are available.

Esker Hills Golf & Country Club

Tullamore, Co. Offaly. ☎ (0506) 55999. ℻ (0506) 55021. ⓦ globalgolf.com.eskerhills ☐ Daily. ⓔⓔ Holes: 18. Par: 71. 🌣 🌣 AE, MC, V.

The lakes and trees, valleys and plateaux of this parkland course provide a challenging round of golf. Group discounts are offered.

Glasson Golf & Country Club

Glasson, Athlone, Co. Westmeath. ☎ (0902) 85120. ℻ (0902) 85444. @ glasgolf@iol.ie ☐ Daily. ⓔⓔⓔ Holes: 18. Par: 72. 🍴 🌣 🏠 🌣 🏌 AE, DC, MC, V.

Lough Ree forms part of this very beautiful and enjoyable parkland course, located 10 km (6 miles) north of Athlone. Visitors can obtain tuition and group discounts.

Greenore Golf Club

Greenore, Co. Louth. 【 (042) 937 3678. FAX (042) 937 3678. ☐ Daily (by appointment). ⒠⒠ Holes: 18. Par: 71. �🍴 💺 🚩

A flat, "semi-links" course with panoramic views of Carlingford Lough and the Mourne mountains. Rivers, ponds and pine trees provide extra challenges for the golfer.

Headfort Golf Club

Kells, Co. Meath. 【 (046) 40146/ 40857. FAX (046) 49282. ☐ Daily. ⒠⒠ Holes: 36. Par: 72. 🍴 💺 🔒 💺 🚩 📋 AE, MC, V.

Situated in the historic town of Kells, this is one of Ireland's most scenic championship parkland courses.

Killin Park Golf Club

Killin, Baird-a-Chrinn, Dundalk, Co. Louth. 【 (042) 933 9303. ☐ Daily. ⒠⒠ Holes: 18. Par: 69. 🍴 💺 💺 🚩

Castletown river runs through this rolling parkland course with its mature trees and views of the Mourne mountains. Group discounts are available to visitors.

Laytown & Bettystown Golf Club

Bettystown, Co. Meath. 【 (041) 982 7170. FAX (041) 982 8506. ☐ Mon–Fri. ⒠⒠⒠ Holes: 18. Par: 71. 🍴 💺 🔒 💺 🚩 📋 MC, V.

Recent improvements in layout and design have created a formidable and testing course for all golfers. Tuition and group discounts are offered to visitors.

Moor-Park Golf Course

Mooretown, Navan, Co. Meath. 【 (046) 27661. ☐ Daily. ⒠⒠ Holes: 18. Par: 72. 💺 🚩

The Hill of Tara and Skryne stand in the background of this challenging parkland course, which has all-weather greens and artificial lakes. Group discounts are offered.

Mount Temple Golf Club

Mount Temple, Moate, Co. Westmeath. 【 (0902) 81841/81545. FAX (0902) 81957. @ mttemple@iol.ie ☐ Daily (by appointment). ⒠⒠ Holes: 18. Par: 72. 🍴 🔒 💺 📋 MC, V.

A traditional championship course with links-style greens but parkland features. Playable throughout the year, the course has spectacular views of the Midlands countryside. Visitors are offered tuition and group discounts.

Mullingar Golf Club

Belvedere, Mullingar, Co. Westmeath. 【 (044) 48366. FAX (044) 41499. ☐ Mon–Fri. ⒠⒠ Holes: 18. Par: 72. 🍴 💺 🔒 💺 🚩 📋 AE, MC, V.

This parkland course is over 100 years old and has beautiful mature trees lining its fairways. Tuition and group discounts are available to visitors.

Nuremore Hotel Golf & Country Club

Carrickmacross, Co. Monaghan. 【 (042) 9661438. FAX (042) 9661853. @ nuremore@tinet.ie ☐ Daily (by appointment). ⒠⒠ Holes: 18. Par: 71. 🍴 💺 🔒 💺 🚩 📋 AE, DC, MC, V.

A championship-length parkland course, with picturesque views of the surrounding countryside. Tuition is available to visitors.

Portarlington Golf Club

Garryhinch, Portarlington, Co. Offaly. 【 (0502) 23115. FAX (0502) 23044. ☐ Mon–Sat. ⒠⒠ Holes: 18. Par: 72. 🍴 💺 📋 MC, V.

The River Barrow flows through the centre of this parkland course with its flat fairways, mature and young trees, lakes and abundant wildlife. Located just outside town.

Seapoint Golf Club

Termonfeckin, Drogheda, Co. Louth. 【 (041) 982 2333. FAX (041) 982 2331. @ golflinks@seapoint.ie ☐ Daily. ⒠⒠⒠ Holes: 18. Par: 72. 🍴 💺 💺 🚩 📋 MC, V.

This championship links course, 35 minutes north of Dublin airport, is playable all year round and features water hazards and manicured greens. Visitors are offered tuition and group discounts.

Slieve Russell Hotel, Golf & Country Club

Ballyconnell, Co. Lavan. 【 (049) 952 6444. FAX (049) 952 6640. ☐ Sun–Fri. ⒠⒠⒠ Holes: 18. Par: 72. 🍴 💺 🔒 💺 🚩 📋 AE, DC, MC, V.

Opened in 1992, this has become one of the finest parkland courses in the country. It played host to the 1996 Smurfit Irish PGA Championships and the 1997 Quinn Direct Charity PGA Trophy. Tuition is available.

South Meath Golf Club

Langwood, Trim, Co. Meath. 【 (046) 31471. ☐ Daily. ⒠ Holes: 9. Par: 70. 🔒 💺

Situated close to Trim Castle, this parkland course designed by Eddie Hackett has wide fairways, generous greens and mature trees.

NORTHERN IRELAND

Ardglass Golf Club

4 Castle Place, Ardglass, Co. Down. 【 (01396) 841219. FAX (01396) 841841. @ golfclub@ardglass.force9.co.uk ☐ Mon–Fri. ⒠⒠ Holes: 18. Par: 70. 🍴 💺 🔒 💺 🚩 📋 AE, MC, V.

A scenic seaside course providing a challenge for the serious golfer and an enjoyable game for the novice. Tuition and group discounts are available to visitors.

Belvoir Park Golf Club

73 Church Road, Newtownbreda, Belfast City. 【 (01232) 491693. FAX (01232) 646113. ☐ Mon–Fri. ⒠⒠⒠ Holes: 18. Par: 71. 🍴 💺 🔒 💺 🚩

This championship parkland course, situated 5 km (3 miles) south of Belfast, has mature trees and a demanding finish at the 18th hole. Visitors are offered tuition and discounts.

Cairndhu Golf Club

192 Coast Road, Ballygally, Larne, Co. Antrim. 【 (01574) 583324. FAX (01574) 583324. @ cairndhu@globalgolf.com ☐ Sun–Fri. ⒠⒠ Holes: 18. Par: 70. 🍴 💺 🔒 💺 🚩 📋 AE, DC, MC, V.

A very scenic parkland course to the north of Larne overlooking the sea and the Glens of Antrim.

Castle Hume Golf Club

Blleek Road, Enniskillen, Co. Fermanagh. 【 (01365) 327077. FAX (01365) 327076. ☐ Daily. ⒠⒠ Holes: 18. Par: 72. 💺 🔒 💺 🚩 📋 MC, V.

Host of the Ulster PGA Championships from 1996 to 1998, this parkland course is challenging but picturesque, with its abundant trees, water hazards and bunkers.

Clandeboye Golf Club

Tower Road, Conlig, Co. Down. 【 (01247) 271767. FAX (01247) 473711. ☐ Mon–Fri. ⒠⒠⒠ Holes: 18, 18. Par: 73, 70. 🍴 💺 🔒 💺

One of Ireland's top golf clubs, this championship parkland course has hosted many high-ranking tournaments and there is a secondary course for an easier round.

Downpatrick Golf Club

73 Saul Road, Downpatrick, Co. Down. 【 (01396) 615947. FAX (01396) 617502. ☐ Daily. ⒠⒠ Holes: 18. Par: 70. 🍴 💺 🔒 💺 🚩

This challenging parkland course has superb views of the Ulster countryside and across to the Isle of Man on a clear day.

Foyle International Golf Course

12 Alder Road, Londonderry, Co. Londonderry. 【 (01504) 352222. FAX (01504) 353967. ☐ Daily. ⒠⒠ Holes: 18. Par: 72. 🍴 💺 🔒 🚩 📋 MC, V.

Situated 3 km (2 miles) north of the city, this championship parkland course has a number of water hazards to challenge all golfers. Tuition and group discounts are available.

Galgorm Castle Golf Club

Ballymeena, Co. Antrim. 【 (01266) 46161. FAX (01266) 651151. @ golf@gallorncastle.uk ☐ Daily. ⒠⒠ Holes: 18. Par: 72. 🍴 💺 🔒 💺 🚩 📋 MC, V.

This 220-acre parkland course was designed to championship standards. It is set in the delightful grounds of one of Ireland's most historic castles.

Kilkeel Golf Club

Mourne Park, Ballyardle, Kilkeel, Co. Down. 【 (016937) 65095. FAX (016937) 65095. ☐ Mon–Fri. ⒠⒠ Holes: 18. Par: 72. 🍴 💺 🔒 🚩

This parkland course, at the foot of the Mourne mountains, co-hosted the 1999 British Amateur Open along with Royal County Down. The club offers discounts to groups.

Kirkistown Castle Golf Club

142 Main Road, Cloughey, Newtownards, Co. Down. 【 (01247) 771233. FAX (01247) 771699. @ kirkistown@aol.com ☐ Sun–Fri. ⒠⒠ Holes: 18. Par: 69. 🍴 💺 🔒 💺 🚩 📋 AE, MC, V.

Built around an historic moat, with magnificent views of the Isle of Man, this is a parkland course with the open style of a links and challenging holes requiring a variety of shots.

Mahee Island Golf Club

Mahee Island, Comber, Newtownards, Co. Down. 【 (01238) 541234. ☐ Sun–Fri. ⒠⒠ Holes: 9. Par: 68. 🍴 💺 🔒

This championship parkland course is located next to an old monastery and offers scenic views of Strangford Lough Islands and Scrabo Tower. It has excellent greens.

Newtownstewart Golf Club

38 Golf Course Road, Newtownstewart, Omagh, Co. Tyrone. 【 (016626) 61466. FAX (016626) 62506. @ newtown.stewart@bnet ☐ Daily. ⒠⒠ Holes: 18. Par: 70. 🍴 💺 🔒 💺 🚩

Situated 1.6 km (1 mile) west of Newtownstewart, this very friendly and scenic parkland course offers its visitors group discounts.

Portstewart Golf Club

117 Strand Road, Portstewart, Co. Londonderry. 【 (01265) 832015. FAX (01265) 834097. @ portstewart.golf@bnet.co.uk ☐ Mon–Fri. ⒠⒠⒠⒠ Holes: 9, 18, 18. Par: 64, 72, 64. 🍴 💺 🔒 💺 📋 MC, V.

This championship links course, with great views of the sea, has one of the finest opening golf holes in the world.

Royal Belfast Golf Club

Station Road, Craigavad, Holywood, Co. Down. 【 (01232) 428165. FAX (01232) 421404. ☐ Daily. ⒠⒠⒠ Holes: 18. Par: 70. 🍴 💺 🔒 💺 🚩

A beautifully-kept parkland course with mature woodlands and bunkered greens, providing a stern test of golf. Tuition is available.

Royal County Down Golf Club

36 Golf Links Road, Newcastle, Co. Down. 【 (013967) 23314. FAX (013967) 26281. @ royal.co.down@virgin.net ☐ Sun–Fri. ⒠⒠⒠⒠ Holes: 18, 18. Par: 71, 72. 💺 🔒 💺 🚩 📋 AE, DC, MC, V.

There are two 18-hole links courses at this world-renowned venue – one a championship course, the other less demanding.

Royal Portrush Golf Club

Dunluce Road, Portrush, Co. Antrim. 【 (01265) 822311. FAX (01265) 823139. @ rpgc@dnet.co.uk ☐ Sun–Fri. ⒠⒠⒠⒠ Holes: 18, 18. Par: 72, 70. 🍴 💺 🔒 💺 🚩 📋 MC, V.

The championship links course, Dunluce, is one of the most challenging courses in the world, requiring great skill and concentration.

General Index

Page numbers in **bold** type
refer to main entries.

Road Maps

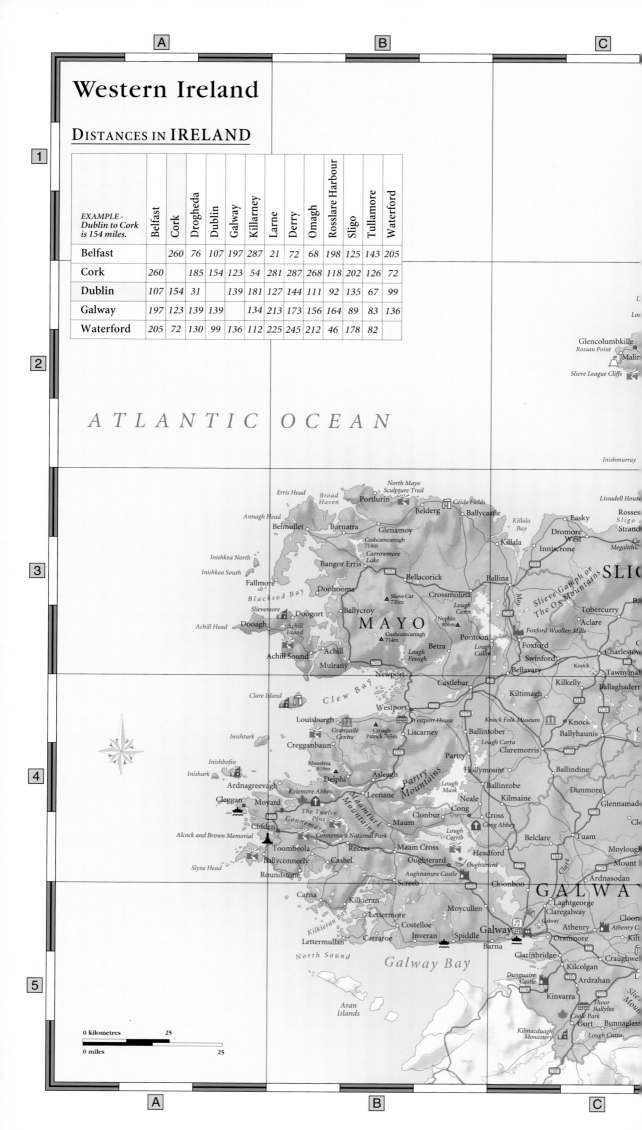

Western Ireland

DISTANCES IN IRELAND

EXAMPLE - Dublin to Cork is 154 miles.

	Belfast	Cork	Drogheda	Dublin	Galway	Killarney	Larne	Derry	Omagh	Rosslare Harbour	Sligo	Tullamore	Waterford
Belfast		260	76	107	197	287	21	72	68	198	125	143	205
Cork	260		185	154	123	54	281	287	268	118	202	126	72
Dublin	107	154	31		139	181	127	144	111	92	135	67	99
Galway	197	123	139	139		134	213	173	156	164	89	83	136
Waterford	205	72	130	99	136	112	225	245	212	46	178	82	

ATLANTIC OCEAN

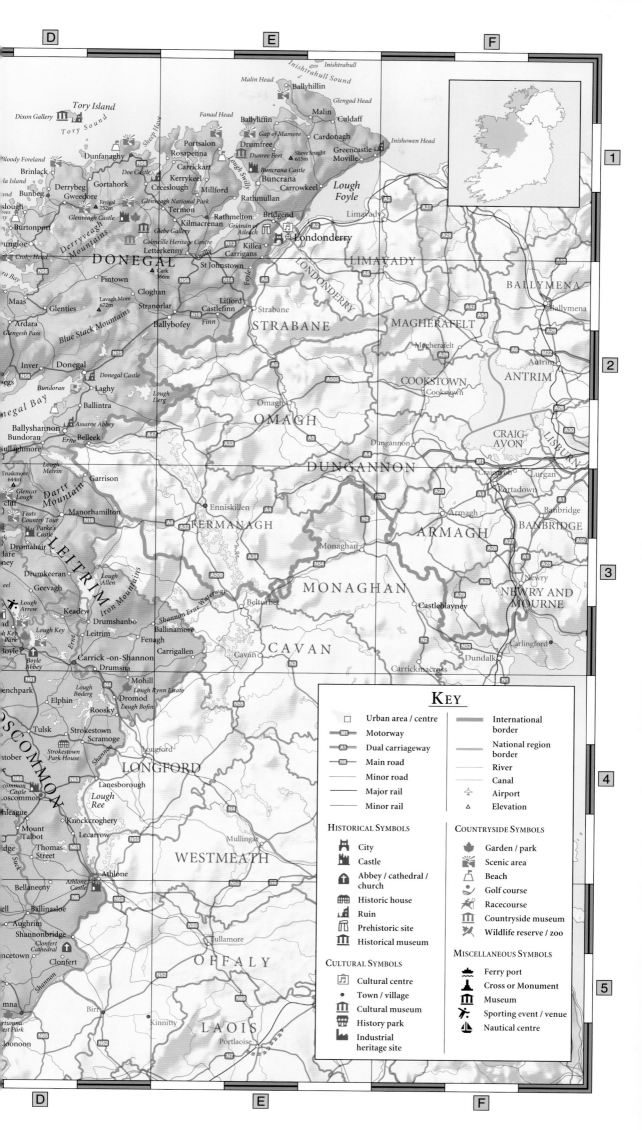

Northern Ireland

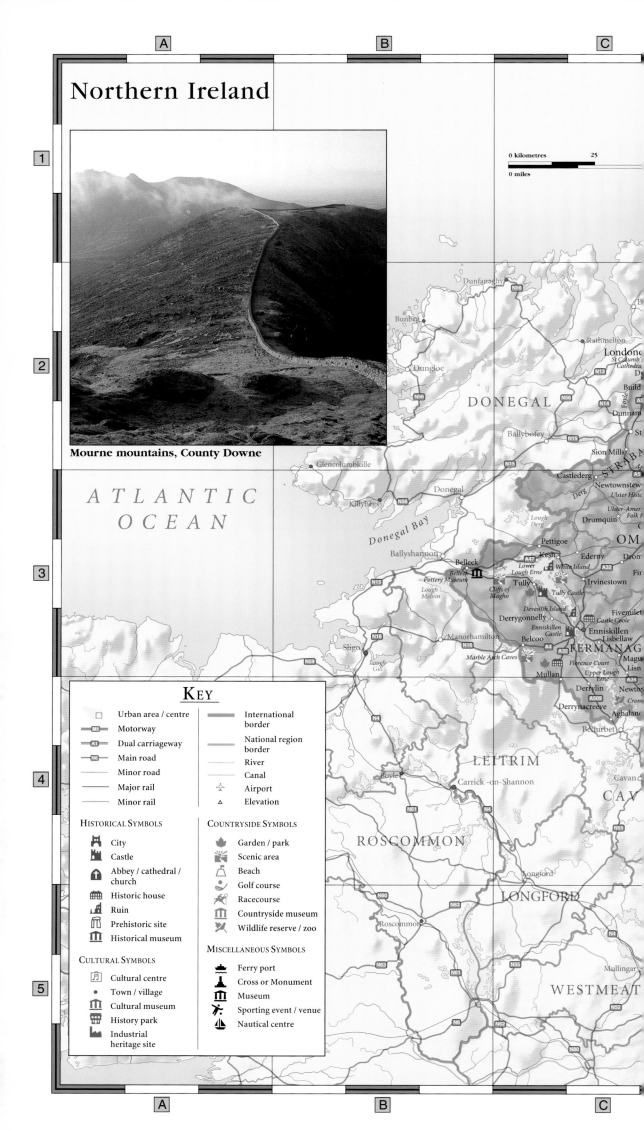

Mourne mountains, County Downe

ATLANTIC
OCEAN

0 kilometres   25

0 miles

Map labels:

Dunfanaghy · Bunber · Rathmelton · Londond · St Columb's Cathedral · Build · Dungloe · Dunloe · DONEGAL · N13 · N14 · Dunnam · Ballybofey · N15 · St · Sion Mills · STRABA · Glencolumbkille · Castlederg · Newtownstew · Ulster Histo · Derg · Donegal · Ulster-Amer · Folk · Killybegs · N56 · Lough Derg · Drumquin · OM · Donegal Bay · Pettigoe · Ballyshannon · Belleek · A47 · Kesh · Ederny · Drom · Lower Lough Erne · White Island · A32 · Fir · Belleek Pottery Museum · N15 · Cliffs of Magho · Tully · Tully Castle · Irvinestown · Lough Melvin · Devenish Island · Fivemile · Castle Coole · Derrygonnelly · Enniskillen Castle · Enniskillen · N16 · Manorhamilton · Belcoo · Lisbellaw · Sligo · Marble Arch Caves · A4 · A32 · FERMANAG · Magu · Florence Court · Upper Lough Erne · Lisn · Mullan · Derrylin · Newto · A509 · Crom · N59 · Derrynacreeve · Aghalanc · Belturbet · N4 · LEITRIM · Cavan · Boyle · Carrick-on-Shannon · CAV · N61 · N4 · N55 · ROSCOMMON · Longford · N60 · LONGFORD · Roscommon · N4 · N63 · N63 · Mullingar · N61 · WESTMEAT · N55 · N52 · N6 · N62 · N80

KEY

☐ Urban area / centre
M1 Motorway
A1 Dual carriageway
N6 Main road
Minor road
Major rail
Minor rail

International border
National region border
River
Canal
✈ Airport
△ Elevation

HISTORICAL SYMBOLS

City
Castle
Abbey / cathedral / church
Historic house
Ruin
Prehistoric site
Historical museum

CULTURAL SYMBOLS

Cultural centre
• Town / village
Cultural museum
History park
Industrial heritage site

COUNTRYSIDE SYMBOLS

Garden / park
Scenic area
Beach
Golf course
Racecourse
Countryside museum
Wildlife reserve / zoo

MISCELLANEOUS SYMBOLS

Ferry port
Cross or Monument
Museum
Sporting event / venue
Nautical centre

Lough Erme, County Fermanagh

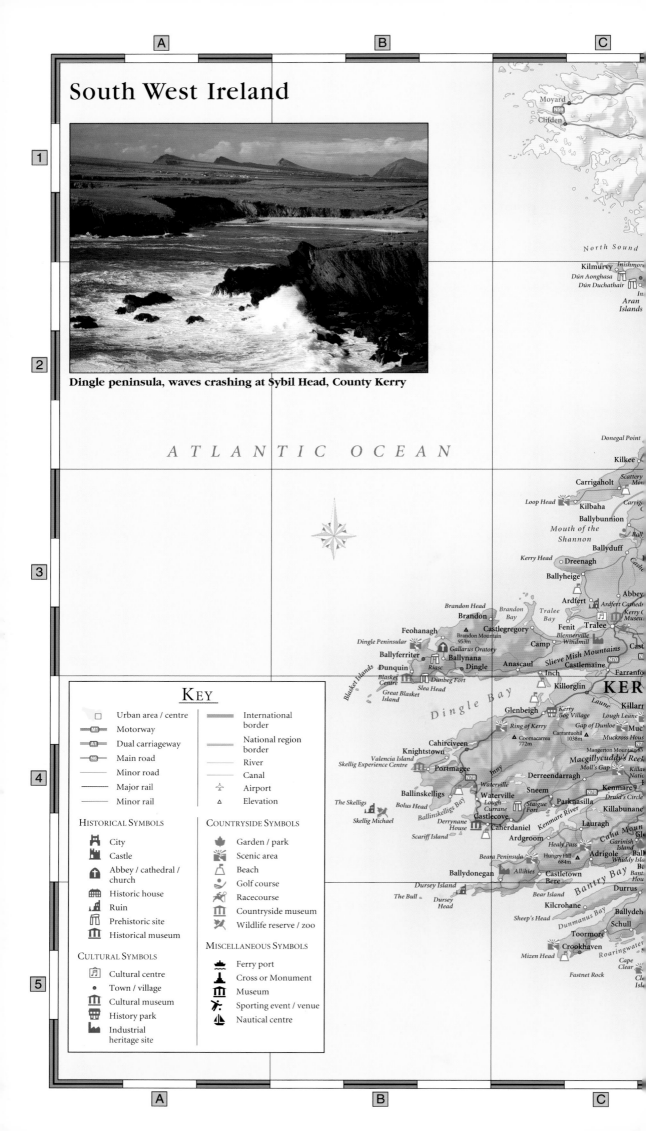

South West Ireland

Dingle peninsula, waves crashing at Sybil Head, County Kerry

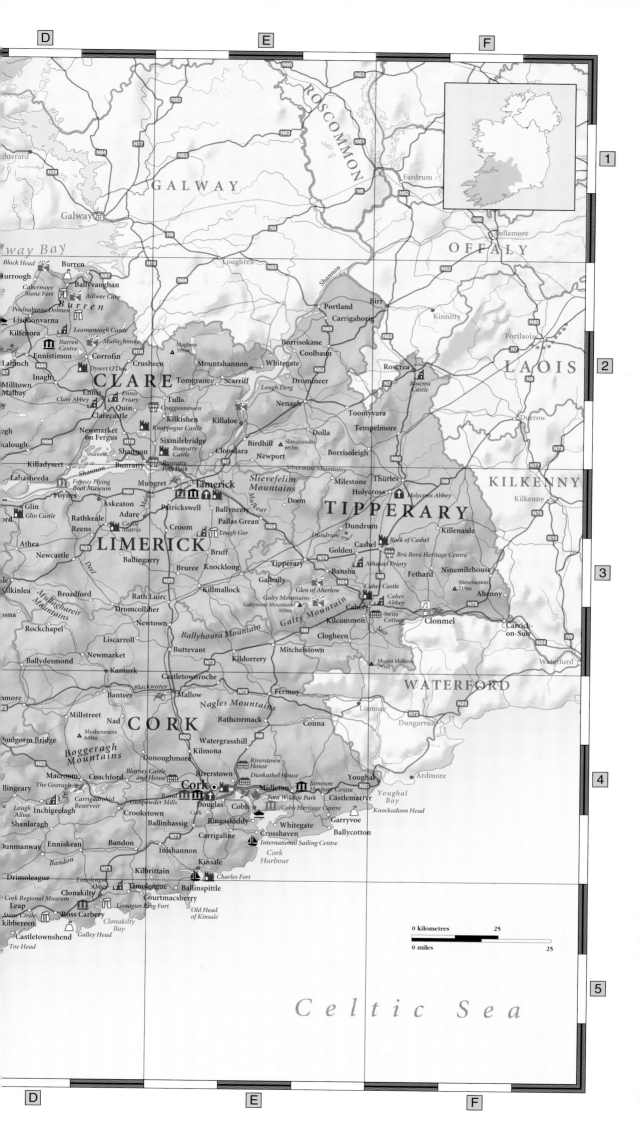

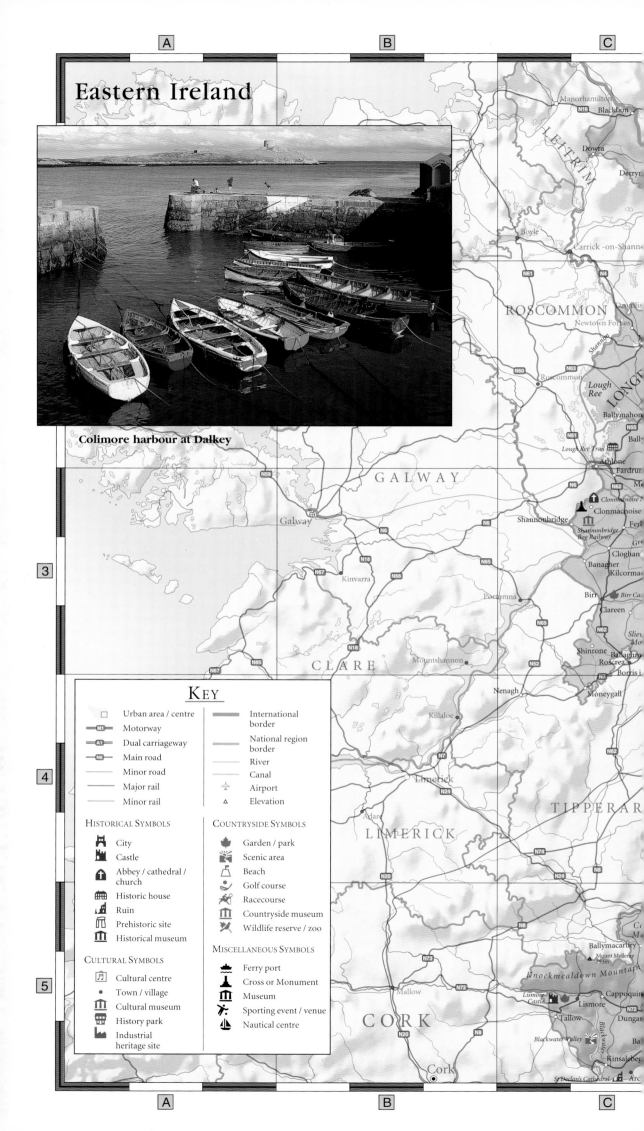

A

B

C

Eastern Ireland

Colimore harbour at Dalkey

LEITRIM

Manorhamilton

N16 Blacklion

Dowra

Derryr

Boyle

Carrick -on-Shann

N61

N4

ROSCOMMON

Newtown Forbes

N60

Roscommon

N63

Lough Ree

LONG

Ballymahon

N61

N55

Ball

Lough Ree Trail

Athlone

Fardrun

N59

GALWAY

N6

Clonmacnoise

Clonmacnoise

Galway

N6

Shannonbridge

Shannonbridge Bog Railway

Ferl

Cloghan

Banagher

Kilcorma

N18

N65

N67

Kinvarra

N66

Birr

Birr Ca

Clareen

Portumna

Slie Mo

N65

Shinrone

Ballaghn

Roscrea

N18

Mountshannon

N52

Borris i

CLARE

Nenagh

Moneygall

N67

N85

Killaloe

N7

N62

N7

Limerick

N24

TIPPERAR

Adar

N20

LIMERICK

N74

N8

N24

N73

CORK

Ballymacarbry

Mount Melleray

Mallow

N72

Knockmealdown Mountai

Lismore Castle

Cappoquin

N20

N8

Tallow

Lismore

Dungan

Blackwater Valley

Blackwater

Kinsalebe

Cork

St Declan's Cathedral

Arc

KEY

□ Urban area / centre
M1 Motorway
A1 Dual carriageway
N6 Main road
Minor road
Major rail
Minor rail

International border
National region border
River
Canal
✈ Airport
△ Elevation

HISTORICAL SYMBOLS
City
Castle
Abbey / cathedral / church
Historic house
Ruin
Prehistoric site
Historical museum

CULTURAL SYMBOLS
Cultural centre
• Town / village
Cultural museum
History park
Industrial heritage site

COUNTRYSIDE SYMBOLS
Garden / park
Scenic area
Beach
Golf course
Racecourse
Countryside museum
Wildlife reserve / zoo

MISCELLANEOUS SYMBOLS
Ferry port
Cross or Monument
Museum
Sporting event / venue
Nautical centre

3

4

5

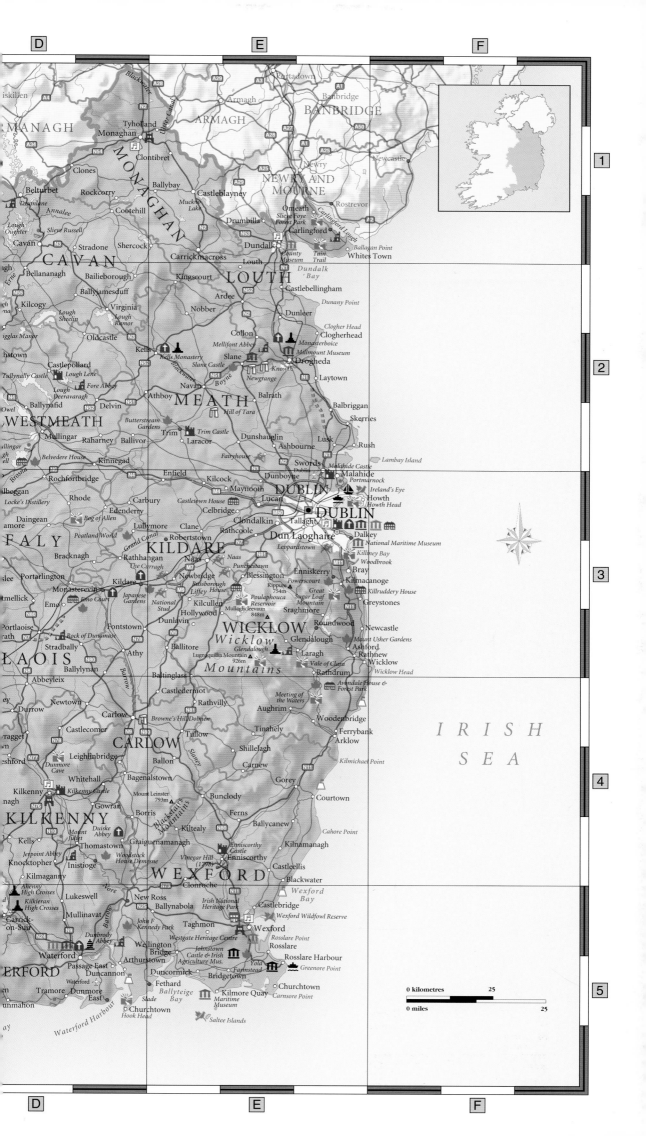

Gazetteer Index

KEY TO THE INDEX

🛐 Abbey, cathedral, church • 🤸 Golf course • 🏛 Museum

💥 Area of natural beauty • 🏰 Historic city • 🏛 Prehistoric site

⚔ Battle • 🏛 Historic house • 🏇 Racecourse

🏰 Castle • 🏛 History park • 🏚 Ruin

⚒ Cross, monument • 🏭 Industrial heritage • 🤾 Sporting event, venue

🎵 Cultural centre • 🏘 Interesting building • 🦅 Wildlife park, zoo

🍁 Garden, park • ≣ Local edifice

Acknowledgments

DORLING KINDERSLEY would like to thank the following people whose contributions and assistance have made the preparation of this book possible.

MAIN CONTRIBUTORS

LISA GERARD-SHARP is a writer and broadcaster who has contributed to numerous travel books, including the *Eyewitness Travel Guide to France*. She is of Irish extraction, with roots in County Sligo and County Galway, and a regular visitor to Ireland.

TIM PERRY, from Dungannon, County Tyrone, writes on travel and popular music for various publishers in North America and the British Isles.

ADDITIONAL CONTRIBUTORS

Robin Blake, Sue Gordon, Douglas Palmer, Christina Park.

EDITORIAL AND DESIGN

PUBLISHER Douglas Amrine
ART DIRECTOR Gillian Allan
SENIOR MANAGING EDITOR Louise Bostock Lang
MANAGING EDITORS Vivien Crump, Helen Partington
MANAGING ART EDITORS Jane Ewart, Steve Knowlden
PRODUCTION Marie Ingledew

Marion Broderick, Margaret Chang, Martin Cropper, Guy Dimond, Fay Franklin, Yael Freudmann, Sally Ann Hibbard, Annette Jacobs, Erika Lang, Michael Osborn, Caroline Radula-Scott.

ADDITIONAL PHOTOGRAPHY

Peter Anderson, Joe Cornish, Andy Crawford, Michael Diggin, Steve Gorton, Anthony Haughey, Mike Linley, Stephen Oliver, Magnus Rew, Anthony Souter, Clive Streeter, Matthew Ward, Alan Williams.

ADDITIONAL ILLUSTRATIONS

Richard Bonson, Brian Craker, John Fox, Paul Guest, Stephan Gyapay, Ian Henderson, Claire Littlejohn, Gillie Newman, Chris Orr, Kevin Robinson, John Woodcock, Martin Woodward.

ADDITIONAL PICTURE RESEARCH

Miriam Sharland.

INDEX

Hilary Bird.

SPECIAL ASSISTANCE

Dorling Kindersley would like to thank all the regional and local tourist offices in the Republic and in Northern Ireland for their valuable help. Particular thanks also to: Ralph Doak and Egerton Shelswell-White at Bantry House, Bantry, Co Cork; Vera Greif at the Chester Beatty Library and Gallery of Oriental Art, Dublin; Alan Figgis at Christ Church Cathedral, Dublin; Labhras Ó Murchu at Comhaltas Ceoltóirí Éireann; Catherine O'Connor at Derry City Council; Patsy O'Connell at Dublin Tourism;

Tanya Cathcart at Fermanagh Tourism, Enniskillen; Peter Walsh at the Guinness Hop Store, Dublin; Gerard Collet at the Irish Shop, Covent Garden, London; Dónall P Ó Baoill at ITE, Dublin; Pat Cooke at Kilmainham Gaol, Dublin; Angela Shanahan at the Kinsale Tourist Office; Bill Maxwell, Adrian Le Harivel and Marie McFeely at the National Gallery of Ireland, Dublin; Philip McCann at the National Library of Ireland, Dublin; Willy Cumming at the National Monuments Divison, Office of Public Works, Dublin; Eileen Dunne and Sharon Fogarty at the National Museum of Ireland, Dublin; Joris Minne at the Northern Ireland Tourist Office, Belfast; Dr Tom MacNeil at Queen's University, Belfast; Sheila Crowley at St Mary's Pro-Cathedral, Dublin; Paul Brock at the Shannon Development Centre; Tom Sheedy at Shannon Heritage and Banquets, Bunratty Castle, Co Clare; Angela Sutherland at the Shannon-Erne Waterway, Co Leitrim; Máire Ní Bháin at Trinity College, Dublin; Anne-Marie Diffley at Trinity College Library, Dublin; Pat Maclean at the Ulster Museum, Belfast; Harry Hughes at the Willie Clancy School of Traditional Music, Miltown Malbay, Co Clare.

ADDITIONAL ASSISTANCE

Kathleen Crowley, Rory Doyle, Peter Hynes, David O'Grady, Mary O'Grady, Madge Perry, Poppy.

PHOTOGRAPHY PERMISSIONS

THE PUBLISHER would like to thank all those who gave permission to photograph at various cathedrals, churches, museums, restaurants, hotels, shops, galleries and other sights too numerous to list individually.

PICTURE CREDITS

tl = top left; tc = top centre; tr = top right; cla = centre left above; ca = centre above; cra = centre right above; cl = centre left; c = centre; cr = centre right; clb = centre left below; cb = centre below; crb = centre right below; bl = bottom left; bc = bottom centre; br = bottom right.

Every effort has been made to trace the copyright holders and we apologize in advance for any unintentional omissions. We would be pleased to insert the appropriate acknowledgments in any subsequent edition of this publication.

The publisher would like to thank the following individuals, companies and picture libraries for permission to reproduce their photographs:

AKG, London: National Museum, Copenhagen/ Erich Lessing 30cl; ALLSPORT: David Rogers 32cb; Steve Powell 51tc.

BORD FÁILTE/IRISH TOURIST BOARD: Brian Lynch 28–29c, 29tl, 256-257c, 288c/b, 330tl, 330tr; BRISTOL CITY MUSEUMS AND ART GALLERY: 36bl;

BRITISH LIBRARY: *Richard II's Campaigns in Ireland* Ms.Harl.1319, f.18 41tl; BRITISH MUSEUM: 37bl.

CENTRAL BANK OF IRELAND:*Lady Lavery as Cathleen ni Houlihan,* John Lavery 15t; CHESTER BEATTY LIBRARY, Dublin: 89t; BRUCE COLEMAN COLLECTION: Mark Boulton 23tr; Patrick Clement 22clb, 22bl; Adrian Davies 22br; Rodney Dawson 23cl; Frances Furlong 22tl; David Green 268bl; Pekka Helo 23cr; Jan Van de Kam 232bl; Gordon Langsbury 22cl, 232cr; John Markham 338br; George McCarthy 23tl, 23bl, 23br, 160tl, 269bl; MR Phicon 22crb; Eckhart Pott 23cb; Hans Reinhard 23tcb, 194tl; Kim Taylor 23tc, 338t, 364tl; R Wanscheidt 23cbr; Uwe Walz 22cr, 229cb; G Ziesler 269br; COLLECTIONS: Michael Diggin 20b, 21b, 224t, 224-225c, 314b, 334-335; Robert Hallmann 317cr; Julian Nieman 19b; Ray Rampton 185br; Michael St Maur Sheil 5t, 183t, 185bl, 257tl, 347t; Joan Tordai 254b; George Wright 184tl; COLLECTIONS/Image Ireland: 121b; Bob Brien 20t, 415; Thomas Ennis 18c, 316tl, 360b; Errol Forbes 18b; Alain Le Garsmeur 142b, 224bl, 225ca, 315b, 340-341, 344c, 345b; John Lennon 21c, 222t; John Scovell 414; Geray Sweeney 287b, 288t, 315t; COOLEY DISTILLERY: 347b; CORBIS: 75cra; Jan Butchofsky-Houser 20c, 178-179; Corbis-Bettmann 346b; Richard Cummins 92-93, 185t, 192-193, 218-219, 294-295; MacDuff Everton 110-111; Derek Hall/Frank Lane Picture Agency 236-237; Catherine Karnow 68-69, 204-205; Richard T Nowitz 18t; Purcell Team 242-243; Michael St Maur Sheil 144t, 145cra, 210-211, 317b; Tim Thompson 21t, 122-123, 262-263, 304-305, 380-381; Adam Woolfitt 144cl; Michael S Yamashita 272-273, 298-299, 373, 410-411; CORK EXAMINER: 33tl; CORK PUBLIC MUSEUM: 39cla; JOE CORNISH: 23cla, 274b, 364tr; CRAWFORD MUNICIPAL ART GALLERY: *The Meeting of St Brendan and the Unhappy Judas,* Harry Clarke 212bl.

DERRY CITY COUNCIL: 350tr; MICHAEL DIGGIN: 24tl, 181b, 195cr, 196cla, 197tr, 229tl, 264bl, 293t, 296tr, 296cl, 297cla; BILL DOYLE: 276bl; GA DUNCAN: 50cb, 50bl; DUNDEE ART GALLERIES AND MUSEUMS: *The Children of Lir,* John Duncan 31tc.

ET ARCHIVE: 31bl, 184-185c; MARY EVANS PICTURE LIBRARY: 11 (inset), 28tl, 30tr, 30bl, 30br, 31cla, 38bl, 41bc, 42bl; 48bl, 57 (inset), 89cl, 105bl, 135 (inset), 145c/crb, 316bl/br, 346t, 377br.

FAMINE MUSEUM, Co Rosscommon: 281tr.

GILL AND MACMILLAN PUBLISHERS, Dublin: 49bl; RONALD GRANT ARCHIVE: *The Commitments,* Twentieth Century Fox 27br; GUINNESS IRELAND LTD: 118bl, 118br, 119tl, 119tr, 119bl, 119br; VK GUY LTD: Mike Guy 143t/b, 182b, 184tr, 223t, 282-283, 287t, 344t, 352-353; Vic Guy 183bl, 222c.

ROBERT HARDING PICTURE LIBRARY: 170-171; Roy Rainford 225t; CHRISTOPHER HILL PHOTOGRAPHIC

LIBRARY: Jill Jennings 322-323; ANGELO HORNAK LIBRARY: 328-329; HULTON GETTY PICTURE COLLECTION: 26clb, 27tr, 43t, 46br, 46cbl, 50crb, 144bl/br, 145bl; Reuter 51crb, 70bl.

IMAGES COLOUR LIBRARY: 59tl; 301bc; INPHO, Dublin: 32cla, Billy Stickland 32br, 144-145c, 145br, 164-165; Lorraine O'Sullivan 33br; IRISH PICTURE LIBRARY, Dublin: 42cla, 45tl, 48tl; IRISH TIMES: 156br; IRISH TRADITIONAL MUSIC ARCHIVE, Dublin: 29bl.

JAMESON IRISH WHISKEY: 109b, 346cl; JARROLD COLOUR PUBLICATIONS: JA Brooks 70br; MICHAEL JENNER: 224br, 254t, 255c, 256t, 286b, 325cr.

KATZ PICTURES: Mansell/Time Inc 44bl, 49cra, 99bl, 362bc; TIMOTHY KOVAR: 90bl, 289cb.

LAMBETH PALACE LIBRARY, London: Plan of the London Vintners' Company Township of Bellaghy, Ulster, 1622 (ms. Carew 634 f.34) (detail) 43cra; FRANK LANE PICTURE AGENCY: Roger Wilmshurst 232bc; LEEDS CITY ART GALLERY: *The Irish House of Commons,* Francis Wheatley 44cla; LENSMEN, Dublin/National Maritime Museum of Ireland: Susan Kennedy 184bl; DAVID LYONS: 19t/c, 182tl, 184cla, 222b, 223c, 224cl, 225cb, 254c, 286t/c, 310-311, 314t/c, 315cb, 317t.

HUGH MCKNIGHT PHOTOGRAPHY: 121t; TOM MACKIE: 142t/c, 182cr, 183c/br, 223b, 230-231, 250-251, 255t, 266-267, 345t/c, 418; MANDER AND MITCHESON THEATRE COLLECTION: 28cl; ARCHIE MILES: 268br; JOHN MURRAY: 55bl, 116cl, 148c; © MUSEUM OF THE CITY OF NEW YORK: Gift of Mrs Robert M Littlejohn, *The Bay and Harbor of New York 1855,* Samuel B Waugh 46–47c.

EDMUND NÄGELE: 150-151, 416; NATIONAL GALLERY OF IRELAND, Dublin: *WB Yeats and the Irish Theatre,* Edmund Dulac 26tr, *George Bernard Shaw,* John Collier 26cr, 120c, *Carolan the Harper,* Francis Bindon 28tr, *Leixlip Castle,* Irish School 45cla, *The Custom House, Dublin,* James Malton 45bc, *Queen Victoria and Prince Albert Opening the 1853 Dublin Great Exhibition,* James Mahoney 47bl, *The Houseless Wanderer,* JH Foley 80tl, *Pierrot,* Juan Gris © ADAGP, PARIS and DACS, London 2000 80tr, *For the Road,* JB Yeats 80cla, *The Taking of Christ,* Caravaggio 81cra, *The Castle of Bentheim,* Jacob van Ruisdael 81cl, *Judith with the Head of Holofernes,* Andrea Mantegna 81crb, *The Sick Call,* Matthew James Lawless 81bl, *Convent Garden, Brittany,* William Leech, © Barbara V Mitchell 82t, *A View of Powerscourt Waterfall,* George Barret the Elder 82b, *A Group of Cavalry in the Snow,* Ernest Meissonier 83tl, *Virgin and Child Hodigitria,* Constantinople 83cra, *Guards at the Door of a Tomb,* Jean-Léon Gérôme 83cla, *Peasant Wedding, Pieter Brueghel the Younger* 83br, *Jonathan Swift, Satirist,* Charles Jerval 95tr, *James Joyce,* Jacques Emile Blanche ©

ADAGP, Paris and Dacs, London 2000 106bl, *Interior with Members of a Family*, P Hussey 154br, *William Butler Yeats, Poet*, JB Yeats 307tl, *The Last Circuit of Pilgrims at Clonmacnoise*, George Petrie 336tr; National Gallery, London: *Beach Scene*, Edgar Degas 107b; National Library of Ireland, Dublin: 27cla, 27crb, 35b, 38tl, 38clb, 40bl, 42tl, 42clb, 44clb, 45cl, 46tl, 46bl, 47crb, 47tl, 48clb, 49tl, 49crb, *St Stephen's Green*, James Malton 56–7,163tr, 216cra, 326b; National Museum of Ireland, Dublin: 36tl, 36clb, 36cb, 36crb, 36–7c, 37c, 37clb, 37br, 38cla, 39cb, 39br, 59bl, 57cr, 65crb, all 76–7, all 124-125, 316tr; The National Trust, Northern Ireland: *Lord Castlereagh* after Lawrence 378tl, *Hambletonian*, George Stubbs 379tl, 379cra; The National Trust Photographic Library: Mathew Antrobus 367b, John Bethell 382tl, Patrick Pendergast 366bl, Will Webster 368-369, 373br.

Nature Photographers: B. Burbridge 233b; Paul Sterry 232cl; Northern Ireland Tourist Board: 32tr, 350, 367t; Norton Associates: 86bl.

The Office of Public Works, Ireland: 208bl, 330cl, 331tl, 331cr, 332br, 336tl.

Oxford Scientific Films: Frithjof Skibbe 232tl.

PA Photos: David Cheskin 288-289, 289crb. Walter Pfeiffer Studios, Dublin: 29tr, 29cra, 29c, 29cr, 29crb, 29br; Photo Flora: Andrew N Gagg 232br; Popperfoto: 50cla, 50br, 51tl, Reuter/Crispin Rodwell 51tr; Powerscourt Estate, Enniskerry: 157c; Public Record Office: 346-347c.

The Reform Club, London: 46cla; Report/Derek Spiers, Dublin: 50tl, 50tr, 374bl, 374br; Retna Pictures: Craig Barritt 289bl; L Flusin/Stills 289br; Chris Taylor 28bl; Jay Blakesberg 28br; Retrograph Archive, London: Martin Ranicar-Breese 78c; Rex Features: 51ca, 289t; Ken McKay 289cra; Sipa Press 51clb, 51br, 51bl.

Severin Archive: Ian Yeomans 185cb; Shannon-Erne Waterway: 309bc; The Slide File, Dublin: 16b, 17t/c, 22cla, 22cra, 26cla, 33cra, 33clb, 33bl,

36cla, 52cla, 52bl, 53cb, 54cla, 54cra, 54cb, 54bl, 55cra, 89tr, 89br, 96tl, 136cla, 138-139, 145t, 149br, 160cl 160br, 177br, 185bc, 225b, 229br, 271tl, 275tr, 276cb, 276br, 277bc, 292br, 297tr, 302tl, 302b, 306tr, 313b, 320tl, 324tl, 332tl, 336–7c, 338cra, 346tl, 347cr, 364clb; Sportsfile, Dublin: 33tc.

Tate Gallery Publications: *Captain Thomas Lee*, Marcus Gheeraedts 42br; Rick Tomlinson: 185ca; Topham Picture Source: 45br;The Board of Trinity College, Dublin: Ms.1440 (Book of Burgos) f.20v 41clb; Ms.58 (Book of Kells) f.129v 4t, *The Marriage of Princess Aoite and the Earl of Pembroke*, Daniel Maclise 40cla, Ms.57 (Book of Durrow) f.84v 59cra, Ms.57 (Book of Durrow) f.85v 71cr, Ms.58 (Book of Kells) f.129v 72cra, Ms.58 (Book of Kells) f.34r 72cl, Ms.58 (Book of Kells) f.28v 72crb, Ms.58 (Book of Kells) f.200r 72b, Ms 58 (Book of Kells) f.27v 316-317c; Trip: R Drury 162c; Ulster Museum, Belfast/Courtesy Trustees of the National Museums & Galleries of Northern Ireland: *The Festival of St Kevin at the Seven Churches, Glendalough*, Joseph Peacock 34, *The Relief of Derry*, William Sadler II 42–3, 43crb, 48cla, 349crb, 374clb.

Ian Vickery: 184clb; Viking Ship Museum, Strandengen, Denmark: watercolour by Flemming Bau 39tl.

Waterford Corporation: 39bl, 40tl, 40clb, 41bl; © Writers Museum, Dublin: 26tl.

Peter Zöller: 14, 16t, 23cra, 52tc, 52cr, 53cra, 53bl, 172br, 252, 278–9, 281bl, 284, 312, 333tr.

Front endpaper: all commissioned photography with the exception of Peter Zöller: tl, cla, br.

Jacket: all commissioned photography with the exception of: Mary Evans Picture Library front flap t; The Board of Trinity College, Dublin front cover bl and spine; Ulster Museum, Belfast/ Courtesy Trustees of the National Museums & Galleries of Northern Ireland front flap b.

Dorling Kindersley Special Editions

Dorling Kindersley books can be purchased in bulk quantities at discounted prices for use in promotions or as premiums. We are also able to offer special editions and personalized jackets, corporate imprints, and excerpts from all of our books, tailored specifically to meet your own needs.

To find out more, please contact: (in the United Kingdom) – Special Sales, Dorling Kindersley Limited, 9 Henrietta Street, Covent Garden, London WC2E 8PS; Tel. 020 7753 3572. (In the United States) – Special Markets Department, Dorling Kindersley Publishing, Inc., 95 Madison Avenue, New York, NY 10016.

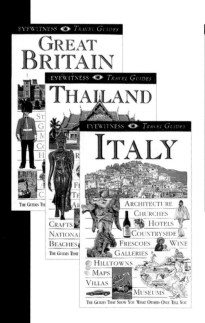

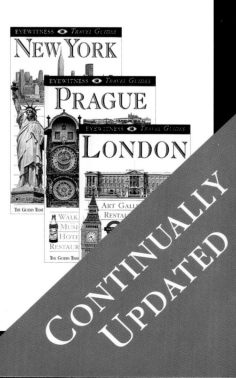